Case Teaching Notes

to accompany

Problems & Cases in Health Care Marketing

John T. Gourville
Harvard Business School
Department of Marketing

John A. Quelch
Harvard Business School

V. Kasturi Rangan
Harvard Business School

McGraw-Hill Irwin

Boston Burr Ridge, IL Dubuque, IA Madison, WI New York San Francisco St. Louis Bangkok Bogotá Caracas Kuala Lumpur Lisbon London Madrid Mexico City Milan Montreal New Delhi Santiago Seoul Singapore Sydney Taipei Toronto

Irwin

Case Teaching Notes to accompany
PROBLEMS & CASES IN HEALTH CARE MARKETING
John T. Gourville, John A. Quelch and V. Kasturi Rangan

Published by McGraw-Hill/Irwin, an imprint of The McGraw-Hill Companies, Inc.
1221 Avenue of the Americas, New York, NY 10020.

1 2 3 4 5 6 7 8 9 0 QSR /QSR 0 9 8 7 6 5 4 3

ISBN 0-07-295199-0

www.mhhe.com

The McGraw-Hill Companies

Problems and Cases in Health Care Marketing
Teaching Notes

PART I

Developing a Marketing Strategy

PART II

Developing New Products

PART III

Launching New Products

PART IV

Managing Distribution

PART V

Managing Communications

PART VI

Managing the Brand

PART VII

International Marketing

HARVARD | BUSINESS | SCHOOL

9-602-063
SEPTEMBER 17, 2001

STEFAN THOMKE

Millennium Pharmaceuticals, Inc. (B)

Paul Pospisil, Associate Director of Business Development and Strategy, angled his tall frame into the airplane seat. Soon over the Atlantic Ocean, with the British Isles receding into the horizon, he reached for the airphone. "Yes, I'm returning from Cambridge," he said. "Cambridge?" asked the confused secretary at Millennium's headquarters. "Yes, Cambridge, England. Can you put Kevin [Starr] or Steve [Holtzman] on the line?[1]"

It was early June of 2000. Millennium was flying high. Over the past year, it had continued forming alliances to strengthen the company financially. Senior management had refused the tempting Lundberg deal because of what it felt was a "poor strategic fit," with agribusiness being too far afield from its focus on becoming an integrated pharmaceutical firm. Millennium further felt that its scientists would lack the passion for the project and that Lundberg was poorly prepared for it. Instead, the recent acquisition of Cambridge-based firm Leukosite further strengthened Millennium's downstream capabilities while simultaneously adding six potential drugs to its development pipeline. It was now awaiting approval from the Food and Drug Administration on its very first drug candidate in December 2000.

Moreover, Millennium was negotiating a five-year agreement with Aventis, the European pharmaceutical giant[2]. Under the proposed partnership, the two companies would work as equals in identifying targets and developing new drugs in the field of inflammation and would jointly commercialize the resulting products. Such a partnership between a biotech and pharmaceutical company, extending from drug discovery down to commercialization, would be unprecedented in biotech history. Aventis would have to pay $200 million for rights to Millennium's gene and drug discovery technology and invest $250 million in Millennium stock. (At senior management team's insistence, all deals would have to bring in at least $200 to 500 million.)

Despite Aventis' keen interest, Millennium remained aware that it lacked important capabilities needed to achieve the partnership's objectives. Planning exercises indicated that it would need new lab space, more than 35 experienced medicinal chemists and new information technologies. It would take at least one year to hire these chemists, and another year to integrate the newcomers into a cohesive team.

---

[1] Kevin Starr is Chief Financial Officer and Steven Holtzman is Chief Business Officer at Millennium.

[2] Aventis was created in 1999 from the merger between Germany's Hoechst AG and France's Rhone Poulenc.

Professor Stefan Thomke and Research Associate Ashok Nimgade prepared this case. HBS cases are developed solely as the basis for class discussion. Cases are not intended to serve as endorsements, sources of primary data, or illustrations of effective or ineffective management.

It was a testimony to Millennium's success that a major pharmaceutical firm would accept its reassurance that it would somehow build new capabilities and acquire the necessary knowledge in the allotted time. However, the tight schedule and milestones spelled out in its intense negotiations left no time for developing these capabilities internally. Again, senior management started to search for suitable acquisitions. Millennium conducted a study of 60 acquisition candidates, looking at the quality of scientists, availability of personnel, transaction cost, and location. Cambridge Discovery Chemistry (CDC) in England, a wholly owned subsidiary of Oxford Molecular Group, eventually emerged as the frontrunner.

The subsidiary had 85 chemists and boasted high quality people in an attractive and fairly accessible location. CDC was already known to Millennium scientists who had enjoyed a fruitful collaboration with its chemists on an earlier project. However, Starr estimated that more than $50 million might be needed to acquire CDC. It was also unclear if Millennium could absorb the resources into its own programs should the deal with Aventis fall through. Many details still had to be negotiated before papers could be signed and there was a 50/50 chance that either party would back out of the agreement.

Paul Pospisil was sent to Cambridge as a key part of negotiations with Oxford Molecular which was very interested in selling the division right away. Much to his surprise, though, Pospisil learned that another potential buyer already existed, eager to make a bid for CDC. On his flight back to Boston, he reflected on Millennium's options. They could wait on the acquisition until the Aventis agreement was signed but by then CDC would possibly be sold. On the other hand, if they made a bid for CDC right away, what would happen if the Aventis agreement fell through? With these thoughts in mind, he waited for Starr or Holtzman to pick up the phone.

5-603-106
FEBRUARY 5, 2003

TEACHING NOTE

Millennium Pharmaceuticals, Inc. (A) & (B)

Case Synopsis

Millennium Pharmaceuticals, a leading biotechnology firm, has pharmaceutical and technology alliances with large firms, including Bayer AG, Monsanto and Eli Lilly & Company. Central to its strategy and success in forming alliances is a technology platform for experimentation in drug discovery, considered to be one of the finest in the industry. At the same time, Millennium is using the technology platform to fundamentally rethink how it can discover new drugs and eventually become an integrated pharmaceutical company. This dual strategy – developing and selling its technology platform through alliances and leveraging these alliances to build downstream drug development capabilities -- is being challenged in August 1999, when the European agribusiness conglomerate Lundberg is proposing a technology alliance to Millennium's senior management.

Teaching Objectives

The Millennium case has been used in MBA and executive courses in managing product development, innovation, strategy and healthcare at HBS and elsewhere. Not only does the case address the role of new technologies in changing drug discovery but it also describes a model for smaller but growing firms to participate and profit from these technological changes. Specifically, it addresses how novel alliance structures can be used to exploit technological innovations which, in turn, can result in resources and opportunities for building downstream R&D capabilities. By looking at which alliances do and do not fit with Millennium's strategy, students develop a general framework for assessing potential partners. The framework can then be applied to the proposed Lundberg alliance. As such, the case study was designed for a broad audience from diverse industries but does provide "rich" details on drug development which are necessary for a thoughtful case discussion.

I teach this case in the third and final module of the second-year elective *Managing Product Development* (see module overview note **Managing Development Networks,** HBS No. 603-091). The module addresses development networks at three levels: between firms, within firms and between products. Millennium is specifically designed to address R&D issues between firms but also links the

---

Professor Stefan Thomke prepared this note was for the sole purpose of aiding classroom instructors in the use of Millennium Pharmaceuticals, Inc. (A) and (B), HBS Nos. 600-038 and 602-063. It provides analysis and questions that are intended to present alternative approaches to deepening students' comprehension of business issues and energizing classroom discussion. HBS cases are developed solely as the basis for class discussion. Cases are not intended to serve as endorsements, sources of primary data, or illustrations of effective or ineffective management.

discussion to the other two course modules where the roles of technology platforms for experimentation are discussed[1].

Specifically, the teaching objectives are:

- Appreciating how innovative technology platforms for experimentation can transform the development of new products in general and drug discovery in particular.
- Learning how to manage the tension between exploiting (upstream technology platforms) and exploring new capabilities (downstream product development) and its link to a company's strategy.
- Understanding the selection, design and management of R&D alliances.

The case is particularly effective in teaching students about the role of alliances in growing a small company. Because Millennium *depends* on these alliances to finance its growth and to build downstream product development capabilities, its management faces these issues in exaggerated form. Executives have found the case extremely useful in rethinking their companies' alliance strategies and finding opportunities for innovation. In fact, students usually come to class expecting a technical discussion on how Millennium is trying to revolutionize drug discovery. At the end of the class, they understand that the way Millennium's alliances were selected, designed and managed was equally important in growing the company.

Recommended Assignment Questions

Prepare: Millennium Pharmaceuticals, Inc. (A) (HBS Case No. 600-038)

Millennium Pharmaceuticals, a leading biotechnology start-up in the field of genomics, has followed a model of using strategic R&D alliances to finance its development of technology platforms. Fundamental to the strategy is Millennium's ability to dramatically change the new drug development process, its organization and, ultimately, the underlying economics. As the firm has grown very rapidly, it now faces important strategic issues.

Preparation Questions:

1. How has the biotechnology industry changed over the last few years? How has Millennium competed since it was founded in 1993? How has it managed its rapid growth?
2. How would characterize the Millennium model (technology, strategy, organization and culture)?
3. What has been Millennium's alliance strategy? How has it differed from other biotechnology firms? How could Millennium do this?
4. As CEO Marc Levin, would you pursue the Lundberg alliance? Why or why not?

[1] Other cases that address the role of new technologies for experimentation in product development are: S. Thomke and A. Nimgade, "BMW AG: The Digital Auto Project (A) and (B)." Harvard Business School Case # 699-044 and 699-045; S. Thomke and A. Nimgade. "Bush Boake Allen." Harvard Business School Case #601-061; and S. Thomke, A. Nimgade, and P. Pospisil. "Eli Lilly and Co.: Drug Development Strategy (A) and (B)." Harvard Business School Cases #698-010 and 698-026.

Recommended Material

An optional background reading is the article titled "Mastering the Value Chain: An Interview with Mark Levin of Millennium Pharmaceuticals," by David Champion, *Harvard Business Review*, June 2001: 109-115. The article provides a good overview of the strategic thinking at Millennium. For more background on practical aspects of alliance making, instructors will find the book *Strategic Alliances: An Entrepreneurial Approach to Globalization* by M. Yoshino, and S. Rangan (HBS Press, 1995) useful in teaching this case[2].

Case Analysis

The Lundberg decision raises some fundamental issues about how Millennium intends to grow and leverage its technology. By offering the company hundreds of millions of dollars for a technology transfer, Lundberg's cash would buy more time for Millennium's management to meet its strategic goal of becoming a drug development firm. On the other hand, it would also distract the company and contribute little to building needed downstream development capabilities. I have found that this decision is not only an excellent entry point into the case issues but also acts as a catalyst for a much broader question: what is Millennium's strategy and how will it get there?

This Analysis section begins by examining Millennium's technology platform and its potential impact on drug discovery. Next, we turn to how Millennium has equally tried to innovate in the way they design and manage its alliances. The section closes with an analysis of Levin's options with the Lundberg deal.

Innovations in Drug Discovery: Millennium's Technology Platform

One of the challenges of teaching this case to a non-pharmaceutical audience is to convey a basic sense of Millennium's innovations but not to let the technology get in the way of a more general discussion of the company's management issues. Students need to have an appreciation of the immense scientific task that the company is trying to accomplish but detailed knowledge of the science itself is not necessary to appreciate the general learning of the case.

What Millennium is trying to accomplish As the case states, part of the excitement for new technologies in drug discovery stems from the fact that the traditional way of finding cures for diseases has been extremely effort-intensive and expensive. Typically, for each successful drug that made it to market, a firm began with roughly 10,000 starting compounds. Of these, about 1000 would make it to more extensive *in vitro* trials (i.e. outside living organisms in settings such as a test tube), of which 20 would be tested even more extensively *in vivo* (i.e. in the body of a living organism such as a mouse) before ten or so compounds made it to human clinical trials (see case, pages 2-3). The entire process represented a long and costly commitment, with the human trials closely monitored by the US government[3]. Advances in mapping the human genome and in new drug discovery technologies

[2] The body of published academic research on the management of alliances is rather large and reviewing it would be beyond the scope of this teaching note. The book *Strategies of Co-operation: Managing Alliances, Networks and Joint Ventures* by J. Child and D. Faulkner (Oxford University Press, 1998) provides a good summary of several decades of research into cooperative strategy. For an additional practice-oriented book, see *Alliance Advantage: The Art of Creating Value through Partnering* by Y. Doz and G. Hamel (Harvard Business School Press, 1998).

[3] A widely-cited study of pharmaceutical drugs developed between 1972 and 1987 found that the expected capitalized development cost per marketed drug was on average 230.8 million (1987) dollars, with total development times well above ten years (see J. DiMasi, R. Hansen, H. Grabowsky and L. Lasagna, 1991, "Cost of innovation in the pharmaceutical industry",

have not only provided potential "shortcuts" to this process but also opened up a rich lode of pharmaceutical drug leads[4]. Specifically, researchers have estimated that current drug therapy is based on less than 500 molecular targets, but there are somewhere between 5,000 to 10,000 targets that could potentially lead to new drugs. In other words, there are at least ten times as many molecular drug targets than what has been used in the last 100 years of medicine[5]. Millennium's genomics-based approach has tried to reverse the traditional development process by first identifying and understanding the role of genes implicated in causing a disease. This should allow for selecting drug candidates based on their ability to intervene in disease initiation and progression—thus targeting the root genetic basis of illness. The firm's strategy relies on combining many advanced discovery technologies (such as combinatorial technology and high-throughput screening) as well as other computer, informatics, and robotics technology – in the aggregate referred to as its "technology platform." This platform would allow for discovering and processing huge amounts of information about genes, making many new targets possible. Proprietary lab technology includes software for analyzing gene function, and machines that decode DNA sequences (the various technologies and approaches are discussed in pages 6-8). It is important to emphasize the enormity of the task – many very large pharmaceutical firms and governments were working towards the same goals with significantly more resources and experiences in some of these areas.

The industry's challenge, however, was not just designing integrated technology platforms but also addressing the dramatic changes required for organizing and managing the science of discovery itself. Commenting on the impact on experimentation and knowledge creation, Dr. Edward Scolnick, president of Merck Research Laboratories, noted that:

> In traditional biology, you start with a hypothesis about how a specific biological process works. You then do an experiment to collect data to test your hypotheses. You essentially try to understand a system by building up your knowledge one component at a time. The difficult part was in understanding how one biological process might be related to another. Genomics essentially turns the process on its head. We can now measure the expression of 10,000 genes all at once and use software algorithms to sort through the data to identify what's related to what. This is referred to as "systems biology." The problem is that nobody is trained in this stuff. And it takes an entirely different mindset and skill set than how we have traditionally done basic research.[6]

What helped Millennium right from its start was access to leading scientists from nearby MIT and Harvard University.

New experimentation technologies for drug discovery Millennium was in a position to develop a technology platform because of the changing economics of experimentation in innovation in general

---

Journal of Health Economics 10: 107-142). Various other studies have shown a trend that has caused much concern in the pharmaceutical industry: the cost and time of new drug development have increased significantly, reaching about $800 million in a recently released study by the Tufts Center for the Study of Drug Development, primarily due to increases in the costs of running expensive clinical trials

[4] For teachers and students that are interested in the bigger implications of genomics, see J. Enriquez and R. Goldberg, "Transforming Life, Transforming Business: The Life-Science Revolution", *Harvard Business Review*, March 2000 and J. Enriquez, *As the Future Catches You*, Crown Business, 2001.

[5] A recent estimate came up with 483 targets that are in use today (see J. Drews, "Drug Discovery: A Historical Perspective," *Science*, vol. 287, p. 1960-1964, March 2000.

[6] Quoted from G. Pisano, A. Leamon, K. Slack and R. Martinez, 2002, "Discovering the Future: R&D Strategy at Merck," *Harvard Business School Case Study* No. 601-086, October 2002.

and drug discovery in particular. Traditionally, testing has been relatively expensive, so companies limited the number of experimental iterations. To overcome this, managers essentially had two choices: they could try to make each experiment more efficient, or they could attempt to: change the fundamental economics of experimentation through new technologies and process innovation. New technologies (simulation, combinatorial chemistry, etc.) that slash experimentation cost and time not only bring much needed capacity but can also make possible "what-if" experiments that, up to now, have been either too expensive or nearly impossible to run. What if a drug was designed in a particular way? By employing new experimentation technologies, it's possible to explore the assumptions that underlie a design, how they could be changed and what the consequences would be, positive and negative. The technologies also enable companies to fundamentally rethink their processes, organization and management of innovation. When I teach Millennium, these changes have already been addressed in the two other course modules in *Managing Product Development* and thus students tend to bring them up right away[7].

How Millennium plans to change drug development When students try to understand what Millennium is "selling" as part of its alliances, they realize that isn't just a physical "technology platform" but also a different way of managing discovery. The case describes three major strategies to shorten development times and increase productivity (case page 11-12). The company has by no means achieved its objective of being "twice as fast and half as expensive" but at least senior management has recognized the challenge. As CEO Levin explained in an interview with the *Harvard Business Review*:

> "...companies must find new ways to make the entire drug development process – finding and testing leads – much faster and more cost-effective. That's what our R&D technology can do. We've already dramatically accelerated the process of identifying leads. It wasn't too long ago that a scientist might spend half a year working on just one lead. She'd sit at a bench, do a few experiments, and report the results six months later. By thanks to our technology, our scientists can spend their time designing automated experiments and analyzing results rather than carrying out the experiments manually. Indeed, if you go into any Millennium-run laboratory, you're not going to see a lot of scientists at work because the process has become so automated that most the actual experimentation is carried out by robots. One scientist can now look at dozens of experiments in the space of a week rather than just the one she did."[8]

One reason why large pharmaceutical firms are forming partnerships with Millennium is because it can provide the results from changes in upstream discovery – validated targets – which then serve as inputs to these firms' downstream product development efforts. However, it also becomes evident that as Millennium is building downstream capabilities to become an integrated pharmaceutical company itself, Levin and his team will eventually compete with their potential partners.

Fit with company strategy The role of its technology platform for discovery becomes very important in the discussion of Millennium's strategy. If Levin's strategy was to become the leading specialist for discovery technologies and process (but *not* products), it should continue to exploit its current platform and explore new upstream capabilities that are outside the scope of large

---

[7] For more information on these course modules, see S. Thomke, "Building Capabilities for Experimentation, Learning and Prototyping," HBS module overview note no. 603-089 and S. Thomke, "Product Development Process Design and Improvement," HBS module overview note no. 603-090. For a full explanation of the research and managerial implications, see S. Thomke, *Experimentation Matters: Unlocking the Potential of New Technologies for Innovation*, HBS Press, June 2003.

[8] Quoted from D. Champion, 2001, "Mastering the Value Chain: An Interview with Mark Levin of Millennium Pharmaceuticals," *Harvard Business Review*, June 2001: 109-115.

pharmaceutical firms. However, if Millennium intends to develop and market its own drugs – as the case indicates – Levin needs to transform the company from a technology specialist into a product developer. This will require people, money, capabilities and, of course, late-stage drug candidates that the company doesn't have in 1999.

Innovations in Alliance Making: Millennium's R&D Network

Integral to Millennium's strategy has been the use of strategic alliances. Because of its deal flow, the company has managed to show operating financials that were significantly better than its peers in the biotechnology industry. Chief Business Officer Steven Holtzman was regarded as the principal architect of the company's alliance strategy and enjoyed an excellent reputation within the industry. In personal interviews, I learned that Holtzman approached alliance-making the same way that Millennium's scientists approached drug discovery: find new ways of structuring partnerships such that they created more value for all parties involved. As a result, Millennium not only focused on technology and process innovations but also became an innovator in designing and extracting value from alliances.

Type of alliances Senior management distinguished between two types of partnerships: technology and pharmaceutical alliances. In a *technology alliance,* the primary objective is to "sell" the technology platform through a transfer to its partners and receive primarily money in return. For example, when Millennium transferred its technology to Monsanto (case, page 9), it received $118 million in up-front fees and another $100 million over five years based on achieving milestones that were spelled-out in the agreement. To facilitate the transfer, it created nearby Cereon Genomics, a Monsanto subsidiary, in which it "cloned" its technology platform in an agricultural setting. Other than money and learning how to transfer technology most effectively, Millennium got little else out of the partnership. In a *pharmaceutical alliance,* the objective is to supply discovery capabilities (e.g., target identification) to its partners for money as well as to build downstream capabilities and retain the rights needed to bring new drugs to market. These agreements were much more complicated to structure and large partners had to be convinced that Millennium should be treated as an equal partner. For example, its alliance with the German industrial giant Bayer AG (case, page 10) involved a very competitive screening process before an agreement was drawn up for a partnership that was the largest of its kind in the biotechnology industry. While pharmaceutical alliances were more consistent with Millennium's strategy, they were also more difficult to achieve as the company would become a competitor to its larger partners.

Millennium's innovative approach to alliance-making Central to Millennium's alliance strategy was a departure from the industry model of making alliances. Holtzman and Levin understood that the traditional full-time equivalent (FTE) model of funding would not get the company closer to its goal of selling drugs[9]. As a result, negotiations with potential partners not only focused on money, but also on intellectual property and ways of aligning both partners' objectives more closely. They also understood that the structure of alliances had to be aligned with anticipated appropriation and coordination issues[10]. Specifically, alliance agreements between Millennium and its partners tended to be long and explicit, drawing upon some of the most talented lawyers in the industry and Holtzman's ability for thinking through "big picture" issues along with attention to detail. When I teach this case, I draw out the differences between conventional partnerships and alliances à la

[9] The FTE model is described on page 7, paragraph 5 of the case. It is comparable to a consulting model where biotechnology companies bill its partners for time, equipment and materials but typically do not retain the rights for their work.

[10] This is also supported in empirical work by R. Gulati and H. Singh, "The Architecture of Cooperation: Managing Coordination Costs and Appropriation Concerns in Strategic Alliance", *Administrative Science Quarterly,* 43 (1998): 781-814.

Millennium (see **Table TN-1**). Students need to be clear that the company's innovation efforts aren't just aimed at its technology platform and the drug development process but also at designing partnerships.

Table TN-1. Differences between conventional and Millennium's partnerships

Issue	Millennium's Approach	Conventional Practice of Biotechnology Companies
Governance	Joint governance of some alliances Partners become stakeholders in M.	Company works for paying partner
Benefits	Downstream development capabilities M. gets rights to some patents Funding of M.'s R&D activities	Mostly funding of R&D activities
Incentives/funding	Variable payments linked to achieved milestones; measure outputs Partners lose rights if they don't meet milestones	Full-time equivalent (FTE) funding; measures inputs
Intellectual Property	Rights that aren't of immediate interest to partner stay with M.	Rights usually stay with partner that pays for research

Fit with Millennium strategy In the selection of R&D alliance partners, senior management needs to have a clear framework for assessing the suitability of a potential partnership. The case doesn't articulate such a framework but is designed so that students can develop one by following Levin's and Holtzman's concerns. In fact, I selected the Lundberg decision as the pivotal issue in the case to get students to think about the various factors that contribute to good alliances (**Table TN-2** lists a set of possible factors). Because Millennium is a growing company that needs to move rapidly, the opportunity cost of weak alliances is higher than in established firms. Without a clear framework for assessing fit, the company may not have the time or resources to deliver on the vision of becoming the drug development company of the 21st century.

Table TN-2. Framework for assessing alliance fit[11]

Assessing Fit	Question
Strategic fit	Are the respective objectives compatible? For how long?
Resource fit	Are the partners willing to contribute the resources and competences necessary for competitive success? Do they have the resources?
Cultural fit	Can we understand each other and communicate? Do we share the same business "logic"?
Organizational fit	Can we bring the decision-making and control mechanisms used by the partners into line?

The Lundberg Decision

Millennium's strategy comes in the form of a partnership offer from Lundberg[12], a multinational agribusiness concern and one of the largest privately held companies in Europe. Its senior

[11] I am indebted to Professor Michael Yoshino for sharing this taxonomy with me.

management is eager to access the company's technology platform and apply it to livestock and agricultural produce – businesses in which Millennium has no experience. The proposed alliance would draw on the successful Monsanto experience, generate large sums of cash (hundreds of millions of dollars), and exploit Millennium's technology leadership in discovery. On the other hand, it is not clear whether it would lead to any new downstream capabilities for drug development.

While important in itself, the Lundberg decision should be used to set up a discussion about Millennium's innovation and business strategy. In theory, the company has enough money to decline the proposed partnership; if it does, however, should it turn away *all* technology alliances in the future? If so, can it build downstream development capabilities and bring a drug to market quickly enough, before other pharmaceutical companies close the technology gap? After all, large companies come to Millennium because of its technology platform and denying them access would eventually make it less attractive as a partner. If Millennium failed to bring a successful drug to market before it ran out of cash, this strategy would also bet the company. Moreover, there would be little work for Steve Holtzman and his business development team.

These issues need to be addressed as part of the case discussion. Specifically, students can choose between the two options briefly discussed below.

Option 1: Accept Lundberg Alliance The potential of applying Millennium's technology platform to livestock and agricultural produce, particularly after the Monsanto experience, makes this partnership very attractive to Lundberg. It may also open up new opportunities that Levin and his team have not seriously considered. There is little financial or technical risk since Lundberg will bear the costs, and the partnership with Monsanto has already taught Millennium's management how to transfer its technology. In the worst case, Millennium will walk away with hundreds of millions of dollars that can be invested into its R&D.

Option 2: Decline Lundberg Alliance Students will propose that this isn't a question about money; it is about strategy and focus. Senior management has already decided that it wants to develop new drugs and thus needs to build downstream capabilities as quickly as possible. Its current alliances are already stretching employees and adding another partnership will be a serious distraction. Exploiting its technology platform across many diverse industries (livestock, agriculture, human health, etc.) would go squarely against its strategy. Starting with page 1 of the case ("I never thought of Millennium as just a technology company"), the objective of becoming a firm with pharmaceutical products is stated throughout the case study.

Teaching Suggestions

I suggest that the instructor covers the material in roughly the reverse order in which it was presented in the Analysis section. The teaching plan has been used in various settings (second year MBA courses, general management and customized executive education programs) and has proven to be very effective, with broad levels of participation. I have only used the (B) case once because the discussions were rich enough for the entire 80-minute class period.

It is very important that the complexity of drug development and its technology is addressed before the case discussion begins. During the class introduction, I usually explain to students that this case is about technology, process *and* business innovation. While the advances in drug

---

[12] Even though the dilemma and its specific details are real, the name "Lundberg" is a disguise for a well-known privately held company.

development are complex yet fascinating, they shouldn't distract from the general lessons that can be drawn from the case.

Block 1: The Lundberg Decision (20-25 minutes)

An effective way to start class discussion is to focus on the Lundberg alliance. Before class begins, I usually list both two options on the center board (see Exhibit TN-2). After explaining the options, an informal class poll will reveal student positions. Experience has shown that the responses can vary significantly. I have had classes where most students wanted to accept the alliance whereas other classes were mostly against it. Over the years, I have also learned that few students have a good framework to assess the alliance, and the variance in initial positions has confirmed this. In my best class ever (executive education), most participants wanted to accept the alliance but realized at the end, *after a framework for assessing fit was developed,* that it was a poor recommendation. Participants told me later that this eureka effect had such an impact on them that they later went back and reassessed their company's alliance portfolio. This experience taught me that it is best if I can get as many students as possible to accept the Lundberg alliance when class begins.

To achieve this, I usually begin by asking: "Who is on side of money and would support accepting the alliance?" and mention the decline option last. After the poll, I invite students to explain their positions (see **Table TN-3** for sample responses). About 10-15 minutes into the discussion, the instructor needs to shift the discussion towards Millennium's strategy.

Table TN-3. Sample comments on Lundberg Decision

Accept Lundberg Alliance	Decline Lundberg Alliance
• Financially attractive (>US$ 200 mill.); alliances are only source of revenue	• Current financials are sound; need to focus on meeting targets of existing alliances
• Leverages experience with Monsanto (Cereon Genomics)	• Does not fit M.'s strategy of becoming pharmaceutical company; distraction
• Exploits M.'s core competence (its technology platform)	• Alliance will result in few new capabilities for M.
• Will probably increase value of stock options; motivates employees	• Employees already show signs of burnout; M. requires focused execution instead of more deals
• Lundberg's senior management is extremely motivated; strong bargaining position for M.	• Lundberg's middle management have not been involved yet
• Cereon experience should allow for a smooth transfer of technology platform	• Lundberg's senior management is poorly prepared; already signs for downstream implementation problems
• Wall Street wants to see continued strong financials	• M.'s scientists may not want another technology transfer since it could be a dull activity

There is a small risk that most students support the same option and class dynamics are slow. If that happens, the instructor needs to be proactive at balancing the discussion.

Questions that move students toward *accepting* the alliance:

- *Question*: "Other biopharmaceutical companies are starving for money. How can Millennium decline such a deal?"

- *Question:* "Lundberg's senior management really wants this alliance. Isn't this the ideal negotiation position to be in?
- *Question:* "Would you turn down Lundberg at *any* price? What if they double their offer?"

Questions that move students toward *declining* the alliance:

- *Question (against accept)*: "Do you think that Millennium's scientists want this deal?"
- *Question (against accept)*: "Do you think that the world's best scientists come to Millennium to transfer technologies?"
- *Question (against accept)*: "How is this deal going to help Millennium to become a leading pharmaceutical firm? They have money but lack downstream capabilities."

At 20-25 minutes, I stop the discussion and tell students that we need to have a clearer sense of what Millennium is before proceeding. After all, why do large pharmaceutical companies that spend billions on R&D themselves turn to small companies like Millennium for discovery expertise?

Block 2: The Millennium Model (15-20 minutes)

It is important to set some time aside for understanding Millennium as a company and why it exists at all. The purpose of this block is not only to reflect on case facts but also make sure that every student has a solid understanding of the company, how it is organized and what it is trying to accomplish. I have found it very useful to structure the discussion around technology/R&D, strategy, organization and culture and write these categories on the board (see **Exhibit TN-3**)

- *Question*: "Why are the elements of Millennium's model? Please assign them to the four categories on the board?" *Technology/R&D process, strategy, organization and culture.*
- *Question*: "Why are large companies so eager to enter alliances with Millennium?
- *Question*: "Why is Millennium selling? Is it just technology?"
- *Question*: "Why do the leading scientists want to work there?"
- *Question*: "Why would a large pharmaceutical company fund and build a future competitor?"

Block 3: A Framework for R&D Alliances (25 minutes)

Once students have a good grasp of Millennium's model, it is time to take a step back and develop a general framework for assessing alliances. The discussion is started by explaining to students that in order to assess the Lundberg alliance in the context of Millennium's model, we first need to develop a set of criteria against which the partnership's fit can be evaluated. This set should be general enough, so it can be used to evaluate the attractiveness of any alliance. I have found the level of participation to be very high because the discussion draws on students' experience and intuition. As students begin suggesting criteria (e.g., cultural fit between both partners), the instructor needs to follow-up with clarification questions to ensure all students understand it. In Block 4, the criteria will be used to reassess the Lundberg decision (see **Table TN-4** for past student suggestions).

Table TN-4. Sample suggestions from students

Criteria for Assessing Alliances	Lundberg?
• Does it fit with my long term objectives (strategic fit)? • Do both partners get along and share same values (cultural fit)? • Is it financially attractive for us (financial implications)? • Is the partner fully committed to make it work? • Does the partner have the capabilities to make it work? • Have issues of control/governance been addressed? • Wall Street wants to see continued strong financials • etc. (students should suggest and explain 10-15 criteria)	(this column will be used for assessing the Lundberg alliance in block 4)

Students generally are excellent at suggesting a relatively exhaustive set of criteria. If they haven't already discussed the specifics of Millennium's alliances as part of Block 1 or 2, this line of questioning should follow next. (I open up the left sideboard early in the class and collect answers throughout the discussion.) It is important to highlight the innovative elements of Millennium's alliance strategy, as described in the **Case Analysis** section.

Block 4: Revisit Lundberg Decision (5-10 minutes)

Finally, the instructor should take the class through an evaluation of the proposed Lundberg alliance, using the framework that was developed in Block 3. I ask the students to rate each criterion according to the following five-point scale (by showing hands):

++ = criterion strongly supports Lundberg alliance

\+ = some support

0 = indifferent

\- = some opposition

— = criterion strongly opposes Lundberg alliance

After listing all the scores, it usually becomes very clear that the alliance is unattractive for Millennium's senior management. Some students correctly point out that the final decision depends on how much significance is assigned to each criterion, but a strong consensus against the alliance has emerged every time the case has been taught. Because the framework was developed by the students, they also tend to buy into the final recommendation.

To summarize, students should recall the following three major points:

- New technologies for experimentation are fundamentally changing the discovery and development of new medicines. This will lead to breakthrough drugs and fundamentally change the way they are developed.

- With its integrated science and technology platform, Millennium strives to equally be an innovator along *technology, process* and *business development*.

- An alliance portfolio needs to be clearly aligned with a company's strategy and rigorously evaluated using a set of criteria similar to what was developed in class.

(A) Case follow-up: Millennium's senior management team declined the proposed Lundberg alliance. It was a very difficult decision because of money involved. One senior executive told me that they sat at the table, looked in each other's eyes and asked if they really want to do this. As there was little enthusiasm in the room, the decision was made. At the time, the business development team had also started to work on an even more attractive partnership with the European pharmaceutical giant Aventis which is the subject of the optional (B) case.

Optional Block 5: B-Case (15minutes)

The purpose of the (B) case is to focus on the often complicated execution of a R&D alliance. It allows students to go beyond the assessment of fit and to think about the management of contingencies. Specifically, Millennium needs important downstream capabilities that it had promised to Aventis as part of the proposed alliance. Paul Pospisil, a young associate director of business development and strategy, is asked to find acquisition targets that would address the company's deficiency before the alliance agreement is finalized. After a rigorous screening process of sixty candidates, Pospisil selects Cambridge Discovery Center (CDC) in England as the frontrunner. Much to his surprise, a potential buyer already exists and its owner wants to sell CDC right away. Millennium needs to move quickly but there is still a 50/50 chance that Aventis backs out of the proposed alliance.

After giving the students five minutes to read the case, I start out with the decision point (see **Table TN-5**). They should also propose some plans to hedge Millennium's risk by brainstorming on innovative ways to structure the acquisition. The instructor should make it clear that the company's business development team has always been creative at structuring deals and that this should be no exception.

Table TN-5. Should Millennium Acquire CDC Now?

Make CDC Bid *Now*	Wait Until Aventis Deal Is Signed	Alternative Plans
• Have promised capabilities to Aventis already • Potential buyer already exists • M. may be able to absorb CDC if Aventis deal falls through	• Deal has 50/50 chance of falling through • M. does not need CDC if deal falls through • $50 million dollar risk	(students proposals need to address by hedging some of the risk, e.g., by exploring contingencies with seller)

Company Update

Millennium eventually bought CDC and the Aventis deal was successfully closed (see **Exhibit TN-4** for a press release that describes more details). By 2002, Millennium had created more than 20 strategic alliances with leading pharmaceutical and biotechnology companies, which provided close to $2 billion of committed funding. In February 2002, a merger with COR Therapeutics added cardiovascular research and drug development capabilities to the company. The merger also brought INTEGRILIN® (eptifibatide) Injection, a market-leading intravenous anti-platelet drug for patients with severe cardiovascular diseases, into the Millennium portfolio. There are some drug candidates currently under evaluation and the company's future depends in part on their clinical and market success. For more current information, see www.mlm.com. The company's very recent challenges were featured in a *Boston Globe* article (shown in **Exhibit TN-5**).

Exhibit TN-1 Class Flow

Block (1)
The Lundberg Decision
(suggested time: 20-25 minutes)

"How should Mark Levin and his management team respond to Lundberg?"
(1) Accept alliance; (2) Decline alliance

↓

Block (2)
The Millennium Model
(suggested time: 15-20 minutes)

"Why is the M. model? Culture, Organization, Technology/R&, Strategy"
"Why are firms so eager to to enter alliances with M.?
"Why do pharma firms fund a potential future competitor?"

↓

Block (3)
A Framework for Assessing R&D Alliances
(suggested time: 20-25 minutes)

"What are the questions you would ask before entering an alliance?"
"Let us build a framework for evaluating alliances."

↓

Block (4)
Revisit Lundberg Decision
(suggested time: 10 minutes)

"Let us evaluate the Lundberg decision using our framework for evaluating alliance fit."

↓

Optional Block (5)
B-Case
(needed time: 15 minutes)

"What should Pospisil recommend?"
(1) Make CDC bid now; (2) Wait with bid until Aventis deal is signed

Exhibit TN-2 Board Plan

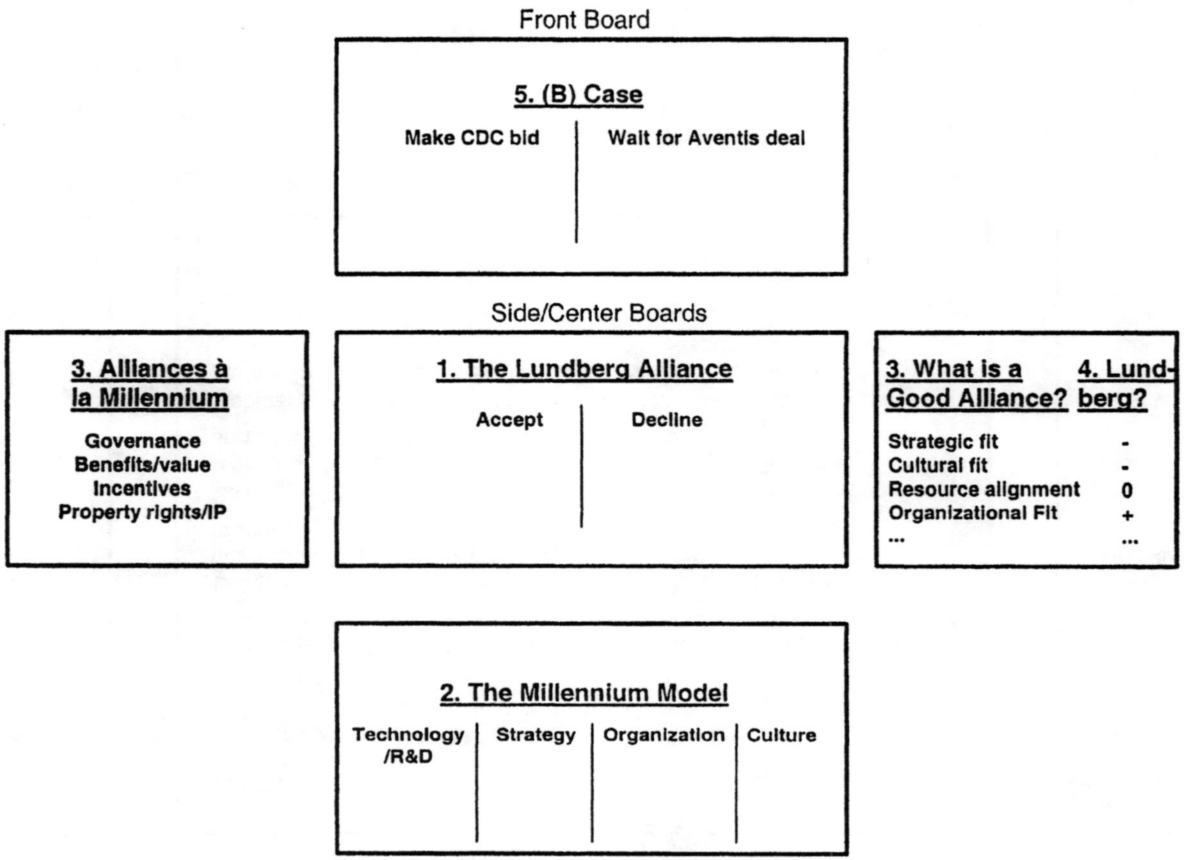

Exhibit TN-3 Center/Side Boards: The Millennium Model – Sample Comments

Technology/R&D

- Build finest science and technology platform for drug discovery (genomics, bioinformatics, etc.)
- Initial focus: target identification
- Later focus: validated targets (further downstream)
- Apply operations management principles to drug discovery
- Development approach:
  - a) 2 x speed at ½ x cost
  - b) Increase predictability to lower late stage failures (front-loading)
  - c) Fast iterations

Strategy

- Focus on downstream capabilities that add most value (e.g., targets to *validated* targets)
- Initial objective: exploit technology platform in diverse industries
- Long-term objective: to become pharmaceutical company with drug products
- Strategic alliances to generate revenues, downstream capabilities and intellectual property
- Reputation as reliable alliance partner that hits milestones

Organization

- Attract world's best scientists and advisors
- Relative flat, little hierarchy but problems because of rapid growth
- High pressure, fast-paced environment
- Management is very accessible and have small offices
- Short distance to leading research institutes (Harvard, MIT, Whitehead)

Culture

- Think tank-like atmosphere
- Informal, casual
- Feels like start-up culture, even with increasing company size
- People are motivated by "hot" science and generous financial rewards (stock options)
- "Spectacular scientists want to come to M. because spectacular scientists work at M." (case, page 5, line 6)

Exhibit TN-4 Press Release: Millennium and Aventis Pharma Close Alliance Agreement And Begin Collaborative Work

CAMBRIDGE, Mass. and FRANKFURT, Germany, July 28 /PRNewswire/ --

Millennium Pharmaceuticals, Inc. (Nasdaq: MLNM) and Aventis Pharma, the pharmaceutical company of Aventis S.A., (NYSE: AVE) today announced the closing of agreements signifying the initiation of a major strategic alliance between the two companies. Closing was expedited upon receipt of notice from the United States Federal Trade Commission (FTC) of early termination of the waiting period under the Hart-Scott-Rodino Antitrust Improvements Act of 1976. Under these agreements, which allow the companies to move forward with a multi-dimensional collaboration, Aventis made a $150 million stock purchase in Millennium at closing.

Millennium and Aventis have formed a unique alliance to jointly develop and commercialize drugs for the treatment of certain inflammatory diseases; jointly develop new drug discovery technologies; and transfer key elements of Millennium's technology platform to Aventis to enhance its existing capabilities. The agreements also provide for the purchase an equity interest in Millennium by Aventis. This is the first biotechnology/pharmaceutical company alliance of its kind and will result in Millennium and Aventis Pharma working collaboratively and exclusively to identify drug targets, develop new drugs in the field of inflammation and jointly commercialize the resulting products in North America. In all other countries, Aventis Pharma will have exclusive rights to commercialize the resulting products, with royalties paid to Millennium.

"We are delighted that all of the elements required to close this major transaction have come together quickly and we are eager to begin implementation of this collaboration. We are committed to working together with Millennium to build the world's leading program for the discovery of drugs for inflammatory diseases, as well as to make technological advances in predictive ADMET that will benefit Aventis Pharma in all of its strategic therapeutic areas," said Dr. Frank L. Douglas, executive vice president and head of Drug Innovation & Approval for Aventis Pharma AG.

"We are enthusiastic to embark upon this groundbreaking relationship with Aventis. We believe that, together, we can develop technologies that will enhance productivity of the drug discovery and development process and ultimately enable us to develop and commercialize a portfolio of breakthrough products to treat inflammatory diseases," said Mark Levin, chief executive officer of Millennium. "This relationship is a true collaborative effort and provides Millennium with our first opportunity to fully participate with one of our major pharmaceutical partners in the entire drug discovery, development and commercialization process."

Four separate arrangements covering Inflammation, Technology Development, Technology Transfer and an Equity Investment are the foundation for this alliance. Under a Technology Transfer Agreement, Millennium will provide Aventis with rights to certain drug discovery technologies in exchange for payments of up to $200 million over a five-year period. Under an Equity Investment Agreement, Aventis will also invest $250 million in Millennium's common stock. A $150 million stock purchase was made at closing yesterday and two additional $50 million purchases will be made in 2001. The combination of the Technology Transfer and the Investment Agreements represent a total of up to $450 million in payments to and investments in Millennium by Aventis. Both the Inflammation and Technology Development Agreements call for joint funding by the two companies.

Exhibit TN-4 (continued)

Aventis S.A. (NYSE: AVE) is one of the world's leading life science companies, focused on two core business areas - pharmaceuticals and agriculture. With global corporate headquarters in Strasbourg, France, Aventis employs around 90,000 people in 120 countries and recorded pro forma sales in 1998 of euro 21 billion (US $ 21.65 billion). Aventis was launched in December 1999 through the merger of Hoechst AG and Rhone-Poulenc S.A. Aventis Pharma AG is the pharmaceutical company of Aventis S.A. Aventis Pharma is dedicated to treating and preventing human disease through the discovery, development, manufacture and sale of innovative pharmaceutical products aimed at satisfying unmet medical needs. Aventis Pharma focuses on important therapeutic areas such as cardiology, oncology, infectious diseases, arthritis, allergies and respiratory disorders, diabetes and the central nervous system disorders. Aventis Pharma has its corporate headquarters in Frankfurt, Germany. Aventis Pharma also encompasses Aventis Pasteur, a world leader in vaccines based in Lyon, France, and Aventis Behring, a world leader in therapeutic proteins headquartered in King of Prussia, Pennsylvania, USA.

Millennium, a leading biopharmaceutical company, applies its comprehensive and integrated science and technology platform for the discovery and development of breakthrough therapeutic and predictive medicine products, with a goal of delivering personalized medicine. Through the industrialization of this gene-to-patient platform, Millennium is also striving to accelerate the process of drug discovery and development. Headquartered in Cambridge, Massachusetts, Millennium currently employs more than 1,000 people.

This press release contains "forward-looking statements." These statements include descriptions of Millennium's operational plans, expectations about future earnings and other results of operations, views of future industry or market conditions, and other statements that include words like "may," "expects," "believes," and "intends," and that describe opinions about future events. Known and unknown risks may cause Millennium's actual results and performances to be materially different from those expressed or implied by these statements. Some of these risks are: uncertainties relating to unanticipated difficulties and delays relating to gene identification, drug discovery and clinical development processes; changes in relationships with strategic partners and dependence upon strategic partners for the performance of critical activities under collaborative agreements; the impact of competitive products and technological changes; uncertainties relating to patent protection and regulatory approval; and uncertainties relating to the ability of Millennium and its affiliates to obtain substantial additional funds required for progress in drug discovery and development. These and other factors are identified and more fully explained in Exhibit 99.1 (entitled "Risk Factors") to the quarterly report on Form 10-Q filed by Millennium with the Securities and Exchange Commission on July 26, 2000.

Exhibit TN-5 *Boston Globe* Article, December 25, 2002 (page E1 of Business Section)

HEADLINE: SHOW US THE MONEY

By Naomi Aoki, Globe Staff

CAMBRIDGE - Two years ago, when the market value of Millennium Pharmaceuticals soared to as much as $12 billion, the company had no marketed products, six drugs in clinical trials, and little or no sales and marketing infrastructure. This year, the ambitious, 9-year-old biotechnology firm began testing four first-of-a-kind drugs in human studies this year - a feat unmatched this year and virtually unattainable for all but the biggest and most profitable biotech companies in the nation. But even though the firm is actually showing signs of delivering on its promise - moving a large number of breakthrough drugs into and through trials year after year with its sights set on becoming an industry powerhouse - investors continue to lose faith.

Millennium's stock, which climbed to $86.50 a share in late 2000, has since suffered a steep and steady descent that no amount of good news seems able to reverse. The stock in recent months has hovered around $10 a share, closing yesterday at $8.55. Its market capitalization stands at under $2.5 billion. "It's a show-me market," said Bill Tanner, an analyst with Leerink Swann & Co. in Boston. "Show me how this is adding to the near-to-intermediate term revenue stream. Show me that you can not only get these compounds into the clinic, but through the clinic and the regulatory process and on to the market." Millennium has one marketed product, Integrilin, a heart drug it acquired when it merged with San Francisco's Cor Therapeutics Inc. this year. The drug is expected by year's end to generate $300 million in sales, revenue that Millennium shares with a marketing partner. Millennium also plans to seek regulatory approval for its cancer drug, Velcade, under an accelerated process, putting the firm on track to bring its second product to market sometime next year.

But by most estimates, the company is still years away from profitability. With a staff of nearly 2,500 people and a dozen drugs in clinical trials, the company is already too large to become profitable based solely on the projected revenue from Integrilin and Velcade. The other drugs in the pipeline are in the first or second of the three phases of human testing usually required for regulatory approval, and likely several years away from reaching the market. Millennium's chief executive, Mark Levin, said the biotech firm is revisiting its forecasts and plans next month to give investors a clearer picture of its path to profitability. To date, the company has said it would reach profitability sometime in 2004, a projection few now believe is realistic.

Dennis Harp, an analyst with Deutsche Banc Alex Brown in New York, said he has crunched the numbers through 2006 and doesn't see the company reaching profitability in that time frame. "Most people believe 2004 is unrealistic," Harp said. "So the question becomes, 'When will they turn profitable?' If not in '04 and not in '06, then when?" Levin argues that the fundamental premise of the business has not changed. Millennium's goals have always been ambitious, and its strategy aggressive. Unlike many of today's successful biotech companies that spent years bringing a product to market and then relied on profits from that product to grow the company, Millennium has managed its growth based on the assumption that it would be a big success.

Its goal is to surpass even the biggest of biotech companies such as California-based Amgen Inc. and Genentech Inc. to rival pharmaceutical giants like Pfizer Inc. and Merck & Co. Levin doesn't want to bring one drug to market, just to be faced with a dearth of drugs in late-stage development. He wants to continuously fuel the pipeline, hedging the odds against failure, to make sure Millennium delivers a steady stream of drugs. On average, only one in five drugs that begin clinical trials reach the market. With $1.7 billion in available cash, Millennium has more on the runway than most biotech firms. And Levin wants to use that runway to secure the company's long-term success, even if that means postponing profitability for a few more years. "If you look at companies founded in 1990 or beyond, none of them come close to what we've done," Levin said. "Now, as we approach profitability, we have to think not only about how we get to break-even but about how we invest in the business to build a major company five to 10 years from now without major gaps in products."

Two years ago, when investors were giddy over biotech, they bought into the Millennium story in droves. They believed Millennium would reach profitability in 2004, or soon afterward. In today's dismal financial climate, however, they are more critical. When Millennium said earlier this month it would seek approval to market Velcade just two years after beginning clinical testing based on results from its phase 2 studies, rather than waiting for its phase 3 study results, analysts questioned whether the company was rushing unprepared into the regulatory process.

When analysts hear Millennium's predictions that sales of Integrilin will grow significantly next year (they are on track to increase by about 30 percent this year), they question the accuracy of the forecasts. And they take a wait-and-see approach when Millennium promises to put three to four first-of-a-kind drugs into the clinic again next year and the year after. Of the four drugs that entered clinical trials this year, two - one for rheumatoid arthritis and another for various cardiovascular complications - would compete in multibillion-dollar markets. The others - both cancer drugs - have the potential to generate smaller but still significant returns. But analysts say it is far too early to tell whether the drugs are likely to reach the market or how lucrative they might be. They note that all but one of the twelve drugs in clinical development were licensed from other companies or brought in through acquisitions. If Millennium is going to reach its goals, they said, it must move more internally discovered compounds into clinical testing, proving that its own discovery engine can fuel its pipeline.

Harp, Tanner, and other analysts said investor sentiment could turn for Millennium if the company gains approval for Velcade under the accelerated regulatory process, if it continues to put three to four new drugs into the clinic each year, and if it successfully moves them through clinical development. In the meantime, however, they wonder if it wouldn't be wiser for the company to follow a more typical path, scaling back some of its development efforts to reach profitability sooner. "In this kind of market, I think everyone would rather have something usual and successful than something record-setting where you don't know what you'll have at the end of the day," Tanner said. "Investors are looking for evidence of value creation - not by cloning a thousand genes, but by taking a drug through clinical testing and into market. Millennium is at least a few years away from really hitting stride there."

Hikma Pharmaceuticals

Teaching Note

Synopsis

Hikma is a Jordanian manufacturer of generic drugs, primarily oral and injectable cephalosporins (cephs), which has expanded internationally through a greenfield plant in Portugal and an acquisition in the United States (U.S.). The case focuses on how sales can be boosted in the U.S. One option is to become an OEM supplier to either a leading U.S. ethical pharmaceutical company or to a large managed care organization with distribution contracts to supply hospitals. A second option is to "go it alone" by investing in developing the Hikma-owned West-ward brand in the U.S.

Objectives

1. To demonstrate how a small company from an emerging market can compete internationally in an increasingly global industry.
2. To explore the criteria which internationalizing companies use to decide the sequence of country markets which they enter.
3. To highlight the tradeoffs that small foreign companies confront when trying to establish a foothold in the large U.S. market.

Teaching Suggestions

There are two ways of starting the class. One option is to ask what Said Darwazah should do in the United States and whether his goal of $100 million sales by 2000 is doable. A second option is to take a chronological approach and ask the class first how Hikma got started and why it has been successful.

If the second approach is followed, the first third of the class should be devoted to Hikma's historical development, how Samih Darwazah was able to establish the company's credibility in Jordan and the Middle East, and why and how he changed his vision for the company and began to look beyond the Arab world.

This note was prepared by John A. Quelch for the sole purpose of aiding classroom instructors in the use of Hikma Pharmaceuticals, HBS No. 598-019. It provides analysis and questions that are intended to present alternative approaches to deepening students' comprehension of business issues and energizing classroom discussion .

The second third of the class should be devoted to Hikma's entry into Europe, why Portugal was selected as the base and why Hikma's efforts in Europe have not yet borne fruit. This leads naturally to the final area of discussion: why Hikma has decided to pursue the North American market and whether Hikma has the skills, resources and determination to succeed.

So far, Hikma has done an effective job of turning West-ward around. However, Hikma now faces important strategic decisions on how to grow the U.S. business. Ideally, Said Darwazah would like to retain Hikma's independence and build the West-ward brand in the United States. However, his ambitious sales goal (and unused capacity in Portugal) probably require that he sign a three or five year OEM deal with either Northaid, a large U.S. drug company, or Sanitas, a large managed care provider, to achieve scale and profit margins (that could then be reinvested in building the West-ward brand).

Assignment Questions

1. How was Samih Darwazah able to build a successful pharmaceutical company in Jordan?

2. Why did Darwazah decide to extend Hikma's reach beyond Jordan and the Arab world?

3. Appraise Hikma's efforts to date in Europe.

4. Why did Hikma decide to pursue the U.S. market?

5. What strategic options are open to Said Darwazah and West-ward in the United States? What would you recommend?

Analysis

1. How was Samih Darwazah able to build a successful pharmaceutical company in Jordan?

Some students attributed Hikma's success to Darwazah's leadership:

- He was educated in the U.S., trained with a U.S. multinational company, and therefore knew how to run a high quality pharmaceutical firm.
- He had a vision—to create a pharmaceutical company to serve the Arab world.
- He identified the niche opportunities that led Hikma to specialize in manufacturing cephs and later in manufacturing generics for the world market.

Early in Hikma's history, Darwazah secured support and capital from an Italian joint venture partner and permission from Fujisawa, a Japanese drug manufacturer, to make some of their drugs under license in Jordan. Later, Darwazah was able to persuade Fujisawa and other MNCs to grant marketing licenses to Hikma to sell their drugs in other Arab markets beyond Jordan.

Darwazah faced many obstacles in attempting to start a drug manufacturing operation in Jordan:

- Jordan was a small country (4.3 million people) with a modest per capita annual income ($1,620).

- Multinational drug companies were already marketing their products in Jordan and these companies commanded more credibility among the Jordanian medical community than a fledgling Jordanian drug company.

- There were no other domestic drug manufacturers in Jordan so Darwazah had difficulty finding qualified personnel to staff his operation.

On the other hand, there were some benefits to Darwazah from starting out in Jordan:

- As a small market, Jordan was hardly a priority for any MNC. No MNC would assign its best managers to Jordan. As a result, Hikma was able to secure manufacturing and marketing licenses from MNCsnot only for Jordan but also for other Arab countries.

- Since drugs are high value, low bulk products, transportation costs to ship drugs from Jordan to export markets would account for a very small percentage of total costs. At the same time, Hikma's real estate and personnel costs in Jordan were probably low.

- There were well-educated Palestinians and Jordanians available to staff Hikma's operations.

2. **Why did Darwazah decide to extend Hikma's reach beyond Jordan and the Arab World?**

Initially, Hikma's expansion beyond Jordan was opportunistic. Hikma was invited to bid on government procurement tenders offered by other Middle Eastern and North African countries. Hikma later decided to expand beyond the Arab world. The reasons were:

- The Gulf War disrupted commerce in the region. Hikma needed to diversify geographically to minimize business risk.

- Hikma's success in Jordan spawned the emergence of local competitors which put pressure on Hikma's market position in its domestic market.

- In the face of a globalizing industry, Hikma had to broaden its geographical reach to build the sales volume and scale necessary to survive.

- Other Arab countries such as Saudi Arabia adopted protectionist measures to defend their own fledgling drug manufacturers, making it difficult for even an Arab competitor to penetrate their markets.

- Hikma needed to build sales internationally to keep its senior managers motivated and give them opportunities to expand their responsibilities.

- The weaker patent protection in the Arab world enabled Hikma to develop generic versions of patented cephs earlier than they could be developed in the West. This gave Hikma the opportunity to become a global supplier of generic injectable cephs. Hikma attracted enough skilled researchers and technicians not only to develop generics but also to improve upon the original drugs.

3. **Appraise Hikma's efforts to date in Europe.**

Hikma decided to focus on Western Europe for the following reasons:

- Hikma's efforts in Muslim markets beyond the Arab world such as Indonesia and Malaysia did not succeed. The government-controlled health services in these countries were not accustomed to procuring and importing generic drugs.

- Most Hikma managers had European or North American education and experience, rather than experience in Asia.

- The market integration program within the European Community (EC) promised the possibility of a single drug filing in Brussels securing access to a market of 330 million people.

- Hikma was able to secure investment grants, tax incentives and an IFC loan by locating its manufacturing operations in Portugal.

Hikma wisely build its new plant in Portugal to meet U.S. Food and Drug Administration standards (so that its output could be exported to the U.S.). Early on, Hikma Portugal was able to secure marketing licenses for other drugs to keep its sales organization occupied, pending injectable ceph production coming on stream. However, Hikma Portugal was not as successful as quickly as had been expected. The reasons were:

- EC regulations prevented generic drug manufacturers from working on formulations of patented drugs until they came off patent.

- Despite the promise of market integration, the convenience of pan-European drug licensing through a Brussels regulatory board did not materialize.

- It proved hard for Hikma to sell its products in Western Europe because government procurement on behalf of each national health service tended to favor national or established European manufacturers.

4. Why did Hikma decide to pursue the U.S. market?

- For Samih Darwazah, having studied in the U.S., it must have been a special moment to return, leading his own Jordanian company.

- The U.S. was a large and competitive market. In Darwazah's words: "If you can make it there, you can make it anywhere."

- Hikma's long experience in international markets prepared the company for entering the tough U.S. market.

- As an expert niche manufacturer of generic oral and injectable cephs, Hikma had something to offer the U.S. market.

- Hikma needed to find an alternative outlet to Western Europe for the production from its Portuguese operations.

- The U.S. market was more open and fair than the markets in either Europe or Asia.

- Generic drug penetration was higher in the U.S. than in Europe or Asia, thanks to the "drug product selection law" requiring substitution, the public concern about escalating health care costs and the many drugs coming off patent.

- Acquisition candidates (like West-ward) were available for foreign companies to acquire to gain a foothold in the U.S. market.

5. What strategic options are open to Said Darwazah and West-ward in the United States. What would you recommend?

After acquiring West-ward, Darwazah was able to restore the quality of its manufacturing operations and secure recertification from the FDA. Sales increased from $12 million in 1990 to $15 million in 1996, by when West-ward had recovered to 80 percent of its peak performance. since Hikma acquired West-ward, 35 ANDAs had been applied for and granted to West-ward by the FDA.

Said Darwazah's ambition is to grow West-ward sales to $100 million by 2000 of which $70 million would be injectable cephs imported from Hikma Portugal and distributed in the U.S. The remaining $30 million would be of other generic drugs, manufactured by West-ward, some of them under license. The West-ward manufacturing facility is not good enough to make injectable cephs and there are no plans to upgrade the plant to do so.

Although **Exhibit 4** shows that Hikma would need to sell in branded product only 37% of the generic ceph volume required to achieve the same absolute profit (0.60/1.60), West-ward has very limited resources and perhaps a negative brand reputation. It is unlikely that West-ward could go it alone, build its own name brand and still achieve the $100 million goal by 2000. Hikma's ability to supply generic injectable cephs is an important capability but Hikma is not unique in this regard, and Hikma's current capability may lose value with the passage of time. To achieve the desired level of sales, Hikma will probably have to contract as an OEM or private label supplier with either a major U.S. drug manufacturer (like Northaid) or a large managed care organization (like Sanitas). Perhaps the profits generated by one or more of these contracts could be reinvested to build the West-ward brand over time.

Both Northaid and Sanitas seem like attractive, reliable customers. However, both want to sign contracts of such size that Hikma's and West-ward's independence would be diminished. both also want exclusive arrangements, adding to the business risk. Further comparison of the two offers reveals the following:

- Northaid already has joint venture experience with West-ward. In fact, Northaid accounted for 10 percent of West-ward's 1995 sales. Sanitas has also tested West-ward's ability to deliver quality product through a one year contract to supply Sanitas with generic drugs.

- Northaid is willing to buy $30 million in generic drugs manufactured by West-ward in addition to $60 million in purchases of injectable cephs. Sanitas is not interested in procuring other generic drugs from West-ward, but its demand for injectable cephs could reach $200 million by 2000, which would require a doubling of plant capacity in Portugal.

Most students believe that Sanitas will demand lower prices and greater delivery reliability than Northaid. However, as a distributor, Sanitas will assuredly need a supply of injectable cephs, whereas Northaid's strategy, and the relative importance it places on injectable cephs as part of that strategy, may change over time. It is worthwhile taking a vote in the class as to which firm will be the better partner for West-ward.

The Aravind Eye Hospital, Madurai, India: In Service for Sight

Teaching Note

Synopsis

In Madurai, India in 1976, a retired eye surgeon named Dr. Govindappa Venkataswamy ("Dr. V.") fulfilled a lifelong dream by creating a private, non-profit hospital to provide quality eye care to citizens of India. Motivated by a deep desire to "serve God and humanity," and guided by an acute business sense, Dr. V. eventually transformed a simple 20-bed unit into a technologically advanced, 1,224-bed complex - one of the biggest hospitals of its kind in the world. Primarily through cataract surgery, Aravind restores vision to some 75,000 individuals each year who hail from the elite and poor classes alike. Dr. V.'s inspiring leadership, combined with brilliant social marketing and excellence in operations, has turned Aravind into a self-sustaining social enterprise.

The case explores how Dr. V.'s high-volume, low-cost approach to eye surgery has enabled the self-sustaining Aravind to provide free treatment to two-thirds of its patients. It also describes the hospital's "eye camp" system, whereby poor villagers are regularly offered free screenings, transportation to Aravind, surgery, and follow-up care. The case closes with Dr. V. pondering what he considers to be his biggest challenge in the next three years: how to "spread the Aravind model to every nook and corner of India, Asia, and Africa."

Use

This case can be used to illustrate the general management challenges in non-profits. It is best taught towards the concluding part of a course on non-profit management or general management. Because of its strong emphasis on leadership and the process of constructing and articulating a vision/mission/and strategy, it can be effectively taught in a strategy course as well. At HBS, it is taught as part of the Marketing Strategy module in the introductory marketing course.

This note was prepared by Professor V. Kasturi Rangan for the sole purpose of aiding classroom instructors in the use of Aravind Eye Hospital, 593-098. It provides analysis and questions that are intended to present alternative approaches to deepening students' comprehension of business issues and energizing classroom discussion.

There are at least three important analyses areas that all students need to fully understand before they make a good recommendation on what Dr. V. should do.

1. Students need to understand the Operations Model.

2. Students need to understand the Marketing Model, and

3. Students need to understand how and why the Service Model works at Aravind, both at the customer level and at the employee level.

A rich understanding of the above issues, combined with an appreciation for Dr. V.'s vision and management style, should provide enough background for students to address future steps and recommendations on hospital operations, efficiencies, and expansion plans.

Teaching Questions

1. Can you identify the key factors that have led to Aravind's success?

2. What has Dr. V.'s role been in all this?

3. How do you evaluate the quality of service at the free hospital? At the paying hospital?

4. What has been the role of Aravind's clinical and support staff in all this? Are they dedicated and altruistic or do they have an ulterior motive?

5. Are there any weaknesses at all with the Aravind model of delivering eye care?

6. How are its satellite hospitals at Tirunelveli (best labeled T-Valley) and Theni doing?

7. How are its eye camps performing?

8. How should Dr. V. expand the Aravind model to other parts of India, Asia, and Africa?

Analyses

The Operations Model

1. See case page 3, bottom paragraph. Extra-Cap ECCE took 30 minutes and Intra-Cap ICCE took 20 minutes. Compare that to Aravind's efficiency. See case page 10, bottom paragraph. Dr. Natchiar took about 15 minutes for an ECCE procedure. Aravind's ECCE efficiency is almost two times: 30/15.

See case page 11, the second to the last paragraph from the bottom. It says that a team of 5 surgeons and 15 nurses could do 150 ICCE cases in 5 hours. That is equivalent to 30 cases per hour for 5 surgeons, or 6 cases per hour for each surgeon, or 10 minutes per case per surgeon. Here again, Aravind doctors are twice as skilled: 20/10 = 2. The Aravind doctors seem to be twice as efficient in performing the surgery.

2. Aggregate Efficiency factors: See case page 4, top paragraph under India. 8.000 opthamologists operate on 1.2 million cataracts every year. That is, 1.2 million/8,000 = 150 operations/doctor and 1.2 million/42,000 eyebeds = 28 operations/bed.

Now compare that to Aravind statistics: See Exhibit 5 on page 19.

Total # of surgeries at the Madurai Hospital = 39,557 and total # of cataracts = 31,167. Aravind has 30 surgeons on its staff (bottom line of page 5). Therefore, 31,167/30 = 1,039 operations/doctor and 31,167/724 beds (from Exhibit 6) = 43 operations/bed.

So the Aravind team is 7 times more productive in terms of surgeries per doctor, and 1.5 times more effective in terms of bed utilization. Their superior skills account for only twice the efficiency. What accounts for the rest? How did the leverage go from 2 to 7?

3. Aravind runs a superb Operation. Look at the opening paragraph in the case. Aravind operators had a computerized patient entry system. It took the receptionist only about 2 minutes per patient to register them into the system. That is indeed phenomenal—that too in a third world country, backwater town. Dr. V. himself supervised the patient entry! Also read the bottom paragraph on page 10, "Even while she was operating, she explained to me in a methodical step-by-step fashion the 7 critical things she had to do to ensure a successful operation and recovery." Aravind has converted its surgical skills to a "routinized procedure" much like a time and motion assembly line worker. Read the description on the second, third, and fourth paragraphs on page 10 of the case under A Visit to the Aravind Eye Hospital. See page 13 for the Eye Camp description. All this points to a hospital with phenomenal dedication to efficiency, economy, speed, and routinizing.

Aravind runs a simply amazing assembly line operation. It is no different from McDonald's.

Be it the paying hospital or free hospital or camp, the steps are all similar:

1. Registration
2. Vision recording
3. Preliminary examination
4. Testing of tension and tear duct function
5. Refraction
6. Final examination
7. Optical shop for those who need it

Even inside the surgical theatre the patient flow configuration is focused on efficiency:

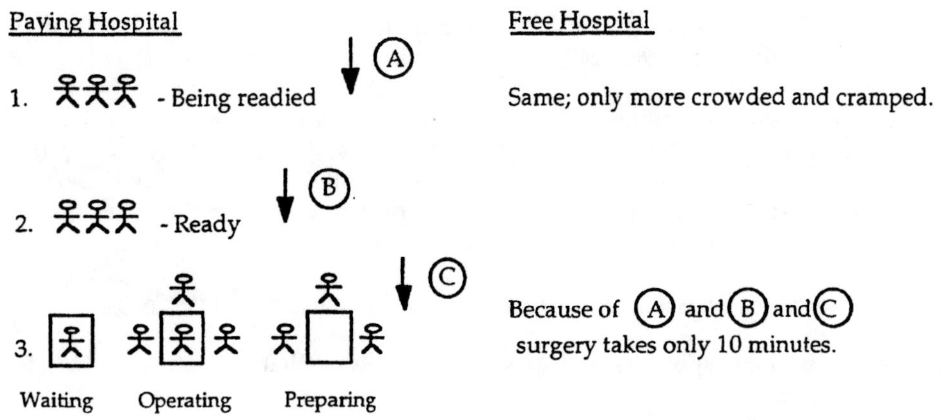

4. Study Aravind's management and staff development program.

The Dr. Natchiar and Dr. V. quotes on page 7 of the case:

"....Brother always believed in pushing the mind and body to its highest effort levels. So we would have to work twice as hard for half the salary.... But what we lost in earnings was made up by the tremendous professional support that Brother gave us. We were encouraged to attend conferences, publish papers, buy books, and do anything to advance our professional standing in the field."

"We have a lot of very capable and intelligent people, all very well trained in theoretical knowledge. But knowledge by itself is not going to save the world.... What we need is dedication and devotion to the practice. When doctors join us for residencies, we gradually condition them physically for long hours of concentrated work."

The Thulasi quote on the bottom of page 9 of the case:

"Our nurses are paid Rs 12,000 a year on average, which is not bad at all given that our staff is recruited and trained from scratch by us. They don't come from nursing school; we provide the training for them. It is like getting a prestigious degree and job training all in one."

All this indicates some very disciplined training and commitment. This is the spiritual part that Dr. V. alludes to. Aravind Eye Hospital is indeed a focused factory much like McDonald's. Cataract surgery (like hamburgers) is the main menu item. (Exhibit 5 points out that 80% of all their surgical procedures are for cataract removal.) The Aravind staff does this with relentless energy, enthusiasm, and commitment.

5. He exhorts himself and his staff to very high levels of effort and discipline. Dr. V. can perform 50 operations at a stretch with crippled hands (page 5). He admires Christ and Gandhi and Magic Johnson all in the same breath because he admires the work ethic and discipline they bring to their activity. Each of his heroes are willing to work at superhuman levels to achieve their goals.

The Marketing Model

1. From Exhibit 5 one can see that of the 569,335 patients who came to Aravind, 191,000 (34%) were from Eye Camp. This is clearly attributable to their outreach programs and social

marketing. Of the remaining 378,335 patients, paying patients are 241,643 (42%) and free patients visiting the hospital are 136,692 (24%).

It is difficult to imagine why 241,643 patients would pay to go to Aravind, when free treatment is available at the same hospital. This has to be the Aravind reputation, quality, service, and other such related factors. So it is the Reputation and Quality of Service that attracts them. The free patients visiting the hospital do so probably because they have heard of Aravind's "free" service. It is "word of mouth" that seems to do it.

2. <u>Aravind has mastered the Demand General Mechanism - Eye Camps</u>

—Run by local sponsors who have community affiliations and therefore feel obliged to deliver the patients.

—They organize the human resources to publicize and execute the camp and also pay for patients' food and logistics.

—Aravind used its failures of the formative years to understand why camp patients did not show up for surgery (see page 13). Aravind's market research revealed that 24% could not afford food and transportation, 13% could not leave family, 11% feared surgery, 10% could not go because of a lack of escort, etc. Now patients are "captured" at the camp and transported immediately. Cohort comfort is provided, both during the trip and at the hospital. Patients from the same village are bussed together, treated together, and housed together.

Its outreach program and the strategy of using its Sponsors to pay for all the social marketing costs is indeed a very very clever one. It gets the involvement of the local community. The sponsors feel good about it, and they are the ones who have deep access to consumers. Small tricks like bussing patients from the same village together, accommodating them together in the free hospital, and the 65 patient study (see page 13) are all reflections of some deep thinking given to this task. The Saturday/Sunday camp ritual and how it has been thoroughly routinized even while including the service of senior doctors like Dr. Nam is indeed interesting.

Moreover, Aravind has an outside sales force (camp organizers) who are allotted territories to work with (see Exhibit 12). Their camp organizer meeting, and Dr. V.'s evaluation of the yield, "Why only 14 surgery cases from a catchment of 100,000?" (page 15, second full paragraph), is indicative of the sales focus that drives the organization. The camp organizers help well-motivated sponsors become efficient in organizing and bringing in patients in big numbers.

Paying Patients

—Aravind has nicely price-segmented the market. The 30% paying patients subsidize the 70% non-paying patients. The paying patients are provided better service facilities:

Bed <u>vs.</u> coir mat

Private rooms <u>vs.</u> public ward

ECCE <u>vs.</u> ICCE

•Clearly differentiated product between the paying and free sections at Madurai. The paying hospital is one block (physically) away from the free hospital.

•From Exhibit 5 one can see the variety of specialized procedures that Aravind offers: Retinal detachment, Vitreous surgery, Laser and Xenon photocoagulation, etc.

•Clearly different comfort levels and service. See Exhibit 2.

•The paying hospital is obviously more spacious (see case pages 5 and 6 under History). It has 80,000 square feet for 250 beds, whereas the free hospital has 36,000 square fee for 350 beds (not including the 250-bed expansion in 1991).

•In addition, Aravind's connections to St. Vincent's, New York, and the Illinois Eye and Ear Infirmary all add to its reputation as a top-notch teaching and research institution.

•Exhibit 7 and 8 show that Aravind has a healthy gross margin of 50%. But its leaders are visionary enough to re-invest that on equipment and research (Natchiar quote on page 7 and Dr. V. quote on page 8).

Vision and Leadership

But in order for the operations and marketing model to work, the entire organization must line up behind Dr. V.. It is very clear from the case how he has been able to motivate his staff to superhuman levels. Dr. V. has strong commitment and dedication, but his greatest achievement is how he has been able to translate that for his team. Here are some thoughtful quotes on leadership quality from the September 19, 1994 issue of *Fortune* (pages 241, 242).

"The indispensable first quality, Bennis says, is a guiding vision, a clear idea of what he wants to do. 'All the leaders I know have a strongly defined sense of purpose. And when you have an organization where the people are aligned behind a clearly defined vision or purpose, you get a powerful organization.' Thomas Carlyle had it right: All history is biography—so great companies are indeed the direct reflection of their leaders.

The most exemplary leaders are also pragmatic dreamers. Banker Walter Wriston once told Bennis that he regarded his long-term plan for Citicorp as a dream with a deadline.

The best leaders have a potent point of view. Bennis quotes Mike Eisner, Disney's lion king, as saying: 'You know, we don't have a vision statement, but we have a strong point of view. What amazes me is that it's always the person with the strong POV who influences the group, who wins the day. Around here, a powerful POV is worth at least 80 IQ points.'

The leader's character is made up of a tripod of forces: ambition and drive; competence and expertise; integrity and moral fabric. All three are needed, and all three have to be in balance, or the tripod topples. Get a leader with only drive but not competence and integrity, and you get a demagogue. Get seduced by someone who has ambition and competence but lacks integrity, and you get a destructive achiever.

Leaders are people who do the right things. Managers are people who do things right. There's a profound difference. When you think about doing the right things, your mind immediately goes toward thinking about the future, thinking about dreams, missions, visions, strategic intent, purpose. But when you think about doing things right, you think about control mechanisms. You think about how-to. Leaders ask the what and why question, not the how question. Leaders think about empowerment, not control. And the best definition of empowerment is that you don't steal responsibility from people."

IN SUMMARY, ARAVIND HAS WORKED OUT A WONDERFULLY INTEGRATED MANAGEMENT MODEL, COMBINING VISION (COMMITMENT), OPERATIONS, AND MARKETING EXCELLENCE.

Figure 1

What has all this led to? Two things:

1. Customer satisfaction, and

2. Employee satisfaction.

Customer Satisfaction

The paying patients at Madurai are happy because they know they get quality eye care from some of India's most renowned ophthalmologists at a "breakthrough" hospital.

The free patients are happy because they get back functional vision. The statistics on page 12 and Exhibit 9 are revealing. Some students will argue that the free patients only get non-IOL or ICCE operations, and only one of six patients on page 12 got back a 20/20 vision. But the real question to ask is, "What was the starting point?" Patient #3, who couldn't even register hand movements, can now actually see. That must be a big improvement in quality of life. The hospital tracks back post-operative complications by patient to individual surgeons. They have pre- versus post-operation comparisons of vision recovery. The FREE patients are taken quite good care of. The poor patients get the same doctors as the paying patients. The operating staff is rotated. Even Dr. Nam (a retina surgeon) goes to the eye camp on a Sunday!

Employee Satisfaction

Initially Dr. V. got commitment by asking his family members to join in his cause. (Dr. Natchiar quote on page 7.) But later on, he simply bumped up salaries (see Thulais quote on page 9). This is probably necessary because now the hospital has 30 eye doctors, of which only 13 are from Dr. V.'s family, and a number of the second generation members might not share the same commitment to social service. Fortunately for Aravind, however, their finances are very strong (salaries only 12% of revenues). So a mixture of prestige and money is currently being used to motivate its surgeons. Aravind's satisfied employees drive higher customer satisfaction, and customer satisfaction in turn motivates higher quality employee effort.

Figure 2

Employee Satisfaction	Customer Satisfaction
- Prestige	- Continuous Process Improvement
- Research Training	- Service Quality
- Training	- Benefit Segmentation
- Equipment	- Referrals
- Specialty Clinics	- Results
- Compensation	
- Social Ideals/Goals	
- Variety of Surgical Challenges	

So What's Wrong with Aravind?

While the Madurai Hospital is doing yeoman work, the bed occupancy rate at Tirunelveli and Theni leaves much to be desired (See Exhibit 6).

Bed Occupancy Rate	*Paying*	*Free*
Madurai	265/324 = 81.5%	396/400 = 100%
Tirunelveli	**51/200 = 25.5%**	**154/200 = 77%**
Theni	**10/40 = 25%**	**28/60 = 47%**

The question is, why are those two hospitals doing so poorly?

Tirunelveli: The catchment population is not of the size to suite the Aravind model. Madurai is the district headquarters of nearly 3.5 million people. Tirunelveli is a much smaller town. Moreover, the physical infrastructure has eliminated the differentiation between the paying and free sections. See. Dr. Ravindran quote on page 9. Unlike Madurai, where the paying and free hospitals are separated by a (city) block, at Tirunelveli they are both combined. This takes away the perception of quality difference that paying patients would like to experience. If one goes back to the chronology of the Madurai hospitals (pages 5 and 6), the 250-bed paying hospital was established first in 1981. This established the reputation of the Aravind name. Only after the paying clientele was developed was the free hospital constructed. At T-Valley they were constructed together.

Theni: Probably, a wrong choice. The hospital was set up because Dr. Nam wanted a hospital for his rural town (top paragraph, page 8). There were no demographic studies that would indicate this as a good site for Aravind.

From an analysis of Case Exhibit 4, one can see that the proportion of free treatments are declining. Is Aravind losing its service focus?

Table 1

	1	2	3	4	Col. 3/ Col. 3 & Col. 4	Col. 4/ Col. 4 & Col. 2
Year	Paying Outpatient	Paying Surgery	Free Operations	Free Surgery	%Free/Total Outpatient	%Free/Total Surgery
1977	15,381	980	2,366	0	13.3%	0.0%
1978	15,781	1,320	18,251	1,045	53.6%	44.2%
1979	19,687	1,612	47,351	2,430	70.6%	60.1%
1980	31,334	2,511	65,344	5,427	67.6%	68.4%
1981	39,470	3,139	75,727	8,172	65.7%	72.2%
1982	46,435	4,216	79,367	8,747	63.1%	67.5%
1983	56,540	4,889	102,781	11,220	64.5%	69.7%
1984	69,419	5,796	104,799	11,954	60.2%	67.3%
1985	89,441	7,194	153,037	17,586	63.1%	71.0%
1986	111,546	8,202	164,977	19,623	59.7%	70.5%
1987	121,828	9,971	180,181	21,562	59.7%	68.4%
1988	182,274	12,702	232,838	23,635	56.1%	65.0%
1989	203,907	15,103	290,859	25,867	58.8%	63.1%
1990	227,243	17,896	338,407	31,162	59.8%	63.5%
1991	241,643	19,511	327,692	31,979	57.6.%	62.1%

Note decline in percentages of Free Patients in both categories. Are we losing the ability to focus on the poor?

Eye Camps

As can be seen from Tables 2 and 3, there is a wide variation in the number of patients per camp. In general, the yield from camps is declining. The # of outpatients per camp are nowhere near the 476 (of 1983) or 427 (of 1988). There is a big difference in the efficiency of the camp sponsors. Moreover, Madurai camps yield 354 patients/camp but Tirunelveli yields only 197 and Theni 191. This can be calculated from the footnote under Exhibit 11.

The important question is, "Is Aravind taking on too much camp activity and expanding into areas that compromise its basic business formula?" This suspicion is further fueled by the Sundar quote on page 15 "We don't have to sell the idea of Eye Camp to anyone. There are far more individuals, businesses, and social organizations that need our services than we can effectively offer."

Table 1

Analysis of Exhibit 10

Year	Screening Camps	Operating Camps	Outpatients Seen	Operations	Year	Outpatients Per Camp	Operations/ Camp
1978	118	0	18,251	1,045	1978	155	9
1979	215	0	47,351	2,430	1979	220	11
1980	198	10	65,344	5,427	1980	314	26
1981	140	13	75,727	8,172	1981	495	53
1982	205	9	79,367	8,747	1982	371	41
1983	204	9	101,469	10,975	1983	476	52
1984	247	21	103,177	11,796	1984	385	44
1985	475	18	153,037	17,586	1985	310	36
1986	516	13	164,977	19,623	1986	312	37
1987	506	12	180,181	21,562	1987	348	42
1988	536	9	232,838	23,635	1988	427	43
1989	818	2	290,859	25,867	1989	355	32
1990	884	3	203,805	20,852	1990	230	24
1991	707	3	191,000	20,818	1991	269	29
	5,769	122	1,907,383	198,535		4,667	478

Yield of Camps 1978-91

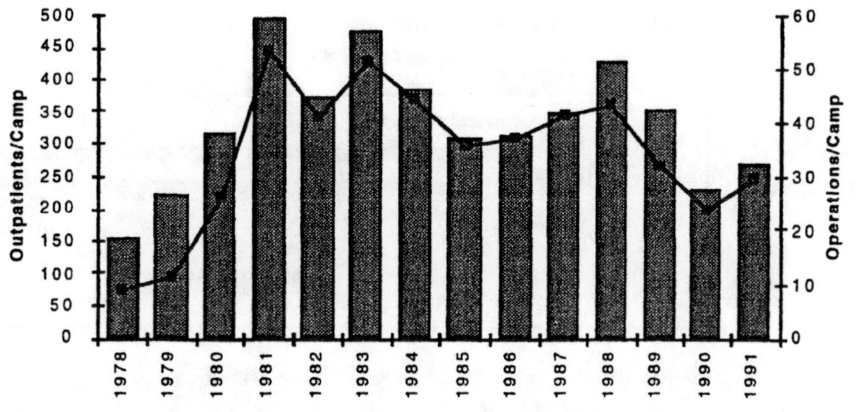

The author would like to thank Tom Kosnik for the above graph.

Table 2

Exhibit 11 Analysis: 1991 Eye Camps

Name of Organization	Number of Camps	Source	Total Outpatients	Total Surgery	Source	Outpatients/ Camp	Surgery/ Camp
Lions	105	LIO	42,439	5,210	LIO	404	50
Rotary	42	ROT	17,629	2,010	ROT	420	48
Vivekananda	190	ViV	30,899	2,897	ViV	163	15
Bhagavan ...Seva	20	SEVA	7,114	1,519	SEVA	356	76
Jaycees	18	Jay	3,823	319	Jay	212	18
Banks	27	Banks	4,854	389	Banks	180	14
Mills & Factories	28	Mills	10,543	1,019	Mills	377	36
ASSEFA	6	ASSEFA	900	109	ASSEFA	150	18
Schools & Coll.	50	Schls	8,577	492	Schls	172	10
Hospitals	12	Hosp	4,291	1,031	Hosp	358	86
Trusts	16	Trusts	6,329	1,258	Trusts	396	79
Youth and Fans	37	Youth	6,291	392	Youth	170	11
Other Religious	41	Relig	12,696	1,362	Relig	310	33
Other Voluntary	75	Volunt	23,356	1,981	Volunt	311	26
Others	40	Other	11,259	30	Other	281	1
	707		191,000	20,018		4,258	521

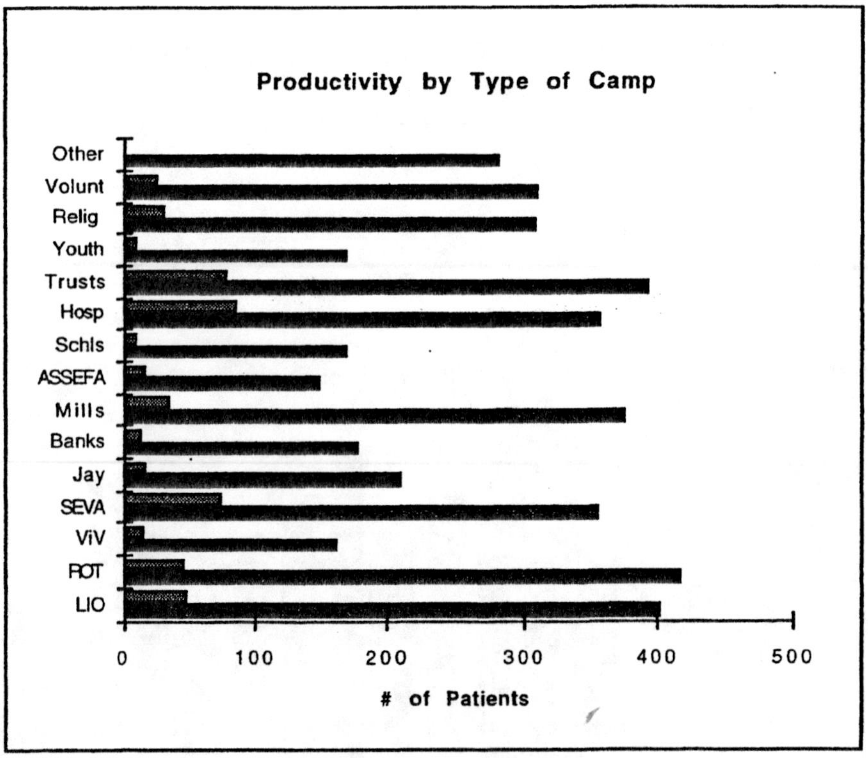

The author would like to thank Tom Kosnik for the above graph.

Action Plan

So, what should Aravind do? Follow Dr. V.'s vision of "spreading the Aravind model to every nook and corner..." or, regroup and refocus? A dispassionate analysis would certainly indicate that

- Theni should be closed down

- Tirunelveli should be reorganized

- Coimbatore is probably a good decision. It has the characteristics that made Aravind successful.

- Eye camp activity should focus on high yield camps. Regardless of sponsor enthusiasm, some camps are not conducive to Aravind's style of volume.

On the other hand, one can argue that Dr. V.'s vision and mission are simply to cure blindness, not to be the "cataract McDonald's" of the world! The operations and social marketing are a means to an end, not the end in itself. But can he achieve the latter without the management? One can argue that the 3 gears of Figure 1 (page 7 of teaching note) have to help each other. Vision and commitment can start up businesses and organizations, but sustaining them requires functional expertise offered by the other two wheels. Moreover, if Dr. V. would like his good work to continue after he retires from the scene, it is all the more important to shore up the management side. What happens to Dr. V.'s family? Will they show the same commitment? How about the second generation of doctors? It is refreshing to see that Aravind has indeed moved to make its salary scales attractive. Look at the Thulasi quote on the bottom of page 9. They certainly should not match private sector salaries, but can go up some more to attract talented clinicians and nurses. After all, Aravind has the reputation. Exhibit 7 indicates a gross margin of 50%. Stipends and salaries are a mere 12%. Even if they went to 18% or 20% or so, (i.e., a 50% salary raise), Aravind would still be able to maintain a healthy margin of 40-45% for reinvestment in equipment and research. If the Aravind efficiency permeates, say, the Indian medical system, blindness can actually be eradicated in a decade or so.

Figure 3

Eradicating Blindness in India

Current Model

- Blind Eyes (1992)	20 million
- Additions each year	2 million
- Operations each year	1.2 million
- Blind Eyes (2001)	28 million (i.e., 20+(2-1.2)x)

Projection

All surgeons in India work at Aravind Efficiency:

8,000 doctors x 1000 surgeries in 1 year:

- Operations each year	8 million
- Blindness eradicated	3 to 4 years (by 1995)

All surgeons in India work at 50% Aravind Efficiency:

- Operations each year	4 million
- Blindness eradicated	in 10 years

Investments in bed capacity will be needed to perform the volume of surgery indicated, but brick and mortar investment would be a monumental waste because once the backlog is cleared, one needs only a 1.2 million-patient capacity every year. That's why the eye camp model is so attractive. One has to creatively think of a hub and spoke system.

Teaching the Case

Aravind is an inspiring story. Students are touched and impressed by Dr. V.'s achievements.

The case needs good, thoughtful analyses, and is best structured to discuss the "What will you do?" question last. It is useful to follow the order of the teaching questions on page 2 of this teaching note. Students who in general recognize Aravind as a very successful model will learn by understanding the operations and marketing part of the overall picture. It is very useful for them to see the model underlying Figure 1.

The discussion on service quality, the differentiation between the paying and free hospital, and what's in it for the employees (who slog away for a low salary) is a very interesting one; instructors should not short-change that part of the discussion. Also, few students see the weaknesses in the Aravind model. It is quite a revelation to many that such a successful business could actually be committing mistakes. But they are, and they seem to be moving away from their basic assumptions of the very successful Madurai venture. Only after students discuss this in detail, should one ask for an action plan. Very creative solutions are offered, but instructors should press students on the consistency of their plans, with respect to their analyses. In short, I advocate four major class discussion themes:

Theme 1: Madurai success factors

Develop, synthesize, and summarize Figure 1

Theme 2: Service quality, delivery, and employee motivation

Develop, synthesize, and summarize Figure 2

Theme 3: Weakness

Theme 4: Action plan

5-503-046
DECEMBER 5, 2002

TEACHING NOTE

Abgenix and the XenoMouse

Synopsis

Abgenix has spent 7 years and $40 million developing a class of genetically-engineered mouse (the XenoMouse) that has the ability to produce human antibodies that are useful in the treatment of human diseases, such as cancer, arthritis, etc.

To date, the company has made money by licensing the XenoMouse technology to leading pharmaceutical and biotech companies. These companies identify a specific disease target (e.g., thyroid cancer) that they are trying to hit with an antibody. Abgenix then sells exclusive rights to use the XenoMouse technology to develop antibodies for that specific disease. For this right, the licensing company agrees to pay an upfront fee, development milestones fees, and a royalty on the sale of the resulting drug, should it gain FDA approval. To date, Abgenix had entered 17 such licensing arrangements, with many more expected.

At the time of the case, the company is debating whether it should move from a pure-licensing strategy to one in which it (sometimes) plays a more direct role by co-developing and co-marketing the drug. The tradeoffs the company faces involve level of risk (licensing brings in revenues even if the drug proves unsuccessful) versus greater upside potential (co-development provides greater returns should a drug gain FDA approval). The present debate involves a promising new cancer drug (codenamed ABX-EGF) and two standing offers—one that involves licensing and one that involves co-development.

Use

This case is useful at several levels. These include:

- It exposes students to the high-risk, high-reward nature of biotechnology.
- It generates a discussion about risk diversification in new product development. In fact, students may come to different conclusions if they view the decision about this promising drug as a one-shot deal or as part of a larger, multi-shot approach to drug development.
- It highlights the pressures in this industry to "forward integrate." Given the shape of the value curve (Case **Figure C**), there is enormous pressure in drug development to remain

This note was prepared by Professor John T. Gourville for the sole purpose of aiding classroom instructors in the use of Abgenix and the XenoMouse, HBS No. 501-061, written by Professor Robert J. Dolan. It provides analysis and questions that are intended to present alternative approaches to deepening students' comprehension of business issues and energizing classroom discussion. HBS cases are developed solely as the basis for class discussion. Cases are not intended to serve as endorsements, sources of primary data, or illustrations of effective or ineffective management.

involved through commercialization. In teaching the case, one can contrast the drug industry with industries where most of the value is created early in the product development process.

- Finally, it allows for a discussion of company evolution. This can be thought of as "What does the company want to be when it grows up?" There are indications in the case that Abgenix wants to be a Fully Integrated Biotech Company (FIBCO). Does this make sense and, if so, is this the right drug to be doing it with?

In past teachings, the case has proven effective because (1) it presents an interesting industry, (2) it offers plenty of qualitative and quantitative data to ground the class discussion, (3) there is a strong difference of opinion about which option should be pursued, and (4) the discussion generally prove enlightening for the students.

Analysis

There are four main areas of discussion in this case. These include:

1. A general discussion of the pros and cons of the three options presented in the case. This debate helps identify issues that are critical for resolving the case.
2. A more detailed economic analysis of the two standing offers from Pharmacol and BioPart.
3. An assessment of the risk inherent in bringing this product to market. This discussion has two parts. The first involves the value curve inherent in this industry. The second involves the single-shot versus multi-shot perspective of drug development.
4. An assessment of what this company wants to be in the future. If it wants to be a licensor of technology, what should it do? If it wants to be a FIBCO, what should it do?

1: Which Offer Should Abgenix Take?

It is recommended the instructor begin by asking students which option they would take if they ran Abgenix. Based on information in the case, the three options can be summarized as follows:

A. An offer from Pharmacol—a large, well-regarded, well-established pharmaceutical firm—to license the XenoMouse technology to develop ABX-EGF.

B. An offer from BioPart—a much smaller biotech firm with a good reputation for innovation and managing the regulatory process—to jointly develop and market ABX-EGF.

C. The option of "Doing Phase II by itself and Then Deciding." Under this option, Abgenix would incur the cost of Phase II trials on its own.

Reasons For and Against Pharmacol

Many students will support the Pharmacol proposal, primarily because it guarantees some revenue and it fits with the company's current licensing strategy. More completely, reasons for supporting the Pharmacol offer include:

- No downside. Pharmacol pays at least $18 MM regardless of FDA results.
- Greater total sales due to the highly accomplished salesforce of Pharmacol.

- A royalty on sales of 10%, as opposed to the normal 4% to 6%.
- Upside potential in excess of $400 MM.
- Consistency with its stated licensing strategy. As Geoff Davis, Abgenix's CTO states on case page 8, "We have always had a strategy of being out by the end of Phase II."
- There are thousands of potential licensing agreements (case page 1).
- Abgenix does what it does best (R&D) and Pharmacol does what it does (FDA and Sales).

However, others will offer reasons not to go with Pharmacol. These include:

- ABX-EGF has too much upside potential to simply license it to another firm.
- Pharmacol offers Abgenix little else besides money.
- The value curve demands that Abgenix retain commercialization rights to ABX-EGF.
- It is not clear how much of a priority Pharmacol will place on ABX-EGF.

Reasons For and Against BioPart

Other students will support the BioPart proposal because it offers higher upside potential and it allows Abgenix to develop skills in the areas of late-stage drug development, regulatory approval, product launch, and marketing. More completely, reasons for BioPart include:

- Much greater upside potential—$900 MM versus $400 MM.
- Ability to develop skills that Abgenix currently lacks.
- Abgenix has many other licensing agreements that it can fall back on, if this product fails.
- Abgenix is currently cash rich, with $500+ MM in the bank (see **Case Exhibit 2**).
- If Abgenix wants to be a FIBCO, they will have to take this step at some time.
- This is how Amgen and other large biotechs became FIBCOs.

However, naysayers will quickly point to the downside of the BioPart deal. In particular:

- Should ABX-EGF not gain FDA approval, Abgenix will lose $35 MM.
- Overall sales will be only 80% of what they would have been with Pharmacol.
- BioPart does not have the clout that Pharmacol does.
- Do you really want to fail with such a high-profile product?

In this discussion, some students may question the likelihood of FDA approval if Abgenix goes with BioPart versus Pharmacol. Some students will argue that the odds of success should be better with the larger and more sophisticated Pharmacol. However, the case makes it clear (case page 10) that the likelihood of success will be 40% regardless of whom Abgenix goes with.

Reasons For and Against "Going it Alone"

Finally, some students will argue for "going it alone" (at least through Phase II), allowing Abgenix to gather more information with little risk. These students will argue that the value curve suggests that there is much value to be gained by getting to the end of Phase II. Further, they argue that Pharmacol and BioPart are not likely to go anywhere.

However, those against this plan will argue that there *is* something to lose. First, Abgenix will incur the costs associated with the Phase II trials, which could amount to as much as $35 MM (the sum of the first two years of expenses calculated under the BioPart plan). Second, it is not clear that the value creation curve for ABX-EGF will match that shown in **Case Figure C**. As mentioned on case page 11, "Management felt it was highly likely that the development program would at least enter Phase III" regardless of whom Abgenix went with. If this is true, and if Pharmacol and BioPart know this, it is unlikely they would improve their offers after Phase II is completed. This may partly explain why Pharmacol is willing to offer a hefty 10% royalty at this early stage.

Summary

As this discussion is taking place, it is helpful to capture the major decision factors on a side board. Based on the reasons for and against each option, these can be summarized as (1) economics, (2) risk tolerance, (3) long-term goals, and (4) opportunity to learn.

Before leaving this discussion, the instructor should get a sense of where the class stands. The instructor should ask for a show of hands for each option. If many students still choose Option 3, "go it alone," the instructor might force these people to make a decision by asking, "OK, its 2 years down the line, Phase II has been successful, and the same two offers still stand. Who do you choose now?" Based on past experience, there will be a fairly even split between going with Pharmacol and BioPart.

2: The Economic Analysis

In tandem with the first area of discussion—which option to choose—students will raise the issue of the costs and benefits of each option. Given the uncertain nature of the drug development process, this leads to three sets of numbers: (1) a worst case scenario, in which the drug fails to gain FDA approval, (2) a best case scenario, in which the drug does gain FDA approval, and (3) and expected value, which weighs these two outcomes by their likelihood of occurrence. Based on a few simple main options in the case, licensing to Pharmacol and BioPart offers.

Pharmacol Analysis

The data needed to analyze the Pharmacol offer are contained on case pages 10 and 11, and in **Case Exhibit 3**. The nature of the licensing agreement has Abgenix liable for no expenses and has Pharmacol responsible for the following payments to Abgenix:

- $5 MM upon signing the licensing agreement.
- $5 MM upon beginning Phase II trials, which was virtually guaranteed.
- $8 MM upon beginning Phase III trials, which was again, virtually guaranteed.
- $10 MM upon FDA approval, which had a 40% likelihood.
- If approved by the FDA, a 10% royalty on the sales laid out in **Case Exhibit 3**.

It is also noted on case page 10 that it would take 5 years to get ABX-EGF to market if everything went as planned. This 5 year window suggests that the timing and probability of the above payments, if spread over the approval and sales window, could be as follows:

Year 0 (i.e., start of Year 1):	$5 MM, guaranteed
End of Year 1:	$5 MM, guaranteed
End of Year 3:	$8 MM, guaranteed
End of Year 5:	$10 MM, 40% probability
Years 6-15:	10% of sales, 40% probability

These payments and probabilities are summarized in **Exhibit TN-1**. Ignoring discount rates, this implies the following revenues for Abgenix:

Worst Case (i.e., FDA rejection):	$ 18 MM
Best Case (i.e., FDA approval):	$ 409.50 MM
Expected Value	$ 174.60 MM

With discount rates, these figures are reduced. **Exhibit TN-2** presents worst-case, best-case, and expected value outcomes at discount rates of 0%, 5%, 10%, 15%, and 20%.

BioPart Analysis

As with Pharmacol, all of the data required to do an economic analysis for the BioPart proposal are contained on case pages 10 and 11, and in **Case Exhibit 3**. The salient points of this agreement are as follows:

- BioPart would pay Abgenix $5 MM upon signing.
- BioPart would pay Abgenix $5 MM upon start of Phase II trials, virtually guaranteed.
- Abgenix and BioPart would share all other costs and revenues equally.
- Shared costs in years 1-5 would be:

Year 1	$10 MM, guaranteed.
Year 2	$20 MM, guaranteed.
Year 3	$25 MM, guaranteed.
Year 4	$35 MM, guaranteed.
Year 5	$35 MM, 40% probability.
Pre-launch	$15 MM, 40% probability.

- If approved by the FDA, likely sales at 80% of those outlined in **Case Exhibit 3**.
- If approved by the FDA, likely COGS and S, G & A at 35% of sales.

These payments, costs, and probabilities are summarized in **Exhibit TN-3**. Ignoring discount rates, this results in the following results for Abgenix:

Worst Case (i.e., FDA rejection):	$ 35 MM Loss
Best Case (i.e., FDA approval):	$ 931.90 MM Gain
Expected Value	$ 351.76 MM Gain

With discount rates, these figures also are reduced. **Exhibit TN-4** presents worst-case, best-case, and expected value outcomes at discount rates of 0%, 5%, 10%, 15%, and 20%.

Summary

The economic analyses of Pharmacol and BioPart can be summarized as shown in **Figure TN-1**. In short, there is a 60% chance that a drug based on ABX-EGF will not gain FDA approval and a 40% chance that such a drug will gain FDA approval. Therefore, with a 60% likelihood, the Pharmacol offer will produce $18 million in revenue, while the BioPart offer will result in a $35 million loss for Abgenix. Clearly, in this regard, the BioPart offer represents a must riskier option. To bring this point home, the instructor can ask students to take the role of Abgenix's CEO, Scott Greer, and explain to his Board of Directors why the company lost $35 million with BioPart when it could have made a minimum of $18 million with Pharmacol.

Figure TN-1 Summary of Economic Analysis for Pharmacol and BioPart

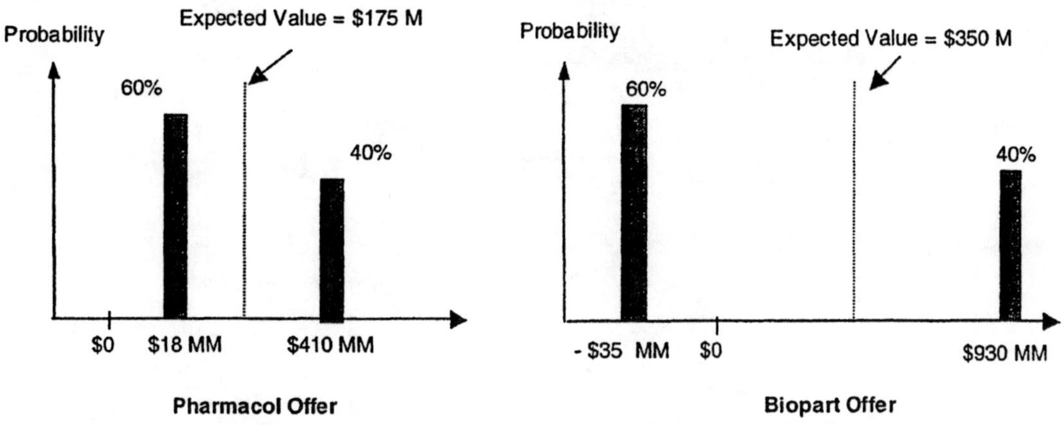

Source: Author

However, with a 40% likelihood, Abgenix stands to earn $410 million from the Pharmacol deal, but $930 million from the BioPart deal. This much greater upside makes the BioPart offer very attractive. It should be noted that some students will argue that once these figures are discounted, the economics become less favorable for BioPart, as reflected in **Exhibits TN-2** and **TN-4**. Nevertheless, most students will agree that Pharmacol represents the "safer" option and that BioPart represents the option with greater potential.

3. Is This Just About the Economics? An Assessment of Risk

After a detailed analysis of the economics, some students will be satisfied that they have all the information they need to come to a decision. However, other students will feel that the class has missed several important points. To encourage a broader discussion, the instructor can ask, "Is this decision just about the economics? What else is involved?" This should raise at least two higher-level issues. The first is a question of how much risk the company is willing to take on. The second is whether to view this decision in the context of a single product or many products.

How Much Risk is this Company Willing to Take On?

To help answer this first question, it is useful to refer to the curve found in **Case Figure C.** When plotting "value created" against "stage of development," the curve is quite flat through the beginning of Phase II. During Phase II clinical trials, the value perceived by the potential licensee or buyer increases dramatically. Then, following Phase II, it flattens off again. This pattern suggests that much of the value created in the drug development process occurs during Phase II trials. This is also reflected on case page 7, where it is stated:

> Phase II is the inflection point where you get the big bump in value. In Phase II, you have shown it effective to a statistically significant degree. Sure, there are things to still work out in Phase III and with the FDA.

This thinking can easily be captured by redrawing **Case Figure** C on the board and adding a few details, as reflected in **Figure TN-2.** In this figure, it clear that handing off in the form of a license early in the process is low risk. However, it also generates only a fraction of the value Abgenix might receive by holding on though Phase II trials. In contrast, holding on through Phase II trials creates a lot more value, but greatly increases the risk of failure.

Figure TN-2 Risk Profile for Abgenix's Drug Development

Source: Author.

The end result is that there is tremendous pressure to forward integrate in this industry. This pressure can be contrasted with that which exists in something like the software industry, where much of the value is created early in the development process. Rather than a curve that climbs late in the development process, the value curve climbs early in the software development process and then flattens out. Students should be asked to think about how different shapes of the value creation curve will affect the logic of licensing versus in-house development or co-development.

Is This a One-Shot Deal?

The second issue relevant to this discussion involves how broadly to consider the decision at hand. If considered in isolation (only ABX-EGF) the relevant economics are as presented in **Figure TN-1.** However, some students will argue that this decision needs to be made in the context of a portfolio of products. First, Abgenix has 17 licensing agreements with many more possible. As a result, the current decision likely will not make or break the company. Second, Abgenix has a total of four products under internal development that it has high hopes for. While any one of these four products may seem risky (when viewed in isolation), as a group they present far less risk. This is the power of diversification—as long as the upside potential on these products is large enough, the company can tolerate several product failures along the way.

Such thinking is reflected in **Figure TN-3.** While the probability of losing money is 60% in the one-product scenario, it decreases considerably as one increases the number of products one builds into the portfolio. For instance, with two products, the chance that both fail is 36% (i.e., 0.6^2). With four it drops to 13%(i.e., 0.6^4). And with 10, it drops to less than 1% (i.e., 0.6^{10}). As a result, as the number of products in the development portfolio increases, the worst-case and the best-case scenarios become meaningless and the expected values become increasingly more important. And given the two options currently under consideration, the expected value of the BioPart offer ($350 million) is twice as large as the expected value of the Pharmacol offer ($175 million).

Figure TN-3 The Effects of a Change in Perspective Regarding Risk

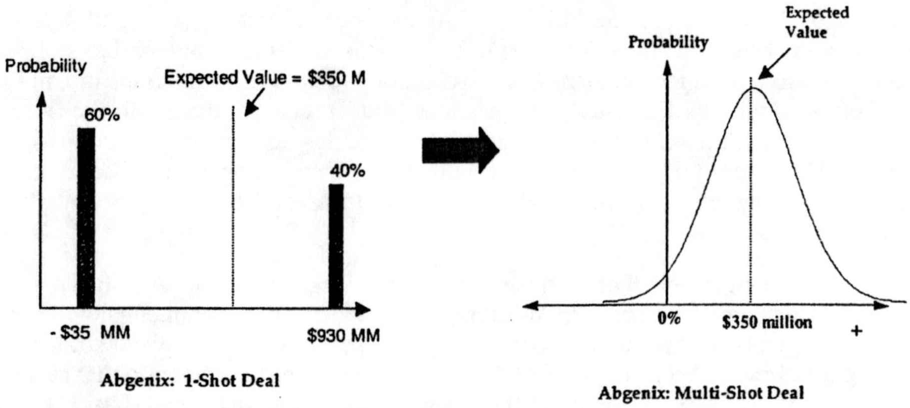

Source: Author.

Summary

At the end of this third section, students should have gained a sense that industry pressures encourage forward integration in this marketplace. In addition, how one views the decision at hand may greatly influence perceptions of risk. If viewed in isolation, the decision of whether to go with BioPart of Pharmacol is a choice between a risky and a safe alternative. However, if viewed as part of a larger development effort, the risk associated with BioPart tends to be diversified away. Therefore, the discussion at hand has less to do with ABX-EGF and more to do with Abgenix's overall approach to product development, leading to the final area of discussion.

4. What Does the Company Want to Be?

This final area of discussion raises the level of discussion yet another notch. Rather then view the ABX-EGF decision in the context of a single product or in the context of a portfolio of products, the decision can be analyzed at the level of long-term company goals—i.e., what does the company want to look like in 5, 10, or 20 years? Such a discussion can be grounded in the drawing shown in **Figure TN-4**. In particular, if Abgenix is content being a licensor, why even consider BioPart? But if Abgenix wants to be a FIBCO, why would it not take the BioPart offer?

Figure TN-4 Where does Abgeniz want to Play in the Long-Term?

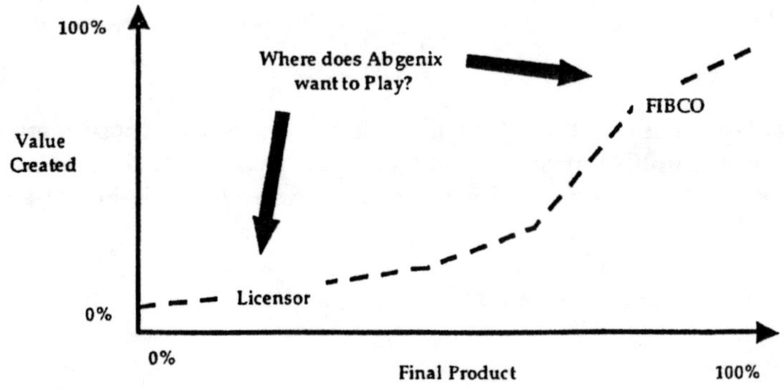

Source: Author.

Several issues are valuable to discuss in this area. The first is, "How did the Amgen's and Genentech's of the world become FIBCOs?" As laid out on case pages 3 and 4, these companies initially pursued licensing strategies, in much the same way that Abgenix has done to date. For instance, Genentech used recombinant DNA technology to produce human insulin, but then licensed the marketing rights to Eli Lilly. Only later did it take a drug all the way through to commercialization. Similarly, Amgen spent years licensing its promising products before it took Epogen and Neupogen through to commercialization. Using Amgen and Genentech as examples, one could view Abgenix's current decision as part of the evolution of any potential FIBCO in this industry.

It is also important to note that both Genentech and Amgen still employ a mixed strategy when it comes to product development. In addition to products they commercialize themselves, they continue to take on collaborators, to whom they license products. This mixed strategy suggests that even if Abgenix were to become a FIBCO, it might not or should not abandon its currently licensing strategy for some products. To help get these issues out, an instructor could ask, "How has Amgen approached this issue?"

As for those in charge of Abgenix, there seems to be some evidence in the case that they aspire to become a FIBCO. The mere fact that they are seriously considering the BioPart offer makes this evident. Other evidence include the quotes from Ray Withy, Abgenix's Chief Business Officer, who states, "Are the preclinical results so compelling that we have already created lots of perceived value? Or, on the other hand, is there so much potentially on the table that we should not be thinking about handing off at all?" Finally, some students will argue that the raising of $600 million in funds suggests that the company is planning of doing something more than just licensing the XenoMouse.

Given this, the instructor can ask whether ABX-EGF is the right product to be using to make this transition. Some students will say 'no.' They will argue that ABX-EGF is too much of a high profile, high potential product to "learn with." Instead, these students will argue for picking a lower profile product that provides all of the learning, but little of the visibility or risk should it fail to gain FDA approval.

Others will argue that this is exactly the 'right' product to learn with. First, they will note that the case says that the odds of success are the same regardless of whether Abgenix goes with BioPart or Pharmacol. Second, they will argue that the effort and cost of learning will be similar regardless of the potential of the product. Therefore, Abgenix may as well learn on that product that provides the largest upside potential. In their thinking, "Why give away a potential blockbuster via licensing? If you are going to take a chance on commercialization, do it with a product that maximizes returns." Finally, even if this product fails to gain FDA approval, Abgenix will have learned a tremendous amount about the late-stage development and regulatory process that it can apply to the next potential blockbuster it develops.

Summary

The net result of this last section is that students generally agree that those managing Abgenix would like to see it become a FIBCO at some point in time. In light of this, ABX-EGF probably provides a good platform for them to make the transition. However, this in not an "either - or" decision. As with Amgen and Genentech, most students agree that in addition to retaining certain high-potential products for commercialization, Abgenix should retain a portfolio of licensing agreements for those products that stand a better chance of success with a licensee.

What Happened?

In July 2000, Abgenix entered into agreement with Immunex (disguised as BioPart, in the case) to jointly develop and commercialize ABX-EGF. Through fall 2002, Immunex and Abgenix were conducting Phase II clinical trials targeted at colorectal, prostate, lung, and renal cancer. They also had begun Phase I trials for the treatment of kidney, pancreatic, non-small cell lung, and esophageal cancer. Throughout this process, Abgenix and Immunex shared all costs and efforts, as per the agreement in the case. In annual reports and in other public statements, Abgenix and Immunex remained optimistic that ABX-EGF would prove to be a major drug breakthrough.

Similarly, in August 2000, Abgenix entered into a co-development agreement with Sangstat for ABX-CBL, another of the drugs that Abgenix had been developing. Sangstat was given exclusive worldwide license for the marketing and sale of ABX-CBL, development costs would be shared equally, as would any potential profits from sale of a ABX-CBL product. Also, Abgenix would be responsible for manufacturing ABX-CBL. Through fall 2002, ABX-CBL had been through Phase II clinical trials.

In addition, Abgenix had retained the rights to several other promising products and continued to conduct early stages trials. These products include ABX-IL8, for the treatment of pulmonary disease, and ABX-MA1, for the treatment of melanoma (skin cancer). However, in May 2002, Abgenix announced that ABX-IL8 was found to be ineffective as a treatment for pulmonary diseases, putting the product in doubt for that application.

At the same time, Abgenix was continuing to license the XenoMouse technology to a number of biotech and pharmaceutical firms. All together, these licensing agreements generated revenues in the range of about $30 million per year. These revenues were offset, however, by ever increasing development costs for those drugs that Abgenix had decided to co-develop. Research and development costs in FY 2001 were $96 million, up from $50 million in FY 2000, and $19 million in FY 1999. Research expenses were on track to exceed $120 million in FY 2002.

To fund these ongoing efforts, Abgenix raised another $230 million in the fall of 2000 in a private placement of common stock. This was in addition to the $600 million mentioned in the case. By fall 2002, the company held slightly over $450 million in cash and other short-term assets.

Teaching the Case

With this case, students come to class with strong opinions about what Abgenix should do—opinions largely driven by economics. For the first half of the class discussion, the instructor should play into these strong opinions and allow the many issues, especially economic, to come out. In the second half of the class, the instructor should raise the level of discussion to look at the larger picture of the direction of this company.

At the start of class, it is recommended that the instructor start by asking, "So, if you were Scott Greer, what would you do?" This leads to qualitative comments (e.g., BioPart allows for learning) and quantitative comments (e.g., Pharmacol guarantees $18 MM in revenue). These comments should be captured on the board under the headings "Pharmacol," "BioPart," and "Go it Alone."

As more and more of the economics come out, the instructor should use a fresh board to walk through the financial analysis (see **Exhibits TN-1** through **TN-4**). While there will be some disagreement regarding the timing of certain payments or costs, there is general agreement as to the magnitudes of the financials for both offers—resulting in Pharmacol being perceived as the safer option and BioPart as the one with much greater upside.

Before leaving the first area of discussion, the instructor may wish to take a vote to see where the class stands. In all likelihood, there will still be much disagreement. To help move away from a pure economic focus, the instructor might ask, "Is this just about the economics of the two offers? What are we missing?" This leads naturally to the second half of the case discussion, which focuses on the bigger picture facing Abgenix. The instructor can encourage a discussion about, "Why does this pressure exist to forward integrate?, Is this really a risky decision?, What is so attractive about being a FIBCO?," and "Is this the right drug to be learning on?" These questions should allow for the type of discussion laid out previously in this note.

A potential board plan for this discussion is provided in **Exhibit TN-5.**

Suggested Preparation Questions

Some suggested preparation questions for this case are:

1. Does Pharmacol or BioPart represent a better way to go for Abgenix? Why?
2. What factors would you focus on in choosing a partner? Which of these factors are most important? Why?
3. What should Scott Greer do?
    - go it alone through the end of Phase II trials?
    - sign with Pharmacol?
    - sign with BioPart?
    - something else?
4. What are the major risks you see in your decision? How can these be managed?

Exhibit TN-1 Economic Analysis for the Pharmacol Proposal (all $ figures are in millions)

	Year															
	0	1	2	3	4	5	6	7	8	9	10	11	12	13	14	1
Pharmacol Payment ($)	**5**	**5**	**0**	**8**	**0**	**10**										
Probability (%)	***100%***	***100%***	***100%***	***100%***	***100%***	***40%***										
Pharmacol Revenue ($)							20	70	135	250	330	450	540	620	700	
Royalty (%)							*10%*	*10%*	*10%*	*10%*	*10%*	*10%*	*10%*	*10%*	*10%*	*1*
Abgenix Royalty ($)[1]							**2**	**7**	**13.5**	**25**	**33**	**45**	**54**	**62**	**70**	
Probability (%)							***40%***	***40%***	***40%***	***40%***	***40%***	***40%***	***40%***	***40%***	***40%***	***4***
Abgenix Costs ($)	0	0	0	0	0	0	0	0	0	0	0	0	0	0	0	
Revenues:																
Minimum ($)[2]	5	5	0	8	0	0	0	0	0	0	0	0	0	0	0	
Maximum ($)[3]	5	5	0	8	0	10	2	7	13.5	25	33	45	54	62	70	
Expected Value ($)[4]	5	5	0	8	0	4	0.8	2.8	5.4	10	13.2	18	21.6	24.8	28	

Notes:
1. "Abgenix Portion" reflects the 10% royalty paid on Pharmacol Sales
2. "Minimum" includes only those payments that are 100% certain.
3. "Maximum" includes all payments regardless of probabilities.
4. "Expected Value" is a weighted average of payments and is calculated as [Royalty or Payment] x [Probability]

Source: Author.

Exhibit TN-2 Discounted Economic Results for Pharmacol Proposal (in millions)

Discount Rate	Worst Case Scenario	Best Case Scenario	Expected Value
0%	$18.00	$ 409.50	$ 174.60
5%	16.67	234.77	103.91
10%	15.56	142.24	66.23
15%	14.61	91.09	45.20
20%	13.80	61.66	32.94

Source: Author.

Exhibit TN-3 Economic Analysis for the BioPart Proposal (all $ figures are in millions)

	Year															
	0	1	2	3	4	5	6	7	8	9	10	11	12	13	14	15
oPart Payment ($)	**5**	**5**	**0**	**0**	**0**	**0**										
Probability (%)	***100%***	***100%***	***100%***	***100%***	***100%***	***40%***										
ug Sales ($)[1]							16	56	108	200	264	360	432	496	560	560
Abgenix Portion (%)							*50%*	*50%*	*50%*	*50%*	*50%*	*50%*	*50%*	*50%*	*50%*	*50%*
genix Portion ($)							**8**	**28**	**54**	**100**	**132**	**180**	**216**	**248**	**280**	**280**
Probability (%)							***40%***	***40%***	***40%***	***40%***	***40%***	***40%***	***40%***	***40%***	***40%***	***40%***
rtnership Costs ($)	-0	-10	-20	-25	-35	-50	-5.6	-19.6	-37.8	-70	-92.4	-126	-151.2	-173.6	-196	-196
Abgenix Portion (%)	*50%*	*50%*	*50%*	*50%*	*50%*	*50%*	*50%*	*50%*	*50%*	*50%*	*50%*	*50%*	*50%*	*50%*	*50%*	*50%*
genix Portion ($)	**-0**	**-5**	**-10**	**-12.5**	**-17.5**	**-25**	**-2.8**	**-9.8**	**-16.9**	**-35**	**-46.2**	**-63**	**-75.6**	**-86.8**	**-98**	**-98**
Probability (%)	***100%***	***100%***	***100%***	***100%***	***100%***	***40%***	***40%***	***40%***	***40%***	***40%***	***40%***	***40%***	***40%***	***40%***	***40%***	***40%***
venues:																
Minimum ($)[2]	5	0	-10	-12.5	-17.5	0	0	0	0	0	0	0	0	0	0	0
Maximum ($)[3]	5	0	-10	-12.5	-17.5	-25	5.2	18.2	35.1	65	85.8	117	140.4	161.2	182	182
Expected Value ($)[4]	5	0	-10	-12.5	-17.5	-10	2.08	7.28	14.04	26	34.32	46.8	56.16	64.48	72.8	72.8

Notes:
1. "Drug Sales" are 20% less than those sales shown in Case Exhibit 3, as per the text on page 11 of the case.
2. "Minimum" includes only those payments that are 100% certain.
3. "Maximum" includes all payments regardless of probabilities.
4. "Expected Value" is a weighted average of payments and costs.

Source: Author.

Exhibit TN-4 Discounted Economic Results for BioPart Proposal (in millions)

Discount Rate	Worst Case Scenario	Best Case Scenario	Expected Value
0%	($35.00)	$ 931.90	$ 351.76
5%	(29.27)	497.83	181.57
10%	(22.99)	216.04	72.62
15%	(20.79)	152.71	48.61
20%	(17.62)	86.32	23.96

Source: Author.

Exhibit TN-5 Potential Board Plan for Abgenix and the XenoMouse

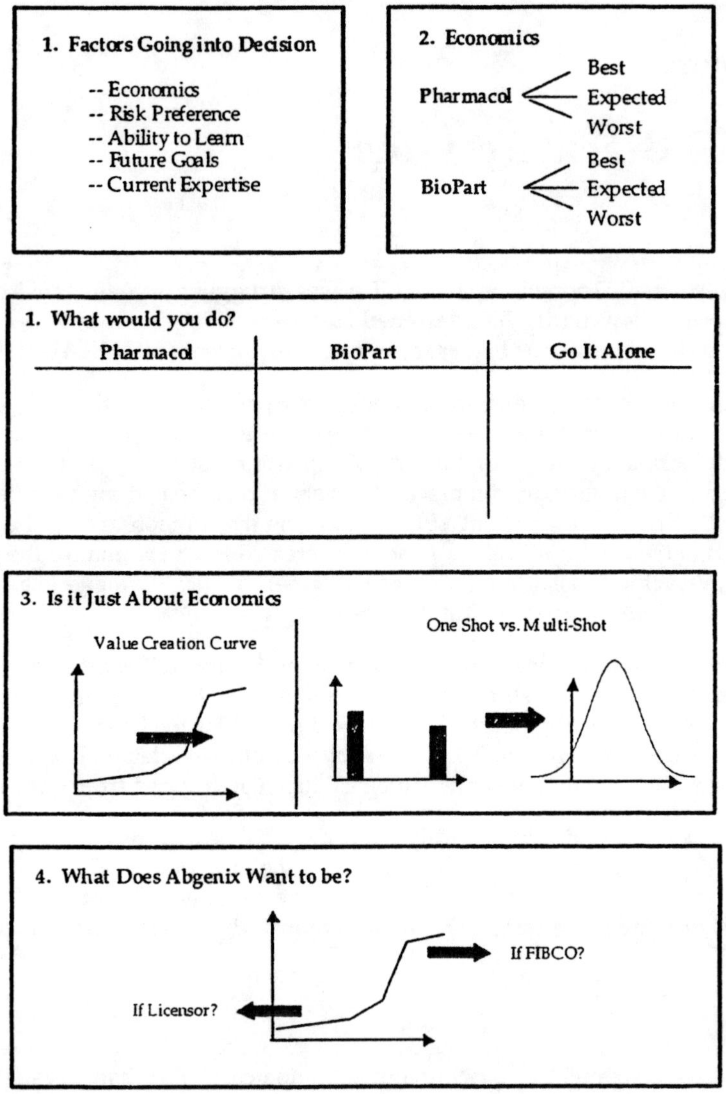

Source: Author.

5-503-092
APRIL 25, 2003

TEACHING NOTE

CardioThoracic Systems

Synopsis

In April 1998 CardioThoracic System (CTS) was struggling to gain traction in the marketplace. The small Silicon Valley startup had designed and been selling for 15 months a device that allowed cardiac surgeons to perform "cardiac artery bypass graft surgery" (CABG) on a beating heart.

Traditionally, the 330,000 heart bypass surgeries performed in the U.S. each year involved a "sternotomy" and a "heart-lung machine." To expose the heart of the patient, the surgeon would make a 12-inch incision down the middle of the patient's chest and spread the rib cage 6-inches apart (the sternotomy). Then, the surgeon placed the patient on a heart-lung machine, which temporarily oxygenated and circulated the patient's blood, allowing the surgeon to stop the heart to operate on it. Both the sternotomy and the stopping of the heart created great trauma for the patient, resulting in a hospital stay averaging 7 days, a 6% risk of major neurological damage (e.g., stroke, coma, death), and a 30-50% risk of minor neurological damage (e.g., "pump head").

The 1st generation CTS device, brought to market in January 1997, offered surgeons a way around these complications. First, it eliminated the need for a wide chest incision. Second, it allowed surgeon's to work on a beating heart, eliminating the need for the heart-lung machine and leading to the procedure being referred to as "off-pump" bypass. In fact, data collected on the first 2,000 CTS off-pump patients showed that major neurological damage dropped from 6.0% to 0.1%.

Nonetheless, surgeons were not readily adopting CTS' beating heart device. Through April 1998, only 400 of 3,000 surgeons had been trained in the use of the CTS beating heart procedure. Additionally, these surgeons used CTS' technology in only 10% of the bypass surgeries they performed. At the time of the case, CTS was wondering what it had to do to increase sales.

Use

At HBS, this case is taught as a technology adoption case. CTS had developed what appeared to be a superior alternative to the traditional CABG surgery, only to find that doctors were reluctant to adopt. Why? The answer lies at several factors, each of which offers insight into the marketplace acceptance (or lack of acceptance) of many new, innovative products.

This note was prepared by Professor John T. Gourville for the sole purpose of aiding classroom instructors in the use of CardioThoracic Systems, HBS No. 899-281, written by Entrepreneurial Studies Fellow Diana S. Gardner under the supervision of Senior Lecturer Michael J. Roberts. It provides analysis and questions that are intended to present alternative approaches to deepening students' comprehension of business issues and energizing classroom discussion. HBS cases are developed solely as the basis for class discussion. Cases are not intended to serve as endorsements, sources of primary data, or illustrations of effective or ineffective management.

The first critical factor is whether there is a recognized need for the new product—i.e., do customers feel the need to switch. For CTS, it is not clear that surgeons and hospitals view the current "on-pump" solution as "broken." The second factor is the distribution of the costs and benefits associated with the innovation. In the case of CTS, a disproportionate percentage of the immediate cost of adoption fell on the surgeon. The third factor is the complex, drawn-out nature of the adoption process—e.g., surgeons first needed to be aware, then convinced to learn, then convinced to trial, then convinced to retry, then convinced to adopt as a regular routine, etc.

Together, these factors suggest three things. First, the value created by any new technology needs to be adequately communicated to those customers who stand the most to gain. What seems evident to product developers often is not evident to the target market. Second, it is in the best interest of a firm to minimize the behavior change required by those expected to adopt the innovation. Third, product adoption is not a simple step function on the part of a customer. Rather, it is a series of small steps and the failure to achieve any one of those steps will lead to non-adoption.

Analysis

There are four main areas of discussion in this case, each of which will be discussed in turn. These include:

- What do you think of the underlying innovation?
- How has CTS done to date? Why?
- What does the adoption process look like?
- How should CTS define success?

1. What Do You Think of the Innovation?

This case is best begun at the level of the "beating heart" innovation—understanding what it offers patients, doctors, and hospitals. Thus, the instructor can begin the discussion by getting the class to assess the underlying technology, perhaps by asking, "Is beating heart surgery a great breakthrough?" This should get the class to assess the relative merits of the beating heart concept as well as the size and timing of the market opportunity facing CTS. Students' responses can be captured on the board under two broad headings—"Great Idea" and "Questionable Idea."

Reasons students likely will give in support of off-pump bypass include:

- Fewer Complications – Perhaps the most compelling benefit of the off-pump procedure is the reduced risk of major and minor neurological complications. As the case mentions on page 12, an assessment of the first 2,000 CTS patients revealed that the incidence of stroke decreased from 6% to 0.1%. Presumably, the rate of other complications also is less.

- Faster Recovery – A second major benefit students will cite is faster recovery for the patient. As mentioned on case page 4, relative to traditional on-pump CABG, the beating heart, off-pump procedure led to 50% shorter hospital stays.

- Lower Cost – Relative to on-pump bypass, off-pump bypass led to 30% lower hospital costs. For a procedure costing $36,000 (page 3), this is a substantial savings for a hospital.

- Cutting Edge Technique – Finally, some students will note that this innovation provides a means for "hot-shot" surgeons to make a name for themselves, providing a strong incentive for adoption for those doctors.

In contrast, other students will argue that the beating heart procedure stands little chance of widespread adoption. At the very least, some will question whether the beating heart market is financially attractive. Their reasoning will include:

- Marginal Gains – One concern students will cite is the relative success of traditional bypass. As mentioned on case page 6, "The old-fashioned way (CABG) has an impressive track record: its mortality rate is 4% or less for most of the 900 U.S. medical centers. And recent studies show the repairs can last 15 years or more in 90% of patients." This quote suggests that the gains a surgeon can expect from adopting this procedure are not worth the effort. In a sense, the old traditional system is "not broken."

- Learning Curve – A second major concern students will raise involves the cost to surgeons of adopting this procedure. In the long-run, their success rate may improve, but in the short term, they will be less proficient in performing bypass surgery. It should be noted here or at some other point in the case discussion that a disproportionate share of the cost (e.g., increased time, complications, effort) required for product adoption falls on the surgeon as opposed to the hospital.

- Added Up-Front Cost – Students also will raise the question of the up front cost of the CTS device. The 1st generation unit cost $2,500 and the 2nd generation unit cost $1,000. These costs are known and immediate, whereas the benefits are uncertain and in the future. This may cause some hospitals to delay adoption.

- Uncertainty of Benefits – While CTS is confident that its procedure reduces complications and the cost of a bypass, these benefits are still uncertain. Until there is documented proof of these benefits, surgeons and hospitals may question the procedure.

- Market Size – Finally, students may question the size of this market for CTS. First, the pricing for the CTS device is $1,000. Second, the entire bypass market was 330,000 patients per year. Best-case scenario, this suggests a total market of $330 million (330,000 x $1,000). Split between four major device makers, this suggests maximum revenues of under $100 million per year for CTS. This math should be captured on a sideboard as shown in **Figure TN-1**. Realistically, however, one might expect competition to erode devices prices to, say, $500 per device [note that the pricing of the CTS device has already dropped for $2,500 to $1,000 in less than a year] and for the beating heart procedure to capture 50% of all bypass surgeries. This suggests potential revenues closer to $25 million per year for CTS, a number that will be unattractive for many students.

Figure TN-1 The Potential Market for Beating Heart Bypass

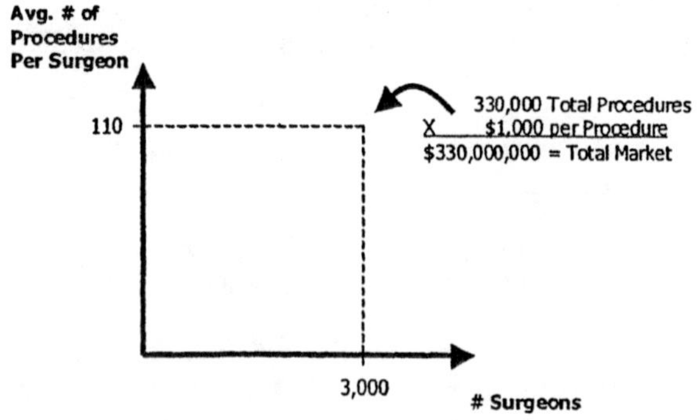

Source: TN Author

In the end, this first discussion can be wrapped up with the instructor summarizing the arguments for and against the success of the "beating heart technology." The reasons "for" are primarily objective in nature—i.e., the off-pump procedure offers objectively better outcomes than the traditional on-pump procedure. The reasons "against" are more subjective and deal with the incentives of the various players to adopt this innovation. The interested parties may not see sufficient benefit to warrant the required behavior change.

2. How Has CTS Done to Date and Why?

After a high-level discussion of the underlying technology, it makes sense to delve into CTS' performance to date. This can be done by asking, "How has CTS performance been to date?" While there may be some support for their performance (e.g., they have converted 400 surgeons; they sold 8,000 units in 1997; they have 50% of the beating heart market), most students will agree that CTS has not done as well as it might have hoped.

In particular, CTS trained only 400 of the 3,000 cardiac surgeons in the United States, these surgeons averaged only 20 CTS procedures per year, and given that CTS was targeting high volume surgeons (200 to 250 bypass procedures per year; page 12), this represented less than 10% of their cases. This implies two problems. First, CTS was having difficulty getting surgeons to trial the CTS procedure (supported by the text on page 13) and it was having trouble getting those trained in the procedure to use it more broadly. This thinking can be captured on the "market sizing diagram," as reflected in **Figure TN-2**.

Figure TN-2 CTS Performance to Date

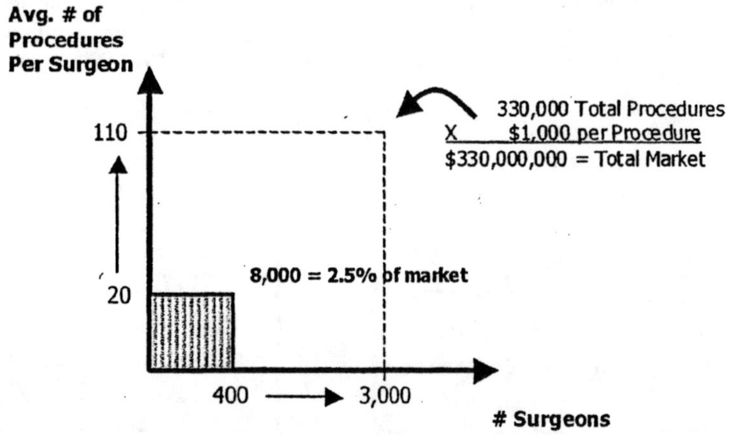

Source: TN Author

Having quantified CTS' performance, students should next be pushed to identify the reasons behind this lack of success. Most will focus on the physical product CTS was trying to sell and claim that it just did not meet the surgeons' needs. This should be explored in detail and can be done by focusing on each of the three generations of products CTS has produced, as reflected in **Figure TN-3**.

1st Generation: MIDCAB I CTS' 1st generation product was introduced in January 1997 at a price of $2,500. It had two important characteristics. First, it allowed surgeons to operate on the one or two blood vessels on the front of the heart. Second, it was designed to support MICS or "minimally invasive cardiac surgery." Many students will identify these two features as problematic for product adoption. In particular:

- Not Enough Vessels – As noted on case page 4, 80% of the 330,000 bypass surgeries done in the United States each year were done on 3 or more vessels. By limiting surgeons to only one or two vessels, the CTS device was useful in only 20% of bypass surgeries. [Note, the instructor may wish to merely capture this thought at this point. It will re-emerge in the analysis of the 2nd generation product, where it can be analyzed in greater depth.]

- Required Too Many Changes – The combination of the MICS and the beating heart surgery created too many changes for surgeons to be comfortable with the CTS procedure. As noted on case page 10, "Our first generation device asked the surgeon to make several radical changes at once."

Here it is useful to get students to articulate what these many changes were. They included: (1) operating through a small incision, (2) operating from the side of the heart, (3) surgeons could no longer touch the blood vessels with their hands, and (4) operating on a beating heart. What is important about this set of features is that (1), (2), and (3) are associated with the MICS or "minimally invasive" part of the procedure. Only feature (4) is associated with the actual "beating heart" aspect of the surgery. This suggests that CTS may have overbuilt its 1st generation product by adding features that surgeons do not want or need. As stated on case page 10:

> "... doctors want a "safety valve." In the event that something went wrong in the operating room, they wanted to be able to fall back to their "classic" and more familiar technique. With traditional open-heart surgery, surgeons could see if something went wrong because everything was exposed—the heart was right in front of them. With the chest "closed," they couldn't do this."

Figure TN-3 The Three Generation of CTS Devices

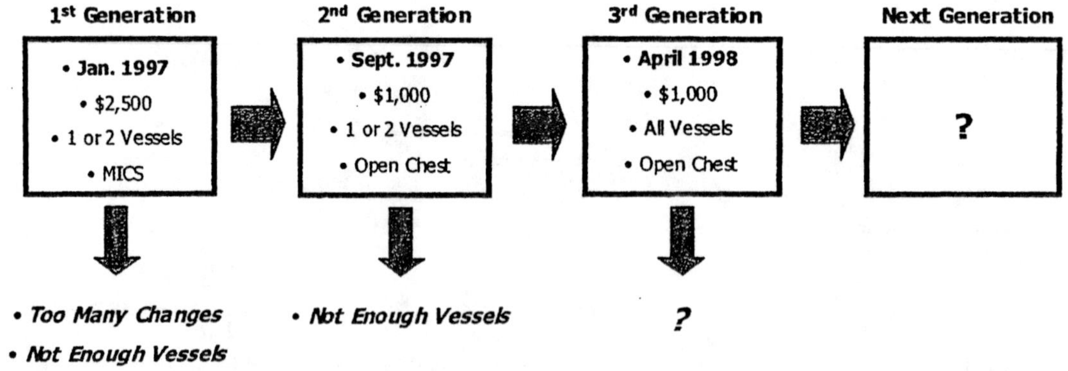

Source: TN Author

2nd Generation: MIDCAB II Given surgeons' reluctance to adopt the 1st generation product, CTS introduced a new version in September 1997 at a price of $1,000. This 2nd generation product reverted to the traditional 12-inch chest opening. Most students will argue that this was a good move. In particular, it eliminated many of the "radical changes" required in the 1st generation product.

One way the instructor may choose to frame this 2nd generation device is to ask if CTS "dumbed down" the device. For instance, the instructor could ask, "So this is a good thing? Going from a small opening to a massive chest opening? How do you feel about this if you are the patient? Is this a step forward or a step backward?" At this point, it is important for the students to recognize that this "step backward" is essential for product adoption. Unless a doctor feels comfortable performing the procedure, he won't attempt it. At this early stage of product adoption, the seemingly desirable MICS aspect of the device was more a hindrance than a desired feature.

At the same time, however, students will point out that this 2nd generation system still limited access to one or two vessels. At this point, students should be asked, "How big a problem is this?" The answer is that it is a huge problem, for at least several reasons:

- Nearly 80% of the 330,000 bypass surgeries performed in the United States each year involved the replacement of three or more vessels (case page 4), meaning that only about 66,000 bypass surgeries were for 1 or 2 vessels.
- Cardiac surgeons tended to replace all diseased vessels (case page 4), regardless of the extent of the disease. This "complete revascularization" philosophy went against the growth of these one or two vessel bypass operations.
- Interventional cardiologists first saw all patients and tended to treat one and two vessel patients themselves via an angioplasty. As the use of stents continued to improve the success rate of angioplasties, it was likely that cardiac surgeons would see fewer and fewer one and two vessel patients.

These factors combine to suggest that CTS still had not gotten it right with its 2nd generation product. Nonetheless, CTS did sell 1,400 units of this device in the 4th quarter of 1997.

3rd Generation: OPCAB Finally, students should be asked to assess the current (3rd) generation CTS product. Many students will argue that CTS had finally "gotten it right." It had retained the "open chest" aspect of the 2nd generation product and incorporated the ability to operate on all the diseased vessels of the heart. To strengthen the impact of the discussion that comes next, the instructor should try to build this "CTS has finally gotten it right" perspective as best they can.

Next Generation. If time is available, the instructor may wish to close this part of the discussion by asking students to speculate on what the next generation product from CTS might entail. Some students will argue that CTS will or should return (in the longer term) to the MICS aspect that was available in the 1st generation product. However, this should only be done after surgeons have become fully comfortable with the beating heart procedure. This discussion reinforces the concept of "minimal behavior change" with successive generations of an innovative product.

3. What Does the Adoption Process Look Like?

During the next stage of the case discussion, the goal is to shift students' focus from the physical attributes of the CTS product to the steps necessary to gain adoption from doctors. In the process, students should come to recognize that having the right product is not sufficient to ensure adoption. Rather, the adoption process is a series of many small steps, any one of which can result in failure.

This can be done by asking students, "Now that CTS has the right product, sales should take off? Right?" The answer is "No!" To get to this conclusion, the instructor should encourage the class to map out exactly what has to happen for a surgeon to adopt CTS' beating heart procedure. An example of this process is captured in **Figure TN-3** and is described in detail below. Each step of the way, students should be asked to assess how good a job CTS has done at that stage and to estimate the rate of successful surgeon conversion. It should be noted that the steps identified in any given case discussion will vary across student groups, based on their familiarity with the product adoption process and their willingness to dig deep into consumer behavior. Regardless, the instructor should be able to build a lengthy adoption process that has many of the aspects reflected in Figure TN-4.

Figure TN-4 The Adoption Process for Beating Heart Bypass

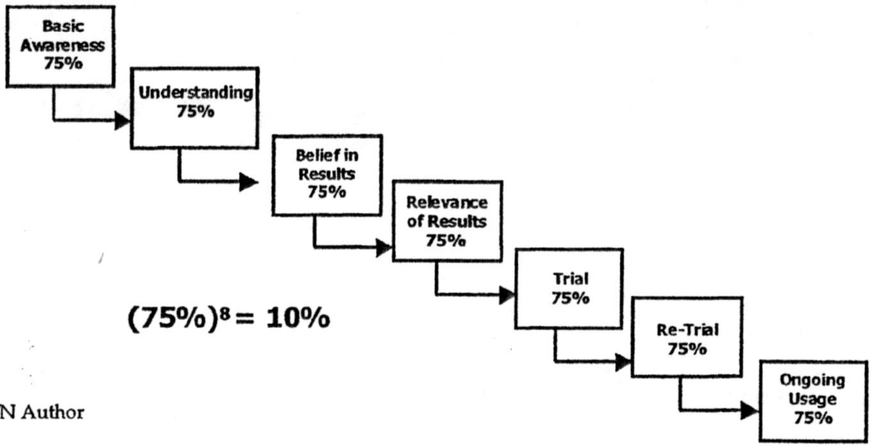

Source: TN Author

Basic Awareness. The first step in any product adoption process is "Basic Awareness"—i.e., in this case, surgeons must be aware of the existence of the procedure. Most students will agree that virtually 100% of surgeons will be aware of beating heart bypass, partly due to CTS' efforts and partly due to the general hype around beating heart bypass and MICS.

Understanding. The next step required is sufficient "Understanding" to recognize the proposed costs and benefits. Here, it is not enough to be aware that beating heart bypass exists, but that it offers potential benefits over traditional bypass surgery. The importance of this step is noted in CTS' own comments on page 13, "We thought they came to these training sessions to learn *how* to do the procedure, but in reality, they came just to see what it was all about." This comment suggests that CTS had not done a great job of communicating the details of the beating heart procedure to most surgeons.

Belief in Results. After surgeons become aware of the reported benefits of CTS' beating heart procedure, they need to believe them. As noted in the case, the traditional on-pump procedure had a long track record of success. Thus, there is the striking need for clinical proof of the improved outcomes and lower hospital costs associated with beating heart transplants, something that CTS was only just beginning to collect.

Belief that the Results are Relevant. As noted on page 12, while surgeons may finally accept the benefits of the beating heart procedure, they may not accept that those benefits apply to them. As noted, "...they say, 'well, a 6% stroke rate is the *average* for the *average* doctor: my numbers are better.'" This a very tough hurdle to overcome. While CTS can collect complication rates at the aggregate level (e.g., for a region or for a hospital), it will have difficulty collecting complication rates for individual doctors.

Training. The final stage of the *education phase* of product adoption involves teaching the actual technique of the surgery. To date, CTS has tried a two-day and a one-day seminar to accomplish this task, with limited success (at most, 10-20% of those attending attempted the procedure). Part of this stems from CTS' confusion as to the role of these seminars. While CTS viewed them as training seminars, surgeons viewed them as information seminars. In any case, students should agree that CTS efforts at training have not been particularly successful.

Trial. Following education, surgeons still need to incorporate the beating heart procedure into their daily routines. This begins with "trial"—an attempt to perform a beating heart procedure on an actual patient. It is important to note that this "trial" will likely be uncomfortable for most surgeons—e.g., it will take longer than the traditional bypass, it will create more anxiety, and it may lead to an increased likelihood of a complication. This is all part of the learning curve that surgeons will likely experience. The fact that this "trial" will lead to a worse outcome needs to be brought out, perhaps as shown in **Figure TN-5.**

Re-Trial. Trial is then followed by "re-trial," the ongoing attempts at the beating heart procedure. It is likely that CTS will lose many surgeons at this phase of the adoption process. In particular, rather than resulting in immediate benefits, beating heart bypass will only lead to better outcomes as a surgeon becomes proficient in the procedure. This is also captured in **Figure TN-5.**

Ongoing Usage/Replacement. The final stage of product adoption is the ongoing usage of beating heart procedure by a surgeon. The procedure needs to become part of the surgeon's regular repertoire. It should be noted that even for the 400 surgeons who were using CTS' beating heart procedure, this stage did not appear to have been reached. As pointed out on case page 12, the 400 surgeons trained in the CTS procedure average only 20 beating heart procedures per year, a small fraction of their total bypass surgeries. Therefore, one could conclude that CTS still has work to do with these surgeons to assure full product adoption.

Figure TN-5 The Impact of Product Trial on Surgeon Performance

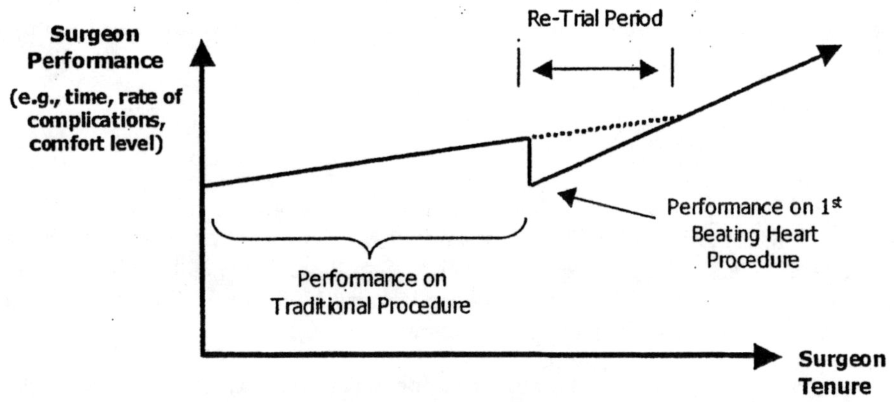

Source: TN Author

Summary

The goal of this third area of discussion is to gain a more complete understanding of what has to happen to convert a customer—in this case, a surgeon. By mapping out the product adoption process, it should become obvious that CTS is supporting only some of the steps in the adoption process. In addition, even assuming very respectable conversion rates for each one of these steps, the net conversion rate can still be quite small. For instance, if CTS manages to convert 75% of surgeons at each stage of the adoption process, the net conversion rate is only about 10% (0.75^8).

4. How Should CTS Define Success?

The last area of discussion need only take the final five or ten minutes of the class and should focus on how CTS should define success. To get to this discussion, the instructor can refer to the complex product adoption process and comment, "Given all that has to happen for a surgeon to adopt, couldn't we argue that CTS is doing well? How would you define success for this company in, say, two years?"

One possible dimension on which to assess success would be the scope of adoption. Is it narrow, but deep, meaning that a small group of surgeons use CTS' beating heart procedure in the majority of their surgeries. Or is it broad, but shallow, meaning that most surgeons use CTS' procedure, but only in a small percentage of cases. Of these two outcomes, which is more desirable from CTS' perspective?

A second dimension on which to assess success might be overall sales or share of the total bypass market. Should CTS be happy if beating heart bypass comes to represent 10% or 20% of bypass cases within several years, or does that number need to be closer to 50%.

Finally, CTS might gauge success based on relative adoption of the various beating heart procedures. What if CTS retains 50+% share of the beating heart market, but that market only grows to represent 10% or 20% of the total bypass market?

In the end, this last section clearly will be more opinion than fact. However, students' thinking of what constitutes success should reflect the realization that what CTS and its competitors are trying to do is really difficult. They are trying to replace a well-accepted medical procedure that has been around for decades and has a very high success rate with a radical new procedure that is more complex, offers a steep and painful learning curve, and that improves success rates by only a few percentage points.

What Happened?

In August 1999, CTS was purchased by Guidant Corporation, a world leader in the treatment of cardiovascular disease with 1999 sales of $2.3 billion and with a significant position in cardiovascular stents and cardiac pacemakers. The purchase price was $313 million, or $19.50 per share of CTS stock (note that CTS IPO'd for $18 per share in 1996). Between January 1997 and the time of the acquisition, CTS had shipped over 40,000 beating heart bypass systems.

By 2002, the concept of off-pump bypass surgery appeared to have caught on with doctors and hospitals. Overall, the practice of "off pump bypass" surgery grew rapidly to represent about one-third of the roughly 500,000 bypass surgeries done in the U.S. in 2002. As might be concluded from the case, the reasons for this growth included the belief in a lower rate of major neurological (e.g., stroke, coma, death) and minor neurological complication (e.g., impaired cognitive functioning).

However, the benefits of the off-pump procedure relative to the more traditional "on pump" CABG were still unclear. For instance, one study reported in the August 2002 issue of *Annals of Thoracic Surgery* (p. 394-399) compared 8,069 traditional bypass surgeries to 2,320 off-pump surgeries that were conducted at a single hospital between 1994 and 2000. The study found that patients in the traditional surgery group were twice as likely (2.5% vs. 1.1%) to have a stroke as the patients in the off-pump group. But another study reported in *The New England Journal of Medicine* in January 2003 compared low risk patients who underwent either the traditional on-pump procedure with the new off-pump procedure and found no long-term difference in complications. Based on these and other studies, it appeared that for relatively low-risk bypass patients, the advantage of off-pump over on-pump surgery was questionable. However, for higher risk patients (e.g., older, overweight, impaired kidney functions, etc.), the advantages of off-pump were much more pronounced.

Finally, in addition to Guidant, all of the major manufacturers outlined in the case (i.e., Medtronic, U.S. Surgical, Genzyme) continued to develop and sell devices to aid in off-pump, beating heart surgeries. While detailed revenue figures were tough to come by, Guidant could be used as a benchmark. In 2002, Cardiac Surgery Products accounted for $91.9 million of Guidant's $3.2 billion in revenues (*2002 Annual Report*, p. 28), with its latest generation heart stabilizer (now called the AXIUM™) being one of three major products accounting for this $91.9 million. This suggested that sales of Guidant's beating heart platform amounted to between $20 million and $40 million per year. In the end, it appeared the innovation of beating heart surgery had caught on, but Guidant's ability to generate major revenues from that innovation was somewhat limited.

Teaching

Ideally, the discussion of this case has two halves of roughly equal proportions. The first half addresses the *obvious* issues in the case. Namely, the medical rationale behind the beating heart procedure and CTS' failure to generate the types of sales it had expected. These issues have already been detailed in section (1), which should take about 15 to 20 minutes to discuss, and section (2), which should also take about 15 to 20 minutes to discuss.

At the end of this first half, many students will be left with the sense that beating heart bypass has lots of potential and that CTS has failed to capture sales because their products did not fully meet the needs of most surgeons. However, these students will feel that with the introduction of the 3rd generation product, this will soon change. If this type of attitude develops, the instructor should try to build and extend it. At the end of this first half of the case discussion, it is desirable to have students excited about CTS' prospects now that they have a product that fully meets the needs of most bypass surgeons.

This leads to the second half of the case discussion, covered in section (3), which should take about 30 minutes, and section (4), which should take about 10 minutes. The goal of these sections (especially section 3) is to dig deep into the steps necessary for product adoption. In particular, given the complexity of the adoption, the small (but significant) benefits of off-pump bypass over on-pump bypass, and the well-entrenched nature of the existing solution, the process of product adoption will likely be quite low even under the best of circumstances.

In the end, students should come to appreciate that changing any entrenched behavior is slow and effortful. And until CTS begins to support the full product adoption process, sales will continue to languish.

A potential board plan is presented in **Exhibit TN-1** and possible preparation questions are presented below.

Suggested Preparation Questions

Some questions for this case are:

1. What do you think the diffusion of this product will look like? Of this class of products?
2. What or who are the obstacles to adoption for the CTS product? Of these, which is most critical?
3. What can CTS do to maximize the speed of adoption?
4. What should CTS do in the near term?

Exhibit TN-1 Potential Board Plan

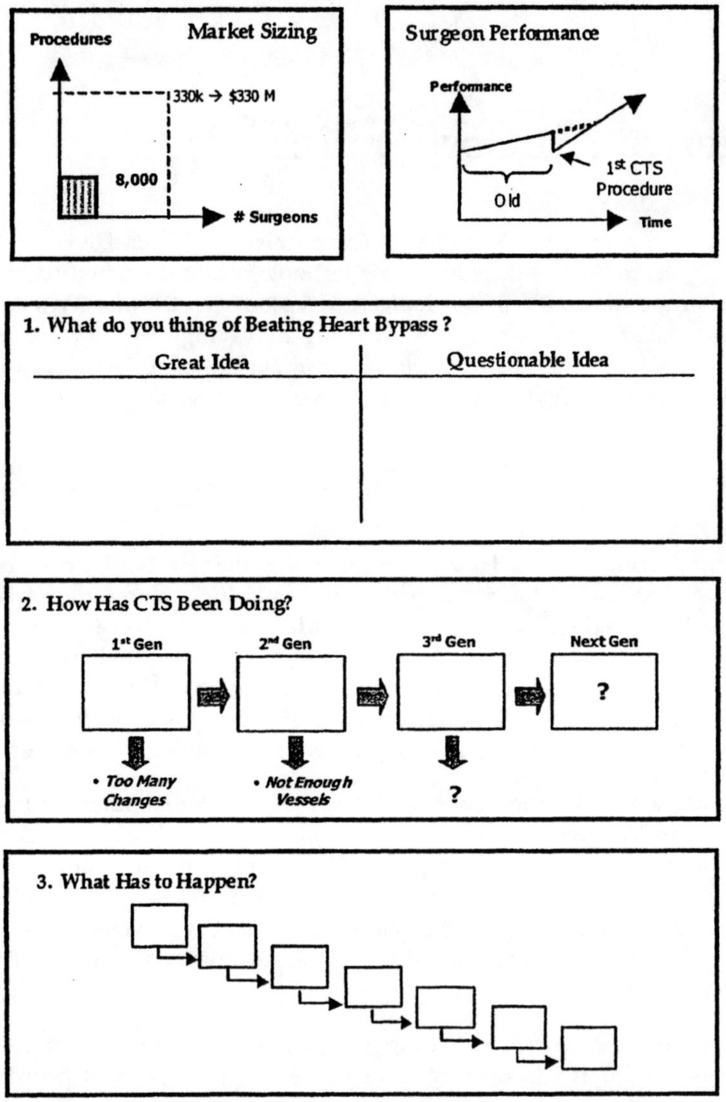

Source: TN Author

9-699-013
REV: JULY 23, 2002

STEFAN THOMKE

Innovation at 3M Corporation (B)

In a conference room in 3M's Performance Chemicals and Fluids Division, the division's five-member team assigned to find markets for a new technology was deep in discussion on a darkening mid-December afternoon in 1997. Mary Sonnack, division scientist and 3M internal consultant on innovative market research, had opened the meeting by saying, "We are drowning in wonderful technologies at 3M for which we lack markets. But our current experiment with Lead User research with this division's rapid cooling technology may show other divisions how to turn technologies into breakthrough products."

Technology in Search of a Market

Sonnack was referring to 3M Hydrofluoroether® (HFE), a fluid developed by a team of researchers at 3M Speciality Fluids charged with replacing chlorofluorocarbons (CFCs). Greg Sherwood, also at the meeting, had first worked with HFE as part of his mechanical engineering Master's thesis, discovering some properties that could make it a formidable heat transfer fluid. At low temperatures, when conventional heat transfer brines—such as those found in European grocery refrigeration—moved like sludge, HFE continued to flow almost like water. Sherwood subsequently developed a way to pipe HFE around for flexibly transferring cooling to wherever it was needed.

As wonderful as the new technology was, like many 3M technologies it sat on the shelf. Then, in August 1997, Sherwood's divisional market development supervisor, Mary Zettel, had contacted Sonnack in order to establish a rapid-cooling Lead User team. The team, tongue-in-cheek, referred to itself as, "A Rapid-Cooling Technology in Search of a Market" Team[1]. Sherwood reminded the Lead User team at the outset: "HFE costs $250 per gallon . . . at that cost, no one will buy it. What we need is a way to bury the high cost into a system that would ideally sell itself. That is our primary challenge for creating a market."

After an intensive research process using the stages of the Lead User methodology, which involved the review of industries ranging from pharmaceuticals to food transportation, the team narrowed its search to the food industry—a wide arena. Kathy Williams, the team's management

[1] Lead User team members of the "Fast Cooling in Search of a Need" project—all from the Performance Chemicals and Fluids Division—included: Mary Zettel, market development; Greg Sherwood, research specialist; Linda Tsai, corporate marketing; John Pignato, technical service; and Steve Pignato, regional sales representative. Kathy Williams, U.S. and international market operation manager, was the team's sponsor.

Professor Stefan Thomke and Research Associate Ashok Nimgade prepared this case. HBS cases are developed solely as the basis for class discussion. Cases are not intended to serve as endorsements, sources of primary data, or illustrations of effective or ineffective management.

sponsor, had encouraged the team not to narrow options too prematurely. An initial starting point had been supermarkets, of which there were some 50,000 in the United States; the search subsequently included restaurants, numbering around 600,000. To understand these markets, some team members had fanned across the country to selectively interview and observe potential HFE users at work.

A manager at one New Orleans restaurant mentioned that the central compressors never broke down in summers—only peripheral ones did. Later tours of restaurants and supermarkets revealed the same phenomenon. This observation inspired the team to think about how, in case of refrigeration breakdowns, rapid cooling fluid might be piped from a central compressor to a peripheral area. This would never have been brought up by the customers as a need; only probing under the surface revealed it. Further investigations showed that restaurant chains drove innovation, since the potential of these large customers drove sellers of new products to make their first pitches to them.

Preparing the Lead User Workshop

The team ultimately decided to focus the Stage IV workshop on a promising commercial area, albeit one where 3M lacked internal expertise: commercial kitchens. The division found a manufacturing partner, Maytag, which had been very interested in the HFE technology. Although best known for its dishwashers, the Midwest-based, $3+ billion company also fielded refrigeration products and a variety of other major kitchen appliances for the food service industry.[2] Maytag invested over $150 million annually for product innovation.

Now, during the December meeting, the team pondered the value its ideal product or products would add to commercial kitchens. They considered workflow, minimizing traffic to cooler; the ideal point for cooling; ways to minimize food handling; shapes of appliances. The discussion then turned toward identifying relevant Lead Users to invite to the Stage IV workshop in the spring, intended to center around designing the commercial kitchen of the future.

Linda Tsai suggested, "What about this Royal Caribbean Cruise ship food director for whom food safety was highly critical?"

John Pignato laughed across the table. "Food safety is a joke! It will never drive sales of refrigeration," he claimed. "Even in some fine restaurants I've seen chefs licking spoons or bowls—not to mention not wearing hairnets. I've heard stories of how food safety monitoring can be quite haphazard, depending on the mood of the inspector: their measurements for temperature compliance depend so much on whether they place their meters near a fan or under a bottom shelf."

Mary Zettel added: "How about this innovative kitchen architect from California we found on the Internet? He's a professor of design, he loves to cook, he's written a book about designing kitchens. He even designed a deli and bakery with quick disconnect appliances! I think he may qualify as a lead user."

After 90 minutes of discussion, Sonnack glanced at her watch. "In the interest of time," she said, "I suggest we all bring suggestions to our meeting next week. Let me remind you that thinking about what we can learn from these lead users is key to a successful Stage IV workshop. The Medical-Surgical Division invited some of the leading experts in their respective fields but many of the things

[2] Maytag Annual Report, 1998.

the team learned had already been discovered during earlier stages of the process. So, in the spirit of continuous improvement, let's spend more time thinking about the 'right' lead users."

In the closing minutes, Zettel raised another challenge:

> We face another dilemma: how to keep the entire project within the projected six months. Look at how long it took the Medical-Surgical Division—a whole year! We've run into the holiday season crunch time for the restaurant business, which may delay our ongoing data collection a few weeks. I'm certain, now that four months have gone by, that our supervisors will become increasingly impatient. We don't want to impose any more upon the personal time you are already donating."

Sonnack thought back to the year-long Lead User process she had undergone with the Medical-Surgical Markets Division. That first Lead User project at 3M had gained a lot of publicity and some controversy. It was through a presentation by Sonnack that Mary Zettel had heard of Lead User methodology. Sonnack smiled, "In a way your task is much simpler since you already have the technology and are now working backwards to find a market."

"Or markets . . .," replied Zettel.

Innovation at 3M Corporation (A) & (B)

Teaching Note

Synopsis

The case describes the 3M Medical-Surgical Markets Division's experience in escaping the cycle of incrementalism in its innovation process with the aid of a new process called "Lead User research." Initially perceived as a new methodology for understanding future customer and market needs, a team from the Division applies Lead User research to the field of surgical infection control and discovers not only new product concepts but also a promising new business strategy.

The case is set in 1997 when 3M's Medical-Surgical Markets Division remains a world leader in the surgical drapes market. Despite its world dominance, however, overall the unit is stagnating. In the past decade it has introduced only one major successful product. Now, Senior Product Specialist Rita Shor has been charged with the mandate of developing a new breakthrough product within the existing business strategy.

The Medical-Surgical Markets Division has found from prior experience that its market research, while providing an abundance of invaluable data, does not always provide sufficient information for conceptualizing breakthrough products. Shor, however, has heard of a new process for learning about unarticulated customer needs and their solutions. This process—known as Lead User research—seeks to tap into expertise of certain innovative customers that experience market needs ahead of other consumers. Necessity has mothered surprising new innovations through the hands of these lead users, and hopefully, the new process provides a way for funneling these innovations into corporations.

Through the help of consultants, Shor has launched a Lead User study within her division in September 1996. Along the way, following a change in senior management, Shor's team meets resistance from skeptical superiors, many of whom are used to working with more traditional approaches that are quantitative and have more predictable outcomes. Drawing on expertise of a dozen lead users gathered from backgrounds as diverse as cosmetics to surgery, the team comes up with three innovative product concepts in the infection control area. The fourth recommendation, however, creates tension in the business unit as it involves a departure from the unit's current strategy statement. In an intense debate, Shor's team members are split over whether to even present the revolutionary fourth recommendation to senior management.

This note was prepared by Professor Stefan Thomke and Research Associate Ashok Nimgade, M.D., for the sole purpose of aiding classroom instructors in the use of "Innovation at 3M Corporation (A)" and "Innovation at 3M Corporation (B)", HBS case Nos. 9-699-012 and 9-699-013. It provides analysis and questions that are intended to present alternative approaches to deepening students' comprehension of business issues and energizing classroom discussion.

The optional (B) case focuses on deepening the understanding of the Lead User concept and process, particularly the search for lead use experts, and can be used in a breakout group session. The 3M Performance Chemicals and Fluids Division is looking for a market for an innovative refrigeration technology—one of 3M's thousands of innovative technologies languishing for want of a market. The students are asked to help with the difficult but crucial task of selecting a set of lead users for its product concept workshop.

Teaching Objectives

The 3M case has been taught to MBA students in the second-year HBS elective course "Managing Product Development" and fits into a module on research methodologies for the very early phases of product development (sometimes referred to as "the fuzzy front-end"). In particular, the case addresses the following themes:

- **Breakthrough products and services:** the 3M case series illustrates the difficult managerial and process issues that firms face in their attempt to overcome incrementalism and develop new breakthrough products and services.

- **Lead User research**: the series has very detailed step-by-step descriptions and examples of how to conduct Lead User research studies, preparing students to use the process in their own academic projects or later in their professional careers.

- **Managing change**: the case material and the class discussion address the challenges of introducing new and unproven processes into a successful organization.

Suggested Reading Assignment

Stefan Thomke and Ashok Nimgade, "Note on Lead User Research," Harvard Business School Note No. 9-699-014.

The note provides a general description of the Lead User research process and its concepts, using brief examples from business practice. *Length*: 12 pages.

Suggested Assignment Questions

1. How has 3M's innovation process evolved since the company was founded? Why, if at all, does 3M, known as a "hothouse" of innovation, need to regain its historic closeness to the customer?

2. How does the Lead User research process differ from and complement other traditional market research methods?

3. Has the Medical-Surgical team applied the Lead User research process successfully? Why or why not?

4. What should the Medical-Surgical Lead User team recommend to Dunlop: the three new product concepts or a new business strategy? What are the risks to the new Lead User process at 3M? What are the risks to the Medical-Surgical business unit?

Analysis

1. Innovation at 3M's Medical-Surgical Markets Division

- The large 3M Corporation strives to maintain an innovative edge through splintering off decentralized units based on new core product technologies. However, an increasing proportion of 3M's business has come from incremental product changes ("...blue Post-it note instead of just a yellow one"; case p. 1). In the 1990s, in an attempt to move away from this philosophy of incrementalism through extensions of pre-existing product lines, 3M sought to produce 30 percent of sales from products that did not exist four years ago.

- The Health Care Group at 3M provided an umbrella for all health-related product divisions (producing over 10,000 health-related products). By the mid-1990s, the Medical-Surgical Markets Division, with over a hundred million dollars in yearly sales, owned almost the entire surgical drapes market. This arena, however, remained a no-growth sector, largely because of the high cost of 3M products in many overseas markets. By 1996, the division had gone almost a decade without a breakthrough product. The surgical drapes section of the Medical-Surgical Markets Division had discovered the hard way that technological excellence by itself meant little. In the early 1990's for instance, the changing managed care environment, however, banished an innovative virus-proof gown into a tiny niche.

- To identify market needs and trends, 3M product developers in the Health Care unit, for instance, utilized several tools including: data from medical sales representatives, consumer focus groups, customer evaluations of currently marketed products, site visits by 3M technologists to hospitals, and data on risk factors for diseases. Such data, however, reinforced the cycle of incremental product changes as it focused on information from traditional 3M customer bases.

- The information obtained through its traditional research process was not necessarily proprietary, however, and customers were somewhat blind about their own needs. In addition, in recent decades, innovators at 3M (typically autonomous "skunkworks" teams comprised of primarily technical individuals) started inventing for the sake of invention: as a result, thousands of patented 3M technologies awaited markets and produced no income for 3M.

2. Lead User Research

Lead User research, pioneered by Professor Eric von Hippel of the Massachusetts Institute of Technology (MIT), provides a means of finding market opportunities by systematically tapping the expertise and experience base of lead users[1]. The premise is that certain consumers experience needs ahead of the market segment (see **Figure TN-1**) in which they operate and that some of these will seek to innovate on their own. Lead users may lead in either the *target* or *analogous* markets. Some lead users may be involved with just one or more of the important *attributes* of the problems faced by

---

[1] For more information on academic research that led to this process, see Eric von Hippel, *The Sources of Innovation*, Oxford University Press, 1988.

users in the target market. By tapping the expertise of these so-called "lead users," manufacturers could find invaluable sources of innovation. Already, lead users had created innovations such as white-out ("liquid paper") and the sports drink Gatorade.

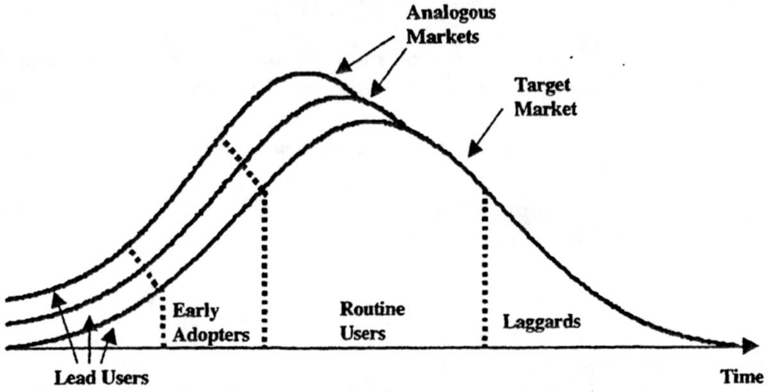

Figure TN-1. Position of lead users relative to target and analogous markets.

More formally, lead users are defined the following way:

- Lead users have new product or service needs that will be general in a marketplace, but they face them months or years before the bulk of the market encounters them.

- Lead users expect to benefit significantly by finding a solution to their needs. As a result, they often develop new products or services themselves because they can't or don't want to wait for them to become available commercially.

- Lead users are not the same as "early adopters"—users who are among the first people to purchase an existing product or service (see **Figure TN-1**). Lead users are facing needs for products and services that do not exist on the market.

2.1. Lead User Research Process

The potential benefits of Lead User research include: access to richer and more reliable information on emerging customer needs and innovative solutions to those needs; development of better products and service concept; breaking the cycle of incremental product extensions. Specific managerial challenges to successfully using the Lead User process and include: difficulty in predicting the process path and outcome; difficulties in assessing the contribution of any given individual's participation in the process; and the need for a high level of commitment needed in terms of quality and quantity of human resources.

Experience has shown that three elements remain necessary for success in the Lead User process: supportive management, use of a cross-discipline team of highly skilled people, and a clear understanding of the principles of Lead User research. Typically, the four to six people comprising a team come from marketing and technical departments and spend up to a third of their time on the Lead User project. This high level of immersion fosters creative thought and sustains project momentum. The Lead User projects can take up to five or six months with four stages involved (for a more detailed explanation, refer to either case **Exhibit 4** or the "Note on Lead User Research," HBS Note No. 9-699-014):

- ***Stage I: Project Planning (up to 4-6 weeks).*** In contrast to incremental innovation projects, this start-up phase is necessary to build firm-level support and establish new relationships outside normal business practice which are necessary to succeed with breakthrough innovations. During this phase, the team also identifies the types of markets and new products of interest, the desired level of innovation, and key business constraints. Part of this stage is marked by informal interviews with lead use industry experts to get a feel for market trends.

- ***Stage II: Trends/Needs Identification (up to 5-6 weeks).*** Typically a four-day team workshop at the beginning of this stage allows team members to digest the information collected during Stage I and get a sense of the "conventional wisdom" relating to trends and market needs. Thereafter, focused interviews with relevant lead use experts helps the team achieve this stage's ultimate goal here of selecting a specific need-related trend that can be addressed by a new product or service.

- ***Stage III: Preliminary Concept Generation (up to 5-6 weeks).*** Here the team generates preliminary concepts involving ideal attributes and features that will best meet customer needs in its chosen area of focus. These concepts come from lead users in *target* and/or *analogous* markets who are interviewed throughout this stage. The team also informally assesses the business fit of concepts being conceptualized.

- ***Stage IV: Final Concept Generation (up to 5-6 weeks).*** Activity in Stage IV centers around a workshop with invited lead users to move preliminary concepts developed in Stage III toward completion. Having a diverse but interrelated collection of wisdom and talent together in one room allows for efficiently generating alternative product concepts as well as rapidly evaluate the concepts in terms of technical feasibility, market appeal, and management priorities. After the workshop, the team refines the concepts emerging from the workshop and presents recommendations backed by solid evidence about why customers would be willing to pay for them on proposed products or services to senior managers.

Because it draws primarily on qualitative input, product and service concepts from Lead User research can and should be later verified using more conventional methods that rely on quantitative analysis (for example, market tests or conjoint methods that trade off specific product attributes).

2.2. Lead User Research at 3M

Although the Lead User research process is described as having four discrete phases, in practice, these often overlap with each other. More important than strict adherence to the letter of the manual is incorporation of the way of thinking "outside the box." The case shows that a commitment to finding lead users in unusual places and working with them in new ways also requires *substantial* commitments on part of senior management. This was especially the case with the Medical-Surgical Division's project, which, because of lack of experience with the process (a formal description was not even ready at the time) and not to mention costly international trips, stretched out a full year. In addition, 3M's management was not used to committing substantial human resources so early in product development, even though it might prove more cost-effective. In Rita Shor's words, "3M pours a hundred thousand dollars at the drop of a hat for a production problem late in the product development process, but it is unused to doing so for such an early stage," (case p. 7, top paragraph).

Not surprisingly, therefore, tension in this case has developed between the assembled team and the new management under Dunlop whose mandate was merely to manage the division conservatively by stopping the financial hemorrhage—a mandate that would involve the termination of experimental projects with uncertain outcomes. To throw salt on Dunlop's wound, the unpredictability of the outcome from using the new and unproven Lead User process ended up leading to the final radical recommendation that challenges the division's current business strategy.

Fortunately for the new process, support for Lead User research existed at high levels within 3M, particularly among those disenchanted with how traditional strategic planning drew too much on managers far removed from new product development. The hope was that the Lead User process might help get 3M back to its roots of working more closely with customers to develop breakthrough products and services.

Some of the contrasts between the traditional 3M development process and Lead User research are outlined in the following table:

Traditional 3M Development Process	Lead User Research Process
• Developers, in recent decades, lack direct contact with customers.	• Puts developers in direct contact with users.
• Developers are not directly accountable for understanding customer needs.	• Focus on a few individuals (Lead Users and lead use experts) with extremely rich need and solution-specific information.
• Marketing research is outsourced to third parties or "thrown over the wall."	• Allows developers to learn from users outside traditional business focus.
• Traditional methods are linear and tend to support primarily incremental innovations.	• Pushes developers toward leading edge with potentially radical new concepts.
	• Can be complemented with traditional market research techniques (during validation).

Table TN-1. Comparison of traditional 3M product development and Lead User process.

3. The Team Recommendation: Evolution or Revolution

The first three recommendations provided by the Lead User team are traditional product development recommendations; they might ultimately have been generated by the more traditional procedures. (Readers of the case, of course, are not expected to pass judgment on the technical merit of these recommendations.) The fourth recommendation, however, goes beyond the initial objectives of the team and management by suggesting a change in the Medical-Surgical Division's strategy, by recommending that the division enter the new but related field of infection containment (upstream prevention).

The crux of the case discussion involves the appropriateness of the fourth recommendation and the risks and benefits that it creates for both, the new Lead User process and 3M. The case opens up a plethora of questions, and a Pandora's box for a conservative senior manager like Dunlop. Several key questions emerge however: Should the Lead User team even present this recommendation? Would the team appear insubordinate, especially in face of a change in upper management? Should the team even risk the existence of the new process at the company, at a point when it is barely getting started? Maybe it is wiser to wait until 3M has more experience and confidence in the new process. There are obviously tradeoffs (see **Table TN-2**) that have to be identified and carefully managed.

Conservative Approach: Three Product Concepts	Radical Approach: New Business Unit Strategy
• Mandate from management.	• Team was charged with finding breakthroughs; Medical-Surgical business needs growth.
• Should not risk new process; Dunlop may use "revolution" against new method.	• Team is empowered and should report all relevant information.
• Need to validate method at least once before basing major strategic decisions on it.	• Fits the defiant 3M culture.
• Not enough data yet to make such drastic recommendation.	• Fits 3M's new strategic mission even though Dunlop does not buy into it.
• Three concepts appear very promising and are enough of a "success" already.	

Table TN-2. Comparing possible team recommendations.

Teaching Suggestions

The case has been successfully taught in an elective course on "Managing Product Development" in Harvard's MBA Program. Experience has shown that a 80-minute class discussion leaves only enough time for either the (B) case or a summary lecture—a choice that the instructor has to make. If there is additional time, the (B) case can be used in discussion groups to clarify the principles of Lead User research. It is best to start the class with the team's recommendation to management. The following plan is for an 80-minute class.

Block (1)
The Team Recommendation

(suggested time: 25 minutes)

The purpose of this block is to confront students directly with the team's dilemma. To increase the classroom tension around this issue, I ask students to submit electronically their answers to assignment question four (see p. 3) prior coming to class (new product concepts or new business strategy?). The instructor can achieve a similar effect by holding an informal poll in class before the discussion begins. Experience has shown that students will favor both options equally (50/50), with a slight bias towards the recommendation for a new business strategy. The class discussion should focus on the appropriateness of including this final recommendation. To start the class, I also show a short video about the stage IV workshop where the lead users and lead use experts are introduced. The discussion is opened with the following introduction, followed by a question:

Q: *"The team has concluded its stage IV workshop which has resulted in three very promising product recommendations (two incremental and one radical). However, as part of their research and discussions in the workshop, they have also discovered that many more opportunities exist outside their current business unit's strategic focus. It appears that the most promising venue—infection prevention—would require the division to rewrite its business unit's strategy and change directions. What should the team recommend to Dunlop?"*

Students should not be expected, of course, to comment on the technical merits or demerits of each of these initial recommendations. The class discussion should be focus on the appropriateness of including this final recommendation and the students should be asked to state the reasons for their recommendation.

Students in the conservative, "play-it-safe" camp will point out that the team is under mandate from senior management, and that they need to validate the new process before making major strategic decisions based on it. Students in the more radical camp will argue that the team was charged with finding breakthroughs and should not hold back relevant findings. Furthermore, they will point out that 3M's history and culture encourages and thrives upon the spirit of "defiance." The major arguments in support of the conservative and radical approaches are summarized in **Table TN-2** in the analysis section.

Note that some students may have a tendency to "warm up" to the revolutionary approach too quickly. The instructor may have to work against such a trend in order to keep up the discussion dynamics. One way to do this may be by asking students to picture themselves with their jobs at stake in a business unit run by Dunlop, an executive who is close to retirement and who may therefore not even mind if the unit gets sold.

Note that some hybrid suggestions may also crop up in the discussion. Some students may suggest, for instance, presenting the first three recommendations as well as bits of information relevant to upstream infection containment (or prevention) that may lead senior management to reach their own conclusions about expanding the business unit charter or even creating a new business unit. The instructor should encourage students to develop alternative plans in addition to the ones proposed.

To understand the tension around incrementalism and more radical approaches, the discussion can also include the change in strategic directions at 3M, going back to early parts of the case when 3M senior management set forth as a corporate objective an increase in innovations truly new to the world.

Q: *What has been 3M's approach to innovation? Why has incrementalism worked so well for them? Why suddenly push people towards more radical innovations?"*

Incrementalism has worked well for 3M because it has allowed for leveraging off preexisting product platforms such as Post-it® notes and Scotch® brand tape. This approach can reduce development costs while at the same time exploiting the company's preexisting marketing channels and relationships. Major reasons for pushing for more radical innovations include increased competition, the change in the consumer environment, as perhaps epitomized by the managed care environment, which makes it imperative for 3M to find solutions to match the quickly changing times, and, of course, the impetus of growth which requires new and faster growing market segments. Some students may also observe that many of 3M's legendary product platforms were discovered through informal relationships with lead use customers. After many years of incremental products, however, 3M needed new platforms.

Block (2)
Traditional 3M Development Versus Lead User Research Process

(suggested time: 20 minutes)

The purpose of this block is to deepen the student's understanding of the Lead User research process—managing the process output was the topic of **Block (1)**. As opposed to asking students about the new process in the absence of a reference process, it is best to characterize 3M's current product development process first which, after all, has been in part responsible for giving 3M its reputation as an innovator. One might start this block by asking students to quickly enumerate the problems, including external market pressures that the Medical-Surgical business unit faces.

Q: *Why has it taken so long for the Medical-Surgical business unit to learn about the new product and market opportunities revealed through the Lead User process?*

(Follow-up Question: *What is different about Lead User research?)*

This discussion sets the groundwork for understanding why Lead User research is different and lead to a table similar to **Table TN-1**. After all, the new process provides access to the type of customers who have faced market needs in advance of other customers. From teaching the case, however, I have found that many students do not immediately grasp the difference between "lead users" and "leading-edge customers." The difference that one should highlight is:

- As opposed to leading-edge customers who provide need-related information, lead users provide need- and solution-related information because they have innovated themselves. The solution-related info is what makes the difference.

- Lead users can be found in *target* or *analogous* markets. Lead use experts in a target market are often useful in identifying important attributes that can be used to find Lead Users (with respect to a given attribute) in analogous markets.

Thus, relying solely upon traditional input from customers leaves a company with a possible blind spot in surveying the market and may forgo the opportunity of finding the solution to a need. Mainstream customers typically have difficulties expressing latent needs or are constrained by their own product experiences ("I don't know if I like the product until I see and use it"). But even if one does find a way to get to unarticulated needs, the solution is not always obvious. The principal theme of Lead User research is to find users that have both—information on needs and solutions.

Block (3)
3M's Rollout Strategy

(suggested time: 15 minutes)

The purpose of this final discussion block is to develop an effective rollout strategy to using the new process that will result in acceptance outside the Medical-Surgical division. While the discussion will be limited to Lead User research, the lessons should be general enough to have students think about managing change in R&D organizations in general. To start off this block, the instructor may ask students to put themselves in the place of 3M senior management.

Q: *As Chuck Harstadt, the VP for Corporate Marketing, how would you successfully roll out the new Lead User research process?*

(Back-up Question: *How will you make sure that conservative managers such as Dunlop do not block the acceptance of this experimental process?)*

Students will likely enumerate several tactics that Harstadt can use. A common suggestion is to use a very successful "demo project", such as the Medical Surgical team's, and have senior managers and team members present the results to other divisions. This of course creates a substantial time burden on some employees and only senior management can free up enough resources to have the kind of impact that is necessary for a successful rollout (see **Table TN-3**).

Successful 3M-Wide Rollout Strategy		
Stakeholders	**Incentives/Motives**	**Methods**
Senior Management	• Financial results.	• Demonstrate how breakthrough products can affect bottom line. • Evidence from other firms. • Allow senior managers to take credit for new innovation strategy.
Middle Management	• Employee productivity. • Motivation. • Project performance.	• Seminars, pilot studies. • Senior management involvement. • Regular updates of progress.
Scientists/Engineers	• Ease of work. • Empowerment. • Flexibility. • Interesting work.	• Interaction with previous users. • Share excitement and praise efforts. • Trust them.

Table TN-3. Understanding methods for rolling out the new process.

The instructor may find it helpful to distinguish methods by the various stakeholders: senior management, middle management, and technical personnel (scientists, engineers). In general, senior management needs to be won over through demonstrating a potential impact on corporate profitability. Middle management may require seminars and pilot studies that demonstrate the utility at a project level. And technical personnel may require a palpable sense of excitement and purpose, as can be demonstrated through success stories of previous users, that makes their work more interesting. Students will quickly agree that scientists and engineers are easily won over for a process that allows them to do more breakthrough work. However, management needs to be very careful about asking them to follow the Lead User research process in addition to their already busy workloads. With student input, the instructor can develop a table similar to **Table TN-3.**

Q: *At 3M, which stakeholders would you focus on first? What senior managers should be involved and at what level? How do you disseminate the mixed experiences of Shor's team?"*

Quite likely, most students will agree that the senior management will require convincing before the new process has any future in the company. At 3M, the support of Chuck Harstadt, VP for Corporate Marketing, provides a good starting base for the new methodology. In practice, heartfelt support is also required at all other levels. The support of middle management is crucial, especially given that these individuals are ultimately responsible for shielding Lead User team members from additional work obligations. And finally, of course, commitment on part of participating scientists and engineers is crucial, given the deep level of thinking and probing required. The 3M experience has shown that sometimes Lead User team members must meet on evenings and weekends because of scheduling difficulties or work obligations, especially when members come from different parts of the company.

(B) CASE

(only if about 15 minutes are left in class)

The (B) case complements the (A) case: While Shor's team has been searching for a breakthrough technology to meet market needs, here, a Lead User team led by market development supervisor Mary Zettel is trying to find a new market for a pre-existing technology—a problem that many firms face if their R&D personnel have little contact with users. The (B) case also points out one of the weaknesses of the 3M product innovation process, which has led to thousands of inventions that are languishing for lack of markets. An invention, after all, only becomes an innovation when it provides economic value to someone. Here, the new Lead User process has been brought in to help rectify this 3M weakness.

The discussion can focus on two levels: improving the process (i.e., learning from past mistakes) and understanding the concept of lead users.

Q. *After having learned from the experience of Shor's team at the Medical-Surgical unit, what should Zettel and her team do in order to be more effective?*

Table TN-4 lists Zettel's own observations when she was interviewed for the (B) case.

IMPROVING THE EFFECTIVENESS OF THE LEAD USER RESEARCH

- Ensure support for the process at all levels.
- Ensure that the Lead User team would be shielded as much as possible from extra work.
- Maintain a focus to speed up things. Zettel was fortunate that she laid out objectives (designing a kitchen of the future using the new technology) at the very beginning and stuck close to the mission. Shor, on the other hand, had faced a far more abstract goal.
- Create artificial deadlines to ensure the project would finish in 6 months as opposed to the 12 months that Shor's team needed. Zettel found this useful, since even after just after four months bosses would get impatient and start piling work back onto the Lead User team members.
- Allow for total immersion. Zettel's team did not diffuse its energy through worldwide travels through a longer length project.
- Keep the team streamlined and easy to work with. Use value adders and high performers rather than big names with matching egos.
- Make the work attractive – for instance, through meeting at restaurants.
- Work with facilitators who are well-trained in the methodology.

Table TN-4. Zettel's observations for more effective Lead User research process.

The instructor may want to use them as a guideline for the kinds of discussion points that can be expected from students. To understand the concept of Lead Users more deeply, the instructor can also ask students to help with the search for lead use experts that could be part of a workshop.

Q. *What lead users should be invited to the workshop? Are the examples discussed in the case really lead users?"*

It is important to emphasize the difference between lead users and early adopters who do not hold information on solutions to unarticulated needs. Each proposal can be discussed using the definition provided earlier in this note:

- Lead users have new product or service needs that will be general in a marketplace, but they face them months or years before the bulk of the market encounters them.

- Lead users expect to benefit significantly by finding a solution to their needs. As a result, they often develop new products or services themselves because they can't or don't want to wait for them to become available commercially.

- Lead users can be found in *target* or *analogous* markets. Some lead users may be involved with just one or more of the important *attributes* of the problems faced by users in the target market.

- Lead users are not the same as "early adopters"—users who are among the first people to purchase an existing product or service. Lead users are facing needs for products and services that do not exist on the market.

The following experts were considered by the team as potential sources of information: a former president of a commercial cooking products leader, a professor of design (identified through the internet as having written on designing the kitchen of the future—in his opinion the most vital things in a kitchen are water and cooling), a Consumer Reports editor, a Royal Caribbean Cruise ship food director for whom food safety was highly critical, and an engineering designer from an industrial association called the "Multi-unit Architecture and Engineer Committee." Eventually the professor of design turned out to be the most useful source of information and was a good example of a lead user.

Update
(5 minutes)

The discussion can be concluded with an update, which is provided in presentation form on **Exhibit TN-3**.

Summary Lecture
(15 minutes)

To provide closure to the case discussion, the instructor can go through a short lecture that summarizes the principles behind Lead User research to students. The slides (**Exhibits TN-4** through **TN-13**) contain enough information to fill a short lecture and the instructor should feel free to pick and choose.

Exhibit TN-1 Class Flow

Block (1)
The Team Recommendation
(suggested time: 25 minutes)

"Regarding the final recommendation for rewriting the business unit's strategy, what do you recommend?" (Poll students.)

↓

Block (2)
Traditional 3M Development vs. Lead User Research Process
(suggested time: 20 minutes)

"Why has it taken so long for the Medical-Surgical business unit to learn about the new product and market opportunities revealed through the Lead User process?"

↓

Block (3)
3M's Rollout Strategy
(suggested time: 15 minutes)

"As Chuck Harstadt, the VP for Corporate Marketing, how would you successfully roll out the new Lead User process?"

↓

Update
(suggested time: 5 minutes)

↓

(B) Case
or
Summary Lecture
(suggested time: 15 minutes)

Exhibit TN-2 Board Plan

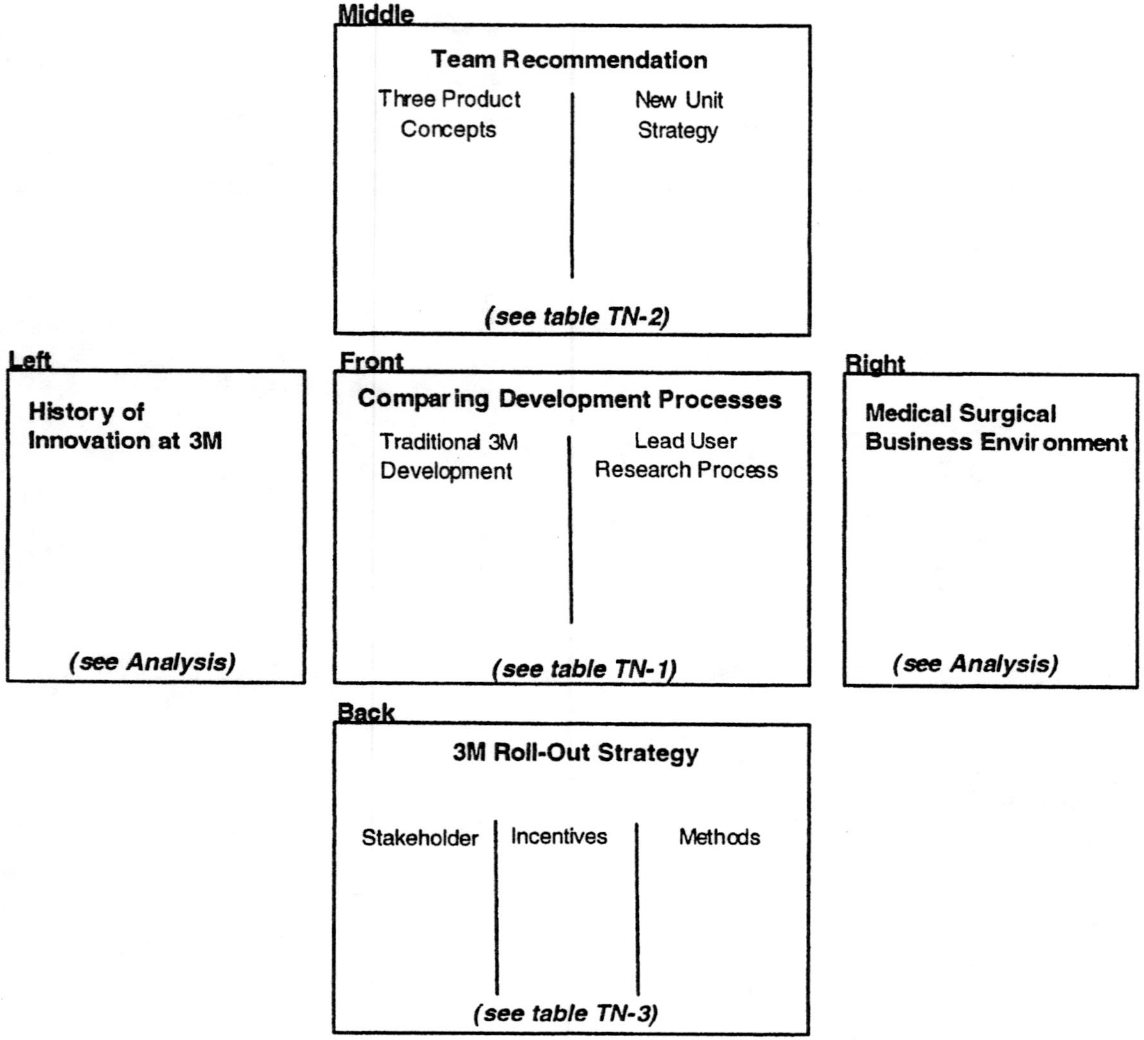

Exhibit TN-3 Update

Innovation at 3M: Update (10/98)

- *The two projects described in the cases led to breakthroughs at the product and strategic level.*
- *Six projects completed at 3M in five divisions.*
- *Planned roll-out of Lead User research process to 55 divisions during the next three years.*
- *Establishment of 3M Center of Excellence, responsible for Lead User training material and coaching.*
- *3M is partnering with other firms to do joint Lead User studies (ex.: Bell Atlantic, Maytag, LL Bean).*
- *On-going academic research on quantifying the benefits of Lead User research process.*

Exhibit TN-4 Summary Lecture—Slide #1

General Principle of Lead User Research

"Extremes versus Means"

- ***Identification*** *of functionally novel products and service concepts should be done at the <u>leading edge</u> of markets and applications.*
- ***Evaluation*** *of commercial potential should be done at the "<u>means</u>" of markets and market segments.*

Exhibit TN-5 Summary Lecture—Slide #2

Important Innovations by Consumers

Category	Example
Health Products	*Gatorade*
Personal Care	*Protein-based Shampoo*
Sports	*Mountain Bike*
Food	*Chocolate Milk*
Office	*White-out Liquid*
Computers	*E-mail, Desktop Publishing*
Apparel	*Sports Bra*

Exhibit TN-6 Summary Lecture—Slide #3

World Wide Web: A Lead User Innovation

- *Berners-Lee did not set out to invent a contemporary cultural phenomenon ("It was something I needed in my work").*
- *He simply wanted to solve a problem that was hindering his efforts as a consulting software engineer at CERN.*
- *His innovation was to apply the idea of hypertext to the growing reality of networked computers.*
- *He expanded the idea he had developed at CERN and made it available on the Internet in the summer of 1991.*

Source: *Technology Review* (July 1996), p. 34.

Exhibit TN-7 Summary Lecture—Slide #4

Definitions of Innovation Sources

- *An innovation is a user innovation when the developer (firm or individual) expects to benefit by using it.*
- *An innovation is a manufacturer innovation when the developer expects to benefit by manufacturing and selling it.*
- *The Lead User research process targets directly user innovations and funnels them into a firm's development process.*

Exhibit TN-8 Summary Lecture—Slide #5

How Often Do Users Innovate?

Results from academic research*

Study	First Device Used in Field Developed and Built By: Product User	Product Manufacturer
Scientific Instruments	77%	23%
Process Machinery	67%	33%
Tractor Shovels	6%	94%
Plastics	0%	100%

*Source: E.v. Hippel, *The Sources of Innovation*, Oxford University Press, 1988.

Exhibit TN-9 Summary Lecture—Slide #6

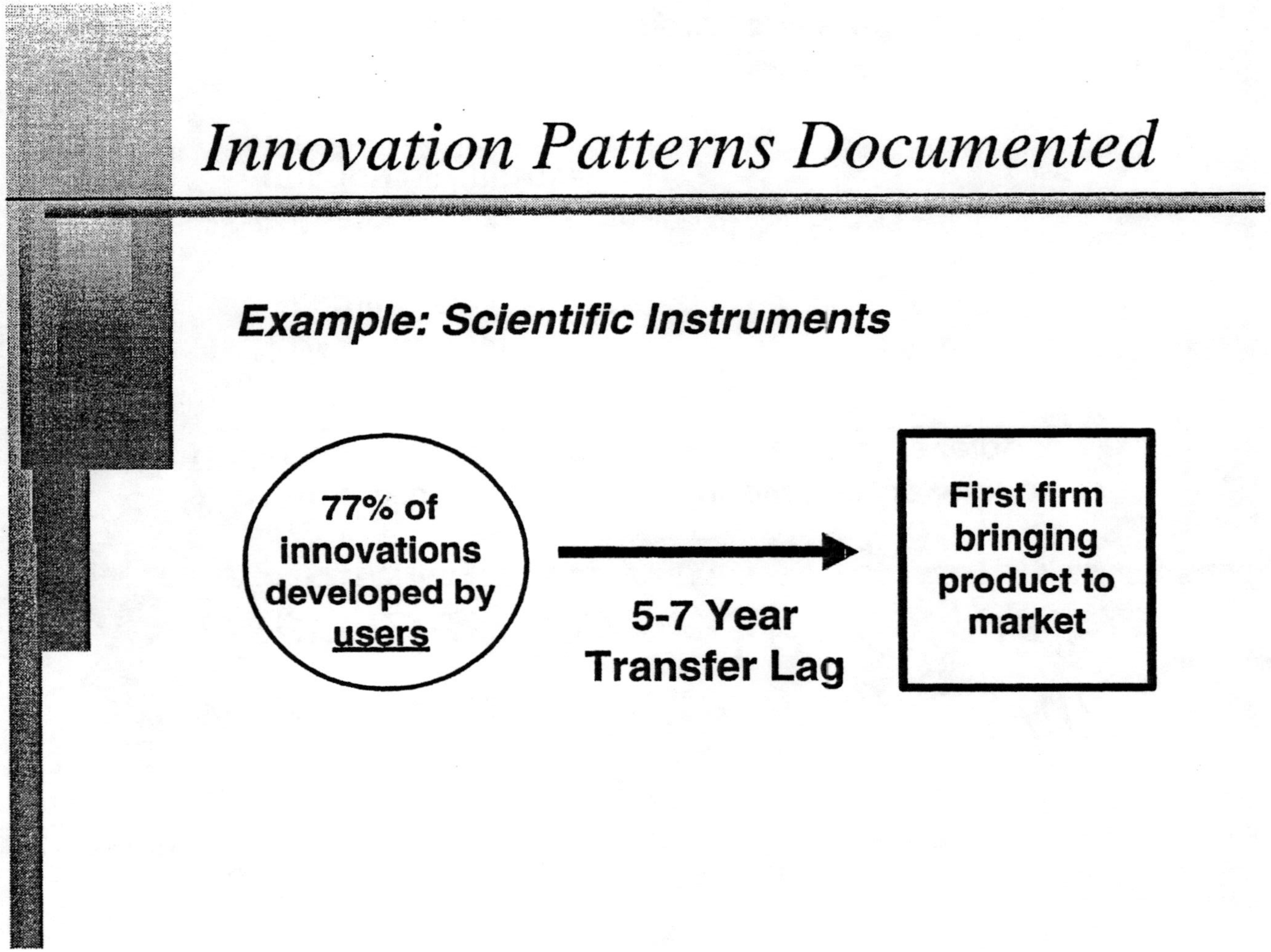

Exhibit TN-10 Summary Lecture—Slide #7

What Kinds of Innovations Will Users Develop and Prototype?

Type of Improvement Provided by Innovation	Innovation Developed By: % User Developed
1. New functional capability	82%
2. Automation of existing function or improve reliability	13%

(Total sample size of innovations studied: n=64)

Source: Riggs, W. and E. v. Hippel, "The Impact of Scientific and Commercial Values on the Sources of Scientific Instrument Innovation," *Research Policy* 23 (July 1994).

Exhibit TN-11 Summary Lecture—Slide #8

Benefiting from Lead Users

- *Lead User innovations form the basis for new products and services of value to manufacturers.*
- *Lead Users:*
  1. *Have new product or service needs that will be general in a marketplace, but they face them months or years before the bulk of the market;*
  2. *Expect to benefit significantly by finding a solution to those needs.*

Exhibit TN-12 Summary Lecture—Slide #9

Adopter Categorization on the Basis of Innovativeness

- *Lead User are <u>not</u> the same as "early adopters" - users who are among the first to purchase an existing product or service.*

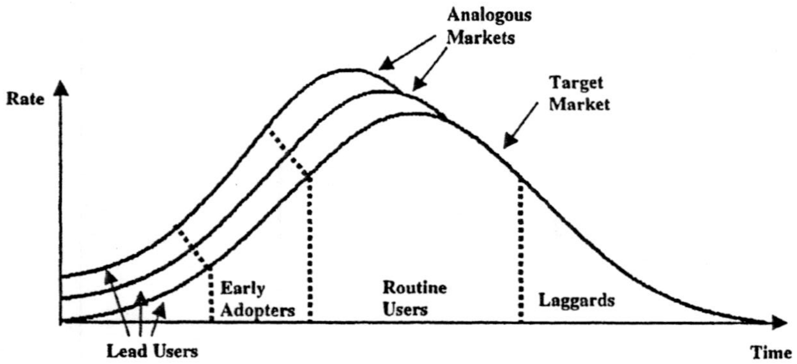

The innovativeness dimension, as measured by the time at which an individual adopts an innovation or innovations, is continuous and maybe partitioned into general adopter categories like the ones shown above..

Exhibit TN-13 Summary Lecture—Slide #10

General Steps for New Product Development with Lead Users

1. *Specify a narrow product/market segment.*
2. *Identify important trend(s) affecting segment (and/or screen innovating users and "back out" market trend).*
3. *Identify Lead Users with respect to trend.*
4. *Developers and Lead Users jointly develop new product concept(s) and specifications.*
5. *Test via traditional methods whether new product concept(s) appeals to routine users at the "means" of market.*

5-502-076
MAY 10, 2002

TEACHING NOTE

The Medicines Company

Synopsis

The Medicines Company was founded in 1996 for the purpose of acquiring or "rescuing" drugs abandoned by other drug companies, completing their development, and bringing them to market. Its first acquisition, in early 1997, was "Angiomax"—a blood-thinning drug used in angioplasty procedures. In December 2000, it received FDA approval for Angiomax. Now it must bring it to market. Complicating this task is the fact that Angiomax is designed to replace heparin, the most widely used blood-thinning drug in coronary medicine. But heparin sells for about $2 per dose while the *cost to make* Angiomax is $40 per dose. This raises a host of issues regarding pricing, target market selection, and consumer trial and adoption.

Use

To start, this is a value pricing case set in a high tech, medical products domain. In determining a price for Angiomax, students must first assess the value created by the drug across three segments of angioplasty patients—i.e., "Low-Risk" patients, "High-Risk" patients, and "Very High-Risk" patients. The results of this assessment will show that Angiomax has a value of $185, $375, and $725 across each of these three segments.

Next, students must assess how much the market is willing to pay for Angiomax. With heparin priced at $2 per dose, resistance to a price even close to the value price for Angiomax will be substantial. This raises an issue common in the launch of new technologies—i.e., how do you replace a well-entrenched, low-priced product with a much higher-priced, superior product?

Third, there is the question of how you go to market? With the need to gain approval from several different individuals in the buying organization (i.e., doctors, pharmacists, administrators), all with different agendas, the sale of Angiomax will be anything but easy. Rather, students need to recognize that diffusion of this product will initially be a series of small victories as opposed to widespread acceptance.

Finally, students can address the logic and long-term viability of the Medicine Company's underlying business strategy of rescuing abandoned drugs. On the surface, it seems strange that a small, upstart company can make money where a larger, more-established drug developer sees little

This note was prepared by Professor John T. Gourville with the assistance of Research Associate Alice Tzou for the sole purpose of aiding classroom instructors in the use of "The Medicines Company," HBS No. 502-006. It provides analysis and questions that are intended to present alternative approaches to deepening students' comprehension of business issues and energizing classroom discussion. HBS cases are developed solely as the basis for class discussion. Cases are not intended to serve as endorsements, sources of primary data, or illustrations of effective or ineffective management.

hope. This raises the question of whether the Medicines Company "just got lucky" with its first acquisition or has a sustainable business model.

Analyses

There are four main areas of discussion that students need to explore in order to develop a "go-to-market" strategy for Angiomax and to understand the logic of the Medicines Company's underlying business model. These main areas of discussions include:

1. An assessment of value created by Angiomax. How much is the product worth?
2. An assessment of a hospital's "willingness to pay" and the drivers of this assessment.
3. An analysis of the likely adoption of Angiomax and plans to influence that adoption.
4. The viability of the Medicines Company's underlying business model. Did the company just get lucky with Angiomax?

We will now cover each discussion area in turn.

1. The Value of Angiomax

A balloon angioplasty is a procedure to restore normal blood flow to arteries in the heart that are clogged by a fatty build-up called "plaque." In an angioplasty, a small incision is made in a blood vessel in the groin and a long flexible tube with a deflated balloon is threaded through an artery until it reaches the clogged artery in the heart. The balloon is then inflated, compacting the plaque against the artery wall and opening the artery to increased blood flow.

Historically, the primary drug used to minimize complications during this procedure has been heparin, a generic blood-thinning drug that has been around for 80 years and that costs about $2 per dose. As reported in the case, there are 700,000 angioplasties performed each year in the United States (case page 5), all of which involve the use of heparin (case Table A). Angiomax has been designed to be a safer alternative to heparin. Its value can be calculated from the degree to which it reduces complications relative to heparin.

To calculate the economic value of Angiomax to a hospital, students will need four pieces of data. These include: (1) the cost of a complication, (2) the patient segments to be analyzed, (3) the relative rate of complications for each of these segments, and (4) the dosage requirement for Angiomax.

The Cost of a Complication = $8,000

As noted in the case (page 10), hospitals are reimbursed by insurance companies at a flat rate of $11,500 per angioplasty. If there are no complications, the cost of the angioplasty is about $9,500. In a small percentage of cases, however, complications do arise. These include: (1) bleeding, (2) the need for a repeat angioplasty, (3) heart attack, and (4) death. Importantly, each of these complications costs the hospital an additional $8,000—an expense that insurance companies do not reimburse and that must be absorbed by the hospital. Thus, the cost of a complication to a hospital is $8,000.

Customer Segments

As can be determined from page 8 of the case, there are three relevant angioplasty patient populations that could benefit from Angiomax. These include:

- "Very High Risk" Patients—those patients who have had a heart attack in the two weeks prior to the angioplasty.
- "High Risk" Patients—those who previously had a heart attack or were admitted to the hospital due to severe chest pains (unstable angina).
- "Low Risk" Patients—all other angioplasty patients.

In terms of numbers, the case notes that 50% of all angioplasty patients are "Low Risk" (Footnote 7, page 8) and that 50% are "High Risk." In addition, 20% of "High Risk" patients can be further qualified as "Very High Risk" patients. This means that the size of the three segments is as follows:

- "Very High Risk" Patients = 10% of 700,000 angioplasty patients = 70,000 patients
- "High Risk" Patients = 40% of 700,000 angioplasty patients = 280,000 patients
- "Low Risk" Patients = 50% of 700,000 angioplasty patients = 350,000 patients

Reduction in Complications across Segments

The benefit of Angiomax relative to heparin for each of these groups can be calculated using the information on page 8 of the case. Case Table C outlines the rate of complications for "High Risk" patients who have received heparin and for those who have received Angiomax. By adding together the incidence of death, heart attack, repeat angioplasty, and major bleeding, students will find that the use of heparin leads to complications in 16.5% of high-risk angioplasties (i.e., 0.2% + 4.2% + 2.8% + 9.3%), while the use of Angiomax leads to complications in only 9.5% (i.e., 0.2% + 3.3% + 2.5% + 3.5%). This leads to a net reduction in complications of 7%.[1]

A similar analysis can be done for "Very High Risk" patients using case Table D. Based on that analysis, the rate of complication for heparin is 21.4% and the rate of complication for Angiomax is 7.8%, for a net savings of 13.6%. Finally, while we do not have rates of complication for "Low Risk" patients, we are told that the relative benefit of Angiomax over heparin is half as great for "Low Risk" patients as for "High Risk" patients (see Footnote 7, page 8). Thus, we can conclude that the reduction in complications is half of 7% or 3.5%.

Dosage Rate for Angiomax

The final bit of information needed to value Angiomax is the dosage level required. As mentioned in the case (page 9), "70% of patients would require a single dose, with the other 30% requiring two or three doses." Taking a weighted average of these figures, a student can easily arrive at an average dosing of about 1.5 doses (i.e., (0.7 x 1) + (0.3 x 2.5) = 0.7 + 0.75 = 1.45).

Putting the Pieces Together

Using these data, a student should be able to calculate the value of Angiomax for any given hospital across each of the three patient populations. These calculations are shown in the following **Table**. Note that these figures represent the highest price a hospital should be willing to pay for

[1] Some students will argue that these are not independent outcomes—e.g., that a patient both can have a heart attack and die. In reality, the statistics presented are independent in that each patient was categorized once based on the most severe outcome.

Angiomax for each of the three patient populations. For instance, from an economic perspective, at a price of $185 per dose, a hospital should be indifferent between using heparin and using Angiomax on "Low-Risk" patients. At prices below $185, it is more economical to use Angiomax. And at prices above $185, it is more economical to use heparin.

Table Objective Value of Angiomax by Patient Segments

	Patient Segment		
	Low-Risk	High-Risk	Very High-Risk
All Complications with Heparin	na	16.5%	21.4%
All Complications with Angiomax	— na	— 9.5%	— 7.8%
Reduction in Complications	= 3.5%	= 7.0%	= 7.0%
Cost per Complication	x $8,000	x $8,000	x $8,000
Savings from Using Angiomax	= $280	= $560	= $1,088
Number of Doses Required	÷ 1.5 doses	÷ 1.5 doses	÷ 1.5 doses
Objective Value of 1 Dose of Angiomax	**= $185**	**= $375**	**= $725**

Applied to the segment sizes developed earlier, this suggests three market sizes. At a price of $185 per dose, a hospital should be willing to use Angiomax for all three patient segments. At $375, it should be willing to use Angiomax on "High-Risk" and "Very High-Risk" patients. And at $725, it should be willing to use Angiomax on "Very High-Risk" patients. This suggests maximum market sizes of:

- At $185: 700,000 patients x 1.5 doses/patient x $185/dose = $194,250,000 ~ $200 MM
- At $375: 350,000 patients x 1.5 doses/patient x $375/dose = $196,875,000 ~ $200 MM
- At $725: 70,000 patients x 1.5 doses/patient x $725/dose = $76,125,000 ~ $75 MM

And if one factors in a cost of goods sold of $40 per dose (case page 9), this suggests maximum gross margins of:

- At $185: 700,000 patients x 1.5 doses/patient x ($185—$40)/dose = $152,250,000 ~ $150 MM
- At $375: 350,000 patients x 1.5 doses/patient x $375—$40)/dose = $175,875,000 ~ $175 MM
- At $725: 70,000 patients x 1.5 doses/patient x $725—$40)/dose = $71,925,000 ~ $70 MM

Graphically, these market size estimates can be drawn as shown in **Exhibit TN-1.** Note, however, that it is more important to generate the analysis shown in the **Table** than it is to generate overall market size estimates. Students <u>must</u> calculate the value of Angiomax for each of the three patient populations. As for the market sizes, depending on the instructor's purposes, it may be sufficient for students to recognize that the theoretical market size is 700,000 patients when priced at $185 (or below), 350,000 when priced at $375 (but above $185) , and 70,000 when priced at $725 (but above $375).

One additional number that may be generated at this point is "$400." The case states that the costs of goods sold for Angiomax is $40 per dose (case page 9). Additionally, the case mentions that the typical "COGS" to "price" ratio in the industry is 1:10 (case page 7). This implies a price of $400 for

Angiomax. While $400 is difficult to justify from an economic standpoint, it does represent an industry benchmark that might influence The Medicines Company's final pricing decision.

As students generate these and other figures through the course of the case, it is useful to capture them on the board in a "value pricing thermometer," as shown below in **Exhibit TN-2.** At this stage of the discussion, the figures generated would likely include the objective value of Angiomax for each of the three patient segments, the expected $40 cost of goods sold for Angiomax, and the corresponding $400 selling price.

Other "Objective" Assessments

Before leaving any discussion about the objective value of Angiomax, there are additional benefits that are difficult to capture quantitatively, but which students likely will raise. In particular, Angiomax appears to outperforms Heparin in the following ways:

- Predictability—Whereas "the anti-clotting effects of heparin was unpredictable" and "its use required very close monitoring" (case page 6), "the effects of a dose of Angiomax are very exacting and very crisp" and "physicians who use Angiomax have been pleasantly surprised by how predictable their results are" (case page 9).

- Speed—Angiomax works faster than Heparin. Angiomax takes 30 minutes to take full effect (case page 9) while Heparin takes 2 to 4 hours (case page 6).

- No Immune Reaction—There is no immune reaction to Angiomax (case page 9) while heparin leads to HIT, a sometimes-fatal immune reaction, in 2% to 3% of patients (case page 6).

Some students will argue that these added benefits of Angiomax over heparin could raise the value of Angiomax above those numbers previously calculated, but by how much is difficult to quantify. However, other students may argue that these benefits are already incorporated in that they reduce the rate of complications. For example, the fact that the effects are Angiomax are more predictable may be one reason behind the reduction in bleeding or death.

In either case, it is important to recognize that Angiomax makes a doctor's job easier. Apart from the pure economic benefits offered by the use of Angiomax, doctors should welcome the faster acting, more predictable results offered by the drug. For a doctor, whose primary concern is the patient, Angiomax should allow for better outcomes. These represent the intangible benefits shown in **Exhibit TN-2.**

2. But How Much Will Hospitals Pay?

The generation of a "value price" for Angiomax is but the first step in arriving at a selling price for the drug. In theory, it establishes the upper bound—the most a rational buyer should be willing to pay for the product. After students have arrived at a value price for Angiomax, they should be asked, "But what price would you charge for the drug?" Any answer to this question must take into account two factors.

Choice of Target Market

The first factor is the choice of a target market. This is the classic skim versus penetrate debate. Some students will want to price Angiomax high and position it as the drug to use for the 70,000 "Very High-Risk" patients. Such a strategy might entail a price approaching $700 per dose. The arguments for such a strategy typically are: (1) a more compelling value proposition, (2) a more focused selling effort, (3) higher margins, and (4) lower production requirements.

Other students will want to price Angiomax much lower (around $150) in the hopes of capturing the complete angioplasty market. In particular, at $150, hospitals have some incentive (e.g., $185 - $150 = $35 in savings per patient) to use Angiomax for the 350,000 "Low-Risk" patients, a moderately strong incentive (e.g., $375-$150 = $225 in savings per patient) to use it for the 280,000 "High Risk" patients, and a very strong incentive ($725 - $150 = $575 in savings per patient) to use it for the 70,000 Very High Risk patients. The primary argument here is one of penetration. If the Medicines Company wishes to foster widespread adoption, it will be much easier at $150 than at $700. Also, it will be easier for the company's salesforce to justify to buyers a "cost of goods sold" to "price" ration of 1:4 than 1:17.

Finally, many students will argue for a middling strategy of a moderate price (e.g., $300) so as to capture both the "High-Risk" and "Very High-Risk" patients. Economically, such a strategy may achieve the same market size as the low-price strategy, yet reduce production requirements.

Subjective Value of Angiomax

The second factor is the hospital's "willingness to pay." The above analysis makes the assumption that hospital personnel recognize the objective value of Angiomax. In reality, there are many reasons to believe that charging anything close to a value price for Angiomax will be difficult. Factors that lead to this conclusion include the following:

- ***The price of heparin.*** The single biggest obstacle to pricing Angiomax anywhere close to its full value is heparin, currently priced at $2 per dose. Some students will argue that the price of heparin should not matter—i.e., that value pricing takes into account the price of heparin. But others will argue that heparin acts as a strong psychological benchmark against which the price of Angiomax will be compared. This is especially problematic given the entrenched nature of heparin in emergency cardiac care.
- ***Doctors' satisfaction with heparin.*** Other students will point to case Figure B to argue that most cardiologists are happy with heparin. On a 1 to 10 satisfaction scale, heparin averages about a 7. Many students will take this to mean that only a small percent of doctors are dissatisfied. Other students will note, however, that at the time of the survey, there was no viable alternative to heparin. With the availability of Angiomax, these ratings of satisfaction for heparin should decrease.
- *Cost Containment* A very real issue that Angiomax faces is "cost containment" or the pressure that exists within hospitals to lower costs (case page 2). With prescription drugs accounting for 9% of all medical expenses and growing at 20% per year, the thought of replacing a $2 drug with a $300 drug will be tough to justify to any hospital. While the Medicines Company can legitimately argue that Angiomax lowers costs by reducing complications, this benefit is "promised," while the cost of the drug is "certain."
- *Dis-Belief in Clinical Data* Some students will question the robustness of the clinical data that the Medicines Company has amassed. In particular, some will question whether 2,161 "High-Risk" patients and 369 "Very High-Risk" patients (case page 8) are large enough samples from which to draw valid conclusions regarding the superiority of Angiomax. For instance, some students will question how the Angiomax complication rate for "Very High-Risk" patients (at 7.8%) can be lower than that for "High-Risk"

patients (at 9.5%). There is no easy answer to this concern, but the instructor might ask students "how large a sample is needed?"

- *Belief about Your Own Ability* Finally, some students will argue that the figures presented in case Table C and Table D represent the complication rates in an "average" hospital and for an "average" doctor and that most doctors do not perceive themselves as "average." For these "above average" doctors, the expected benefits of Angiomax will be much lower than those shown in the two tables. If this view does not come out naturally, the instructor can ask students to "assume that you are a hotshot cardiologist at Massachusetts General Hospital. What do you think of these numbers? Do you believe them? Do they apply to you?"

As these comments are raised, they can be captured as factors that put downward pressure on price. This can be done in two ways. The first uses the "value pricing thermometer" to indicate the downward pressure of the above factors, as shown in **Exhibit TN-2.** The second alternative is shown in **Exhibit TN-3.** As it indicates, the price that The Medicines Company can charge for Angiomax is positively influenced by the clinical studies that it has conducted, but negatively influenced by the five factors raised above. The ability of The Medicines Company to extract value from Angiomax will hinge on its ability to communicate and justify the economic benefits of Angiomax, while reducing or eliminating the relevance of these negative influences.

3. How Do You Get Hospitals to Buy and Use Angiomax?

Following a discussion of product pricing, the case discussion can turn to the question of getting this product adopted in hospitals. There are two parts to this discussion. The first is the recognition of the complexity of the selling task. The second is a strategy for gaining adoption.

The Complexity of the Selling Task

Students need to recognize the difficulties of selling into the complex buying organization represented by the hospital. In particular, as Dr. Stephanie Plent makes clear on page 10 of the case, there are at least three separate entities, with somewhat competing agendas, which need convincing for Angiomax to be adopted. These three entities are:

- *The doctors* are not concerned with price so much as they are with results – i.e., does the drug prove more effective than heparin.

- *The pharmacists* are responsible for determining which drugs the hospital will and will not carry. They have an annual budget for all the drugs they dispense and are rewarded for meeting or beating that budget. As the case says, "replacing a widely-used $10 drug with a $100 drug really kills that budget. Unless they can justify the cost of the new drug to the hospital administrators and get the added expense incorporated into their budgets, it is unlikely they will carry it."

- *The administrators* take the big picture into account – i.e., does the drug make economic sense. It is this group that would be most swayed by the potential for Angiomax to save a hospital money by reducing costly complications.

The case goes on to mention that drug companies rarely have direct access to hospital administrators. Rather, they have access to doctors and pharmacists and must work with them to get a drug adopted within the hospital.

This does not make for an easy sell. The two groups that the Medicines Company does have access to—the doctors and pharmacists—have competing agendas. One cares about benefits, the other cares about price. The one group that the Medicines Company does not have access to—the hospital administrators—is the group that should find Angiomax the most appealing. All of this tends to come out naturally from the students and can be captured by the instructor using the diagram shown in **Exhibit TN-4.**

Gaining Adoption

The next step in this discussion is to develop a strategy for gaining adoption. By the end of this discussion, it is important for students to recognize that the adoption of Angiomax will be a series of small battles:

- Some forward-looking doctors willing to try the drug on a limited basis.
- Other, more conservative doctors will be reluctant to trial the drug until it gains endorsement from the industry's thought leaders.
- Pharmacists will be reluctant to carry large quantities of the drug for fear it will break their budget, but may stock it on a trial basis at the request of particular doctors.
- Progressive administrators will be unlikely to approve the drug for widespread use without some in-house evidence of its economic benefits.
- Other conservative administrators will not adopt until the larger, more recognized hospitals (e.g., Mass General Hospital) adopt its use.
- And even if the drug is adopted, it is likely its use will initially be limited to the "Very High-Risk" angioplasty patients, where its benefit is most pronounced.

This suggests that the Medicines Company needs to work with a small set of forward-looking doctors and pharmacists to showcase the drug's benefits. Perhaps it means providing the drug at a steep discount for a limited period of time. Or perhaps it means seeking out the industry mavericks, those doctors and pharmacists who are always looking for a better way.

In any case, the adoption of Angiomax will likely start with a very limited number of doctors in a limited number of high-profile hospitals who ask their pharmacists to stock this great new drug for use in a select group of very high-risk patients. If the drug proves successful, this should have a cascading effect on trial, as shown in **Exhibit TN-5**. These doctors may expand use to other less risky patients. Fellow doctors may trial the drug for use in their patients. And other hospitals may trial the drug in their hospitals. Over time, evidence will build as to the efficacy of the drug and the Medicines Company will work with doctors and pharmacists to gain acceptance among hospital administrators. An article from *The Boston Globe* highlights how this process took place for a seemingly unrelated surgical product called "FloSeal" (see **Exhibit TN-6**). The adoption of Angiomax may have some of the vary same characteristics as the gradual adoption of "FloSeal."

4. The Sustainability of the Business Model

The final discussion for this case involves the sustainability of the Medicines Company's business model. There is much energy around this topic and instructors should leave time for it to take shape. On one side of the discussion are the nay-sayers—students who question the logic of the business model. Their arguments include:

- The company just got lucky with Angiomax.
- How can the Medicines Company be better at spotting winning drugs than the larger, more sophisticated companies that have abandoned them?
- There are not enough "abandoned winners" to repeat the success on Angiomax. In the company's initial screening, it started with 3,000 candidates and eliminated all but one. Presumably, these 3,000 candidates were among the most promising available. Where is the next batch of 3,000 going to come from?
- Since drugs with blockbuster potential would be kept by their developing companies, the Medicines Company is left with drugs that have limited sales potentials ($100 million to $500 million).
- Already the company has faltered with its second acquisition (IS-159). And it has deviated from its stated business strategy of acquiring late-stage drugs with its third acquisition (CTV-05).

Those who like the business model of the Medicines Company may counter with:

- Angiomax alone may be able to sustain the business for many years. In particular, while it may generate $100 million to $200 million a year as a drug for 700,000 angioplasty patients, it has the potential to generate five times that amount if it can replace heparin in other applications (see case page 6 and case Exhibit 8).
- The Medicines Company is avoiding many of the costs and risks associated with developing drugs from scratch (see case Exhibit 4). By obtaining drugs in late stages of development, it greatly increases the odds of success and lowering the cost of failure. Rather than a 1 in 5,000 chance of success, it is striving for a 1 in 2 chance of success.
- While the large drug companies need blockbuster drugs to survive, the Medicines Company can do quite well with drugs that generate $100 million to $500 million per year.
- Given the blockbuster mentality of the drug industry (see Meanwell quote on case page 3), what is unattractive to a large drug company may be very attractive to the Medicines Company. Thus, there may not be a shortage of abandoned drugs available to the company.

And those who really understand the evolution of the Medicines Company will realize that the company is far different in 2001 than it was in 1997. In particular, whereas the company had a wide-open playing field in 1997, it now had developed expertise in coronary care medicine. Whereas the company was unknown in 1997, it now had a track record of bringing troubled drugs to market. And whereas the company consisted of a handful of employees in 1997, it now consisted of a company with capabilities in drug development, clinical trials, and sales.

This change has several important implications for the company. First, the company now represents a viable partner for any drug company who possesses a drug that might not fit that company's portfolio. Perhaps the company is small and inexperienced at bringing drugs to market and is looking for a partner. Perhaps the company is large and the drug in question does not fit with the expertise of the company. Or perhaps the company is large and the drug does not hold the promise of being a blockbuster. In these cases, the Medicines Company now becomes a destination. Rather than having to search the market for abandoned drugs, the company may now find promising drugs coming to it.

Another important implication for the company is that it now has built expertise and infrastructure in coronary care medicine. Future acquisitions should take this into account. Rather than build a second sales force to call on a separate set of doctors (e.g., pediatricians), it now makes sense to focus its drug acquisition and development efforts on other coronary care products. This allows the Angiomax sales force to leverage its contacts and the goodwill that it has developed over time. [As a note, consistent with this perspective, the company's next acquisition, made in March 2002, was an acute cardiac care drug.]

What Happened?

Angiomax was launched in January 2001. A *Boston Globe* article from January 2002 (see **Exhibit TN-7**) captures the company's efforts and success at marketing Angiomax through the end of 2001. These include:

- Angiomax was priced at $335 per dose.
- Under the guidance of Dr. Stephanie Plent, Senior Director of Medical Policy and Economics, the company produced an interactive CD to explain the economic value of Angiomax. The CD allowed hospital personnel to enter their hospital's own complication rates to determine the value of Angiomax for that hospital.
- As outlined in the case, the company focused on those 700 of 1,300 medical centers that performed 92% of all angioplasties in the United States. By the end of 2001, Angiomax was being used in 260 of these 700 hospitals. [2]
- Many of these 260 hospitals limited use of Angiomax to the 10% to 20% of angioplasty patients who were deemed "Very High Risk."
- Through early 1992, quarterly sales of Angiomax have been as follows:[3]
    - 1st Quarter 2001 Sales = $1.9 million
    - 2nd Quarter 2001 Sales = $2.0 million
    - 3rd Quarter 2001 Sales = $3.5 million
    - 4th Quarter 2001 Sales = $6.8 million
    - 1st Quarter 2002 Sales = $7.7 million
- Through 2001 and 2002, the company has been conducting a new 6,000-person clinical trial to provide clear and compelling evidence of the relative advantage of Angiomax over

[2] Naomi Aoki, "A Drug Maker Weighs the Costs," *Boston Globe*, January 16, 2002, P. E1.

[3] All figure taken from company press releases.

> heparin. In commenting on this trial, Plent noted that "there's no question that if you put Angiomax next to heparin, Angiomax is the better drug. The problem becomes, is the better drug worth the incremental cost to the hospital. If we can prove Angiomax saves money, then we have a slam dunk."[4]

As for the company's other drugs, the following actions were taken:

- As the case mentions, in 1999, the company halted development of IS-159 after problems arose with the drug's formulation.

- In early March 2002, the company acquired the rights to "Clevidipine" from AstraZeneca. This intravenous drug was in Phase 3 clinical trials and was designed for the short-term control of high blood pressure in acute care hospital settings. In commenting on this acquisition, Clive Meanwell noted, "Acquisition of the rights to clevidipine is consistent with our execution of a strategy to build a franchise in acute hospital care. Commercially, the product's ... attributes make it an ideal candidate for ... the control of blood pressure during and after cardiac surgery."[5]

- In late March 2002, the company halted development of CTV-05 after ongoing clinical trials showed that the drug was less effective than expected. At the time, Meanwell noted, "Right now, we have no plans for making significant new investments in the product—rather we intend to focus on our acute care products, [Angiomax] and clevidipine." [6]

Teaching the Case

This discussion of this case has two halves. The first half is a quantitative analysis around the question of what to charge for Angiomax. The second half is more qualitative and involves the process of customer adoption and the logic of the underlying business model. The class discussion should be split equally between these two halves.

With this in mind, it may make sense to open the case with a general question, such as "What do you think of what the Medicines Company has done to date?" Responses will likely come in two forms—either comments about Angiomax or comments about the company. The instructor should capture these on the board as they come out, organizing them under two general headings—"Angiomax Issues" and "Company Issues." After about 10 or 15 minutes, the instructor should then direct the class to focus on one of the two sets of issues—preferably the Angiomax issues.

The instructor can direct students to consider Angiomax by asking, "So, is this a good or bad product?" Typically, someone will raise the issue of value creation and proceed to lay out the economic benefits of Angiomax over heparin. If not, the instructor should explicitly raise the issue. Once the value-pricing framework has been brought out, the instructor can then ask, "But what will hospitals pay?" This should naturally lead to a discussion about the downward pressure on price that exists in this market space.

After a thorough analysis of objective and subjective pricing issues, the discussion can move to the question of promoting adoption. This discussion tends to be more opinion than fact, so the instructor should be sure to ask students to justify their comments. In addition, it can be valuable to do a bit of

---

[4] Naomi Aoki, "A Drug Maker Weighs the Costs," *Boston Globe*, January 16, 2002, P. E1.

[5] Company press release, "The Medicines Company Announces Acquisition of Rights to Clevidipine," March 6, 2002.

[6] Company press release, "The Medicines Company Announces Results of Phase II Bacterial Vaginosis Study," March 26, 2002.

role playing at this point—e.g., assigning one student to play the role of an Angiomax sales person and asking others to play the roles of doctor, pharmacist, or administrator. This helps to bring out the complexity of the selling process.

Finally, the instructor should leave enough time to discuss the company's underlying business model. Experience with the case suggests that there is a lot of energy around this discussion and that many students are quite critical of what the Medicines Company is trying to do. If this proves to be the case, the instructor should solicit favorable opinions (e.g., "Does anyone like what the company is attempting to do?"). In the end, the class generally concludes that this will be a very tough model to keep going. However, with some pushing by the instructor, the class may begin to see that with a success or two, the company's business model becomes easier to implement, as laid out previously.

A potential board plan for this discussion is provided in **Exhibit TN-8**.

Suggested Preparation Questions

Some suggested preparation questions for this case are:

1. What is the value of Angiomax to a hospital?
2. What price should the Medicines Company charge for a dose of Angiomax? Why?
3. What do you think the adoption profile will look like for Angiomax? Will this be an easy sell or a tough sell? Why?
4. If you were the Medicines Company, how would you promote adoption?
5. What do you think of the Medicines Company's business model of "rescuing" abandoned drugs?
6. If Angiomax is a success, how might this business model change?

Exhibit TN-1 Sizing the Angioplasty Market for Angiomax

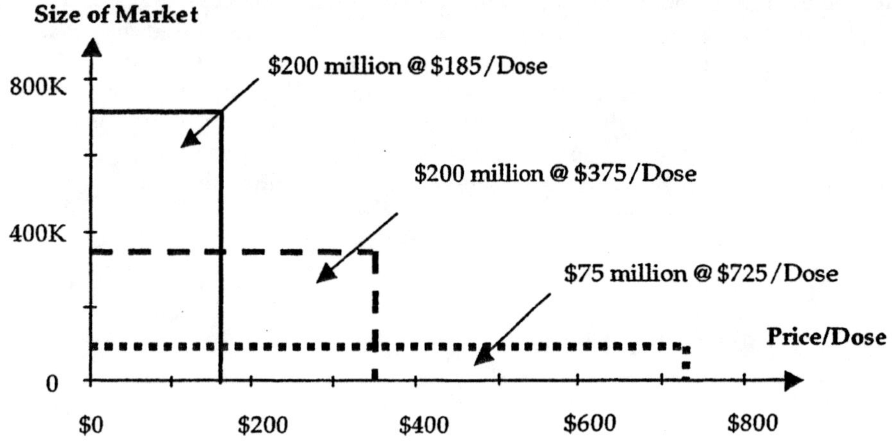

Exhibit TN-2 The Value Pricing Thermometer

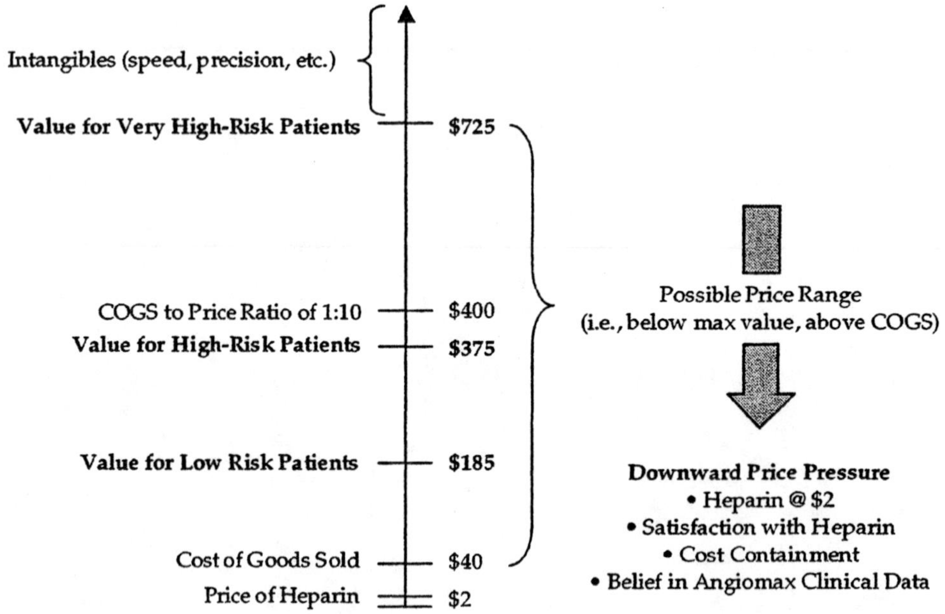

Exhibit TN-3 The Influencers on "Willingness to Pay"

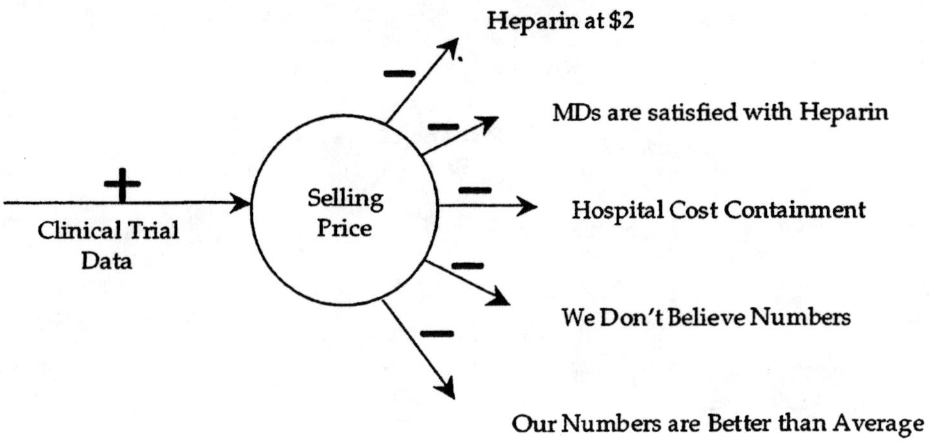

Exhibit TN-4 The Nature of the Buying Organization

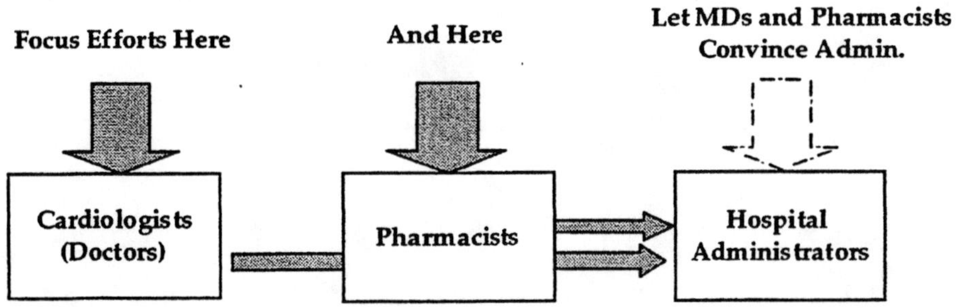

	Cardiologists (Doctors)	Pharmacists	Hospital Administrators
Agenda:	- Good patient care - Ease of use - Predictability	- Cost: $2 vs. $300 - Can I get it budgeted?	- Net benefit
Likely Receptiveness To Angiomax:	- High - But skeptical	- Very low	- Moderate - Skeptical
Accessibility	- High	- High	- Low

Exhibit TN-5 The Cascading Impact of Angiomax Adoption

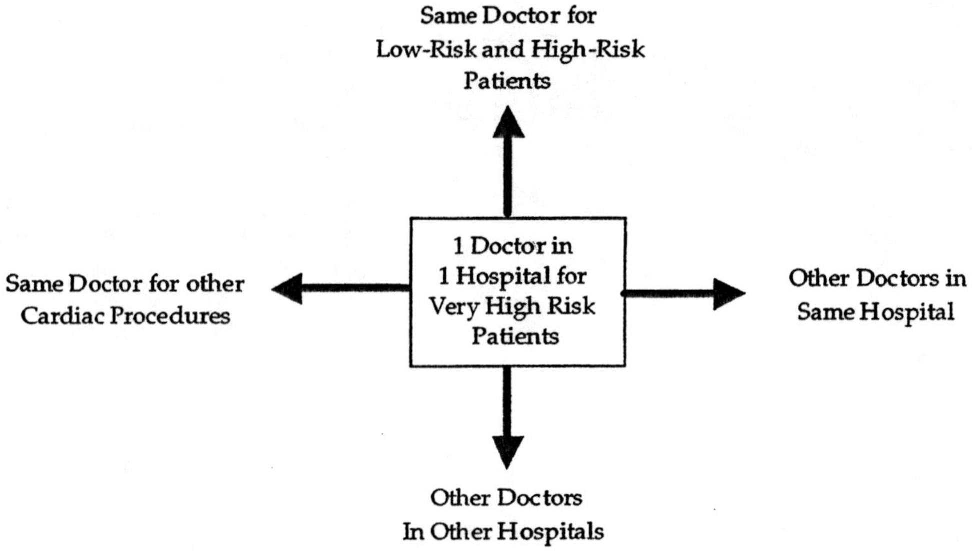

Exhibit TN-6 An Excerpt from *The Boston Globe,* May 23, 2001

Sealing the Deal

'Superglue' FloSeal had FDA Approval. Getting Hospitals to Stock It, However, Was a Challenge

By Naomi Aoki
GLOBE STAFF

Dr. Stephen Brooks was the surgeon on call on the February day paramedics rushed James Rafeld into Cape Cod Hospital in Hyannis. The 19 year-old Coast Guard petty officer had flipped his car, breaking his ribs and shattering his liver.

Brooks did what he could to stop the internal bleeding, packing Rafeld's liver with special cloths to help blood clot and sewing him back up. Two days later, Brooks operated again to remove the packing—a procedure that often causes new bleeding.

This time, he tried a new product, FloSeal, that had been approved by federal regulators just months earlier. He coated the raw areas of Rafeld's liver with it and, he said, watched in amazement as the bleeding stopped almost immediately.

"Dr. Brooks said they superglued my liver back together, Rafeld said. " I was scared by the idea at first. But it worked. It was good ingenuity. I'm feeling great now, and doing everything I used to do."

Brooks, the chief of trauma at Cape Cod Hospital, asked administrators to stock FloSeal and they agreed. It was one of the early successes for Fusion Medical Technologies, the California maker of FloSeal, at a time when the company was struggling to meet the expectations it had set for Wall Street. It also illustrated the importance of decisions by local surgeons in the success of a new product.

Fusion knew that getting new products into hospitals was especially tough these days, given the budget crunches created by cutbacks in reimbursements from managed care and government payers. But the company had expected FloSeal to do better during its first months on the market.

"The financial pressure on hospitals these days is incredible," said Dr. Richard Freeman, associate professor of surgery at Tufts University School of Medicine. "Most companies, especially small companies, are going to have an extremely difficult time getting their products introduced."

Fusion had spent most of 1999 preparing for FloSeal's launch. It evaluated the potential markets for the product—almost any surgical procedure where excessive bleeding might result. It entertained different marketing strategies. ...

When it got word in December 1999 that the Food and Drug Administration had approved FloSeal, its sales force was calling on surgeons within 24 hours.

But the reception was lukewarm, at best.

Cardiac and vascular surgeons were trained to use suturing techniques to prevent bleeding, clamps and pressure to control it. Some interpreted the company's sales pitch as an indictment of their surgical techniques. Others just didn't think they needed a new product to stop bleeding.

Administrators, struggling to cope with ever-tightening budgets, were leery of new products. Most already stocked a number of different products—special types of gels, glues and gauze—to stop bleeding. Some simply slapped moratoriums on new items.

Here and there, however, Fusion began to win some battles. A surgeon would try the product, like it, and persuade hospital administrators to stock it. As surgeons traveled from one hospital to another, they would wage the battle anew, getting FloSeal on yet another hospital shelf.

Brooks said Cape Cod administrators agreed to stock FloSeal, primarily because it worked well on Rafeld but also because it is more cost-effective than many of its rivals—even some with lower price tags. ...

"These are tough decisions that hospitals have to make," Konowitz said. "They operate on slim profit margins, if any. They have to ask, 'Can we afford to use it? Is it effective?' In this case, the answers happened to be yes."

Source: *The Boston Globe,* May 23, 2001, p. D4.

Exhibit TN-7 An Excerpt from *The Boston Globe*, January 16, 2002

A Drug Maker Weighs the Costs

Economic calculations crucial to the success of Medicines Co.'s Angiomax

By Naomi Aoki
GLOBE STAFF

The economic calculations began early. Even before studies proved the drug safe and effective, the Medicines Co. began figuring what the drug would cost to manufacture, what price the market would bear, and whether it could make a profit.

The drug, a blood thinner used in a heart procedure known as angioplasty, had the potential to be better than the standard medication, an 85-year old generic know as heparin. Studies suggested the new drug reduced complications, such as bleeding, heart attacks, and even death.

But it would also be much more expensive—hundreds of dollars a vial instead of the roughly $10 it cost for heparin. In an age of rising health-care costs and stressed budgets, the company knew it would have to prove the drug could prevent enough complications to justify its added cost. If it didn't, no hospital could afford to buy the drug.

"It was really the grating question," said Clive Meanwell, the company's president and chief executive. "Without knowing the economics were there, we couldn't develop the drug."

A decade ago, drug makers rarely worried about the cost of their products. If a drug proved better than existing treatments, doctors and hospitals prescribed it and insurance companies paid for it. But as rising medical and prescription drug costs gave birth to managed care, drug companies found themselves increasingly under pressure to show that their drugs provided value for the money.

"Firms can no longer just develop drugs proven to be safe and effective," said Kenneth Kaitin, director of the Tufts Center for the Study of Drug Development. "They have to demonstrate their drugs provide value for the dollar, not just that they are cost-efficient relative to other drugs but also relative to other therapies—surgery, diet, weight loss. If they can't, they can't get on formularies. And that's the death knell for many products." ...

Increasingly, companies have begun evaluating the economics of a drug early in the development process, weighing whether the potential medical benefits of a project justified its costs and continued development. They hire a staff of health-care economists or outside consultants to analyze the relative cost and medical benefits of their drugs.

Industrywide, drug makers now spend an estimated $300 million a year to establish that the benefits of a new drug outweigh its cost. Without such an economic justification, the drug has little chance of being stocked in hospital pharmacies or reimbursed by managed-care plans.

In the case of a hospital drug like Angiomax, the situation is particularly complex. Hospitals are paid a set fee for a procedure. ... If the procedure goes smoothly, the hospital makes a modest profit. But if complications arise that require blood transfusions or longer hospital stays, the profits are quickly eroded and the procedures often cost more than the fee hospitals are paid.

Proving that Angiomax would prevent enough complications to pay for itself, however, would require evidence. After buying the drug from Biogen, the Medicines Co. put in place a plan to evaluate the drug's economic profile at the same time it tested its safety and effectiveness. The company designed clinical trials to establish head-to-head comparisons between heparin and Angiomax, providing the company with the medical data it would need to establish the real cost of both drugs.

The company's key study to gain regulatory approval showed that there were 22% fewer deaths among patients taking heparin, and 62% fewer incidents of severe bleeding.

Overall, 68 fewer patients per 1,000 suffered complications from Angiomax. Using that data, the company calculated that the reduced complications would save hospitals an average of $500 per patient in standard cases and $1,000 per patient in high-risk cases.

Armed with that data, the company interviewed hundreds of doctors, pharmacists, and hospital administrators, trying to establish the ideal price for

Angiomax—the price at which the company could maximize revenue while offering a value to hospitals.

It eventually settled on $335 a vial. At that price, the theory was that the drug should pay for itself by lowering the overall cost of angioplasties.

The drug won regulatory approval in December 2000, reaching the market a month later. But the company knew the economic battle was just beginning. Many hospitals would want to confirm the Medicines Co.'s finding with their own studies and analyses. Hospital pharmacists had their own budgets to work within—even if the drug lowered overall hospital costs, it was bound to increase pharmaceutical expenses.

The Medicines Co. hired three full-time health-care economists to help craft and implement the marketing strategy. It developed a software program that allowed hospitals to input their own data to help estimate the real costs of using heparin vs. Angiomax. It has completed four studies that analyze the economics of Angiomax against those of heparin ...

All of them have confirmed that at the very least, Angiomax pays for itself. By the end of last year, more than 260 of the 750 hospitals that do nearly all the nation's angioplasties had adopted Angiomax. Revenue from sales of the drug last year is expected to reach nearly $14 million and grow to between $36 million and $41 million this year, according to company forecasts.

Still, cost remains the primary issue in Angiomax sales. Dr. Jeffrey Popma, director of interventional cardiology at Brigham and Women's Hospital, said the Boston hospital uses Angiomax in roughly 10% to 20% of angioplasties, those in which patients are at a high risk of developing complications and appear to benefit most from the use of Angiomax.

But the hospital continues to evaluate whether the drug's use in a broader group of patients is the best medical and economic choice. And before that analysis is complete, he said, he would be reluctant to use the drug on a widespread basis.

"If it were free or the same price as heparin, we would probably use Angiomax in virtually all of our cases," Popma said. "But this is an appropriate drug to study. It needs to establish that it has clear medical benefits as well as clear economic benefits."

The Medicines Co. has worked with hospitals to run countless in-house studies that allow administrators to evaluate Angiomax before adding it to their formularies. And it is in the midst of what Stephanie Plent, the company's senior director of medical policy and economics, describes as "the definitive Angiomax study," a 6,000-person clinical trial designed to put to rest questions of the drug's effectiveness in angioplasties and its potential to reduce costs.

"There's no question that if you put Angiomax next to heparin, Angiomax is a better drug," said Plent. "The problem becomes, is the better drug worth the incremental cost to the hospital. If we can prove Angiomax saves money, then we have a slam dunk."

Source: *The Boston Globe,* January 16, 2002, p. E1.

TN Exhibit 8 A Potential Board Plan for the Medicines Company

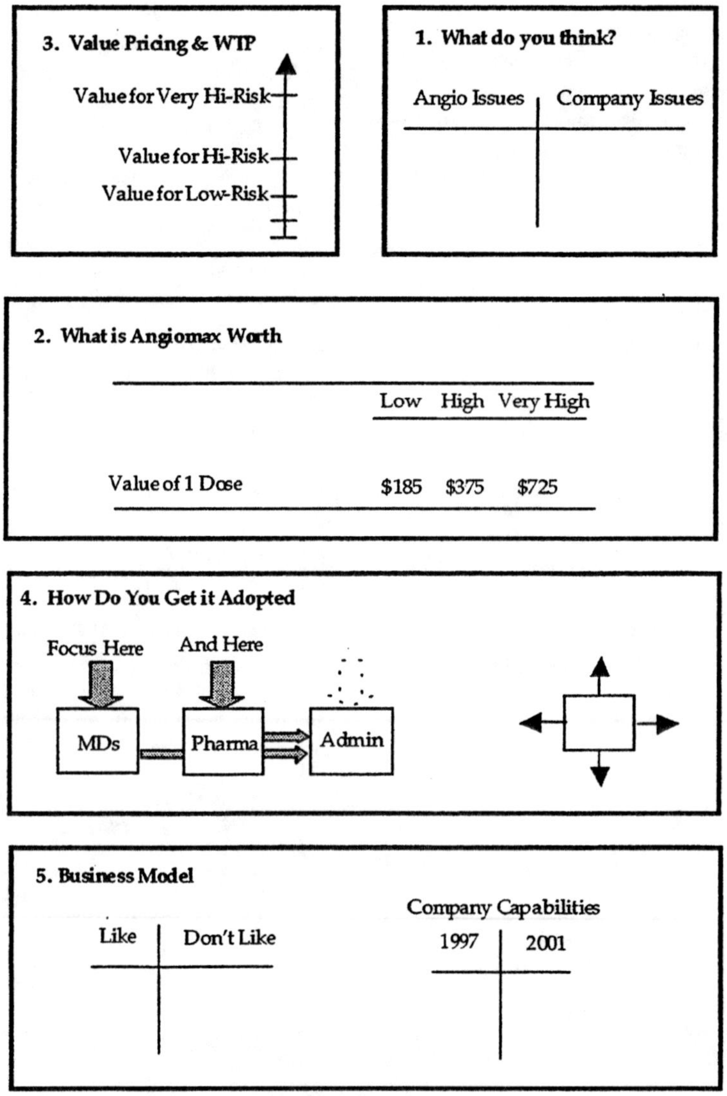

BIOPURE Corporation

Teaching Note

Synopsis

Biopure is a small biopharmaceutical firm with $200 million invested in the development of a revolutionary new "blood substitute" designed to replace the need for donated blood. To date, they have developed two (and only two) products – "Oxyglobin" for the veterinary market and "Hemopure" for the human market. These products are nearly identical in physical properties and production processes. Oxyglobin has just recently been approved for commercial release by the U.S. Food and Drug Administration while Hemopure is still two years away from final FDA approval.

The tension in the case involves what to do with Oxyglobin. Conventional wisdom suggests that the market for Oxyglobin is small and price sensitive, while the market for Hemopure is large and price insensitive. Further, due to the physical similarity of the two products, there is a fear that Oxyglobin will create an unacceptably low price expectation for Hemopure if released first. As a result, Biopure is questioning whether to immediately release Oxyglobin or to delay its release until after Hemopure has established itself in the marketplace? And if Oxyglobin is released now, how should it be brought to market?

Use

At a tactical level, this case explores product line pricing – questioning the ability of a firm to effectively price similar products at different prices to different consumers.

At a strategic level, the case explores issues of "going to market," including:

- Market Potential – How large does a market need to be before it is attractive in its own right? A detailed analysis reveals (1) that the animal market is larger and that the human market is smaller than initially expected and (2) that Biopure faces little competition in the vet market and substantial competition in the human market.

- Reference Pricing – What is the most important benchmark when deciding how to price a new product? While Biopure worries about the impact of Oxyglobin on Hemopure, other benchmarks in the human market may be more important (e.g., the price of donated blood, the price of competitor's blood substitutes, the value of a life).

This note was prepared by John T. Gourville for the sole purpose of aiding classroom instructors in the use of BIOPURE Corporation, HBS No. 598-150. It provides analysis and questions that are intended to present alternative approaches to deepening students' comprehension of business issues and energizing classroom discussion.

- Going to Market – When starting from scratch, how do you decide on price, distribution and a target market? Being a technology-based company, Biopure has spent little to no time thinking about these issues.

With these issues in mind, this case can be used in the pricing module of a principles course or as a "going to market" case in a marketing strategy course.

Analyses

There are four main areas of discussion in this case. These areas include:

1. Reasons for and against immediately launching Oxyglobin.
2. The market potential of Oxyglobin and Hemopure.
3. The impact of Oxyglobin's pricing on Hemopure.
4. The challenge of how to go to market with Oxyglobin.

1. Reasons For and Against Immediately Launching Oxyglobin

To open the case debate, it has proven useful to elicit from students the broad range of reasons for and against immediately launching Oxyglobin. The tone of this debate is very much one of "a bird in the hand is worth two in the bush," with legitimate concerns on both sides of the argument.

Some of the reasons for not launching Oxyglobin at this time include:

- Oxyglobin (with a planned price of $100 to $200) will create downward price pressure on Hemopure (with a planned price of $600 to $800), due to the physical similarity of the two products. Given that margins are much greater for Hemopure, this downward price pressure is unacceptable.

- The potential of the human market is very large and the potential of the animal market is small. Why do anything to jeopardize the human market opportunity?

- There is no foreseeable competition in the animal market, allowing for a successful launch of Oxyglobin in several years (i.e., after Hemopure has been launched).

- Hemopure is bovine-sourced and will be prone to attacks from competitors who have human-sourced products. The existence of Oxyglobin will exacerbate this problem.

- Biopure was founded as a "human products" company. As such, it should not do anything to jeopardize that focus or image.

- Biopure has limited capacity to produce either Oxyglobin or Hemopure. Given that the expected margins on these two products strongly favors Hemopure, why take up valuable production capacity with Oxyglobin.

- A recent round of venture capital financing ($50MM) is sufficient to support operations for the next two years, until Hemopure is projected to gain FDA approval.

At the same time, other students will generate a host of reasons for immediately launching Oxyglobin. These include:

- The timing of Hemopure's FDA approval is still uncertain and there are reasons to believe that Hemopure will take longer than the projected two years to launch. First, Baxter is experiencing difficulties with their human blood substitute. Second, some recent high-profile product failures demonstrate that no biotech product is guaranteed FDA approval. Third, Biopure has yet to receive approval for Phase 3 clinical trials.

- Delaying Oxyglobin means giving up two to three years of revenues, revenues that would help in the launch of Hemopure.
- Oxyglobin and Hemopure were designed for distinctly different markets. While the products may be physically similar, they are not interchangeable, decreasing the potential for cross-market price pressures.
- Oxyglobin will greatly expand the current animal transfusion market, making the animal market very attractive in its own right.
- Oxyglobin has a 2+ year first-mover advantage in the animal market. If launched now, Oxyglobin could gain acceptance among veterinarians and lock up a substantial portion of the market before any competitors can enter.
- Biopure has no experience launching a product of any type and Oxyglobin will allow them to gain some experience in going to market. As stated by Andy Wright, "would you rather make a mistake now with Oxyglobin, or in two years with Hemopure".
- The Oxyglobin marketing team is in place and ready to go.

In summarizing these points, four themes emerge. These themes involve (1) the uncertainty surrounding Hemopure's FDA approval, (2) the potential of the animal versus the human market, (3) the potential impact of Oxyglobin's pricing on Hemopure, and (4) the challenge faced by Biopure in "going to market".

The first of these issues – i.e., uncertainty surrounding Hemopure's FDA approval – is rather straightforward and should be adequately addressed in the initial "launch vs. don't launch" debate. In particular, students should recognize and agree that Hemopure is not a sure bet to gain FDA approval within two years and factor that uncertainty into their subsequent decision making. The remaining issues are more complex and demand further attention.

2. Market Potential

The case is written to suggest that the animal market is much less attractive than the human market. On page 1, Ted Jacobs' states that the "... veterinary market is small and price sensitive. We'll be lucky to get $150 per unit ..." while the "... human market ... is many times larger and we can realistically achieve price points of $600 to $800 ...".

Students should be expected to critically analyze this claim. Based on preliminary analyses that use current levels of animal and human blood transfusions, Jacobs' argument seems to hold. However, more complete analyses suggest that Oxyglobin greatly expands the market for animal transfusions while Hemopure might replace donated blood only in select applications.

2A. The Potential for Oxyglobin

Based on Current Transfusion Levels Some students will mistakenly gauge the potential for Oxyglobin based on the existing level of animal transfusions. If so, these students should estimate a potential market of 300,000 to 350,000 units per year, as shown below. At the suggested price of $150 per unit, this would imply a market potential of $45 to $53 MM per year.

Estimate #1: (based on the statistics on page 5):

	15,000 practices	(number of veterinary practices)
x	800 dogs/yr/practice	(dogs/yr/practice suffering from acute blood loss)
x	2.5%	(% of those dogs who receive a transfusion)
=	300,000 units/year	
x	$150 per unit	
=	$45 MM per year	

Estimate #2: (based on transfusions at primary care vs. emergency care facilities – p. 5):

	242,250 units/year	(= 15,000 practices x 95% primary care x 17 units/year)
+	112,500 units/year	(= 15,000 practices x 5% emergency care x 150 units/year)
=	354,750 units/year	
x	$150 per unit	
=	$53.2 MM per year	

Based on the Potential to Expand the Market Other students will recognize that 300,000 to 350,000 units per year is a very conservative estimate. In particular, they will note that while 30% of the dogs suffering from acute blood loss would benefit from a transfusion, only 2.5% currently receive one (Case page 5). More generally, they will argue that the use of transfusions in the vet market is currently very constrained due to:

- the lack of an adequate donor supply.
- the potential for negative reaction.
- a 84% user dissatisfaction with current transfusion alternatives.

These students will argue that by eliminating these problems, Oxyglobin should expand the animal transfusion market by a factor of 12 (30% vs. 2.5%), bringing demand to 3.6 to 4.3 MM units per year, as shown below. This would imply a much larger market of $540 to $640 MM per year.

Estimate #3: (based on an application rate of 30% instead of 2.5% as per p. 5)

	15,000 practices	(number of veterinary practices)
x	800 dogs/year/practice	(dogs/yr/practice suffering from acute blood loss)
x	30%	(% of those dogs who should receive a transfusion)
=	3,600,000 units/year	
x	$150 per unit	
=	$540 MM per year	

Estimate #4: (similar to Estimate #2, but adjusted upward by a factor of 12 = 30%/2.5%).

	242,250 units/year	(= 15,000 practices x 95% primary care x 17 units/year)
+	112,500 units/year	(= 15,000 practices x 5% emergency care x 150 units/year)
=	354,750 units/year	(total number of units transfused per year)
x	12	(ratio between actual and potential = 30% /2.5%)
=	4,257,000 units/year	
x	$150 per unit	
=	$638.5 MM per year	

As a final caveat, the case identifies Oxyglobin as a canine blood substitute (with dogs representing 50% of the vet market). Some students will speculate that Oxyglobin also may be appropriate for other small animals, especially cats (35% of the vet market), thereby doubling the potential for Oxyglobin. While a possibility (and in reality, Biopure's hope), there is no data in the case to support this assertion.

2B. The Market for a Human Blood Substitute

As a Wholesale Replacement for Donated Blood In the same way that some students will mistakenly look to current transfusions in the vet market to gauge the potential for Oxyglobin, some students will mistakenly look to current transfusions in the human market to gauge the potential for Hemopure. Building off of Case **Exhibit 5**, these individuals may argue for a potential market of 11.3 MM units per year (8.1 MM units for acute blood loss cases and 3.2 MM units for chronic anemia cases). At a price of $600 to $800 per unit (assume $700), this implies a potential market of $7.9 billion per year.

At a minimum, however, these students should recognize the shortcomings of Hemopure for chronic anemia cases. In particular, the high price and short half-life (see case page 6) of Hemopure make it inappropriate as a replacement for the 3.2MM units of donated blood used to treat chronic anemia. Nevertheless, if they view Hemopure as a wholesale replacement for donated blood in all acute blood loss cases, this still implies a potential market of 8.1 MM units and $5.67 billion per year.

As an Alternative in Select Applications Only Other students should argue that $6 to $8 billion vastly overstates the opportunity offered by Hemopure. They will argue that the human market is satisfied with donated blood for most applications. In particular, donated human blood is:

- well-entrenched and widely accepted in modern human medicine.
- readily available through a well-established network of blood collection groups (e.g. the American Red Cross).
- relatively inexpensive, at $125 to $225 per unit (vs. $600 to $800 for Hemopure).
- relatively safe, with little chance of infection (e.g., 1 in 500,000 chance of AIDS).

As a result, these students will argue that Hemopure is only appropriate for applications where donated blood is not readily available <u>and</u> where the loss of blood is life threatening. A good argument can be made that trauma cases fall into this category. Some students also will want to argue that borderline transfusion cases represent a potential market for Hemopure, but the cost effectiveness of Hemopure for these cases is suspect.

<u>Trauma cases</u>. There are 500,000 trauma cases each year where there is the immediate and unplanned need for blood at the scene of the accident (e.g., car accidents, shootings). Currently, in 90% of these cases, the transfusion of blood is delayed until the patient reaches the hospital. This delay is at least partly responsible for the 30% fatality rate in these cases (Case page 4). This delay is due to the inability of paramedic units to efficiently store, type and administer blood "in the field".

Importantly, Hemopure is well-suited for use "in the field" across these 500,000 trauma cases:

- Ease of use by paramedics (e.g., no need for blood typing).
- Easy storage by paramedics (e.g., long shelf life , no refrigeration needed).
- Low price sensitivity of consumer (i.e., trauma victim faces chance of death).

In the 10% of trauma cases where blood was administered "in the field," patients required an average of 4 units of blood each [i.e., 200,000 units administered (Case **Exhibit** 5) to 50,000 patients]. Assuming that the patients for whom a transfusion was delayed also would have required 4 units, this implies a potential market of 2 MM units and $1.4 billion per year, as shown below.

Estimate for Human Trauma Market:

	500,000 cases/year	
x	4 units/case	(average for those who receive blood "in the field"
=	2,000,000 units/year	
x	$700 per unit	(avg. of $600 and $800)
=	$1.4 billion/year	

Borderline Transfusion cases. Some students also will argue that Hemopure is appropriate in "borderline transfusions" cases, described as surgeries in which blood loss is one to two units (case page 4). The case states that in spite of its potential benefit, blood is typically not transfused in these surgeries for fear of disease transmission or negative reaction to the transfusion.

While Hemopure is a disease-free alternative to donated blood, the fact that donated blood is not used in these cases suggests that the cases are not "life-threatening". This calls into question the cost-effectiveness of a $700 per unit blood substitute. Nonetheless, if this demand were to materialize, it could result in 1.5 MM units (1 MM cases x 1.5 units/case) and $1 billion per year.

Together, these two applications suggest a potential market for Hemopure of between 2.0 MM and 3.5 MM units per year and $1.4 billion and $2.45 billion per year. While attractive, these numbers suggest that the market for a human blood substitute is far smaller than might first appear.

2C. The Competitive Environment

The final bit of analysis that is useful to explore when discussing market potential is the competitive environment facing Biopure in both the animal and the human markets.

Animal Market We have estimated the potential animal market to be about 3.6 MM units and $500 million per year. Adding to the attractiveness of these estimates, there are at least two reasons to believe that Biopure will have this market to themselves for the foreseeable future:

- Given the lengthy FDA approval process (that no competitor has yet begun), Biopure anticipates a 2 to 5 year first-mover advantage (bottom, page 8).
- Biopure's most likely source of competition in the animal market would come from its human market competitors - Baxter and Northfield. However, both employ a design that relies on human blood. It is unlikely either company would divert this scarce resource from the production of a high-margin human product to a low-margin animal product.

As a result, students should recognize that Biopure faces no current competition and little threat of future competition in a market that may grow from its current annual demand of ~300,000 units of donated blood to ~3.6 million units of blood substitute. This is reflected in **Exhibit TN-1.**

Human Market In contrast to the animal market, Biopure faces stiff competition in the human market:

- Two competitors have developed products that have already entered Phase 3 trials.
- One of these two competitors is Baxter International, a company with instant credibility in the human blood market due to its past successes with blood related products.
- The products of the two competitors are human-sourced as opposed to bovine-sourced, a fact they likely will highlight when trying to sell customers on their products.

These reasons suggest that Biopure will be fighting for a share of the 2 MM unit per year trauma market. While only speculation, one might guess that Baxter has the size and credibility to capture the largest share of this market (say 50% share), leaving Northfield and Biopure to split the remainder (say a 25% share for each). With a 25% share of the human trauma market, Biopure could expect an annual demand of 500,000 units and $350 MM, as shown in **Exhibit TN-1.**

3. The Impact of Oxyglobin's Pricing on Hemopure.

While a detailed analysis reveals the attractiveness of the animal market, the concern remains that Oxyglobin will create downward price pressure on Hemopure due to the physical similarity of the two products. As stated by Ted Jacobs on page 1:

> "... as soon as we come out with Oxyglobin at $150, we jeopardize our ability to price Hemopure at $800. Hospitals and insurance firms will be all over us to justify a 500% price difference for what they see as the same product."

Implicit in this statement is the assumption that Oxyglobin is the appropriate benchmark for Hemopure. Students should challenge this contention. In doing so, it is useful to establish the potential reference prices for a human blood substitute.

3A. Possible Reference Prices for Hemopure

In assessing the price of Hemopure, there are at several relevant prices and/or costs that might act as a benchmark. These reference prices include:

- **$101.50** = the variable cost of goods sold (COGS) for Hemopure. As stated on page 9 of the case, Biopure has the capacity to produce 150,000 units of Hemopure per year at a cost of $15 million, independent of volume. With raw materials adding $1.50 per unit, this implies a COGS of $100 + $1.50 = $101.50 at full production.
- **$150** = the price of Oxyglobin to the veterinarian (as projected by Ted Jacobs).
- **$175** = the average cost of donated RBCs (avg. of $125 and $225 – Case **Exhibit 6**).
- **$300** = the price of Oxyglobin to the pet owner, given a simple "doubling rule".
- **$350** = the average cost of autologous RBCs (avg. of $275 and $425 – Case **Exhibit 6**).
- **$600-$800** = the planned price of competitors' human blood substitutes.
- **$$$** = the value of a human life – non-quantifiable, but important to consider.

Other relevant reference points for Hemopure might include the COGS for the competing products. Performing a similar calculation to that shown for Hemopure, one could calculate that the projected COGS is $58 for Baxter's HemAssist and $125 for Northfield's PolyHeme. [1]

[1] As an interesting side note, one could predict that the competitors' COGS will rise significantly over time, due to a rising cost of raw material. Currently, Baxter and Northfield use relatively inexpensive outdated human blood as their source material. However, given the relative scarcity of human blood, a market should develop for outdated human blood as production of HemAssist and PolyHeme increase. This should lead to a price increase in their cost of raw material (possibly to that of the cost of fresh whole blood) which will raise their final COGS significantly.

3B. Impact of Oxyglobin on Hemopure

Having considered various reference prices for Hemopure, students should begin to realize that Oxyglobin is one of many benchmarks consumers could use in assessing the price of Hemopure. Arguably, Oxyglobin may be among the least salient of these benchmarks and have little impact on the price acceptance of Hemopure as a result. Support for this contention include:

- For most human blood recipients and transfusion providers, the most visible benchmark will be donated human blood, which is priced at ~$175 per unit.
- For risk-averse blood recipients, a more appropriate benchmark might be autologous blood (both eliminate the risk of infection), which is priced at ~$350.
- For trauma victims in need of blood "in the field," there currently is no alternative to Hemopure and, thus, no appropriate point of reference. Given the significant risk of death, willingness-to-pay among trauma victims and emergency care providers should be very high and unaffected by the pricing of Oxyglobin.
- Assuming Baxter and Northfield successfully launch their products, these products will become the relevant comparison for Hemopure. Currently, they plan to price at $600 to $800 and there is no reason to believe their pricing will be influenced by Oxyglobin.

For these reasons, it appears Biopure's fears may be unfounded. In particular, Biopure appears to be using a "Cost +" mentality when considering price acceptance for Hemopure. In this regard, they fear that consumers will use Oxyglobin's price to infer the COGS for Hemopure.

However, in practice, consumers (both medical providers and patients) will likely evaluate the price of Hemopure in the context of potential and acceptable alternatives. As such, a price of $600 to $800 makes sense in cases of trauma, where (1) acceptable alternatives currently do not exist and (2) alternatives under development will also be priced in the $600 to $800 range. At the same time, a price of $600 to $800 is probably unacceptable in the case of planned surgeries given the ready supply of donated RBCs priced at $125 to $225. In both cases, price acceptance of Hemopure should hinge on the price of alternative treatments and not on the price of Oxyglobin. To make this thinking salient, it is difficult to imagine a paramedic refusing to administer a potentially life saving transfusion of Hemopure because they feel that Hemopure is priced too far above its COGS.

In leaving this issue, students should recognize that the pricing of Oxyglobin and Hemopure are relatively independent. This is especially true given the fact that these two products are not interchangeable in use. As such, Oxyglobin should be priced so at to optimize financial returns in the animal market and Hemopure should be priced (independently of Oxyglobin) so as to optimize financial returns in the human market.

4. Going to Market with Oxyglobin

After a thorough discussion of market potential and of the impact of Oxyglobin's pricing on Hemopure, most of the class will argue that Oxyglobin should be launched immediately. What remains to be determined is how to go to market with Oxyglobin. In this regard, the challenge facing Biopure should not be underestimated. In particular, there are many reasons to suggest that a successful launch of Oxyglobin is anything but a "sure thing":

- The company has never brought a product to market.
- The company is new to veterinary medicine, having been founded as a human products company.
- The company is dominated by engineers and manufacturing types, as evidenced by the organization chart in Case **Exhibit 2.**

- The company has only recently hired someone to take on the role of marketing Oxyglobin and, to date, only seven people have been hired to support him.

- Traditionally, the veterinary market is price sensitive, with veterinarians playing the role of gatekeeper when it comes to recommending treatments to pet owners.

In spite of these shortcomings, Andy Wright and his marketing team must decide on a target market, a distribution strategy and a pricing strategy for Oxyglobin.

4A. Target Market

In terms of a target market, the question facing Biopure is how large a net to cast in the veterinary market. Specifically, do they want to be comprehensive or do they want to be selective in their initial marketing of Oxyglobin.

Comprehensive Approach Some students will argue that Oxyglobin will have immediate appeal across all 15,000 veterinary practices in the United States. As a more convenient alternative to donated animal blood, Oxyglobin eliminates the need for donor animals and for animal blood banks. While this might be true, students should be forced to consider the likelihood of rapid adoption among the broad cross-section of veterinary practices. In particular, given that the vast majority (i.e., 95%) of practices perform an average of only 17 transfusion per year (case page 5), it is not clear how willing these practices will be to trial a revolutionary new blood product.

Selective Approach A more compelling case can be made for Biopure to initially focus its efforts on those practices that perform the greatest number of transfusions. Specifically, while an average of 17 units of canine blood was transfused each year by each primary care practice, an average of 150 units of canine blood was transfused each year by each emergency care practice. In addition, the case states (page 5) that 15% of practices handled 65% of all canine surgeries and that 10% of all practices handled 55% of all canine trauma cases. These "high incidence" practices tended to be the emergency care practices and large primary care practices.

By initially focusing on these "high incidence" practices, Biopure accomplishes several things. First, they reduce the scope of their efforts from 15,000 practices to about 1,500 practices. Second, given their significantly greater reliance on blood transfusions, these practices will see greater value from Oxyglobin than will "low-incidence" practices. Third, these practices are likely to be thought leaders and lead users when it comes to adopting new emergency medical techniques. As such, they may be more receptive to the Oxyglobin sales pitch. Finally, the cost of treatment at an emergency care practice is usually many times greater than at a primary care practice, suggesting lower price sensitivity for Oxyglobin at these locations.

These factors combine to suggest that Biopure should be selective in its initial marketing effort.

4B. Oxyglobin Distribution

The second issue that needs to be addressed is how best to sell and distribute Oxyglobin. Two alternatives are on the table – going through an independent distributor or going direct.

Independent Distributors Going through an independent distributor has the advantages of speed and scale – these distributors have established relationships with the 15,000 veterinary practices and can very quickly introduce Oxyglobin to these practices. For instance, a national distributor with 100 sales reps can reach the 15,000 veterinary practices in far less time than can Biopure with its 3 sales reps. In addition to selling, these distributors would take on the responsibility of physically distributing Oxyglobin to the veterinary practices.

However, there are several drawbacks to going through an independent distributor. First, they typically receive 30% of the selling price of a new product, implying a $30 to $60 charge for selling Oxyglobin. Second, they introduce about 100 new products each year, suggesting that any one new product receives very little attention in their weekly 15-minute meetings with veterinarians. Third, Biopure would still be required to educate these sales reps on the technical specifications and merits of Oxyglobin.

Direct Salesforce In contrast to the intense distribution offered by an independent distributor, Biopure could take on the selling and distribution responsibility themselves. Such an effort has several advantages over an independent distributor. First, any time spent with veterinarians would be fully dedicated to Oxyglobin. Second, a Biopure sales rep would have far greater knowledge about Oxyglobin than a distributor's sales rep could ever have. Given the unique and complex nature of Oxyglobin, this added knowledge could be critical in product acceptance by the veterinarians.

One potential drawback in using a direct salesforce is the length of time it would take to reach the 15,000 veterinary practices. However, by choosing to be selective in their initial marketing efforts, as suggested above, they can limit themselves to about 1,500 practices. Assuming 4 full-time sales reps (i.e., 3 full-time sales reps + 2 half-time efforts from Andy Wright and his director of marketing), each making 4 sales calls per day, this implies that the targeted 1,500 practices could be called upon within a relatively short 20-week window.

Another potential drawback of going direct is that Biopure would take on the responsibility of physical distribution. However, Biopure estimates that they could satisfy this requirement at a cost of $10 to $15 per unit (case page 11), far cheaper than the $30 to $60 that would be charged by an independent distributor.

In the end, given the sophisticated sales pitch required to sell Oxyglobin, the selective distribution that Biopure might initially follow, and the relatively low cost to physically distribute the product themselves, it makes sense for Biopure to go direct with their own salesforce.

4C. Oxyglobin Pricing

A third decision facing Biopure is how to price Oxyglobin. There are several categories of price that students may propose for the Oxyglobin, including:

- Price low (e.g., $100), in response to the high price sensitivity of the broad market.
- Price high (e.g., $200), in response to the lower price sensitivity in the emergency care market.
- Price very high (e.g., $400) so as to limit sales to all but the most price insensitive customers and, in the process, eliminate any lingering fears of negatively impacting Hemopure.

The third option only makes sense if students are still convinced that Oxyglobin's low price will negatively impact Hemopure. If students have convinced themselves that this is not a problem, the pricing decision will likely revolve around the first two options – price low to penetrate the broad market or price high to skim the emergency care market.

In arriving at a price for Oxyglobin, it is helpful to factor in the per unit cost of Oxyglobin. The case states (page 9) that Biopure has the capacity to produce 300,000 units of Oxyglobin per year at a cost of $15 million, independent of volume. With raw materials adding $1.50 per unit, this implies a COGS of $51.50 at full production. In addition, the case states that Biopure can ship Oxyglobin at a cost of $10 to $15 per unit (assume $12.50). Combined, this results in a per unit cost of $64 , implying a $36 gross margin if Oxyglobin is priced at $100 and a $136 gross margin if Oxyglobin is priced at $200. Based on a simple breakeven analysis, this difference in gross margin favors pricing at $200 as long as demand at $200 is at least 27% of demand at $100.

It is also helpful to consider the consumer's willingness to pay, as reflected in Case **Table A** and **Table B.** Two patterns emerge from these tables. First, it appears that veterinarians are more price sensitive than pet owners, especially in non-critical cases. This heightened price sensitivity among veterinarians is important given the "gate-keeper" role that many veterinarians play. Second, when priced at $100, veterinarians willingness to trial Oxyglobin is high for both critical and non-critical cases. However, when priced at $200, willingness to trial drops to 5% in non-critical cases, but remains high (60%) in critical cases.

On first glance, this pattern of sensitivity among veterinarians suggests that a $100 price might make more sense than a $200 price. However, when one considers that the workload of the 1,500 "high incident" practices is heavily skewed toward "critical" cases, the 5% willingness to trial in non-critical cases seems less relevant.

In summary, if Biopure wishes to target the entire 15,000 veterinary practices in the United States, a $200 price might be prohibitively high. However, if they wish to pursue a more selective strategy and focus on the 1,500 "high incidence" practices that handle predominantly critical cases, a $200 per unit price seems to make sense.

Teaching the Case

Given the strong "Go" vs. "No Go" focus in the case, students likely will have formed an opinion about whether Oxyglobin should be launched immediately. As such, it is recommended that you start with a "What would you do?" type of opener with the expectation that the student will provide a rationale for either launching or not launching Oxyglobin. Based on the first student's response to this opener, the instructor should look to solicit the opinion of other students who either agree or disagree with the first student's viewpoint. The instructor should avoid being too directive during this initial debate and should merely attempt to capture the various students comments on the blackboard under the headings "Reasons to Launch" and "Reasons to Not Launch". This initial debate should last about 15 minutes.

As already mentioned, four themes will likely emerge from this initial debate. These four themes involve (1) the uncertainty surrounding Hemopure's FDA approval, (2) the potential of the animal versus the human market, (3) the potential impact of Oxyglobin's pricing on Hemopure, and (4) the challenge faced by Biopure in "going to market". In all likelihood, the first of these themes is self-contained and need not be expanded upon further. The remaining three themes, however, deserve further attention and should be addressed in turn.

After the opening debate, the instructor should focus the class's attention on the issue of (2) relative market potential. The goal of this discussion should be to highlight the fact that the animal market is larger than it first appears and that the human market is smaller and more competitive than it first appears. This discussion might take 20 minutes. Next, the instructor should focus the discussion on the (3) potential impact of Oxyglobin's pricing on Hemopure. This topic might take 15 minutes.

With about 20 minutes left in class and after having discussed issues 1, 2 and 3, the instructor may wish to ask for a show of hands as to whether Biopure should launch or not launch Oxyglobin. Experience with the case suggests that at least 75% of the students will want to launch, citing the market potential of Oxyglobin and the risks associated with Hemopure as the primary reasons. With this being the case, the instructor should transition to a marketing plan for Oxyglobin, perhaps with the question, "So, most of you want to go ahead with Oxyglobin. How would you go about doing it? What would the details be?" This should lead naturally to a discussion of price and distribution.

A potential board plan for this discussion is provided in **Exhibit TN-2.**

Postscript

Oxyglobin was launched in April of 1998 at a price of $150. Rather than go through a distributor, Andy Wright and his sales team sold Oxyglobin directly to the veterinarians, initially focusing on the 750 emergency care veterinary practices and the 750 largest primary care practices. This was done for two reasons. First, these 1,500 practices handled a disproportionate number of canine surgeries and trauma cases and second, the veterinarians in these practices were believed to be the thought leaders in the veterinary community. Product shipment to these practices was handled via Federal Express at a cost of about $10 per shipment.

Among the 1,500 target practices, initial sales were promising and the product received praise from the veterinarians. However, a follow-up investigation revealed that these veterinarians viewed Oxyglobin in one of two fashions. About half viewed Oxyglobin as an everyday replacement for donated animal blood, resulting in the reordering of Oxyglobin on an ongoing basis. The other half viewed Oxyglobin as an "emergency" alternative to donated animal blood. These vets put Oxyglobin on their shelves and only used it in special cases. By the end of 1998, sales of Oxyglobin were approaching an annualize rate of 50,000 units and a coverage across 15 - 20% of veterinary practices.

Suggested Preparation Questions

Some suggested preparation questions for this case are:

1. How do you assess Biopure's potential in the human market? The animal market?

2. What are the biggest obstacles to Biopure's success in the human market? The animal market?

3. How might Oxyglobin be a threat to Hemopure? How might it be an asset to Hemopure?

4. What should Biopure do regarding the commercial release of Oxyglobin? If they release, what price should they set? How should it be distributed?

Exhibit TN-1 Market Analysis Summary of the Animal and Human Markets

Animal Market:

Based on Current Transfusions	Based on Potential of a Blood Substitute

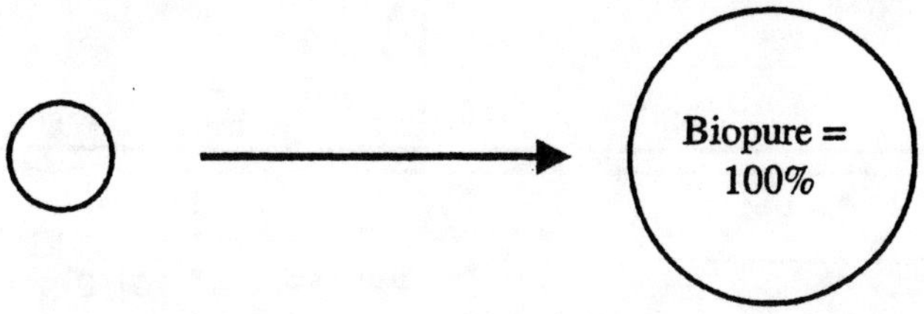

300K to 350K units/year $45 MM to $53 MM/year	3.6 MM to 4.3 MM units/year $540 MM to $640 MM/year

Human Market:

Based on Current Transfusions	Based on Potential of a Blood Substitute

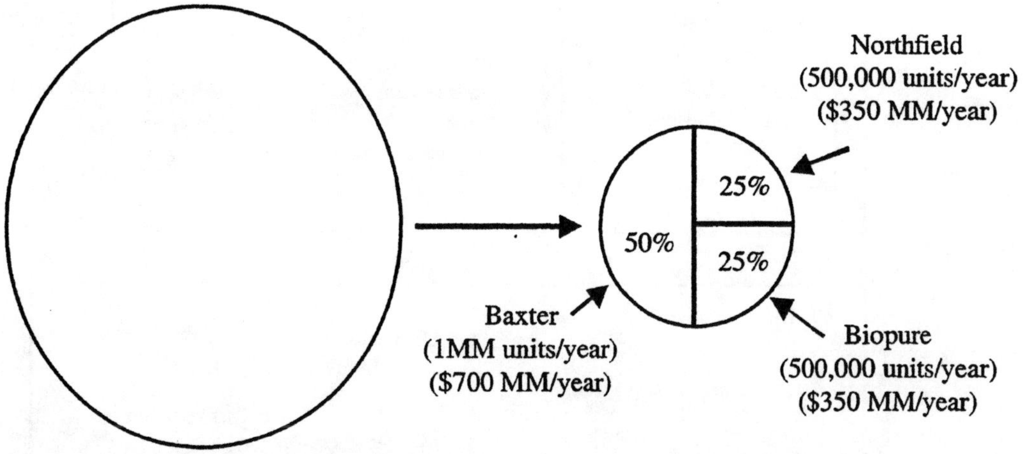

8.2 MM to 11.3 MM units/year $5.7 billion to $7.9 billion/year	2 MM units/year $1.4 billion/year

Exhibit TN-2 Potential Board Plan

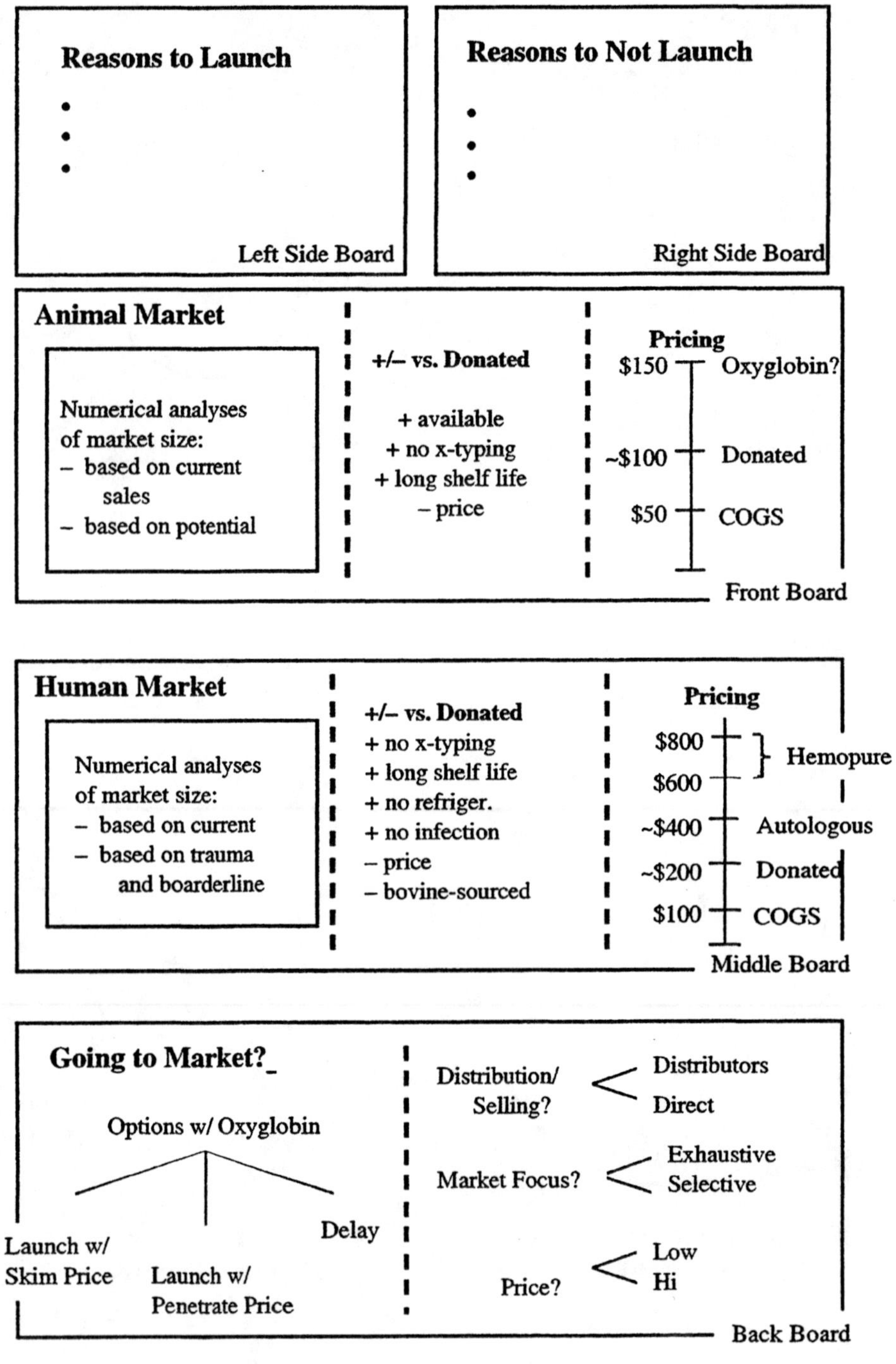

5-503-091
APRIL 10, 2003

TEACHING NOTE

Synthes

Synopsis

Synthes is the leading U.S. maker of orthopedic "implants"—the metal rods, plates, and screws used by doctors to surgically repair severely broken bones. It has a 50% share in a $500 million market, it is widely viewed as having the best-researched, most reliable products available, and it is believed to have the best-trained, most experienced sales force in the industry. Many surgeons regard Synthes' products as the "gold standard," with 80% using its products and over 30% using nothing but Synthes products. One major drawback to all metallic implants, however, is that they must be surgically removed in 20% of adults and 40% of children who receive them.

Into this market, "bioresorbable implants" are slowly being introduced. They are made of plastic-like polymers that gradually dissolve over time, eliminating the need for their removal. But these new implants are not clinically proven and there is a chance that they will lead to incomplete bone healing or infection-like complications in a small, but significant, number of cases. Compounding this concern is the memory of an earlier (1st) generation of bioresorbable implants that proved to be quite problematic, leaving some orthopedic surgeons skeptical of the technology.

Synthes must decide whether to risk its sterling reputation on this new technology. Its options are (1) to ignore this new technology, (2) to develop a line of bioresorbable implants, but sell them only if the market develops, (3) to develop and proactively market a line of bioresorbable implants, or (4) to begin research on the next (i.e., better) generation of bioresorbable products.

Use

This case explores the introduction of an innovative new technology in an environment where product failures are extremely costly (see **Exhibit TN-1** for an example of a costly failure in this domain). Unlike markets where a new product can be gradually improved over time (e.g., computer software), orthopedic implants need to be "near perfect" in their first iteration (see **Exhibit TN-2**). This creates tension for Synthes. Should it risk its hard-earned reputation by coming out with a resorbable product based on an underlying technology that might not be "perfect?" Or should Synthes "wait and see," entering the market only if and when that market develops, recognizing that if it does develop, it may be several years behind the competition.

This note was prepared by Professor John T. Gourville for the sole purpose of aiding classroom instructors in the use of Synthes, HBS No. 502-008. It provides analysis and questions that are intended to present alternative approaches to deepening students' comprehension of business issues and energizing classroom discussion. HBS cases are developed solely as the basis for class discussion. Cases are not intended to serve as endorsements, sources of primary data, or illustrations of effective or ineffective management.

The learning in this case is that the marketplace success of the underlying technology is not independent of Synthes. Rather, given its reputation and influence in the industry, Synthes can increase the odds of successful adoption of resorbable implants by impacting when and where these implants get used. Given its unparalleled access to orthopedic surgeons, Synthes can encourage the use of these implants in "high-probability-for-success" applications and discourage their use in all other applications. Students who do not recognize this interdependency typically argue against entering the resorbables market, while those who do recognize it typically argue for entering.

This case can be used in a high-tech marketing or new product development course to highlight the risks inherent in bringing any new technology to market. If used in this manner, there are at least three interesting angles to explore. The first is the previously mentioned need to be "near perfect" in the first iteration. The second is the realization that being the leader in the current technology can sometimes limit flexibility when it comes to the new technology. In this case, relative to the smaller share firms, Synthes has more to lose if the new technology fails. This creates the interesting dynamic where the firm best able to foster adoption of this new technology (i.e., Synthes) is also the firm that might be most risk averse. The third angle is the above-mentioned interdependency between Synthes and the success or failure of this developing technology.

This case also can be used in a marketing strategy course. In particular, on a tactical level, some will argue that the risks are too great and the rewards too small for Synthes to enter the resorbables market. But on a strategic level, others will argue that resorbable implants will someday be the industry standard and that Synthes should do everything in its power to retain its leadership position by actively developing resorbable products now. Here, the instructor can foster a "marketing myopia" approach to this problem.[1] If Synthes views itself as a "metal implant maker," it will likely avoid resorbables. However, if it views itself as a "mender of broken bones," it may embrace and advance this next generation of orthopedic implants.

Analysis

There are four main areas of discussion in this case, each of which will be covered in turn.

1. What should Synthes do?
2. What are the tradeoffs between the options?
3. What is Synthes impact on the bioresorbable market?
4. How might Synthes introduce resorbables?

1. What Should Synthes Do?

Given the decision focus of the case, students will likely arrive to class with a strong opinion about what Synthes should do. Therefore, it makes sense to tap into this energy and begin class by asking students, "What should Synthes do?" The four options as laid out on page 13 are:

- **Ignore** bioresorbables—as they had in the mid-1980s—and focus its efforts on further improving its metallic implants.

1 See "Marketing Myopia," by Theodore Levitt, *Harvard Business Review*, September-October, 1975.

- Take a **wait-and-see** approach to bioresorbables, allowing other manufacturers to test the waters and educate the market. Under this option, Synthes would spend the $20 million needed to develop (but not market) a line of bioresorbable products.
- Quickly **develop and market** a line of bioresorbable products (initially for fractures of hands, feet, wrists, ankles and, later, for pediatrics) using the currently available polymers.
- Turn its efforts toward the **research and development** of the next (3rd) generation of bioresorbable implants.

As students offer their opinions of these four options, the instructor should record their arguments under a heading for each option. At this stage, there will be "more smoke than fire"—i.e., students will be giving you their opinions, but there probably won't be a lot of deep insights.

However, as students are arguing for their preferred option, a couple of themes will likely emerge and the instructor should capture these. First, many will argue that Synthes should take a hybrid approach, pursuing one of the first three options plus the final R&D option. Such an argument suggests that students recognize/anticipate that resorbable implants will become the next technology platform for implants. This thinking can be captured as shown in **Figure TN-1**, with the critical unknown being "timing"—i.e., "Will this happen quickly or very slowly?"

Figure TN-1 When Will a Viable Market for Resorbables Materialize?

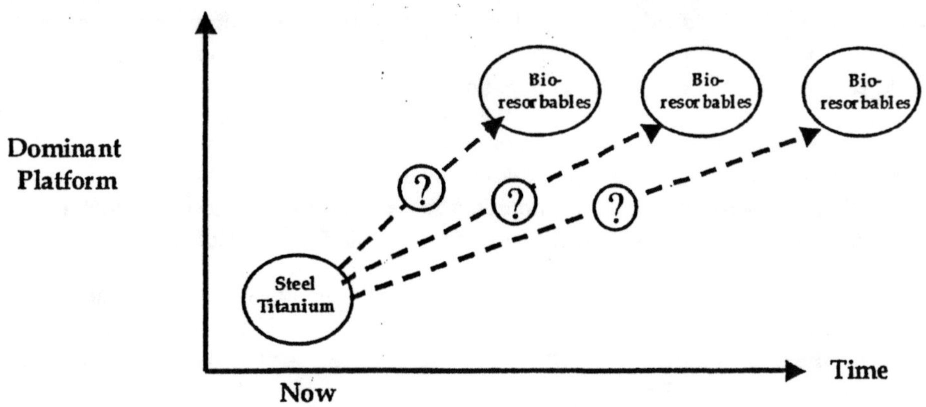

Source: author

Second, behind most students' espoused option will be an underlying belief in the benefit versus risk of entering this 2nd generation market. It is important to capture these reasons. Some students will argue that as the technological and market share leader, Synthes must come out with a line of resorbable products to defend its leadership position. But others will argue that Synthes should not risk its well-earned reputation on a product that is less-then-perfect and that offers only a small increase in sales.

These arguments can be captured under the headings, "Reasons For" and "Reasons Against" entering the resorbables market.

"Reasons For" Entering the Bio-Resorbables Market

The reasons for entering the resorbables market include:

- ***Resorbables make sense!*** One reason for pursuing resorbables is that they provide value to doctors and patients. Provided they work (which is the big "if"), doctors avoid a second surgery to remove the implant and patients avoid another round of pain and recovery. To bring these points home, the instructor should ask students to play the roles of patients and doctors and to give their perspective on resorbables—e.g., If you broke a bone, would you rather have a metal plate or a resorbable plate? What it your child broke a bone? The goal here is to build support for the viability of the concept of resorbables—i.e., if resorbables work as intended, they remove a major headache for patients and doctors.

- ***The technology has improved.*** The current (2nd) generation of resorbables has resolved many of the problems of the 1st generation. They break down more slowly (which should reduce the rate of complications), they are stronger, and they are cheaper.

- ***The margins are 40% better than on metal implants.*** As per the case (page 2), the margin on a metal implant is 50%, meaning a $500 rod will generate $250 in margin. On case page 7, we are told that the COGS for a comparable resorbable implant will be 10% higher and that the selling price will be 20% to 30% higher. Therefore, that $500 metal implant will now sell for $625 ($500 x 1.25) and cost $275 ($250 x 1.10), for a $350 margin—i.e., a 40% increase.

- ***Surgeons seem ready to adopt the technology.*** Seven of 16 leading surgeons reported that they would immediately use resorbables if they were available. Another 6 surgeons said they would use resorbables for specific applications (case page 11).

- ***Competitors are actively developing resorbables.*** J&J, one of the largest players in the orthopedic market, has recently purchased an implant maker, has long had an interest in resorbables, and has begun construction on a research facility to study bio-materials. Biomet has recently introduced a line of resorbables for hand and foot fractures.

- ***Synthes needs to catch up.*** As outlined on case page 13, Synthes is already 2 to 3 years behind the competition in developing resorbables. To delay now would place it 5 to 10 years behind, a huge hurdle to overcome.

- ***Synthes is the thought leader.*** Synthes is widely recognized as the technological and market leader in this field. To avoid resorbables at this point will call that leadership into question.

- ***Synthes must defend its exclusivity.*** Currently, one-third of orthopedic surgeons use nothing but Synthes devices (case page 6). If demand exists for resorbables, these surgeons will have to go outside the Synthes product line to get what they need, providing access for another company's salesperson. In the long run, this may threaten Synthes relationship with these doctors.

- ***If Synthes does not enter, its metal implants will be at risk.*** If resorbables represent the next generation of implants, by not developing a line of resorbable implants Synthes places at risk its metal implant business. As students are fond of pointing out, it is better to cannibalize your own sales than to have someone steal share from you.

"Reasons Against" Developing a Line of Bio-Resorbables

In contrast, some of the reasons against entering the market include:

- ***The risk of failure.*** Perhaps the most salient argument against coming out with a line of resorbables is the financial and reputational risk of a product failure. To date, Synthes has very successfully built its reputation around product quality—the "gold standard" of orthopedic implants. If Synthes were to come out with a line of resorbable implants and those implants failed (e.g., led to complications), this reputation might be tarnished. Note that students should be asked to consider this point of view and to consider how perfect Synthes' resorbables need to be before it creates a problem for the company.
- ***Uncertain timing of market.*** It is unclear how rapidly this market will develop. 1st generation resorbables has been out for over 10 years and barely have sales of $10 million. Some students will argue that there is little reason to believe that the 2nd generation will be much different.
- ***Experts are wary of resorbables.*** While many surgeons seem eager to trial resorbables, those with the most experience with them are reluctant to adopt (case pages 9 and 11).
- ***The $20 million cost.*** As stated on page 13 under the "wait and see" approach, the cost to develop (but not market) a line of resorbables will cost $20 million. Presumably, to market this line of resorbables will add additional costs. Given the uncertain nature of the market, these costs should be avoided.
- ***Limited application/Small market.*** Even if resorbables do get adopted, their use will be limited to the non-weight-bearing bones of the hands and feet and to the bones of children. By one estimate (case page 12), resorbables could replace metallic implants in 25% of all hand and foot surgeries and 20% of all pediatric surgeries within five years. As reflected in **Figure TN-2**, this implies a likely market of only about $33 million per year. Based on these numbers, many students will argue that it is just not worth entering the market.

Figure TN-2 Likely Size of Resorbables Market within Five Years

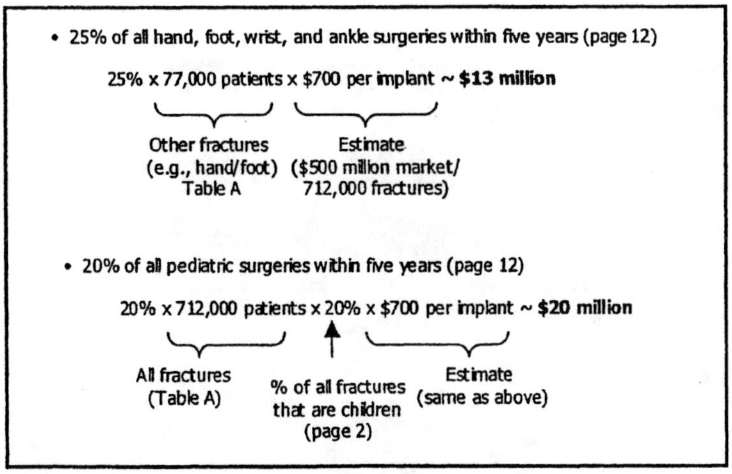

Source: Author's calculations

- ***Ability to quickly follow?*** Finally, some student will argue that should the market for resorbables somehow develop, Synthes could probably leverage its expertise and that of its related organizations [e.g., Synthes Maxillofacial, Synthes Osteobiologics, Stratec (case page 12)] to quickly come out with a line of resorbables in this market. But other data (page 13) suggests that this will not be the case and that to delay now would place Synthes 5 to 10 years behind the competition.

Summary of "For" vs. "Against"

Before leaving this first section of the case discussion, the instructor should attempt to summarize the major points for and against Synthes entering the resorbables market. In particular, the primary reasons for entering include a belief that the market will (eventually) develop and that to maintain and protect its market dominance, Synthes must actively pursue this next technology platform. The primary reasons against are more pragmatic—the predicted market is too small, the cost is too large, and the risk of failure is too great. To emphasize these points, the instructor may wish to capture the spirit of these arguments by writing "Good Concept/Defend Leadership" under the "reasons for" column and by writing "Too Risky" under the "reasons against" column.

2. Assessing the Options

After a thorough discussion of the pros and cons of entering the resorbables market, most of the pertinent case facts and some of the relevant economics should have come out. However, the tradeoffs between the several options likely will not have been made salient [note: since most students think Synthes should research the next generation resorbables regardless of what else they do, the focus at this stage should really be on the first three options]. To help bring these tradeoffs out, I have found it helpful to develop a "what if" discussion. In particular, the instructor can ask the students, "What if Synthes "ignores bioresorbables" and the market does versus does not develop?" The same can be done for "wait & see" and "develop & market." The decision tree in **Figure TN-3** helps to illustrate the consequences of each option conditional on whether the market materializes.

Figure TN-3 Decision tree for Synthes marketing options

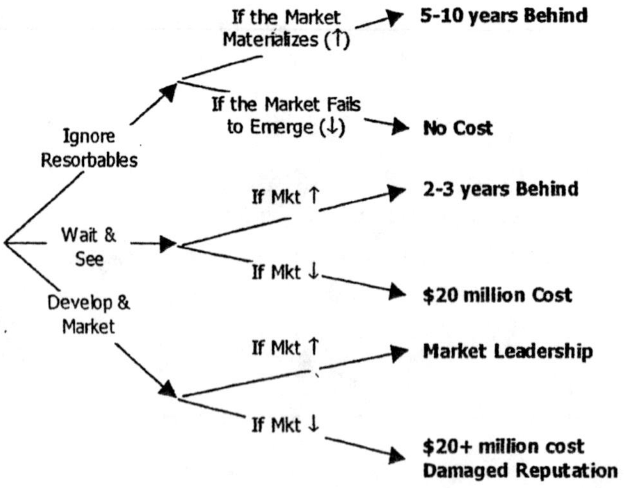

Source: Author

This type of a diagram helps students recognize the tradeoffs between the various options and to debate the consequences of the possible outcomes. If past teaching of the case is any indication, students will be most alarmed by "5-10 years behind," "2-3 years behind," and "$20+ million + damaged reputation." And therein lies the problem. While the "develop and market" option eliminates the dangers of falling too far behind the competition, it opens Synthes up to the risk of a high-profile product failure. This provides a nice jumping point to the final two areas of discussion.

3. What is Synthes Impact on the Bioresorbable Market?

To this point in the case discussion, most students will have been arguing as if the market for bioresorbables will develop or not develop independent of what Synthes does. For instance, some students will argue that Synthes should avoid the resorbables market because it is too uncertain and that the risk of failure is too great, while others will argue that Synthes should enter the resorbables market because it is highly likely to become the next technology platform in implants.

However, given Synthes positioning in the industry (e.g., 50% share, technological leader), a strong argument can be made that the likelihood of the resorbables market developing and being successful is highly dependent on what Synthes decides to do! To encourage this type of debate, the instructor can do one of two things. Preferably, if a student or two has already mentioned this possibility, the instructor should return to those students, perhaps saying, "Earlier you told us that we were thinking about this problem the wrong way. What did you mean?" Alternatively, if the issue has not been raised, the instructor should introduce it, perhaps by asking, "We are arguing as if the market will either develop or not develop independent of what Synthes decides. Is this true?"

This should lead to at least three points of discussion. The first is the **"Perception"** Synthes creates in the marketplace by either entering or not entering the resorbables market. Specifically:

- ***If Synthes enters*** the resorbables market, it sends a strong signal to surgeons that resorbable technology is now ready for use in the implant market. This view is probably strengthened by the fact that Synthes did not enter the market with a 1st generation product. As stated by one surgeon, "If Synthes introduces a new product, I feel safe using it (case page 6)." Thus, Synthes entering the market for resorbables should encourage product trial.
- ***If Synthes does not enter*** the resorbables market, it calls into question whether the 2nd generation technology is viable. In fact, some of those students who feel Synthes should avoid resorbables will argue that Synthes could use its presence in the industry to actively cast doubt on the viability of these 2nd generation products.

The second point of discussion—**"Physical Product"**—involves reasons why Synthes might produce a better resorbable product than that of its competitors, thus assuring a higher likelihood of success. These reasons include:

- Access to the best researchers in the industry, both at Synthes and the AO. [Note that while this is clearly true for metal implants, it may be less true for resorbables.]

- Better understanding of consumer needs. By working closely with surgeons, Synthes should have a better understanding of the performance standards required of a resorbable implant.

The third and, arguable, most important way in which Synthes can impact the success of bioresorbables involves "**Product Usage.**" Synthes, more than any other implant maker, can recommend, influence, and monitor where resorbables do and do not get used. As noted on case page 8, the 1st generation resorbables led to incomplete healing 10% of the time, typically in the case of "stubborn" fractures. This suggests that the choice of when and where to use resorbables could be key to successful outcomes. Reasons to believe Synthes can manage this product usage include:

- ***Synthes/AO credibility.*** Among all implant makers, Synthes is widely viewed as the innovator and thought leader. Part of this is due to its association with the AO and part of it is due to its constant improvement in orthopedic implants. This credibility increases the likelihood that Synthes will be "listened to" by surgeons.
- ***The Synthes' sales force.*** The case notes (page 6) that the Synthes sales reps had a very close working relationship with surgeons, that surgeons and reps consulted with one another several times per week, and that it was not unusual for a surgeon to ask a Synthes rep for advice on a difficult procedure or when using a new implant. This suggests that reps may be able to recommend, almost on a case-by-case basis, where resorbables should and should not be used.
- ***The AO/Synthes training courses.*** One of the major vehicles by which surgeons learned new implant techniques was through the AO/Synthes training courses. This offered Synthes the opportunity to teach the techniques necessary to increase implant success.

In short, in a field were the orthopedic surgeon is the key decision maker, Synthes appears to have the respect of these surgeons. If Synthes chooses, it can leverage that respect to increase the likelihood of success resorbable implants. This thinking can be captured on the board as shown in **Figure TN-4**.

Figure TN-4 Synthes' Influence on the Development of the Resorbables Market

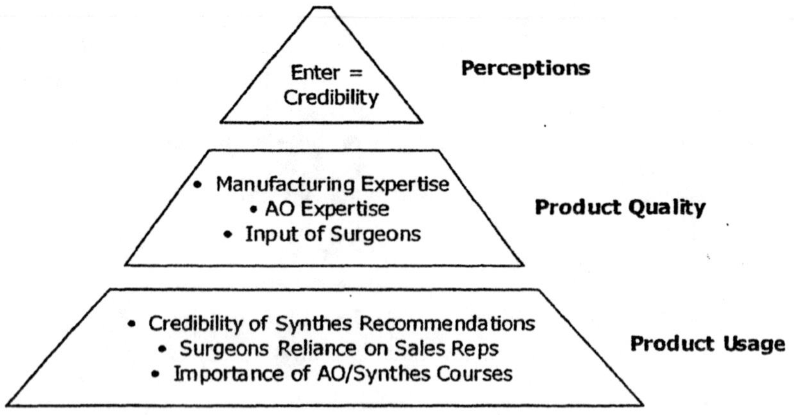

Source: Author

Note that the impact that Synthes can have on the successful adoption of resorbables also can be captured on the previously drawn decision tree (i.e., **Figure TN-3**). Here, the instructor can highlight that by "ignoring" the resorbables market or by practicing a "wait and see" strategy, Synthes will decrease the likelihood that the market will materialize. However, by "developing and marketing" a line of resorbables, Synthes can increase that likelihood.

Finally, Synthes can influence the timing of the resorbables market. Here the thinking is that Synthes can either accelerate or delay the successful adoption of resorbables in the marketplace, but that it can't prevent that adoption. This thinking is captured in **Figure TN-5**.

Figure TN-5 The Development of the Resorbables Market With and Without Synthes

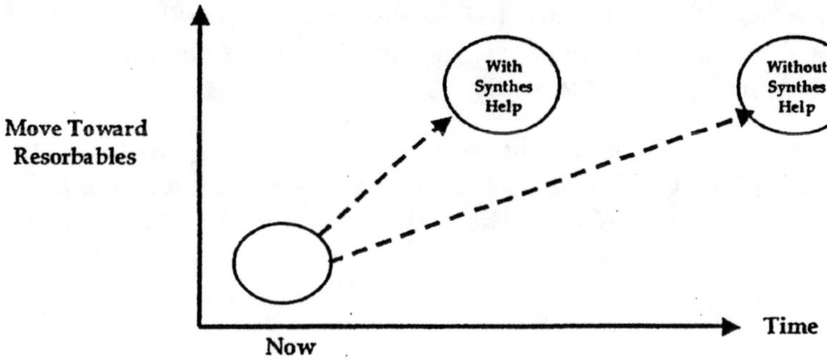

Source: Author

4. How Might Synthes Introduce Resorbables?

The final major area of discussion is, "If Synthes were to actively enter this market, how should it do so?" Here, the thinking is to put into practice the theory espoused in the previous section. If Synthes can increase the potential success in this market through its actions, what should those actions be? Some of the likely responses include:

- Choice of Bones. Limit initial applications to low-risk bones. The case identifies these as the non-weight bearing bones of the hands, feet, wrist, and ankles. Some students will argue for initially focusing on hands and wrists—i.e., the bones that have the least weight placed on them.
- Avoid Children. While the case suggests that the smaller, less-stressed bones of children may be appropriate for resorbables, some students will argue that the risks are just too great with children. It is one thing to tell an adult that their bone has not healed properly, it is something else to tell the parent of a child.

- Sales force. Train the sales force to identify ideal applications. This involves close working relationships with doctors to identify, on a case-by-case basis, appropriate applications.

- Doctors. At first, work with the best doctors to maximize likelihood of success. Also, seek out those doctors who are forward looking and who embrace resorbables.

- Pricing. At least initially, some students will argue for giving away the resorbables to appropriate doctors. This does two things. First, it reduces any cost-based reasons for not trailing resorbables. Second, it controls distribution in a way that might not be feasible if the resorbables were sold outright.

- Branding. Here there may be debate. Some students will argue for protecting the Synthes brand name by coming up with an alternative brand name for the resorbables. The problem is, with Synthes highly trained sales force selling these products into the small, insular community of orthopedic surgeons, it would not take long for medical personnel to link these products to Synthes.

As these recommendations are coming out, the instructor should ask what goals they accomplish. Two goals should quickly emerge. The first is to minimize failure. The second is to learn what leads to success and what leads to failure. Note that this latter goal cannot be achieved in the lab.

Summary

Students (and firms) often view market development as something that happens. According to this thinking, if a product fails, the market was not ready for it, and if that product succeeds, the firm timed the market just right. What is missing from such an assessment is the fact that markets do not develop independent of the firms that are playing in those markets. More than any other implant maker, Synthes decision whether to enter the resorbables market will impact how that market develops. By not entering the market, it will create the perception that resorbable implants are not yet ready for "prime time," which may slow or even temporarily halt the development of this market. However, by entering the market, it helps to validate the concept of resorbables and it offers Synthes the ability to influence adoption.

At another level, this case encourages students to think about the natural progression of markets. While some may argue against entering the resorbable markets at this time, few students will argue that resorbables will fail in the long run. The question then becomes, "When is the best time for Synthes to get into this market?" As the thought leader in this domain, one can make a strong argument that the time should be now, but that the entry should be cautious and controlled.

What Happened?

At the time of this teaching note (spring 2003), Synthes has not yet entered the resorbables market. However, it is actively developing a complete line of hand and wrist implants (and the tools necessary to install them), with the hope of releasing them for use sometime in the next several years.

Teaching the case

This case is a discussion in two parts of about equal length. The first part is more tactical and involves having students assess the options presented in the case—i.e., "What should Synthes do?" This is covered in Sections 1 and 2, above. In this first part, the instructor should try to capture students' opinions in an even-handed fashion, lending weight to both points of view. Also, there should be an assessment of the market size, the cost of developing a resorbables product line, and the likely impact on margins. At the end of this first half of the class, most of the pertinent facts should have been brought out. Before leaving this first part, the instructor may wish to take a vote to see where people stand (the vote could be on which of the first three options each student would endorse). Experience suggests that there will still be a good bit of disagreement regarding which option to pursue.

The second part of the discussion is more strategic in nature and involves Synthes role in shaping the development of this market—i.e., How does Synthes' entry into this market change the odds of success? Here, the students should be pushed to think about how the market for resorbables may evolve with and without Synthes' efforts to develop a product line (Section 3, above) and how Synthes should go about introducing a resorbable product line if it decides to do so (Section 4, above). At the end of this discussion, while some students will still question Synthes entry into this market, all students should appreciate that Synthes has some ability to control the development and success of the resorbables market. Rather than "react to" whatever happens in the market place, Synthes can "drive" what happens in the market place. This naturally leads to the questions, "What business is Synthes in?" (i.e., a metal implant maker or a fixer of broken bones) and "What kind of company does Synthes want to be?"

A potential board plan is presented in **Exhibit TN-3.**

Suggested Questions

1. Are "bioresorbable implants" worth the risk for Synthes? Take a stance and be ready to defend.

2. What are the risks in <u>coming out</u> with a bioresorbable product? What is the worst that could happen? The best?

3. What are the risks in <u>not coming out</u> with a bioresorbable product? What is the worst that could happen? The best?

4. What should Synthes do?

Exhibit TN-1 An Excerpt from *The New York Times,* February 4, 2002

Sulzer Offers $1 Billion Settlement for Defective Implants

By Elizabeth Olson

GENEVA, Feb. 3—Europe's biggest orthopedics maker, Sulzer Medica, has agreed to a $1 billion settlement in an effort to avoid a long legal battle with thousands of American patients who received defective hip and knee implants.

The company had been seeking to settle about 4,000 claims against it to help avoid individual lawsuits with large verdicts that threatened to bankrupt the company. It faced the claims after its unit in Austin, Tex., Sulzer Orthopedics, began recalling the Inter-Op joints at the end of 2000 because a residue of their oil lubricant prevented bonding with the bone, rendering the implants ineffective.

Sulzer Medica, and its parent company, Sulzer A.G. said they would contribute $425 million in cash to the settlement plus an additional $300 million in stock and proceeds from an insurance policy.

"The patients will receive greater compensation, and we can proceed under the assumption that very few will opt out," Stephan Rietiker, chief executive of Sulzer Medica, said in a statement.

The settlement, which must be approved by litigants and a United States district court judge, allows about $200,000 a patient, less than some patients were getting in individual judgments. Last September, a jury in Corpus Christi, Tex., awarded a total of $15.4 million to three women. With two dozen more lawsuits set for trial in state courts, Sulzer said additional large verdicts would drag the company under. It has been trying to find a class-action settlement.

An effort last year to settle the claims for $783 million failed when some claimants refused to go along. Some 31,000 people have received the Sulzer implants, and about 2,800 of them have had corrective surgery to replace the faulty devices. The current settlement arrangement would give each patient roughly twice as much as the previous offer. ...

The proposed accord must be approved by a federal judge in Cleveland, who is scheduled to review the case on May 14. The judge, Kathleen O'Malley, had set the date of Feb. 1 to arrive at an agreement before allowing individual lawsuits to proceed. Last Friday, she pushed the date back to allow the parties more time.

The plaintiffs have until May 2 to agree to the settlement, after which the judge will hold a final hearing.

Source: *The New York Times,* February 4, 2002, page C2.

Exhibit TN-2 Having to Get it "Right" in Version 1

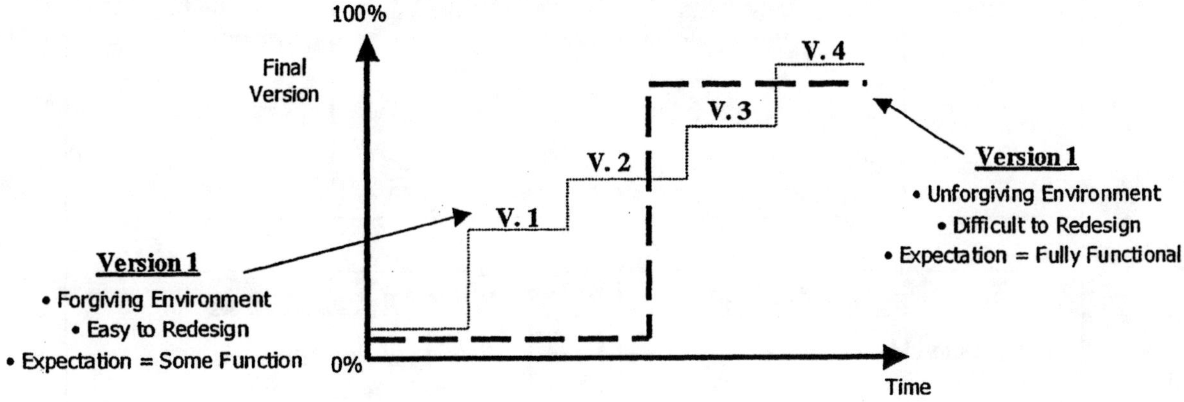

Source: Author

Exhibit TN-3 A Potential Board Plan

What Should Synthes Do?

Ignore	Wait & See	Dev & Mkt	R&D

Reasons For

- Defend Market Share
- Surgeons Want
- Response to Competitors
- High Margins
- Protect Exclusivity

Defend Leadership in Industry

Reasons Against

- Damage to Reputation
- Market is Small
- Expert Surgeons are Concerned
- No Evidence of Demand
- Cost of Development

Too Risky

What If?

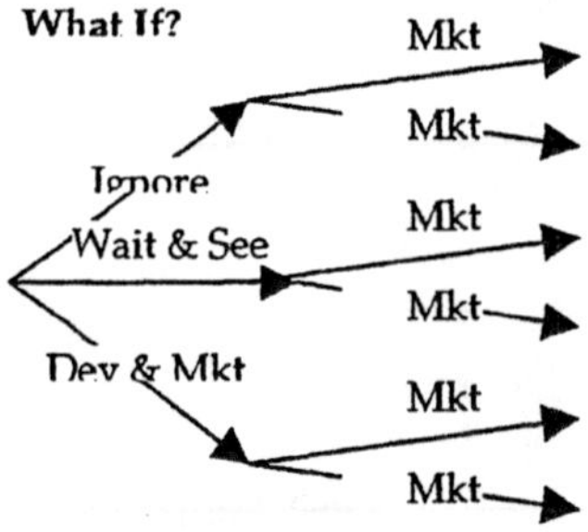

Industry Dynamics

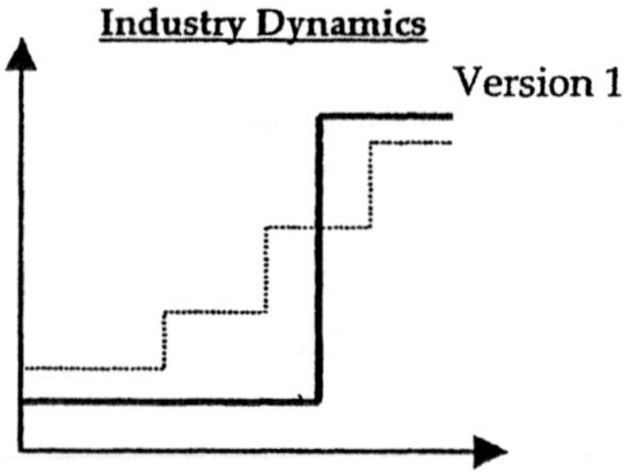

Synthes Role?

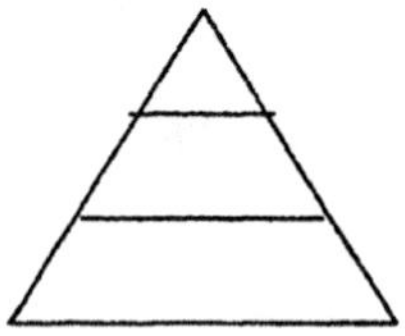

Market Entry Decisions

- What surgeons? All? Some?
- What Applications?
- Pediatrics?
- Sales Force Behavior
- 3rd Generation Polymers
- Reaction to Failure

Merck-Medco: Vertical Integration in the Pharmaceutical Industry

Teaching Note

Synopsis

During the period from 1993-1994, pharmaceutical manufacturers spent approximately $13 billion for the purchase of pharmacy benefit management firms. Pharmacy benefit managers (PBMs) were the 'managed care' arm of the pharmaceutical industry. They typically provided a range of services including pharmacy benefit plan design, prescription drug claim processing, harmful drug interaction reviews, and mail order pharmacy. PBMs' clients were large self-insured employers, insurance carriers, Blue Cross/Blue Shield plans, managed care organizations, and government health plans that provided prescription drug coverage to their employees, retirees, or members.

At the time of the acquisitions, many of the pharmaceutical manufacturers believed that they were positioning themselves for the next level of managed care: disease (health) management. With a disease management approach, the treatment of the patient was analyzed holistically. Total costs and total benefits were weighed to create an optimal quality of life. Drug therapy, although expensive, was often less costly than emergency room visits and surgical interventions and was often a leading recommendation in many disease management programs. Additionally, early intervention with drug therapy could certainly prevent costly and life threatening complications, again tipping the balance toward increased use of pharmaceuticals. In the past, pharmaceutical manufacturers had insufficient prescribing and utilization data to create and support the validity of disease management programs. They believed PBM patient prescribing information databank would overcome this hurdle.

Yet two and half years after the initial euphoria, the success of the PBM purchases were in dispute. Pharmaceutical leader Eli Lilly found itself taking a $2.4 billion write-down on its assets, while another, Merck-Medco, proclaimed the merger of the two firms a success. The case explores the development of pharmacy benefit managers, the rationale that drove the industry-wide purchase of PBMs, and their likely continuing role in the evolving managed care-driven pharmaceutical industry. Students are encouraged to consider what each of the parties brought to the merger and how each has benefited from the merged organization. Further, as the case reports the changes in

This note was prepared by Professor V. Kasturi Rangan and Research Associate Marie Bell for the sole purpose of aiding classroom instructors in the use of "Merck-Medco: Vertical Integration in the Pharmaceutical Industry," HBS No. 598-091. It provides analysis and questions that are intended to present alternative approaches to deepening students' comprehension of business issues and energizing classroom discussion.

the market brought on by industry and government forces, students must re-evaluate and reassess the net benefits of the acquisitions.

Questions

A thorough analysis of the case should address the following questions:

1. What was the rationale for PBMs?
2. Does Medco fit with Merck's strategy?
3. What does Medco bring to Merck? What are the advantages and disadvantages?
4. What does Medco get from the Merck acquisition?
5. Is health management the future?

Analysis

What was the rationale for PBMs?

Prior to the arrival of PBMs, two parallel channels existed—one for the information and financial flow of pharmaceuticals and the other for the physical distribution of products. As seen below, there was no contact between the buyer (the insurance company or self-insured insurer) and the seller (the manufacturer).

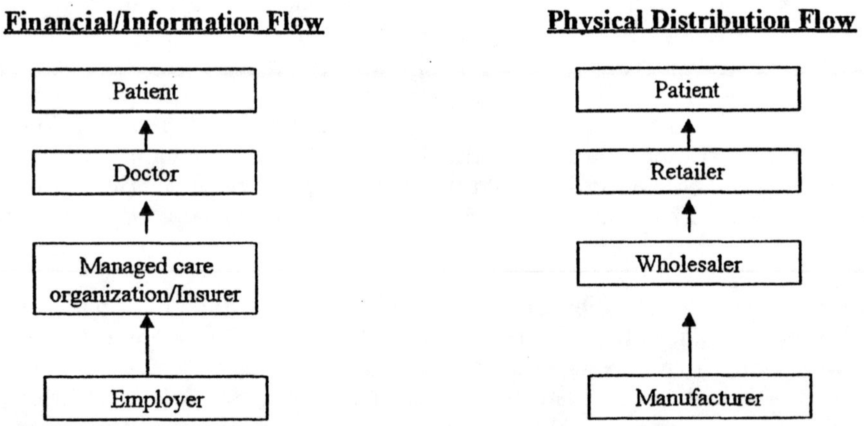

On the financial/information side, employers contracted with a managed care plan or insurer to provide health benefits for their employees. Pharmaceutical needs were determined by the doctor who provided the patient with a prescription which was filled by the patient. The costs of the pharmaceuticals were either the patient's responsibility or reimbursed through the insurance company. On the distribution side, manufacturers distributed their products through wholesalers and retail pharmacies to make products available to patients when they presented a prescription from their doctor. As a result of these two separate channels, there was little awareness and no ability to control the cost of the medication where there was no buyer/seller interface,.

As seen in **Figure B** of the case, PBMs became the "glue" that connected the buyer and seller. As the pharmaceutical industry in specific and the health care industry in general came under increased scrutiny over rising costs, PBMs entered the market—initially offering administration (transactions processing), then formulary management (drug utilization reviews to determine the optimal product selection based on quality and cost, and, ultimately health management.

With the PBM acting as the agent for the payer, it created a balance of power between the physical distributions channel and the information/financial channel, thereby forming a more efficient pharmaceutical market. Students acknowledge that the purchase of a PBM by a manufacturer seems to destabilize this delicate balance. There is a paradox when the manufacturer (the supplier) fulfills this roll. PBMs are supposed to be an agent for the payer—keeping costs down and quality up, but a PBM owned by a manufacturer has a vested interest in the sale of the parent company's products—at the highest prices and largest volumes possible.

How does Medco fit with Merck's strategy?

While students accept the value of PBMs, they question whether the purchase of Medco was a knee-jerk reaction to a rapidly changing market or whether Medco really did fit Merck's strategy at the time. The outstanding question is whether the Medco acquisition fit Merck's strategy or whether the Medco acquisition has been made to fit after the fact. Has Merck-Medco made the best of a bad deal?

Students readily assess Merck's strategy and position in the market at the time of the Medco acquisition. Prior to the rise of managed care, Merck actively avoided dealing with entities that would in any way commoditize its product lines. Merck's ability to do so was based on two factors. The first was the excellence of its direct salesforce. Consistently singled out for excellence, Merck's salesforce had excellent relationships with prescribing physicians that translated into active education and selling time for Merck's products and the creation of a strong Merck franchise among prescribing physicians. The second factor was the strength of Merck's patented products in key therapeutic categories. While Merck was a research and development leader in the industry and had developed strong products in multiple categories, Merck's Vasotec, Zocor, and Mevacor were the leading drugs in the $16 billion cardiovascular category.

Despite these strengths, however, Merck believed that the industry was in the midst of a substantial change that could render Merck vulnerable. Although pharmaceutical represented only 8% of its healthcare costs, it was increasingly singled out for the cost of its products and the margins it earned. The market was commoditizing. The march toward managed care was on. In the early 1990s, it appeared as though prescribing decisions would shift from individual doctors to prescribing committees. In such an environment, personal relationships would become secondary to presentations of efficacy and cost, and Merck would lose much of the value of its saleforce. PBMs had entered the market and were proving effective in shifting share from one product to another. Of specific concern was the success of Bristol Myers's product Pravachol as a preferred product in Medco's formulary. It was clear to Merck that the time had come to become a serious player in the managed care market.

In addition to cost pressure, Merck was also facing increasingly high product development costs further jeopardizing margins. With an investment of over $300 million over ten years before a product reached the market and only 1 in 10,000 projects reaching the market place, research and development costs were escalating. Merck believed that access to a PBM would provide additional input into the R&D process directing development activities and enhancing success rates.

The purchase of a PBM was an opportunity for Merck to buy managed care distribution and influence the shape of the managed care market for pharmaceutical products. Looking at the PBM players, Medco was a good fit with Merck. Merck's product line was concentrated in chronic care illnesses ideally situated to Medco's strength in mail order. Medco's customers base was heavily weighted to "blue chip" clients that covered their employees for life—again complementary to

Merck's chronic care emphasis. Some students, however, will question whether Merck needed to purchase Medco in order to become part of PBM formularies. Merck had market share-leading products with proven efficacy so presumably could have negotiated deals to be highlighted as preferred products.

Finally, Medco was a full service PBM offering "integrated pharmacy services" including an extensive retail pharmacy network, 13 mail order locations. Additionally, as one of the largest national PBMs, it had extensive data on prescribing patterns and had begun to investigate cutting edge health management programs. While this emphasis was also complementary to Merck's thinking, students will again question whether Merck needed to purchase a PBM to access this data. For example, Bristol Myers chose a route of alliances to achieve the same end.

What does Medco bring to Merck?

As discussed above, Medco provides Merck with access to a significant customer base. Merck will need to establish relationships with these 50 million potential patients, especially as two of Merck's top drugs, Vostec and Mevacor, will go off patent in 2000 and 2001 respectively. Generally, when pharmaceuticals go off patent they lose share rapidly. Merck has an opportunity to slow that share loss by converting Medco's patients to Merck's products as chronic care patients are less likely to convert to other medications. However, some students note that Merck did not need to purchase Medco to access its customer base. Merck's products based on their efficacy and pricing would and do command a place not only on Medco's formulary but the formularies of the other leading PBMs.

In the early 1990s, pharmaceutical manufacturers believed that PBMs would bring market share gains. For example, Bristol Myers was able to make significant headway for Pravachol with its preferred position within the Medco formulary. Indeed, prior to the wave of PBM acquisitions, many in the industry believed that PBMs would soon develop closed formularies with a limited number of dispensable products for each therapeutic category. Electronic DUR would not only monitor the threat of adverse drug interactions, but also provide the means to ensure that only those drugs on the formulary were those dispensed. The consent agreement between Lilly and the federal government effectively scotched the closed formulary and created an independent competitive process for drug selection. While the manufacturers sought to downplay the effect of this decision by noting that no single manufacturer had a sufficiently broad product line to fulfill a payer's needs, it undoubtedly left the integrated PBM/drug manufacturer significantly less able to shift significant share.

Medco also brought to Merck significant patient information regarding drug prescribing and utilization behavior. This information represented a significant improvement over Merck's data which consisted of the number of prescriptions written and the doctors writing them. The PBMs' longitudinal data on prescribing and patient utilization behavior provided information on real world outcomes such as patient compliance. This market place feedback then suggested how effective the drug was in its current formulation as compared to the outcomes from the clinical trials in which the patient's use of the drug was carefully monitored. However, as with the ability to shift share, the government regulation also weakened this ownership advantage. The mandated "arm's length relationship" between the PBM and the owner/manufacturer made it difficult for the manufacturer to access the data more efficiently than any other competitor.

Mail order Medco's mail order pharmacy is the jewel that Medco brings to Merck. Through its mail order business, Merck Medco can effectively shift share to Merck Medco's preferred formulary drugs. The process for achieving this is illustrated in the customer examples shown on page 13 in the case. In the retail pharmacy example, the patient goes in to have a prescription filled and has the choice of paying a higher copayment for the prescribed drug or accepting an equivalent generic for the regular copayment amount. In general, the patient will not be willing to wait while the pharmacist tries to contact the doctor to change the selected drug. Additionally, the case patient was suffering from a bacterial infection that required immediate treatment. As a result, the patient may have little interest in saving the amount of the copayment for a single prescription. For that matter, neither does the pharmaceutical manufacturer. For a one-time prescription, worth potentially $20 at retail, there is little value in spending perhaps $10 or more in trying to convert the prescription.

The situation is significantly different for a long-term chronic illness example. Here the savings to the patient, who will need ongoing refills, is significant. Additionally, the process for changing the prescription is painless. The mail order pharmacy contacts the prescribing doctor and after identifying itself and its affiliation with the drug manufacturer, gains approval for the change. The patient and the prescribing physician each receive a letter confirming the change in the prescription and several days later the patient begins receiving the medication through the mail. Not only does the mail service pharmacy save the patient the copay amount, but as a 90 day supply is dispensed rather than a 30 day supply, fewer copayments are necessary. Further, the patient did not have to leave his/her home to receive the needed medication, a condition that could become important for the chronically ill. The mail order pharmacist has a few days to effect the switch because the transaction time is a couple of days anyway. The retail pharmacist has only a few minutes. Additionally, for the manufacturer, there is a financial incentive to effect the change. A chronic care patient may spend in excess of $500 per year at retail, and therefore it is of significant value to spend the $10 to get the patient to convert.

A key advantage for Merck from the Medco acquisition is its mail order pharmacy where there is sufficient savings and benefits for patients, plan sponsors, and producers. Additionally, for all intents and purposes, Medco was the mail order channel with a 55% share, with the next largest mail order business, Baxter Prescriptions, with an 11% share. Other PBM purchasers such as Eli Lilly and SmithKline did not have well-established mail order pharmacies.

The problems created with the Medco acquisition internally are mostly cultural. Merck has always seen itself as a highly scientific organization, creating products to relieve the pain and suffering of others. By contrast, Medco is an upstart organization founded by an investment banker with no previous medical experience. While Merck "makes money by saving lives," Medco makes money at the margin trying to squeeze cost out of the system. If Merck was the Mercedes of pharmaceutical development, then Medco was the "Wal-Mart of pills" and a cultural clash would appear inevitable. The government intervention in the market that limited formulary manipulation, however, worked to assuage the potential for cultural conflict.

From an external perspective, the Medco acquisition caused outrage among the retail pharmacies. Retail pharmacies, who were already facing industry consolidation and the threat of substitute locations such as grocery stores, were constantly being "squeezed" by PBMs and even more specifically by mail order pharmacies. While PBMs exchanged margins for higher volumes on dispensed prescription drugs, mail order pharmacies took patients out of the store entirely, preventing the patient from purchasing other higher margin ancillary supplies (e.g., tissues, toiletries, etc.). Although the retail pharmacist might complain, there was little that they could do to impact the acquisition, "as individual pharmacists often can't afford to buck Medco's clout."

While the above discussion addresses some of the qualitative benefits of the Medco acquisition, it does not address the question of return—what did Merck get for its $6.6 billion purchase? Prior to the merger Merck had 10% of Medco's drug expenditures of $2 billion, or about $200 million. Using Merck's 20% margin, Merck earned about $40 million from its sales through Medco. After the merger in 1993, Merck's share of Medco's $9 billion drug spend had grown to 15% or $1.35 billion. Again applying Merck's 20% margin, Merck earned $270 million from sales of its own products through Medco. Additionally, Merck gain Medco's 7% distributor's margin on the remaining $7.85 billion, or $550 million. The combined earnings accruing to Merck from Medco are, therefore, approximately $820 million.

At the limit, if one assumed that all of the $820 million profit was incremental, Merck faces an eight year payback on its investment. Of course, many students will argue that Merck would have retained the 10% share, so one has to adjust the figures down by about $100 million. But the payback would then be nearly 10 years. Clearly, Merck saw something else—that something was the potential in disease management. Additionally, some students might suggest that Merck's purchase of Medco was defensive and that Merck's share of Medco's drug spend could have been significantly less had a Merck competitor purchased Medco.

What does Medco get?

As a result of the acquisition, Medco received credibility and investment funding. While Medco had been a pioneer in the PBM industry, it was perceived as a newcomer in assessing clinical outcomes. The purchase by Merck legitimized Medco's way of doing business for the broader healthcare industry. Further, the regulatory intervention prevented Merck from "taking over" and Medco was able to continue to expand the boundaries of PBM. The umbrella of Merck's clinical expertise gave Medco access to some of the leading pharmaceutical talent to drive its clinically driven programs such as patient profiling and outcomes research.

The other major benefit to Medco of the Merck acquisition was investment. Subsequent to the acquisition, Merck spent over $50 million on customer service systems and $120 million on upgrades to information and technology. The goal of these investments, which could not have occurred with Medco as a stand-alone company, was to data-mine Medco's patient information in order to create the next domain of PBM, the health management specialists.

Is health management the future?

In the early 1990s, PBMs were at a critical juncture in their development. Beginning as administrators of pharmacy claims, they had progressed through drug utilization review and were beginning to look at health management. Additionally, as transactions processing and drug utilization review had matured, they had become low margin activities.

In the field of health management, the goal was to create the best possible health outcome for the patient. In the treatment of certain diseases such as diabetes and hypertension, early intervention with drug therapy was an effective way to treat the condition. Additionally, early treatment was cost effective as patients avoided costly visits to emergency rooms and in some cases could avoid surgery. Effective early treatment, however, was conditional on patient compliance with pharmaceutical treatment regimens. Patient compliance was often an issue as the patient did not notice a substantial difference in health with or without taking the medication. As a result, missed intake of the medication, while potentially detrimental, was not viewed as a major problem by the patient. Creating behavioral compliance was therefore a key issue in creating an effective health management program.

A key question related to health management is, who is the best player to deliver health management programs? Many patients and payers were suspicious of health management programs sponsored by pharmaceutical manufacturers, especially in circumstances when the health management program recommended drug therapy. Additionally, while the marriage of PBM and pharmaceutical manufacturers provided increased utilization information, patient profiles still lacked the complete medical record indicating other forms of treatment. Indeed, students suggest that the information is necessary but not sufficient given the degree of behavioral modification necessary to increase patient compliance. Doctors and HMOs may be more credible health management agents.

Execution of health management programs was intensive, requiring daily intervention with both patients and physicians. Pharmaceutical companies could not execute such a program as they are not organized for intensive interventions. PBMs, however, are accustomed to contacting patients and doctors, though some students question whether PBMs have the full battery of skills necessary to manage disease protocols and execute programs against them.

The pros and cons of health management are fairly well-balanced. But one has to keep in mind that unlike the initial move to PBMs, which was customer (payer) driven, the health management movement is manufacturer driven. Of course it has value for the customer, but it has to be communicated and consolidated.

Teaching the Case

Merck Medco is a very hard case to teach, on a fascinating channel evolution topic in the industry. Systematically going through the suggested questions, offering brief summaries and recaps at the end of each section, is our recommended approach. This case is more about industry and channels than Merck-Medco in particular. Keeping that in mind, instructors may want to use it as a departure for a lecture on channels evolution.

Becton Dickinson & Company VACUTAINER Systems Division

Teaching Note

Synopsis

Becton Dickinson's VACUTAINER Systems Division (BDVS) produces blood collection tubes and needles for sale to hospitals, commercial labs, and other areas such as physicians' offices and surgicenters. In 1985 the health care industry in general, and hospitals in particular, were affected by government cost control. Within this context, William Kozy, BDVS's national sales director, and Hank Smith, BDVS's vice president of marketing and sales, are negotiating a contract with personnel at Affiliated Purchasing Group (APG), a large hospital buying group. The immediate issue is how to respond to APG's demands concerning pricing, labeling, and distribution terms. But the outcome of the APG negotiations will affect BDVS's negotiations with other purchasing groups, relationships with its current distributors, and the division's traditional marketing and sales strategy. Hence, the longer-term issue is how BDVS should conduct its business in a changing, volatile marketplace.

Use

The BDVS case concerns a drama of shifting power and entangling alliances among a major supplier, buyer, and distributor in a marketplace undergoing significant changes in demand demographics and buying behavior. The case also concerns a crucial and common task in sales and marketing: the conduct of important, high-level, face-to-face contract negotiations. It requires students to analyze what is at stake in the BDVS/APG negotiations, which party is gaining or losing power as the market changes, which of several "demands" is likely to be truly important to each party, and how BDVS managers should respond to the latest (and seemingly final) round of negotiations with APG managers. Thus, the case is suitable for use in the distribution or pricing modules of a general marketing management course, in the procurement section of an industrial marketing course, or in the account management module of a sales management course.

I have tended to use the case as a bridge between the sales management module and a module dealing with issues in channels design and management. This teaching note reflects this dual perspective on the case. I have also used the case with executive groups not in the health care industries. The stakes involved in the negotiations, the case's attention to the process and evolution

Professor Frank V. Cespedes prepared this teaching note as an aid to instructors in the classroom use of the case, "Becton Dickinson & Company: VACUTAINER Systems Division," HBS No. 587-085.

of these negotiations, and the implications of tactical decisions concerning the APG contract for BDVS's marketing strategy, produce an exciting, wide-ranging discussion that can generate insights applicable to marketing and distribution issues in many industries.

In *Going to Market*, Chapter 3 on product, market, and buyer behavior discusses certain aspects of this case, while the issues discussed in Chapter 7 on building channels power, and Chapter 10 on coping with change, are also relevant to this case situation.

Case Analysis

I try to coordinate discussions of the BDVS case among four areas of analysis: (1) What are the important changes in the health care market, and what are the implications for Becton Dickinson (BD) and its BDVS division? (2) How important is the APG contract for BDVS? What's at stake for BDVS in winning or losing this contract? (3) How important is each aspect of the negotiations (pricing, brand name, and delivery terms) for each party explicitly or implicitly involved (APG, its member hospitals, BDVS, BDVS's distributors, and competing suppliers)? (4) Given our analysis, what should BDVS do?

Market Analysis

The case is clear about important changes in the environment in which BDVS competes. Continued increases in the cost of health care caused the U.S. government to legislate so-called DRG criteria for reimbursement to hospitals for many patients (case page 6). Insurance companies and employers have altered payment plans in ways that place additional pressure on hospitals to manage their costs more tightly (case page 7). These developments have resulted in a decline in hospital admissions and the average length of stay (case page 6). Further, since commercial labs compete to perform work for hospitals and clinics, these labs (other important customers for BDVS products) are also more cost-conscious.

Overall demand for the division's products is shifting. Hospital blood testing, which currently accounts for about 70% of demand (case page 4), is forecast to decline through 1987 and then increase "somewhat" in subsequent years. The segment thought to be growing fastest, the nonhospital health care centers, is forecast to grow about 5% annually through 1990, but from a base of only 5% of total demand, as of 1985 (case page 5). These trends have already taken their toll on Becton Dickinson: The company's medical products sales are down 2.4% from 1982 to 1984, its laboratory product sales are down 2.1%, and net income from its health care businesses (which account for over 80% of the corporation's total sales) is down 17% over this period (**Exhibit 1**).

As cost containment has risen in importance, hospital customers have begun to alter their traditional purchasing processes, with consequent changes in who buys and how purchasing is conducted. Traditionally, hospital lab personnel determined what supplies to order and from which vendor(s). For lab personnel, the cost of products such as blood collection equipment was not as important as quality and brand preference, because these personnel have been measured on lab performance, not operating costs, and because these costs (in the pre-DRG environment) were passed on to the patient or insurer (case pages 12-13). These laboratory "bench people" remain important, influential forces in the purchasing process, but hospital administrators and materials managers are increasingly involved. The latter groups tend to be significantly more price sensitive than lab personnel and, in an institution where labor makes up about 70% of hospital costs (case page 5), tend to focus on product categories where there are multiple sources of supply and potential cost savings. BDVS's supplies products, which are ordered frequently and the transactions costs of which can double the costs of product acquisition for hospitals (case pages 4 and 10-11), fall into this category. In addition, hospitals have formed pooled buying groups in order to increase their purchasing leverage with individual suppliers and perhaps attain a critical mass sufficient to make pricing and delivery terms among suppliers especially competitive. APG is clearly among the leading, most sophisticated, and most aggressive of these buying groups.

Competition in the blood collection market is primarily among BDVS and two other firms: Terumo and (a distant third) Sherwood's Monoject division. The following table summarizes case information about each firm's U.S. market share and pricing in tubes and needles:

	U.S. Market			
	Share Position		Average Unit Price	
Company	Tubes	Needles	Tubes	Needles
BDVS	80%	30%	$.08	$.075
Terumo	18	50	.065	.075
Sherwood/Monoject	2	15	n/a	.10

BDVS has maintained its 80% share of the U.S. tube market while increasing its unit prices from $.06 to $.08 in recent years, evidence of the division's strong brand franchise among lab personnel. However, Terumo, a global competitor, has increased its share from 10% to 20% while maintaining its $.065/unit price despite BDVS's price increases, evidence of the firm's aggressive posture toward increased volume and share in a product category where scale economies are significant. BDVS's share in the U.S. needles market has dropped from 40% to 30% while Terumo's share has doubled from 25% to 50% during the past seven years (case page 8). These facts are important because the APG contract covers both tubes and needles, product categories where BDVS has significantly different competitive positions.

In both categories, however, market share and high-volume orders are important. For BDVS, market share is an important aspect of the firm's "quality aggression" strategy (case page 8). A leading share of market allows the company to make large capital investments more readily than lower-share competitors. As one manager notes, "This raises our costs but also forces our competitors to raise their costs even more, since our higher volume allows us to amortize the capital investments over a larger base" (case page 8). The APG contract, for which both Terumo and BDVS are active suitors, is potentially among the highest-volume contracts in the industry.

In other respects, APG represents a microcosm of key market trends for BDVS. As comments make clear (case pages 5, 9, 15, 17), the division's sales strategy (and its market strength) focuses on the laboratory bench people, not on hospital administrators, the constituency served by APG. In fact, a separate salesforce was created as recently as 1980 to help execute this strategy (case pages 8-9): a specialized VACUTAINER salesforce (as opposed to a generalist, full-line BD salesforce) could increase its technical selling abilities by focusing on a product line. This fit with the requirement to sell to lab personnel on the basis of quality and helped solidify BDVS's power in the channel by reinforcing its brand name among end-users. However, purchasing groups such as APG are sold through "Z contracts" (case pages 14-15), which focus on different buying criteria and which, for BDVS's salespeople, mean "less time spent with the bench people and more time with purchasing people" (case page 15).

After buying groups negotiate a contract with the manufacturer, they often renegotiate terms with distributors in order to lower their product-acquisition costs further (case pages 14 and **Exhibit 4**). This practice affects BDVS's traditional distribution strategy, which is more intensive than its major competitors (case pages 11-12) and which has allowed BDVS to service frequent order requirements among hospitals and penetrate many local hospitals that have traditionally done business with a given local distributor (case page 12). Distributors have supported BDVS despite its intensive distribution because the firm's brand franchise is so strong among hospital end-users. However, when BDVS negotiates a contract with a buying group and the buying group then renegotiates delivery terms with distributors (essentially putting this volume out for bid among a number of distributors in a given area), BDVS's distribution policies take on a different aspect:

intensive distribution increases the threat of any one BDVS distributor losing a large account to another, slightly lower-priced distributor in that area. A supplier with more exclusive distribution policies (e.g., Terumo) becomes potentially more attractive, especially to the larger distributors (e.g., ASP), who have significant volumes at stake among hospitals in categories such as blood collection tubes and needles.

Thus, when in 1982 APG sought a standard contract for tubes and needles, BDVS "had resisted negotiating prices and terms directly with APG headquarters and had continued dealing separately with individual hospitals" (case page 16). This is understandable, given the implications for the division's sales and distribution strategy. However, between 1982 and 1985 the passage of DRG legislation, an increase in the power of buying groups, and competitive developments altered the situation.

Importance of the APG Contract

In the context of both BDVS's strategy and larger market trends, then, the negotiations with APG represent "the tip of an iceberg," and the division's response is likely to establish important precedents for the conduct of future business with other buying groups and end-use customers. Faced with APG's demands, some students may argue for simply rejecting the proposed contract. This is a defensible position. But students must understand the significance of the APG contract and what is at stake for BDVS in winning or losing this contract.

APG has grown rapidly from a group representing 20 hospitals in 1975 to one representing more than 500 (which account for more than two million annual admissions) by 1985 (case page 15). These hospitals hold more than 10% of all hospital beds in the United States, including "many large, prestigious hospitals affiliated with medical schools" (case page 15). Thus, APG's potential significance goes beyond its sheer volume. The largest 25% of hospitals in the United States represent about "50% of the market for medical equipment and supplies" (case page 4). Thus, APG's large-hospital membership means it probably accounts for more than 10% of the market for blood collection equipment. Its medical schools' membership offers vendors attractions similar to those of schools and universities in markets such as personal computers: the attraction of developing a customer base among younger users who will later influence purchasing decisions across a spectrum of institutions. Given its growing membership, APG appears to be a trendsetter in the industry and, for its approved suppliers, a "prestige" account providing potential benefits and credibility in selling to other customers in the industry.

Financially, a substantial piece of business is at stake for BDVS. From information in the case, we can calculate the following:

- APG hospitals purchased $6 million in BDVS blood collection products in 1984 (case pages 17-18); since these products represent 70% of BDVS's $90 million in sales revenues (case page 3), APG purchases represent 9.5% of BDVS volume.

- With its current contract, APG is seeking to provide the approved supplier with 90% of the business in tubes and needles among member hospitals. Assuming (conservatively) that a growing APG represents about $6 million in purchases for these products, that means at least $5.4 million ($6 million x .9) is at risk for BDVS. The revenue at risk is in fact larger: The $6 million figure represents only BDVS's sales to APG (where BDVS accounts for about 80% of tubes and 40% of needles purchased by member hospitals); and calculations of the immediate revenue exposed also ignore the aftermarket potentially lost by not reaching the prestige medical schools represented by APG.

Another way to think about the significance of this contract is to consider the costs to BDVS of winning or losing the APG contract. The case tells us that, at the latest negotiating session, APG managers rejected a BDVS proposal "with prices approximately 20% higher than competitors' prices" (case page 18). **Exhibit TN-1** outlines the worst-case financial scenarios for BVDS of winning or losing the contract, assuming that a 20% price reduction (i.e., the worst case) is required to win the contract. The results suggest that, although the immediate effect on sales volume may be more damaging by winning the contract on these terms, the effect on divisional net income is similar whether BDVS wins or loses. Any ability by BDVS to negotiate a deal at something better than a 20% price reduction will improve considerably the "hit" to net income from winning the bid. Further, with BDVS currently accounting for 40% of APG-member purchases of needles and with APG working to deliver 90% of these purchases to the approved vendor, BDVS's incremental sales volume on this contract could be considerable and offset the projected loss in net income from a price reduction. These cost figures deal only with the estimated immediate financial effects of this bid. Should BDVS choose not to negotiate further with APG, Kozy and Smith will still be faced with similar requests from other hospital buying groups, and the potential losses in sales will clearly force price negotiations soon.

Conduct of the Negotiations

Price is only one aspect of the negotiations. APG also wants products covered by the agreement to carry the APG logo (rather than the BDVS VACUTAINER brand name) and to be delivered by distributors affiliated with APG (rather than through BDVS's authorized distributors). These demands considerably complicate the decisions facing Kozy and Smith. Discussions must therefore consider how important each aspect is to each party explicitly or implicitly involved. I like to generate this analysis by putting a simple matrix on the board, highlighting each party and each major component of the negotiations:

	Relative Importance of:		
	Price	Private Label	Nature of Distributors Used
• BVDS - BD			
• APG - Mr. Wilson			
• APG-member hospitals			
• BVDS Distributors			
• Competing suppliers			

Case evidence suggests the following considerations are important in analyzing this array of interests:

For *BDVS*, price is important, as the analysis in **Exhibit TN-1** indicates. As a large, visible group, prices to APG will be precedents for contract negotiations with other buying groups who, because they compete for hospital members (case page 7), will feel pressure to match any deal negotiated by APG for its membership. Perhaps more important for BDVS than price, however, is the private-label demand. The VACUTAINER brand name is, "among the bench people, the best-known brand of blood collection tubes" (case page 5) and clearly an important asset to the company. In a volume-sensitive product category, pricing can be negotiated on an individual basis with different buying groups, and APG as the largest group has the most leverage over this aspect of negotiations. But agreeing to private labeling will set a precedent that Kozy and Smith will undoubtedly want to resist as much as possible, since that demand cuts to the heart of the division's sales strategy and current strength in its channel and within the hospital decision-making unit.

The demand to work through APG-affiliated distributors is also perhaps more important than pricing for BDVS and also more complicated. BDVS's largest distributor, ASP, would lose substantial volume if BDVS assented to this requirement, and ASP accounts for about 40% of BDVS's sales volume (case page 10). By contrast, all BD products account for about 10% of ASP sales, and BDVS products comprise some 25% of this total (case page 11), or about 2.5% of ASP sales. Further, ASP/BDVS relations have improved in recent years (case page 11), but ASP also carries the lines of BDVS's major competitors, Terumo and Sherwood (case page 11). Collectively, six distributors account for more than 65% of BDVS sales volume (case page 10), and these major distributors are not part of the APG-affiliated distribution network being assembled by James Wilson; indeed, some distributors "were reportedly ready to stop supporting (and perhaps sever agreements with) manufacturers that agreed to" the APG distribution program (case page 16).

Clearly, if APG insists on the distribution demand, BDVS is between the proverbial rock and a hard place, potentially forced to choose between the largest distributor and largest buying group in the industry. To some extent, this choice implies a long-term strategic decision about the future evolution of forces within the health care industry. Terumo, by agreeing to the distribution demand (case page 19), has apparently placed its bet. For BDVS, however, distributor support is important to its marketing strategy, as emphasized in comments by divisional management (case pages 11-12) and in the division's promotional literature in **Exhibit 3**: "Our nationwide distribution network is always ready to get you the supplies you need when you need them." Other BD divisions will be interested in this decision: Their products are also carried by ASP and other large distributors, and the presence of the 80% share-of-market VACUTAINER brand on distributors' shelves helps to generate support for other BD products.

For *APG*, price is very important. Lower prices on hospital supply products is a core raison d'être for the formation of a buying group. Whatever else Wilson takes away from a contract agreement, competing with other buying groups for the allegiance of hospital members requires a price discount over what those hospitals can get from suppliers on their own or through other groups. The distribution demand, however, may well occupy a different priority for APG negotiators. Since hospitals typically spend as much on ordering and stocking supplies as on the products themselves (case page 5), there is an opportunity to lower hospitals' product-acquisition costs by developing a low-cost/low-commission network of affiliated distributors. However, this network is primarily a means toward the end of lower product costs, and there are other means for APG to attain this end; one is the now-common industry practice of renegotiating lower commissions among distributors after negotiating a contract with the manufacturer (case page 14). Hence, BDVS negotiators may find there is room for give-and-take concerning the distribution aspects of the contract, especially for the dominant supplier of a large-volume, frequently ordered product category.

The private-labeling issue is more complicated. Wilson has publicly announced that APG hopes eventually to private-label "virtually all" products sold through APG purchasing agreements (case page 16), and this announcement in itself may, for political purposes, stiffen the resolve of APG negotiators on this point. An APG label keeps the group visible to member hospitals, thus fostering loyalty and perhaps increased membership. Private labeling also tends, over time, to erode the power of brand names such as VACUTAINER at member hospitals. At the same time, however, APG negotiators are very concerned with attaining a high degree of compliance among member hospitals for a contract on blood collection products (case page 17). Here, the VACUTAINER brand name is an asset in fostering compliance, as BDVS's relatively successful defense of its position against the 1982 APG contract with Terumo indicates (case pages 16-17). In any case, discussions should recognize how the private-label issue is tied to the issue of compliance and how, in turn, this issue and the entire set of negotiations between APG and BDVS in 1985 occur within an historical context that, among other things, has political and emotional (case page 18) dimensions as well as economic and strategic ones.

For *APG member hospitals,* as noted above, price is probably the most important aspect. The nature of the distributors used is probably the least important, as long as those distributors can provide quick, frequent local deliveries at lower costs. The private-label issue is more complicated: The VACUTAINER brand is recognized and respected among lab personnel, while increased acceptance of private-label brands probably suits the longer-term objectives of hospital materials managers.

For *BDVS distributors,* all aspects of the negotiations are vital, but the nature of distributors used in fulfilling demand is obviously crucial. Further, as the "gatekeeper" to large accounts via its Z contracts, BDVS, while under increasing pressure from these accounts, has gained channel power relative to its distributors. In this sense, Terumo's acquiescence to APG demands represents a potential opportunity for BDVS with its large distributors, at least one of whom (ASP) has, like APG, expressed a preference for developing more private-label brands (case page 11).

For *competitors* such as Terumo and Sherwood, agreeing to the pricing, private-label, and distribution demands of APG is clearly an attempt to "crack" a large, prestigious account where BDVS is currently the major supplier. Both Terumo and Sherwood have much less to lose than BDVS in across-the-board acquiescence to APG. For Terumo, in particular, the APG agreement represents a chance to continue its penetration of APG-member hospitals begun with the 1982 agreement and perhaps increase volume significantly (and, equally important, decrease BDVS volume) in a volume-sensitive product category.

What Should BDVS Do?

The analysis above indicates the array of interests implicated in the negotiations. For BDVS the negotiations involve not only the terms of a contract but a set of entangling alliances that Kozy and Smith must consider in crafting a response to APG demands. I like to use the figure in **Exhibit TN-2** to emphasize this aspect of the situation. Any decision concerning the APG contract by BDVS must consider (a) the changing balance of power in the industry among suppliers like BDVS, large buying groups like APG, and large distributors like ASP; (b) how the contract's terms will affect BDVS's position with its user-customers and with its distribution network; and (c) how the outcome will affect BDVS's marketing strategy and, in particular, the nature of the value provided by BDVS to customers; this value includes, as well as product performance at a certain price, the breadth of the BDVS product line (case page 3) and the delivery network BDVS has established to carry inventory for that broad product line.

Students' suggestions concerning BDVS's response run the gamut from "stonewalling" APG (i.e., standing pat with the last BDVS proposal of August 1, as described on case page 18) to agreeing to each APG demand on price, label, and distribution terms. The pedagogical goal at this point in the discussion is to link each recommendation to its implications for BDVS's position in the chain of entangling alliances that circumscribe the negotiations. In addition, students should not lose sight of the position of Kozy and Smith, the chief sales and marketing managers of the division: their boss is naturally very interested in the process (case page 1), large important distributors are calling Kozy regularly (case page 18), and they have 14 days to submit a new proposal for what appears to be the largest potential contract available (case page 19). It's time for industry and competitive analysis to issue in specific, actionable recommendations.

Toward the final third of class discussion time, it is useful to ask students to vote on each major aspect of the negotiations. Generally, most students are willing to lower price further, although not by the necessary 20% to match competitors' proposals. The reasoning here is that the BDVS brand franchise and APG compliance concerns warrant some price premium over competition ("Besides, why would APG still want to talk with us if they weren't willing to give some on this issue?"). Fewer students are willing to agree to the distribution demands, reasoning that a choice between a buying group that now accounts for, at best, 10% of divisional volume and six major distributors that account for over 60% of sales should favor the distributors. Fewer still are willing to grant the private-label demand. At this point, I like to summarize the majority opinion and then pose the following scenario:

> It's August 15, and you return to APG's offices on the fifteenth floor of a building in Chicago. You present your final proposal to Wilson: a 5% to 10% price reduction from your last proposal but little difference from the last proposal concerning distribution and branding.
>
> Wilson listens to the details, and then politely responds: "Thank you very much, but our own position remains unchanged. Negotiations are over, and the contract will go to (a competing firm) that has agreed to all of our requests. Can I call a cab to take you back to the airport?"
>
> Given this outcome, what should Kozy and Smith do now? What will Wilson be doing by the time their elevator travels from the fifteenth floor down to the lobby?

This scenario helps to underline a managerial reality: It will not be pleasant for the chief sales and marketing managers to return to Newark without this large contract, regardless of the terms. Biting the bullet may sometimes be necessary, but it never makes for a good meal. The final questions help to crystallize the market and company analyses inherent in the case.

Most students note that Kozy and Smith's first actions should probably be to notify their sales managers and large distributors, and have them issue an all-points alert to the field: Make appointments as soon as possible with lab and (if possible) administrative personnel at all accounts that belong to APG; remind them of VACUTAINER's product performance, and judge what potential price reductions may be required to maintain the business. In effect, BDVS must again defend its position in a manner similar to its 1982 battle (case pages 16-17). Conversely, Wilson will undoubtedly contact administrative personnel at all APG-member hospitals, distributors affiliated with APG, the company awarded the contract, and perhaps the trade press, in order to publicize this "showcase program" (case page 17). He will urge them to contact lab personnel as soon as possible and explain the cost and potential operating benefits of working within the purchasing agreement negotiated by APG. In coming months, this agreement probably will also be highlighted in those APG programs that "brought together doctors, nurses, and administrators from different hospitals to discuss cost-reduction opportunities and develop specific action plans. The program allowed member hospitals to compare their costs by product line, therapy type, and department" (case page 16).

Who will win this battle? In 1982, BDVS won by rallying the bench people and cutting price selectively. But that was before the 1983 DRG legislation and its subsequent impact on cost-consciousness at hospitals. This scenario often helps to clarify the opposing forces at work in this case, to underline the issue of buyer power inherent in the situation, and to generate a discussion that focuses on the forces that can build and erode a company's channel power.[1] Further, a revote after

---

[1]Here, it may be noted that the academic marketing literature on channel power has generally treated this aspect of manufacturer-distributor relations in zero-sum terms. That is, the literature assumes a fixed level of total power and a negative relationship between each party's power. This zero-sum approach follows from the literature's definition of power as dependence. (For a good, still-pertinent review of the literature, see John F. Gaski, "The Theory of Power and Conflict in Channels of Distribution," *Journal of Marketing*, Summer 1984, pp. 9-29.)

The BDVS case, however, indicates how much more complex channel power is. In this situation, BDVS's power relative to its largest distributors has increased significantly, since it can affect those distributors' access to a large and valued account. But BDVS's total power (its power irrespective of its power relative to its distributors) has probably decreased, due to the increasing clout of buying groups. Traditional this discussion often reveals a significantly different set of opinions concerning what BDVS should, and should not, be prepared to offer APG.

What Happened

This is one case where interest in what happened is usually high and where discussing the outcome can be instructive. BDVS came to an agreement with APG that involved making significant price reductions beyond those in its August 1 proposal on the condition that APG "deliver" 90% of its member hospitals' requirements for tubes and needles. The agreement specified that these products would be identified as BDVS brand and not APG private-label. Contract fulfillment would be through BDVS-franchised distributors, although BDVS also agreed to consider a number of APG-affiliated distributors for addition to its current distribution network.

---

conceptualizations of channel power cannot deal with these facets of the situation, which are not uncommon in industrial markets. But these power circumstances clearly are vital to the participants involved and shape their strategic and tactical channels decisions.

Exhibit TN-1 Becton Dickinson & Company: VACUTAINER Systems Division
APG Contract: Economic Analysis

I. Cost of Winning the APG Contract at 20% Price Reduction

Assume that all Z-contract prices will have to be lowered to meet this new price with a large, visible buying group such as APG:

- "By 1985 most BDVS blood collection products and approximately 20% of the division's capillary and microbiology products, were sold through Z contracts" (case page 15).

    - Assume 100% of VACUTAINER sales will be affected and that decreasing prices by 20% will result in decreased net income by the same amount. Since VACUTAINER represents 70% of BDVS sales and 33% of divisional net income (case page 3), the effect will be:

        20% x 33% = 6.6% reduction in divisional net income

        20% x 70% = 14% reduction in divisional sales volume

    - Assume 20% of capillary and microbiology sales will be affected. These two product lines represent 30% of divisional sales and 66% of net income. A conservative estimate is that since Z contracts represent 20% of sales, they also represent 20% of net income. (This is conservative because "often Z contract prices with large buying groups were 30% to 40% lower than list prices" (case page 14); and only 20% of these product lines' sales are covered by Z contracts). A 20% price reduction would then mean:

        20% x 20% x 66% = 2.6% reduction in divisional net income

        20% x 20% x 30% = 1.2% reduction in divisional sales volume

        Total reduction in net income = 9.2%

        Total reduction in sales volume = 15.2%

Note: These estimates may be offset by increasing BDVS's share of APG business from 80% to 90%, especially its share of needles purchased by APG hospitals.

II. Cost of Losing the APG Contract

The worst case would be a loss of the entire APG-member sales volume with BDVS of $6 million. Hence, $6 million/$90 million x .7 = 9.5% reduction in sales volume.

Assuming that APG hospitals (which have been sold on an individual basis by BDVS) buy BDVS products in the same percentages as typical BDVS customers and at average prices, then a 9.5% reduction in sales volume represents approximately a 9.5% reduction in net income.

Note: While it is unlikely that BDVS will lose all of its business with APG hospitals if it does not reach a contract agreement with APG, it is also likely that BDVS would still have to reduce prices to individual APG hospitals in order to retain the business. Hence, the result is likely to be similar to the estimates provided in the above scenario.

Exhibit TN-2 Becton Dickinson & Company: VACUTAINER Systems Division
Entangling Alliances

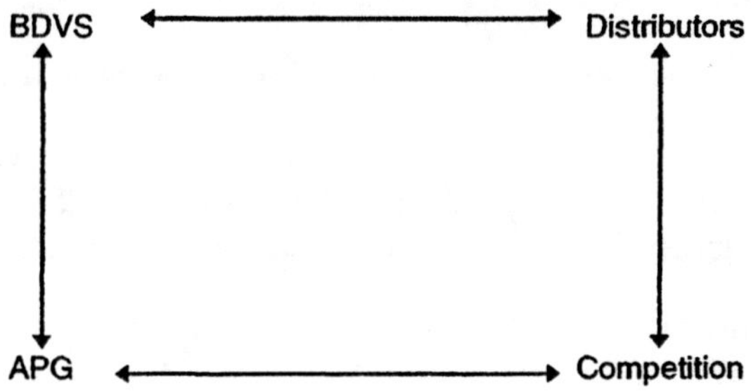

BDVS's response to APG must consider:

- Balance of Power
  - Now
  - Future
- Impact of Contract Terms
  - On BDVS's Position with User-Customers
  - On BDVS's Position with Distribution Network
- Impact on Nature of Value BDVS Provides
  - Product Performance
  - Product Line Breadth
  - Delivery Network for Broad Product Line

CVS: The Web Strategy

Teaching Note

Synopsis

CVS, a major drugstore chain, buys Soma.com, one of three pure-play online drugstores founded in the first half of 1999. At the level of retail detail, the case is about how to integrate Soma into the CVS retail store and direct mail system. There are decisions to be made about whether the online operation must conform to the chain's policies on branding, merchandise assortment, pricing and so on, or whether it should deviate from these policies to more fully exploit the medium. At the industry level, the case is about the effects of information technology on the balance of power in the healthcare market. A policy clash between CVS.com and a pharmacy benefit manager, Merck-Medco, serves to show how market power is shifting as better information becomes available to the drug supply chain.

Uses

This case can be used to teach consumer behavior, if the discussion concentrates on the retail integration questions. It shows how entrenched consumer habits become a drag on new business creation. It was easy in 1999 to envision an online drugstore, but few saw how difficult it would be to motivate customers to visit one. Online shopping meshes badly with the buying process for drugs for acute, urgent medical conditions. For chronic conditions, the fit is closer but still far from perfect. The mail order drug store, Merck-Medco, was better placed to succeed. It did not have to initiate a new behavior, merely to shift the behavior of its customer base from direct mail to the Internet. This careful mapping of channel characteristics into buying habits can be surprisingly informative to students, particularly to those who think that they would never fall for the cavalier consumer behavior assumptions made by so many failed dot.com ventures.

The case can also be used to teach industrial organization from a marketing perspective. The health care industry, and particularly the part that depends on drug therapies, is a delicate balance of market and public policy forces. The case allows a class to try to map these forces, and then invites a discussion of what happens when the Internet disturbs the balance among them. Tension in the case arises from the apparent vulnerability of drugstores and their distributors to disintermediation, and the less obvious strength of the old economy intermediaries who control reimbursement through alliances with insurance plans. Most classes will contain passions on both sides of the issue of vulnerability and invulnerability.

This note was prepared by Professor John Deighton for the sole purpose of aiding classroom instructors in the use of CVS: The Web Strategy, HBS No. 500-008. Some contributions from Professor Carolyn Yoon of the University of Michigan is acknowledged. The teaching note provides analysis and questions that are intended to present alternative approaches to deepening students' comprehension of business issues and energizing classroom discussion.

Possible Discussion Questions

1. At the time of the case, the revenues of online drugstores would have been lost in the rounding error of CVS's income statement. Yet the stock market valued them in the billions. Investors seemed to think that the drugstore industry could be "Amazoned" by Internet-based stores. A few months later, investors thought exactly the opposite. When were they right – then or now? All it would take for e-pharmacies to really hurt the market capitalizations of conventional pharmacies would be for 10% of the revenues of brick-and-mortar drugstores to be lost to the Internet over the next two years. Can you imagine such a scenario? If not, move on to the next question. If yes, list the things that must happen for that scenario to occur.

2. Who is the most powerful player in the prescription pharmaceutical distribution process? The manufacturer? The physician? The PBM? The MCO? The employer? The drug store? The patient? The government? How might that player use the Internet to become even more powerful?

3. How closely should CVS integrate CVS.com into its business? What is your point of view on the choices posed at the end of the case. Should the merchandise strategy on line be identical or different to the store strategy? Would you stock cosmetics? Greeting cards? Electronic greeting cards? Should online pricing conform to store pricing? How about orders placed on line and picked up in a store?

4. What would you do if you were in charge of CVS.com and had to respond to the demands of Merck-Medco?

Teaching the Case

Four blocks of discussion are suggested here. The discussion has a tendency to sprawl unless it is confined quite carefully to these blocks, and this order is probably a good idea.

Block 1

What is the size of the potential market for an online drug chain? Where's the threat to CVS's offline business?

Map out the steps in filling a prescription, and get the class to consider the three candidate sources of online revenue in the light of these steps.

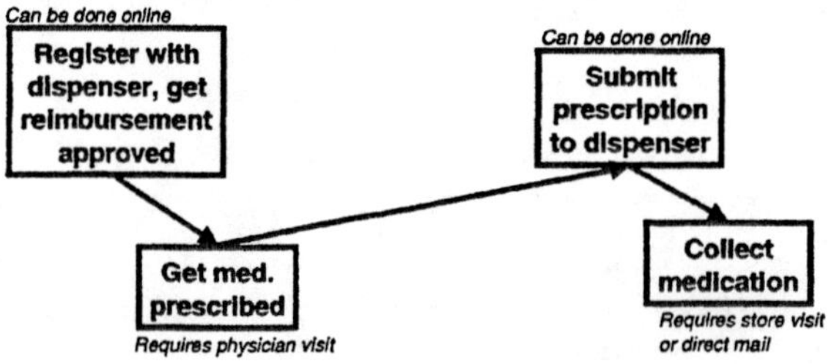

1. *Will patients fill* ***acute*** *prescriptions online? ($50 billion revenue)*

Because the patient has an acute problem, the need here is for same-day service. If patient *is not* registered with the site, no market exists as registration takes 2 days. If patient *is* registered, he or she will want to pick up the medication rather than wait for overnight delivery. The Internet therefore offers no particular advantage to the patient (can submit the prescription online, which might be marginally more appealing than using a telephone, but still has to pick up at store). The store has no incentive to drive its customers to the Web to submit prescriptions if that's not their inclination. The PBM, having no store to solve the problem of speedy pick-up, is not interested in the acute market. *Conclusion*: Not a prospect.

2. *Will patients fill **chronic** prescriptions online? ($50 billion revenue)*

From the patient's point of view, there may be some interest in having chronic medication delivered rather than picked up in stores, but the PBMs have been working hard and successfully to convert insured people to mail order. A third of the chronic medication taken by insured people is already going by mail, and it's the fastest-growing sector of the industry. (Every time a PBM moves a customer from retail to mail order, a drugstore loses the business.) Does the Web have any advantage over direct mail for the patient? Certainly not with respect to receipt of the medicines, as they both ship by mail. It may be marginally easier to place the order at a Website than over the phone, but the gains are minimal, and surely not sufficient to drive consumers to this channel.

There is one niche that may respond to the Web, and that is the people behind the 11% or $11 billion's worth of prescriptions bought at retail and paid for by patients (Exhibit 5). Note that the conversion of these uninsured patients to mail order is much lower (2:11) than insured patients (12:25). Why? The PBMs have had no incentive to convert them because of course the drugs they buy don't pass through a PBM's hands. These drugs move directly from manufacturer to drugstore. Drugstores had no incentive to convert them because they did not want to channel business away from their stores. Now someone does have a wish to convert them. The pure play online drugstores have their sights set on this market, because they can undercut drugstore prices by the cost of the store network. To the extent that they succeed, CVS will have to retaliate by moving its uninsured customers to the Web, but at the cost of cannibalization. *Conclusion*: A defensive move may be necessary.

3. *Will patient/shopper buy front-store items online? ($41 billion revenue)*

If they were buying prescription drugs online, perhaps consumers might be intercepted. If not, they use drugstores as specialist convenience stores for OTC's, cosmetics, photography, etc. *Conclusion:* Not a significant market.

Overall conclusion: At best CVS can attempt to convert uninsured chronic drug consumers to the Web for their prescription and front-store revenues, but only as a defensive move in the event that the pure plays thrive.

- ## Block 2

Where is the power in the pharmaceutical industry? Who decides who gets what medication? Who has the most incentive to drive efficiency in the distribution process? Who has the most incentive to keep health care costs down?

The objective in this block of the discussion is to get the class to come up with the elements of Exhibit A and start to see that there is more at stake here than simply defending CVS's revenues against pure play dot.com incursions. The picture does not emerge easily. If the class is reluctant to take a position on the first question, start probing with the patient and move to the left on the diagram below. Does the patient have power to choose which drugs they consume? No, except to the extent that they make suggestions to physicians. The physician? Constrained by formularies. The pharmacy? Constrained by prescriptions. The PBM? Powerful, but ultimately works for employers, charged with keeping total healthcare costs down. The employer? Here's the seat of power, thanks to the linking of healthcare insurance to employment. Build the flow of power in the prescription drug industry back from the patient to the employer (Exhibit A).

The Exhibit shows that power has devolved from physician to PBM and ultimately to the employer, who contracts with the MCO/PBM to deliver healthy employees at reasonable cost. What gets in the way of reducing employer healthcare costs? The price of prescription drugs, yes, but preoccupation with drug prices might be just a quick fix. You might draw the class's attention to this passage on page 2 of the case: "It was the view of some in the drugstore industry that PBMs and MCOs tended to focus on line item budget management and see prescriptions as a large component of rising health costs, when a broader system-wide view might suggest other ways to reduce costs." Ask what a system-wide view might see?

One big answer is poor patient compliance with drug regimes and poor physician compliance with recommended treatment routines in chronic conditions. For example, an employee with hypertension who fails to take medication can end up in the emergency room at great cost to the employer. Diabetes is another chronic condition whose cost rockets if compliance is poor.

Exhibit A: Power in the Chronic Prescription Drug Distribution System.

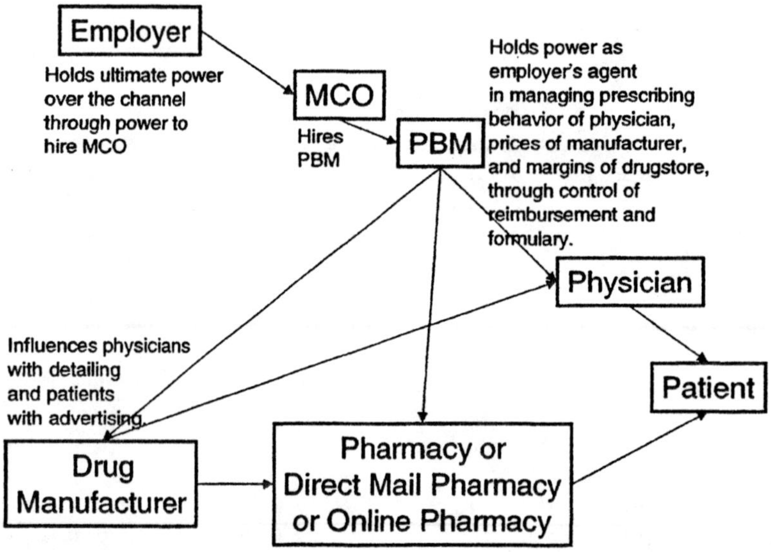

Information on drug consumption and physician prescribing practices can be very helpful to PBMs if they want to intervene to manage employer costs. The Internet supplies a digital trail on prescribing and renewal data, and more important, for communicating one-to-one messages to motivate compliance with treatment plans. So here's the twist – the most important consumer of the benefits of an Internet drugstore is not the end-user of medications, but the employer, who values it as a communication channel to monitor and encourage compliance.

However much employers may want consumers to convert to the Internet channel, is there anything they can do to accelerate diffusion? It may help to consider a recent, very large shift in consumer buying, the adoption of direct mail. It's very important to explore the reasons for the rise in use of direct mail at this stage in the class discussion, and to plant the possibility that the adoption of direct mail is the precursor to the adoption of the Internet channel. The growth of direct mail from zero to 25% of chronic sales was led mainly by Merck-Medco, a merger that put together in one organization the power of a manufacturer, a PBM and a retailer. It happened only in the chronic category, and the reason it happened was to control costs, not to deliver customer value. How did drugstores feel about direct mail? They were furious. It came at the expense of CVS along with the whole pharmacy category, but there was little they could do about it. Now it seems as if the PBM/employer alliance may see value in forcing the pace of growth of another channel, the Internet, and CVS does not want to lose out again.

At the end of this block, try to summarize with the question, 'So why did CVS buy Soma?'

• To grow it rapidly?	Unlikely. Tough to acquire traffic, not a good category for e-retailing.
• To pre-empt the pure play dot.coms?	The threat exists in the uninsured patient category, but it is a long-term threat now that dot.coms are being deprived of funding.
• To fight the incursion of direct mailers into pharmacy territory?	A real threat, but how can CVS.com be used to fight it off?
• Can CVS attack through front-store sales?	This would be an advertising-intensive strategy, expensive. But perhaps CVS can build a one-to-one learning relationship into its site.
• Can CVS attack through chronic prescription sales?	More plausible. A small number of chronic-condition employees make up a large part of health care costs. The Internet permits us to monitor and influence compliance with drug therapies, particularly among patients requiring complex and expensive drug therapy programs. (Note subsequent to the case CVS launched ProCare, a specialty offline pharmacy company targeting this segment.)

Block 3

Can CVS build a one-to-one learning relationship into the front-store experience?

This is a block of discussion that tries to maximize the potential of an interactive drugstore concept. The opportunities are real, but they are predicated on store traffic. In other words, an online drugstore probably has many ways to deliver exceptional customer service and retain trialists, but can it acquire them at a reasonable cost?

What would you do with the greeting cards category if you were not afraid of hurting your store traffic? What would you do to sell cosmetics if you knew the customer well? How does a department store cosmetics counter sell? Can this selling process be moved to a Web interface? How would you become indispensable in OTC medications? How would you integrate with iVillage's pregnancy calendar? What other community sites would you seek out as partners? How would the partnership work?

Block 4

What should CVS do about the impasse with Merck-Medco?

The significance of the conflict between CVS and Merck-Medco is revealed. Merck-Medco is refusing to budge on reimbursement because it is locked in a strategic conflict with CVS. It's a battle between a PBM and a retailer to deliver to employers a reliable system of compliance management that gets employees suffering from expensive chronic conditions like arthritis or hypertension or diabetes to adopt appropriate treatment plans. The PBM's advantage is that it has direct mail relationships with most of the key employees. CVS has to start from scratch to build relationships with these customers.

What Happened?

The attached *Wall Street Journal* article shows that CVS capitulated in the face of the cost of competing with PBMs from scratch, and ceded the prescription business to Merck-Medco, in exchange for an agreement to become the exclusive front-store to Merck-Medco's dispensary.

In 2000 CVS.com and Drugstore.com had revenues in the range of $20 - $40 million a year, while Merck-Medco filled $500 million in on-line prescriptions and aims to double it in 2001.

Attachment

How Merck Unit Beat Dot-coms In Web Foray

***The Wall Street Journal*, 04/13/2000**

By Gardiner Harris
Staff Reporter of *The Wall Street Journal*
The Wall Street Journal B1 (Copyright (c) 2000, Dow Jones & Company, Inc.)
LAS VEGAS, Nev.

Stand in the middle of Merck-Medco's giant mail-order pharmacy here, and you will hear the gears of the Old Economy grinding against the New -- and knocking out some of the New Economy's teeth.

Merck-Medco, a division of venerable Merck & Co., is just the kind of stodgy, paper-dependent company that pesky Internet start-ups were supposed to crush. Its core business, after all, involves reimbursing pharmacies for insured drug purchases and dispensing prescriptions by snail mail. Lightning-fast Internet traffic was supposed to supplant such cumbersome and expensive transactions. But while Web rivals that started up last year amid much fanfare are struggling, Merck-Medco is thriving. It now has its own Web site, and its Internet sales dwarf those of its Net competitors.

Unlike its new rivals, Merck-Medco has managed to dive into the Internet and make money doing it. The number of transactions on the company's Web site increased tenfold last year. Meanwhile, Drugstore.com, a rival that was built with money from some of the New Economy's brainiest people, including Amazon.com's Jeff Bezos and Microsoft's Paul Allen, is burning through its capital at a gold-fever clip.

The Rubik's Cube complexity of the U.S. health-care system helps explain Merck-Medco's success. Even computer geeks have had trouble figuring it out.

But Merck-Medco's success is also part of a growing counterattack by old-line companies on Internet start-ups. The start-ups took for granted that they would make billions snatching sales from old-line companies that weren't on the Net. But old-line companies haven't always cooperated, and many are unveiling Internet strategies of their own this year. Creating an Internet site, it turns out, is the easy part. Getting customers to frequent it is the challenge. As a result, the ability to market an

Internet site to an established customer base has become an ace in the hole for Old Economy companies.

Medco was started in 1969 by union seamstresses who hoped to save pennies on their long-term prescriptions by having them mailed in bulk. The company soon merged with a pharmacy-benefit manager, or PBM, a contractor hired by health insurers and employers to track and control the distribution of drugs. Merck, which is based in Whitehouse Station, N.J., bought the company in 1993.

Most of the work of PBMs – Merck-Medco, PCS and Express Scripts are the giants in the field – involves striking deals with pharmacists and employers. Pharmacists sell prescription drugs to eligible consumers for small fees – usually $5 to $10 co-pays – and PBMs pay the balance out of insurance proceeds. If the PBM doesn't approve the sale –usually because the drug isn't on an approved list called a "formulary" – the customer, insured or not, has to pay the drug's full price. PBMs also have a corner on 90-day bulk prescriptions mailed to patients with chronic medical conditions.

Most customers have no idea a PBM is involved in their drug purchases. Certainly some of the people who launched the early Internet drug sites underestimated PBMs' importance. Peter Neupert, the CEO of Drugstore.com, boasted early last year that his site woul dquickly capture billions in sales from bricks-and-mortar pharmacies by offering better service and privacy. Others predicted the Internet start-ups would do to pharmacies whatAmazon.com is doing to book stores.

But the PBMs responded to the threat of Drugstore.com and the others by simply refusing to deal with them. In the early days, many customers who tried to buy drugs online found that they couldn't get reimbursed. Since roughly 80% of drug sales are handled through PBMs, that cost the Internet sites a huge slice of their target market.

It was also a strategy that infuriated the Internet sites, and they responded by partnering with PBMs. Drugstore.com sold 25% of itself to Rite-Aid, which owns PCS. PlanetRx sold20% of itself to Express Scripts. Hundreds of other drug sites that operate in a legal shadow and sell only a few drugs, like Viagra, were unaffected because such purchases usually aren't reimbursed.

Per Lofberg, Merck-Medco's chairman, says he knew that simply refusing to reimburse Internet drug transactions would work for only a short time. Customers would eventually demand Internet service, and he would have to deliver it or lose them. Faced with the choice of finding a partner or building his own integrated Internet site, Mr. Lofberg took the plunge into site development.

It's a strategy that many other old-line companies have tried without success. But Mr. Lofberg says his company had a key advantage: He is deeply paranoid. "We realized that if we didn't move fast, we'd be in trouble," he says.

A more concrete advantage was that Merck-Medco had recently started investing heavily to improve its mail-order service. Although mail-order prescriptions are the most profitable part of its business, few customers were taking advantage of the service because orders took weeks to arrive.

To speed up the process, Merck-Medco began building an automated drug warehouse in Las Vegas, Nev., in 1994. The building – a combined phone, pharmacy and shipping facility – took three years, $85 million and some very high-tech engineering to construct. Mailed new prescriptions and phoned-in refills are now processed by scores of employees upstairs. Pharmacists check the orders for accuracy and call doctors with questions. Then they punch a button that sends cascades of pills through tubes that end in bottles downstairs.

The bottles and accompanying literature are dropped into bags, addressed and plopped in the mail. For 75% of prescriptions, the entire dispensing and packing process is automated. The rest -- specialty creams, injections and rare pills -- are dispensed by teams of pharmacists. The machines fill roughly 5,000 bottles an hour. Even though they have dispensed millions of orders over the years, the company says, they have never sent the wrong pills.

Equally important, the company set up three calling centers across the country and negotiated with state pharmacy boards to allow prescriptions to be written in one state and dispensed in another.

All this shortened order turnarounds from two weeks to, at most, two days. Nearly three-quarters of all orders are shipped the same day they are received, the company says.

Now, Merck-Medco is constructing a second automated drug warehouse in Willingboro,N.J.

Of course, mailed prescriptions may never overtake the ones that are filled at pharmacies. One reason is that many prescriptions -- perhaps a third -- are needed by patients who can't wait for the mail. Another is the difficulty of getting a paper prescription to the drug provider. Even with faxes, it takes time and effort. Merck-Medco has launched a pilot program in which 2,000 doctors are using Palm Pilots to send electronic prescriptions, but widespread use of such digital tools is probably a long way off.

Still, the mailed prescription market is growing 22% annually and accounted for more than10% of the $125.9 billion U.S. prescription market in 1999, according to IMS Health. Covering nearly a quarter of the U.S. population, Merck-Medco makes money no matter how its customers fill their prescriptions. But if customers cut out the corner pharmacy and use mail order instead, Merck-Medco makes more and employers spend less. Profits and savings are even higher when customers order over the Internet, because Internet transactions are cheaper than phone, mail or fax transactions.

To encourage Web use, Merck-Medco has continuously enriched its site. At Merck-Medco.com, consumers can now get targeted health information, reminders about refills, summaries of their previous orders and detailed descriptions of their insurance-plan benefits. The company plans to offer over-the-counter products on the site soon, and it will allow people who aren't affiliated with it to order products as well.

Nearly 20% of Merck-Medco's customer transactions are now done over the internet -- a ratio the company expects to grow to as much as 75%. This has been accomplished through a bare-bones marketing effort -- brochures in prescription bags, links on employer Web sites -- that cost it almost nothing. Drugstore.com, on the other hand, is spending millions on advertising.

The result: Drugstore.com monthly gets nearly four times as many visitors asMerck-Medco.com, or 1.4 million compared with 352,000, according to Media Metrix, an independent counting firm. But Merck-Medco.com books nearly eight times as much in prescription sales as Drugstore.com quarterly, according to the two companies.

"They generate more visits than we do, but if you can't convert that to cash, who cares?" says Stephen Gold, Merck-Medco's Internet chief.

Mr. Neupert of Drugstore.com says Merck-Medco's Internet strategy is flawed because it is designed to save Merck-Medco money, not serve customers. He predicted that customers will eventually lobby their employers to force Merck-Medco to support the use of Drugstore.com. "Economics control the business. The question is, Who controls the economics?" Mr. Neupert says. "I think it's employees, and employers listen to employees."

Mr. Lofberg says only a handful of employers have ever asked about using sites likeDrugstore.com. As soon as Mr. Lofberg explains the benefits of Merck-Medco's own Internet site, he says, they never mention the Internet pure-plays again.

Mr. Neupert responds that Drugstore.com, as a partner of Rite-Aid, is now able to get Merck-Medco and other PBMs to reimburse his customers, just as any Rite-Aid store does. But Mr. Lofberg denies that, saying Merck-Medco's contracts with Rite-Aid explicitly deny reimbursement for mailed orders such as those sent through Drugstore.com.

In any case, a Drugstore.com spokeswoman says her company has forced the PBMs to change more than the PBMs have forced Drugstore.com to change. Mr. Lofberg happily agreed with this analysis, saying he is willing to reinvent Merck-Medco completely to meet the challenges it faces. As for the Internet entrepreneurs, he says, they assumed theAmazon.com model would work in any industry.

"They had such an easy time getting backers for any idea, maybe they didn't take the necessary care to look at the market," he adds.

5-503-107
JUNE 17, 2003

TEACHING NOTE

Pepcid AC: Racing to the OTC Market

Substantive Issues

Managers at the Johnson & Johnson/Merck Consumer Pharmaceuticals Co. (JJM) are deciding how to introduce a new over-the-counter (OTC) heartburn remedy. Pepcid had been available by prescription for some time, and JJM was following the trend begun in the 1980s of switching a drug to OTC status before its patent expired. The FDA's advisory group has just recommended against allowing JJM to claim that Pepcid in its lower-strength over-the-counter form (Pepcid AC) prevented and relieved heartburn. JJM knew that Pepcid AC's competitors, SmithKline Beecham's Tagamet, Eli Lilly's Axid, and Glaxo Wellcome's Zantac, would be available OTC within months of one another, so speed to market was a significant concern. The case allows the students to analyse the market strategy that JJM pursued in making Pepcid's OTC switch.

Pedagogical Objectives

1. Establish the relationship among positioning, differentiation, and segmentation. Positioning is the sum of differentiation in the mind of the consumer and segmentation, the choice of the proper target market segments.
2. Introduce the concept of life cycle management through the idea that sales of Pepcid, at the end of its life as a prescription drug, will be rejuvenated by the switch to OTC.
3. Explore the annuity value of an OTC product. OTC market shares are "sticky" and even a 1% share, as the net present value of a future stream of income, is a substantial amount in this market.
4. Determine how positioning affects market size. Using the prevention attribute allows Pepcid to create an expanded category.
5. Consider first mover advantage.

This note was prepared by Professors Charles King III and Alvin Silk, and Research Associate Ann Leamon for the sole purpose of aiding classroom instructors in the use of Pepcid AC: Racing to the OTC Market, HBS No. 500-073. It provides analysis and questions that are intended to present alternative approaches to deepening students' comprehension of business issues and energizing classroom discussion. HBS cases are developed solely as the basis for class discussion. Cases are not intended to serve as endorsements, sources of primary data, or illustrations of effective or ineffective management.

Opportunities for Student Analysis

This case provides a rich context for discussing many strategic issues, such as the life cycle management of drugs and the role of joint ventures, in addition to market strategy. This note will focus on the marketing aspects of the problem, but also discuss aspects of the larger picture.

What should JJM do?

A good way to start the discussion is to ask, "What should JJM do?" The FDA's advisors have delivered bad news—they don't see that Pepcid AC is particularly effective at either treatment or prevention of heartburn. The instructor may want to remind students that the FDA's OTC approvals are very limited. Once a claim is approved for a certain dose and a given condition, it could not be adapted to respond to competing claims or the positioning of later rivals without a formal approval process for a new claim. JJM has three possible responses, which the students should mention:

1. **Approach FDA directly and request approval for Pepcid AC just as a treatment for heartburn.** This may be easier to get through the FDA, as prevention requires more understanding and forethought on the part of consumers but could lead to misuse or overuse of the product. With a more direct "cause and effect" connection, with the patients taking the medication to ease a defined condition, approval for a treatment claim may be less risky, especially since the antacids currently available OTC all claim to treat (but not prevent) heartburn. In addition, the results of the BASES concept test favor the claim for treatment as opposed to prevention.

   Drawbacks to this strategy include the flip sides of some of the benefits. The OTC antacids and the H_2-receptor antagonists on their way to OTC all claim to treat heartburn and indigestion. The field is crowded and treatment does not expand the category into new usages or to new customers. The other problem is that Pepcid AC just is not particularly good at treatment. Like the other H_2-receptor antagonists, Pepcid AC takes 30 to 60 minutes to become effective. This is hardly "Pop, pop, fizz, fizz/Oh what a relief it is." Antacids, on the other hand, grant relief in three to 10 minutes.

2. **Approach FDA directly and request approval for Pepcid both as treatment and prevention for heartburn.** This strategy would give Pepcid AC greater differentiation, as a product that prevented heartburn in addition to treating it. If Pepcid AC were first to market, so much the better. If it were not, having the prevention claim would allow it to compete against whatever H_2-receptor antagonist was already there. With the new use and new applications (use before a meal rather than after, something that antacids could not duplicate), Pepcid would have expanded the category into new areas. The category expansion would reduce the impact of Pepcid AC's inevitable cannibalization of both prescription Pepcid and OTC Mylanta.

   This strategy definitely presents increased risk. Given the advisory group's adverse recommendation, it will be more difficult to get the FDA to approve prevention in addition to treatment. Preventative use of Pepcid AC might also mask serious symptoms, an issue of great concern to the doctors who might recommend that patients use the OTC product instead of either a competing OTC treatment or a prescription medication.

3. **Gather more research and approach the advisory board or the FDA at a later point.** The advisory board would much prefer this approach. JJM might indeed obtain better data

through more exhaustive studies, and Tagamet had also been sent back to get more data. The FDA and its advisors would probably be impressed with the company's diligence.

This approach, though, was costly in both time and money. In addition, while Tagamet had been temporarily stalled, Axid and Zantac were also moving quickly toward OTC status. Lastly, JJM believed the data were sufficient to warrant approval. This is important, as Merck prides itself on its reputation as an ethical drug maker.

Why switch Pepcid, anyway?

Once the class has discussed the previous points, the instructor can ask why the company is going through such turmoil in the first place. After all, new prescription drugs took an average of eight years just to get through the FDA's initial approval process. Pepcid was patent-protected for another six years.

In the final analysis, JJM has little choice in the matter. With Tagamet off-patent and generics in the market, the entire class of H_2-receptor antagonists is threatened. Tagamet's U.S. sales had dropped by over $200 million under pressure from generics. Zantac's patent expired in 1997, bringing more generics into the fray. Sales of the remaining prescription-only drugs, Pepcid and Axid, would fall with the increasing availability of OTC and generic versions. Because of the close substitutability of the four H_2-receptor antagonists, Tagamet's patent expiration marked, for all intents and purposes, the end of protection for the entire class of drugs.

There are also benefits to switching to OTC, as drug sales often rose dramatically. In addition, these OTC sales can extend for years into the future, providing an annuity stream.

A useful follow-on question is whether the optimal time to switch is the same for all four drugs. The answer would be no. Zantac, with its market-leading share of high-priced prescriptions, would be better served to remain prescription-only for as long as possible. Pepcid, on the other hand, has barely 20% of the prescription market and thus far less to lose and more to gain.

Students may next consider the question of what would be cannibalized—sales of other prescription medications or of OTC antacids. If sales of Pepcid AC cannibalize not only prescription sales (instead of taking one prescription pill, doctors might have patients take two of the OTC version) but also sales of JJM's antacid, Mylanta, the company might lose more than it expects. In fact, the instructor might ask why JJM bought Mylanta if it was planning to switch Pepcid.

The response touches on the issue of positioning that is central to the case. JJM began clinical trials on Pepcid in 1990, so in 1989, it must have had a good idea of its intended positioning for the product. But Mylanta, with the #4 spot in OTC antacid sales, gave JJM legitimacy in the antacid market. In addition, if JJM could prove that Pepcid AC was effective for prevention as well as treatment, the firm would be in two market segments, not just one. It could tie into Mylanta's history as a claim of legitimacy. This was a pretty large bet, as there was no guarantee that the FDA would approve Pepcid AC's prevention claim, but it positioned the company well to compete if the claim was approved. Finally, JJM contemplated a combined product, Mylanta AC, with the immediate relief of an antacid and the long-term relief of an H_2-receptor antagonist. The acquisition also gave JJM a significant portfolio of OTC products, which enhanced its presence in the OTC market.

Positioning Pepcid

The first question to consider in positioning Pepcid AC is "with whom?" The company has to identify the target market segment, which in this case includes users of antacids and/or prescription ulcer medications.

Having decided which group to target, the instructor could ask what the company should do next. JJM set out to learn as much as possible about who was in the market and how they interacted with the product. A vast majority of antacid users were at least somewhat satisfied with their current products. Women and adults over 50 were the most frequent antacid users, and heavy users made up 25% of the antacid-using population. The prescription H_2-receptor antagonist users and the antacid users did, however, differ in the way they used their product. Prescription users had learned they could prevent the onset of symptoms by taking the product regularly, while antacid users only used their product to treat existing stomach discomfort.

Students next should examine what the concept tests shows about treatment as opposed to prevention. It is noteworthy that BASES was a process that Johnson & Johnson, not Merck, had used. Here is an example, which may be referenced later, of the benefits of a strategic alliance. While Merck undoubtedly knew everything about drug research, Johnson & Johnson knew about consumer research.

If there is time, the instructor may ask the class to describe the BASES I and II protocols to get the salient differences on the board. These would include:

1. BASES I tests the consumers' reactions to the product concept, including both what types of consumers and how many will try it. Using a database of past product tests, BASES I can calibrate the concept scores and produce an estimated market share based on the trial rate times the repeat purchase rate. The repeat purchase rate is more than just a one-time event; it is the repurchase frequency over time. This requires BASES II research to establish.

2. BASES II tests the consumers' reactions not only to the concept but to the product itself. The four stage process includes interviewing mall intercepts to determine a population willing to participate; compiling consumer responses to a standard set of questions on product aspects such as like/dislike, value for money, and purchase intention (before-use data); distributing samples to use at home for those who would try it; and conducting follow-up interviews on the telephone to learn how consumers respond to the same list of questions having tried the product (after-use data).

The class will next discuss what the research found. In both BASES studies, treatment - long lasting relief - was more appealing to the consumers than the promise of prevention. Prevention was more important than treatment, though, for the existing prescription users. The students should explore why this might be and how JJM might evaluate this finding. The case mentions that prescription users have become accustomed to the more complex concept of prevention and value it more highly than do regular antacid users.

Overall, though, prevention appears to be more problematic as a marketing concept than is treatment. The students may want to investigate the reasons behind this, which might include the potential for masking symptoms of a more serious condition and, more importantly, unfamiliarity with the attribute. This is not how consumers are accustomed to taking their antacids. It involves more responsibility on their part, in anticipating a problem and planning for it.

The BASES II study also investigated the cannibalization of both prescription Pepcid and OTC Mylanta that might occur, and found that it would not be substantial. In fact, Pepcid AC surpassed the new (and lower) target for its sales even with the introduction of Mylanta AC, OTC Tagamet, and OTC Axid.

On the strength of these points, JJM would be justified in going to the FDA for treatment only. However, the focus groups and "head-nodder" research raised some questions—and emphasize the importance of outliers. To JJM, the head-nodders were particularly important in identifying concepts that had wide, immediate appeal. With these groups, although few understood the mechanics behind H_2-receptor antagonists, the term "Acid-Controller" as a shorthand for prevention could be grasped intuitively. The attributes of prevention *and* treatment seemed to resonate with these groups.

The class may also explore the relative merits of treatment as opposed to prevention positioning. Prevention certainly appealed to JJM because it opened a new market, provided new benefits, and offered new ways of using the product. A consumer might take Pepcid AC before eating just in case, yet never have truly needed to use it. Treatment, as noted earlier, was a widespread claim and less of a strength for Pepcid AC. It was, however, more intuitively comprehensible to the vast majority of antacid users. Additionally, the BASES research, for which JJM had paid dearly, validated treatment over prevention, even when the consumers had used the product.

From this follows the question, "What do we make of this conflict? Do we trust the positioning for such a high-stakes product to a bunch of ordinary people sitting in a room nodding their heads, or to a whiz-bang program with a fancy name and tons of data behind it?" Students may point out that the head-nodders had already given the researchers an important insight—"Acid Controller" was an intuitive and helpful description of how Pepcid AC worked. Perhaps that was enough?

At this point, the instructor may ask why JJM was interested in the pharmacists and medical community. After all, they were unlikely to use the products themselves. The students should mention that both play pivotal roles in the success of a drug as indirect consumers. Doctors, for instance, are concerned about their lost revenues if patients self-medicate, their lost control over patients' health care, and the efficacy of OTC medications. Patients might use Pepcid AC as a preventative treatment to mask symptoms of a more serious illness, finally coming to a doctor when the situation was advanced. At the same time, doctors were also under severe pressure from health-maintenance organizations to cut costs, and frequently faced severe time constraints. Converting some percentage of prescription patients to an OTC option, especially if they trusted that it performed well, might be a positive change. JJM's research had showed that 30% of physicians would convert their prescription ulcer medication patients to Pepcid AC.

Pharmacists were also important gatekeepers but required special handling. Research had shown they felt themselves neglected by the big pharmaceutical companies and wanted a greater role in patient counseling. Thus, JJM had to reinforce the pharmacists' role as counselor by making them comfortable in recommending Pepcid AC over competitors. JJM also had to ensure that the pharmacists had Pepcid AC in stock. Pharmacists had been hurt by lost sales when Aleve went OTC and they were slow to stock it. If discounters and grocery stores stocked Pepcid AC before the drugstores did, the drugstores would lose not just initial sales but repeat sales as consumers became convinced that "oh, that store doesn't carry it." In addition, drugstores would benefit from ancillary sales of high-margin food, cards, and cosmetics by increasing traffic.

The importance of the pharmacists in steering consumers toward or away from certain drugs is shown in the example of the United Kingdom. The instructor may ask the students to explore this. Because doctors had required pharmacy sales assistants to follow detailed instructions in selling the

OTC versions of Tagamet, Pepcid, and Zantac in the U.K., sales had languished. The sales assistants had urged consumers to use antacids, which were easier to sell, instead.

The class still has not answered the question of whether Pepcid AC should be positioned as a treatment or a prevention. The numbers may help.

How attractive is this opportunity?

By now, the class should understand that the attractiveness of the opportunity depends on the product's positioning. The instructor can ask what the implications are if Pepcid AC is positioned as a treatment. The key point here is that treatment offers little potential for category expansion. Prevention allows Pepcid AC to compete with *both* the antacid and the prescription categories, giving it a larger pool from which to draw. We know that 30% of doctors would recommend Pepcid AC for their existing prescription patients. Now we can get some numbers on the board.

The antacid market is $745 million (Table C on page 6 of the case). The prescription market is $2.9 billion (Table A on page 2 of the case). Thirty percent of H_2-users said they would replace their prescription product with Pepcid AC (page 10 of the case). Thus, Pepcid AC's potential market is Antacid + 30% of the Rx market, or $1.62 billion.

If Pepcid AC gains a 1% share of the market, it would have 1% * $1.62 billion, or $16.2 million. This is not too exciting.

But is Pepcid AC going to be a one-year phenomenon? No—that is part of the reason for the big advertising push. Consider the value Pepcid AC as an *annuity*. (Note the comments in the case about OTC shares being "reasonably stable" (page 6) and Listerine being 100 years old (page 3)!). Taking the net present value of $16.2 million per year at 10% yields $162 million for a 1% market share. Thus a 15% market share in the OTC market is worth $2.43 billion in net present value. Does that get your attention? Now compare this with the alternative in which Pepcid does not enter the OTC market.

If Pepcid stayed prescription only, let's see what happens to its sales when the generics take over. With 1994 sales of $384 million, and assuming the 40% sales drop that Tagamet experienced, Pepcid's sales would fall to $232 million. This is a 14% share of the market Pepcid AC can address (antacids plus 30% of the prescription market). From this, the students can conclude that the OTC market potential is as large or larger than that in prescription. But key to this is the prevention attribute, which allows Pepcid AC to access a far larger market than treatment (antacids) only.

How important is it to be first?

Of course, the numbers are great but how important is it to be first to market? A good way to start this part of the class is to ask, "What is first mover advantage?"

The ensuing discussion should touch upon several points. Specifically, the first mover can create a temporary monopoly, allowing it to build a temporary war chest to purchase or create line extensions or to devise a potent marketing campaign for differentiation. It can also build loyalty among customers, thus increasing switching costs. As an example, think of the number of people who take Advil, rather than its more awkwardly named generic, Ibuprofen. First movers can define preferences, becoming the preferred product. By signing exclusive distribution deals, a first mover can lock up distribution channels and create a barrier to entry. To become the provider of choice for

Wal-Mart, for instance, would confer a huge advantage. Lastly, a first mover can build a reputation as an innovator, especially if its product becomes established as the standard—consider Microsoft.

Is such an advantage sustainable? In some cases, such as becoming the new standard, the answer would be yes. But in many cases, first mover advantage is not sustainable in the long-term. If we look at the example in the case, first mover advantage did nothing to help Tagamet. Despite a later introduction and a higher price, Zantac overtook Tagamet both due to Glaxo's partnership with Hoffman LaRoche's sales force and to the product's characteristics of ease of use and reduced side effects.

This can move the class to consider second mover advantage. Advantages accruing to the second mover include the ability to research and copy the first mover's product and to allow market uncertainties to resolve themselves. In addition, a second mover can learn from earlier mistakes and target a more promising market, create a clearer message, or refine the product (for instance, Zantac's twice a day dosage was preferable to Tagamet's four-times-per-day regimen). Moreover, establishing new markets is expensive, as seen by Pepcid AC's first year marketing expenditure of $75 million. It might behoove a competitor to allow someone else to carry the cost of educating the public about the need for the product, and then arrive with a better solution to a problem that someone else has identified.

Here the instructor may want to ask particular individuals what they would do if they were first or second movers in the H_2-receptor antagonist market and record their responses on the board. First movers might spend large amounts on marketing, perform careful market research, and craft the broadest possible message to imply that this product has defined and claimed the market and that everything else is merely an imitator. Second movers may emphasize the need to show that the product is better than the initiator and offers a more comprehensive solution.

Follow-on questions can inquire about the probable reactions of competitors. How would Tagamet respond if Pepcid AC was first to market? Zantac? Axid? Tagamet and Zantac would likely play on their heritage as the prescription drugs with larger market shares than Pepcid's. Tagamet would say it was first in the market for prescriptions; Zantac that it was "the most recommended by physicians." Axid might proclaim that it was the newest, or did not have Pepcid AC's side effects (ignoring the fact that it had some of its own). All would probably try to speed their OTC versions to market to reduce Pepcid AC's first mover advantage (if indeed any existed).

A final question in this section is what is sustainable. In the end, the only sustainable advantage is having a product that performs well enough, is priced fairly, and is available widely enough that consumers do not feel a need to switch. Here the roles of the doctors and pharmacists come to play. If these parties are recommending against a product, enduring success would be difficult.

Competitive Strategy Context: Joint Ventures

If one is teaching this as part of a competitive strategy course, the preceding discussion may be compressed so that the one that follows can be examined. This is best inserted at the start of the class.

The Role of Joint Ventures: The instructor can ask what role joint ventures can play. In general, they help companies reach a common goal by leveraging one another's strengths in situations where each has complementary abilities. For instance, a manufacturer with knowledge of particular processes might team up with a Japanese firm to enter the market in Japan. Unlike JJM, few joint ventures have a 50/50 control split. Usually one is a more senior partner. This has interesting implications for the JJM venture.

From this, the class can look at the marriage of corporate cultures embodied in JJM. What made observers call it a "marriage made in heaven"? Students may point out the complementary strengths; Merck's in pharmaceutical R&D with its broad product portfolio, and Johnson & Johnson's in its marketing and sales operations. They may also mention the complementary weaknesses, especially in light of an OTC switch for one of Merck's major products. Merck lacked a strong consumer marketing and distribution focus. J&J had not introduced any new large volume products since Tylenol and its product pipeline was barren. Merck, then, had products that it wanted to get to consumers but little expertise in doing so; J&J could get things to consumers but had nothing to deliver. Each really did bring half to the table.

What Happened?

With Pepcid AC

JJM did go directly to the FDA and received approval to launch Pepcid AC as both a treatment for and prevention of heartburn. The formal launch occurred in June 1995. As expected, Tagamet entered six weeks later in August, and Zantac went to OTC in April 1996.

Pepcid AC was the most successful prescription-to-OTC switch in history, with the highest consumption of any switched product. It became the #3 OTC brand overall, and #2 in Wal-Mart, with the greatest number of SKUs of any OTC brand. In Q4 1997, Pepcid AC had a 43% dollar share of the acid reliever category. Note that it had created its own category!

The advertising campaign emphasized findings from the head-nodder research. The first campaign shifted the way that consumers thought about indigestion medication, focusing on its ability to prevent and control heartburn, to allow people to eat the foods they wanted to, and to provide relief for nine hours. Tagamet's launch played on its heritage as a leader in the prescription market. Pepcid's second phase painted Tagamet as an older drug, and thus less desirable.

First Mover Advantage

The instructor should also wrap up the first mover discussion. Conventional wisdom holds that first movers become market leaders in the long-term, citing such examples as Sony Walkman's temporary monopoly, Microsoft's ability to set standards with MS-DOS and Windows, and Wal-Mart's change to the rules of the retail distribution game.

New research[1], however, suggests a contrary view. Previous research focused only on those first movers that survived. Almost half (47%) of pioneers fail. Procter & Gamble claims it invented disposable diapers, but Chux launched its brand ten years before P&G entered the market. Only 11%

---

[1] Peter N. Golder and Gerard J. Tellis, "Pioneering Advantage: Marketing Logic or Marketing Legend?" *Journal of Marketing Research*, 30 (May, 1993), 158-70.

Gerard J. Tellis and Peter N. Golder, "First to Market, First to Fail? Real Causes of Enduring Market Leadership", *Sloan Management Review*, (Winter, 1996), 65-75.

Steven P. Schnaars, *Managing Imitation Strategies*. New York: Free Press, 1994.

of pioneers are current market leaders, and the average market share for pioneers is 10%. The real success appears to be achieved by "early leaders" who enter, on average, 13 years after the pioneers, yet achieve three times their market share.

A number of phenomena explain this. Pioneers often fail to create a mass market. Part of this is due to the products themselves. New products tend to be low-quality and high-priced, as seen in early personal computers, VCRs, and DVDs. They appeal to early adopters, the gadget-minded techno-geek who wants to be first on the block with the new stuff. The general consumer has yet to see any need for this product, or at least a need great enough to offset a steep price. Developing a new market is expensive, in terms of advertising, creating products that consumers can use on the new item (games for PCs, movies for VCRs), and getting the new product right. Subsequent entrants learn from the mistakes of the predecessors. Not only do they learn about the dynamics of the market, but they also are freed from the mantle of high price and low quality that earlier providers may wear.

Yet some first movers thrive. This seems most likely when the first-mover innovates continuously within that product category. This allows a new entrant to become successful, but with a more commoditized item, while the first-mover has defended its market share with a whole new product. Gillette, for instance, has maintained its leadership in razors by innovating, despite the risk of cannibalization. First movers can also impose costs on late-comers by marketing, and they can extend their reach by forming strategic alliances.

As a final comment, research has found that sustaining a leadership position requires five characteristics:

1. A vision of the market that attracts resources and inspires the work force.
2. Management commitment over an extended period.
3. Availability of financial resources.
4. Continuous innovation.
5. Leveraging brand equity.

Suggested Teaching Plan

This case can be taught in a Marketing class or in Competitive Strategy. We have successfully used it in the First-Year Marketing course, in the Branding elective course, and in Executive Education. It can be used to explore questions of product strategy and positioning, competitive strategy, marketing techniques and communications, and/or pharmaceuticals and medicine, so its place in the course depends on how the instructor wishes to use it.

The case's particular use in a course will determine which modules of this note the instructor employs. A marketing strategy course may choose to emphasize the first mover discussion and pay less attention to the details of the BASES research. A marketing techniques course would do the opposite. A course on competitive strategy might emphasize the joint marketing alliance, first mover advantage, and the different marketing approaches that Zantac, Tagamet, and Pepcid might all use, with limited reference to details of market research. The note as written maps out the approach used in First Year Marketing and Branding. To a certain degree, the interests of the class and instructor and the previous cases that have been presented will inform and guide the discussion.

Suggested Assignment Questions

1. Why does Merck want to switch Pepcid to OTC status when the patent is good for another six years? What would be the optimal time to switch? What determines this? Would it be the same for Tagamet, Zantac, Pepcid, and Axid?

2. How will sales of OTC Pepcid affect sales of the prescription version? How will cannibalization affect the sales of JJM's Mylanta antacid? Why did JJM buy Mylanta if it was planning to switch Pepcid?

3. What are the relative merits of positioning Pepcid as a "treatment" as opposed to a "prevention" for heartburn/indigestion? How does the FDA view them? The consumer? JJM? How important is positioning in this market?

4. How attractive is this opportunity?

5. What is first mover advantage? What is the prize for winning the race to market? What are the sources, if any, of its first mover advantage? Are they sustainable?

6. Assess the threat posed by Tagamet's imminent entry. How formidable a competitor will it be? Is there a "second mover advantage" that can be exploited in a prescription-to-OTC switch? If so, what is it? How would these issues apply to the subsequent entry of Zantac and Axid?

7. How can Pepcid simultaneously build and defend its competitive position? How should it respond to the entry of Tagamet? Zantac and Axid? What strategic posture should Pepcid adopt - offensive or defensive, short or long-term? How can Pepcid best exploit its opportunities?

Appendix 1: Closing Slide Presentation

PEPCID AC

- Positioning = Segmentation + Differentiation
  - Market Segmentation
    - Channel (R_x and OTC) *versus*
    - Consumer (R_x, Heavy, Dual, Light)
  - Product Differentiation
    - Treatment *versus* Prevention

PEPCID AC

- Positioning affects
  - Market size
  - Ability to build and defend brand
- Positioning determines
  - Marketing Mix (4 Ps)
    - Product
    - Place
    - Promotion
    - Price

PEPCID AC

- First Mover Advantage
  - Temporary monopoly —> Build "War-chest"
  - Switching costs —> Build "loyalty"
  - Define preferences —> Be preferred product
  - Lock up channels —> Create barrier to entry
  - Innovator —> Build reputation
- Is it sustainable?

PEPCID AC

- Second Mover Advantage
  - Research & Copy
  - Resolve market uncertainties
  - Learn from pioneers mistakes
  - Establishing new markets is expensive

Popular Wisdom

- Most believe market pioneers become long-term leaders
  - Common sense view: "First movers" will dominate a market
- First-mover advantages:
  - Temporary monopoly: Sony Walkman
  - Setting standards: Microsoft DOS & Windows
  - Dictating rules of game: Wal-Mart

First-Mover Advantage?

- New research suggests otherwise
- Previous research ignored survivorship bias
  - Procter & Gamble claims to have created the disposable diaper business
  - But Chux launched its brand in 1950 over 10 years earlier
- What happens if you look at a company when it entered and ask how did it fare?

Appendix 1 (continued)

What *Really* Happens?

- Almost half (47%) of pioneers fail
- Only 11% of pioneers are current market leaders
- Average market share of pioneers is a mere 10%
- Real successes are "early leaders" who enter an average of 13 years after pioneers and achieve 3x the market share of pioneers

Why Do First-Movers Fail?

- Pioneers often fail to create a mass market
  - First products tend to be low in quality, expensive and limited in their applications
    - Personal computers and VCRs
- Developing new markets is expensive
- Subsequent entrants learn from pioneers about structure and dynamics of market
- Pioneers are vulnerable to R&C
  - Sony innovates; Matushita copies

What Can Be Done?

- Need for continuous innovation with product category
  - Innovation allows later entrants to become successful and incumbents to defend share
    - Gillette has maintained leadership in razors through innovation even at risk of cannibalization
- Raise rivals' costs through marketing
- Form strategic alliances

Lessons from History

- Sustaining a leadership position is associated with five factors:
  - → A vision of the market that attracts resources and inspires the work force
  - → Management commitment over an extended period
  - → Availability of financial resources
  - → Continuous innovation
  - → Leveraging brand equity

LifeSpan, Inc.: Abbott Northwestern Hospital

Teaching Note

Synopsis

LifeSpan, Inc., a Minneapolis-based not-for-profit organization, is the parent holding company of three hospitals and several health services corporations. Abbott Northwestern Hospital (referred to in this note as ANH), LifeSpan's premier hospital, adopts a very market-oriented approach to increase its share of a business that is both shrinking in size and becoming increasingly competitive. The company initiates a telemarketing advertising campaign that results in a flood of inquiries. In January 1986, Steve Hillestad, vice president of marketing, requests an expansion of the advertising budget of 1986 to $1.25 million, a hike of 75% over the 1985 budget of $717,000. The board of directors demands some evidence that advertising, other marketing programs, phone calls, and inquiries lead to filled beds and more business. Students must specify if and how Hillestad can justify his request for a substantially bigger budget and whether the board should approve it.

Use

The case has been used with both MBA students and executives. It can be used, as we have positioned it here, in the Marketing Performance Assessment Module of the first-year M.B.A. Marketing Management course. It has also been used as a communication case to emphasize especially the role of advertising and other communication tools in a not-for-profit services setting.

In its present position, the major objectives of the case are as follows:

1. To expose students to the kind of analysis that is necessary for evaluating the role of marketing.
2. To illustrate the difficulties associated with measuring marketing performance.
3. To introduce students to the concepts of efficiency, effectiveness, ethics, and externalities—the 4 E's of marketing performance assessment.

This teaching note was prepared by Assistant Professor Melvyn A. J. Menezes as an aid to classroom discussion of "LifeSpan, Inc.: Abbott Northwestern Hospital," HBS Case No. 587-104.

4. To provide an opportunity to examine how various marketing programs and tools are used in a not-for-profit services setting.

5. To raise the ethical dilemmas posed by the aggressive use of marketing programs in the health care industry.

Analysis

Analysis of the case revolves around four main areas: (1) understanding the health care industry and its various constituents; (2) comprehending what drives the business from an end-consumer perspective (3) acquiring analytical depth regarding ANH's marketing programs, and linking marketing to sales; and (4) examining the ethical dilemmas associated with marketing and other actions in the health care industry.

Health Care Industry

Analysis of the health care industry needs to take into account its size, structure, and unique features. The health care industry was very large ($425 billion in 1985, accounting for 10.7% of the gross national product of the United States), and growing rapidly. Case **Exhibit 1** shows that between 1955 and 1985, the health care industry grew at a compound annual rate of 11.1% (the GNP's compound annual growth rate was 8.0% during the same period). With its rich blend of human and institutional constituents, and their differing ways of operating within it, the health care industry is probably more complex than many industries students have been exposed to in the course, and deserves to be examined in some depth.

The various entities in the system are physicians, insurance companies, government, health maintenance organizations (HMOs) and other alternative health care delivery systems, hospitals, and, of course, end consumers. Within these groups, rapid changes are occurring, and it is important that students identify them. Government regulations are in flux; the number of physicians has recently jumped; the role of consumers in choosing a hospital has become more predominant; and HMOs have emerged as a significant player.

Exhibit TN-1 captures some of the important changes that took place in the health care industry between 1965 and 1985. With regard to government, whose role in health care needs to be carefully analyzed, the very substantial increase in spending in the past two decades led to several reforms aimed at controlling runaway costs. Cost-based reimbursements by Medicare were replaced by Medicare's Prospective Payment System, under which hospitals must now deliver inpatient services for fixed prices based on the diagnosis. When costs exceed the diagnostic-related group (DRG) price, the hospital loses money. In turn, DRG pricing has affected the nature, and possibly the quality, of health care. Needing to provide lower-cost care, many hospitals began to change practice patterns, shifting care from an inpatient to an outpatient basis. ANH's outpatient surgery volume increased from 13% to 44% of all surgical procedures performed at the hospital.

The health care industry has witnessed an astounding growth in the number of physicians. Traditionally in short supply, physicians were in surplus in 1985. Consequently, some became highly entrepreneurial—changing practice patterns, drawing more on the competitive and aggressive aspects of their professional persona—merely in order to survive.

The emergence of health maintenance organizations (HMOs) is also a significant change in the industry. With the coming of HMOs, physicians practicing within them had no incentive to institute extra procedures that would augment their fees.

An interesting and unusual dimension of the health care industry is the dominance of third-party payers such as the government and private insurance companies. Third-party payers played an increasing role in financing personal health care expenses and in 1985 financed 71.6% of those expenses (see **Exhibit TN-2**). In the case of hospital care, third-party payers accounted for as much as 90.7% ($151.2 billion out of $166.7 billion) of expenses.

It is important for students (especially foreign students) to fully understand the roles and strategies of the various players in the system, because the health care system in the United States is quite different from that in other countries. It also may be useful to consider how the U.S. health care delivery system compares with those in some other countries in Europe, Asia, Africa, and South America. Some foreign students infer that in the U.S. health care system, a key objective of some players, such as government and insurance companies, is to discipline some other players, such as physicians, hospitals, and particularly end consumers. The part played by consumers, especially their changing role in hospital selection, is discussed in the next section.

End Consumer

Everyone is a consumer of health care services at some time, and to most people, these services are often very important. In analyzing the end consumers, it is important that they be classified into two broad categories: those who are locked in to an HMO and those who are not. Consumers who are locked in to an HMO typically have far less choice with respect to hospitals and physicians but save money, since HMOs are usually less expensive than other delivery systems.

The trade-off between loss of choice incurred by the rise of HMOs (and other alternative health care delivery systems) and the cost to consumers is a useful topic to explore. Besides HMOs, there are alternative health care delivery systems such as IPAs (individual practice associations) and PPOs (preferred provider organizations). The case does not refer to IPAs and PPOs; for the benefit of instructors, they are new, nontraditional health care organizations that are variations of HMOs and in which the degrees of choice are greater than with standard HMOs and are therefore an attraction. The figure below characterizes these various health care delivery systems with regard to degree of choice and cost to consumers.

Health Care Delivery Systems: Choice and Cost

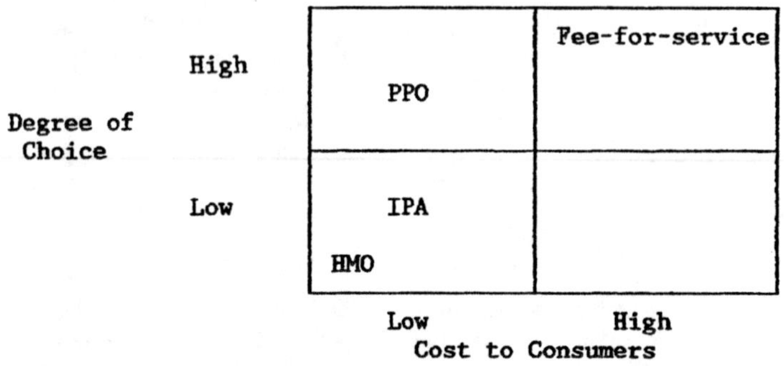

For consumers who are not contracted with an HMO, the decision regarding hospital selection varies according to the context in which the choice is made. The context can be analyzed in terms of at least two important dimensions: the condition of the person's health and whether or not he or she has a physician. The second factor is probably related to the individual's local residency status, that is, whether he or she is an established or recent resident of a particular locality. With respect to the individual's health condition, four levels can be identified: prevention, minor illness, acute care, and emergency.

Students need to realize that although consumers are playing an increasingly important role in hospital selection, the control they exert over this choice probably varies according to the situation. **Exhibit TN-3** shows the main decision maker for each of the eight different situations. With respect to preventive health maintenance, the consumer apparently makes the choice. In the case of an emergency, the decision is made by the consumer, physician, or ambulance driver, depending on the seriousness of the emergency and whether the consumer has a physician. In the case of a minor illness, the decision is probably made jointly by consumer and physician, whereas the physician clearly has a very important role to play in acute care hospital selection.

It is worth noting that both of the parties involved—consumers and physicians—believe that they are the key decision maker in hospital selection. A little more than half the consumers (56%) believe that they are the key decision makers in hospital selection, while most physicians (89%) believe they make that choice for the patient.

The ways in which consumers evaluate the quality of health care provided are complicated and interesting to ponder. Organizations such as Consumers Union, for example, have stated that they cannot offer an appropriate evaluation of the quality of health care services. Hospital mortality rates have been used as a quality index. The federal government's release of mortality rates for all U.S. hospitals in December 1987 was very controversial. Most hospitals called the data misleading and useless because they did not account for the degree of illness among patients who died. Some consumers may evaluate health care quality by using price as a cue for quality. A similar discussion can be had regarding the evaluation of the quality of a physician. For example, do consumers use the age of the physician as a cue for quality?

Most consumers have low price sensitivities for health care. This has to do with the importance they assign to their health along with the fact that they do not, in general, pay directly for health services at the time of consumption. In the case of third-party payments, which account for over 90% of hospital care expenditures, receipt of and payment for health care services are not connected; this is one of the distinguishing features of the health care industry.

It is indeed rather surprising that despite the very significant differences in Twin Cities hospitals in terms of size, occupancy rates, and market shares (case **Exhibit 4**) in 1985, consumers did not perceive there to be much of a difference in the quality of different "brands," that is, most hospitals were considered to be of good and similar quality.

ANH

The next area of analysis concerns ANH's position in the Twin Cities health care marketplace. The Minneapolis/St. Paul (Twin Cities) market is particularly relevant for LifeSpan, since most of its patients are from that market. The Twin Cities market is exceptionally competitive; it is dominated by HMOs, which account for 41% of the market, compared with 11% on a national basis. To make matters worse, during the period 1980 to 1984, the Twin Cities market size shrunk dramatically in terms of number of patients, average length of stay in a hospital, and total inpatient days (based on case **Table A**).

	1980	1984	% Change
Number of patients	361,421	316,695	-12.4%
Average length of stay	7.73	6.28	-18.8%
Total inpatient days	2,794,810	1,989,466	-28.8%

This decline in total inpatient days, coupled with a simultaneous increase in the number of physicians, resulted in intense competition among hospitals, HMOs, and physicians in the Twin Cities. The 25% decline (from 1984 to 1985) in average income of doctors in the Twin Cities provides evidence of this competition.

Despite the competitiveness of the Twin Cities health care marketplace, LifeSpan and Abbott Northwestern Hospital were doing very well in 1985:

- LifeSpan revenues are up 41.0%; $211.5 million in 1985, compared to $149.9 million in 1984.
- Operating margins are up 45.7%; $6.2 million in 1985, compared to $4.3 million in 1984.
- ANH's bed occupancy rate is a very high 71.2%.
- ANH's market share is the highest in the Twin Cities and is rising.

Analysis of ANH's success in this competitive marketplace should differentiate between marketing brilliance and medical excellence. The case indicates that ANH is a high-quality hospital with seven Centers of Excellence [see case under "Abbott Northwestern Hospital" section]. For example, ANH's cardiovascular program is known as the best of its kind in the upper Midwest, and the world's first artificial heart implant in a woman was performed there.

Despite its status as a not-for-profit organization, LifeSpan appears to place a great deal of emphasis on profitability and financial performance. The sentence [under the "Company Background/Management" section] in the case, "While the party line is human service, it is vital that we meet the bottom line," captures some of the culture and values at ANH. There is plenty to discuss regarding what it means to be a not-for-profit organization, and the dimensions on which a not-for-profit organization differs from a for-profit organization. Most of the analysis should, of course, focus on the role of marketing at ANH, specifically in terms of the hospital's performance in 1985. This leads to the next area of discussion—ANH's marketing approach.

Marketing at ANH

ANH's marketing efforts are directed at three broad categories of customers—physicians, end consumers, and HMOs. Since the case does not describe what ANH does with respect to HMOs, this discussion will be about the hospital's marketing activities for physicians and end consumers. ANH appears to strike a good balance between push (physicians) and pull (end consumers).

Support for Physicians. ANH management views physicians as its "retailers" who are "critical in getting patients to the hospital." The vital importance of physicians, especially as a revenue source for the hospital, is clearly recognized. ANH's 400 active physicians bring in 85% of its patients. **Exhibit TN-4** shows how the contribution per active ANH physician can be calculated. On average, each active ANH physician brings in 62 inpatients per year, and ANH receives a contribution of $43,400 per active physician each year. In addition, ANH also receives some revenue and contribution from the outpatient and emergency room admits of these physicians.

To support its active physicians, ANH took several steps:

- Initiated a physician referral system, in which people who did not have a physician or who wanted to change their physician were given the name of an ANH doctor.
- Created a medical staff development program to assist ANH physicians in establishing full-service suburban clinics in communities that needed them. The assistance was extensive, ranging from market research, office site selection, and legal advice to financial support.

- Introduced a product management system.
- Set up a 24-hour toll-free telephone link between physicians and hospitals in rural areas and ANH's subspeciality physicians.

Despite ANH's active efforts to support them, physicians appear to be quite skeptical of ANH's marketing activities, and view some of them as attempts to bypass the doctors and increase the hospital's control (case page 9). Even the physician referral system was not received by physicians with much enthusiasm.

Marketing Activities Directed at End Consumers. ANH's marketing approach has begun to be very end-consumer-oriented. To compensate for its poor location and low awareness level, ANH tries hard to enhance its image, heavily orienting its marketing toward the end consumer. The early-morning welcome by senior executives and the free valet parking are steps aimed at improving patients' first impressions as they enter the hospital. For patients from outside Minneapolis, the Wasie Center—a hotel-like, low-priced facility in the ANH complex—is an added attraction. The hospital uses advertising, Medformation, and WomenCare programs to improve its image. The specific programs need to be carefully reviewed.

Medformation

Medformation is the heart of ANH's marketing effort. It is useful first to examine the objective and strategic role of Medformation before analyzing its economic implications. Conceptually, the role of Medformation is given in **Exhibit TN-5.** Medformation was established to set up a direct contact and link between ANH and the end consumer. People who called Medformation as a result of ads regarding general medical information, cancer, and "other" information received help from ANH without the hospital benefiting from any immediate economic returns. However, most of these people probably were very pleased with the service provided and spoke to their friends about Medformation. In addition, 10% of callers also asked for a physician referral. Medformation operators recommended a physician to each of these persons as well as to all those who called in for the physician referral system. It was expected that both the consumer and the physician would feel kindly toward ANH for that referral. Consequently, when a consumer needed to use a hospital's facilities—either as an outpatient, an inpatient, or in the emergency room, his or her physician was expected to recommend ANH, and the consumer was expected to be positively disposed to ANH thanks to his or her good experiences with Medformation.

Medformation's quit-smoking and weight-loss programs provide good preventive health care. These programs also fit in well with ANH's strategy to provide consumers with an incentive to visit ANH when they are not sick. Some of the attendees (10%) at these programs were referred to one of ANH's physicians.

It can be inferred that some ANH managers, such as Hillestad and Penrod, believe that Medformation has been a great success. They were even contemplating extending Medformation to cover outbound as well. Penrod appears to measure Medformation's success in terms of the number of calls received and the improvement in consumer perception. Some non-ANH industry people as well have been impressed by the Medformation ads. The case states [in the section under "Specific Programs/Medformation"] that the marketing director of a New York hospital offered $100,000 to buy the ads used by ANH.

Medformation Economics. Examining the cost of ads and calls is an appropriate starting point for an analysis of Medformation's economic benefits. Using the information in case **Exhibit 6** and the cost of ads given in case **Exhibit 9,** the response rate (average calls/ad) and the average costs can be calculated:

Average response rate (calls/ad)	= 139.8 (28,667/205)
Average cost/call	= $10.25 ($294,000/28,667)
Average cost/ad	= $1,434.15 ($294,000/205)

In computing the average cost/ad, some students consider only the media costs and disregard the production costs. They usually do this in one of two ways:

1. Based on case **Exhibit 9**:
   Media cost/ad = $270,000/205
   = $1,317.07

2. Based on information in case [section under "Specific Programs/Medformation"]:
   Media cost/ad = $700 (.9) + $7,000 (.1)
   = $1,330.00

To examine thoroughly the link between Medformation and sales, each component of Medformation should be analyzed separately. **Exhibit TN-6** examines the physician referral system. The net present value of the gross contribution to ANH from this system during the first two years is $199,492, and the net contribution (after subtracting the cost of the ads) is $124,916. The gross contribution has three components—inpatients, outpatients, and emergency room. Since the inpatient contribution accounts for more than 86% of the gross contribution, the economic short-run success of the physician referral system is very sensitive to Hillestad's estimate of the percentage of people returning to ANH as inpatients.

Exhibit TN-7 evaluates the contribution of persons who contact an ANH physician through Medformation and shows one way of calculating the break-even number of calls for the physician referral system. The value to ANH of a consumer who contacts one of its physicians is calculated at $121.86. Of those who call for a physician referral, 70% actually contact the physician whose name they have been given. Therefore, the value (in terms of expected contributions) to ANH of each call to the physician referral system is computed to be $85.30.

The break-even calculations for the weight-loss and quit-smoking programs are shown in **Exhibit TN-8**. The objectives of these programs are to provide preventive health care, to bring the consumers to ANH while they are not sick, and to ensure that they have positive experiences at ANH. These programs benefit ANH in at least four different ways:

1. Revenue accrues directly from the program—on average the revenue per person attending is $150 and the contribution to ANH is $90.

2. Attendees who are satisfied with the program and the facilities at ANH will generate positive word-of-mouth publicity. This should lead to increased business in the long run.

3. About 10% of the program attendees are referred to an ANH physician. When these consumers need to select a hospital, it is expected that they will choose ANH.

4. Those program attendees who already have a physician are also expected to be very positively impressed with the facilities and quality of service and to choose ANH when they need to select a hospital or when the physician suggests ANH as a possibility.

The contribution per person attending the program is $98.53. These programs provide ANH with a gross contribution of $79,711, and the cost of the ads is $53,063; the net contribution is $26,648.

Exhibit TN-9 provides a complete analysis of Medformation and its contribution to ANH. The total gross contribution from the program is $492,252, and the cost of the ads is $294,000, leaving a net contribution of $198,252. This just covers Medformation's fixed costs of $175,000 [see case section under "Specific Programs/Medformation"].

In pushing to show that marketing did in fact play a major role in the 1985 performance, many students will focus only on Medformation and WomenCare. More thoughtful students tend to include the role of the product managers, the courteous early-morning welcome, the Wasie Center, and the support provided to physicians as other marketing elements that have helped boost ANH's image, market share, revenues, and profits. Some students argue that these marketing "gimmicks" have not contributed at all and that it is the excellent quality of medical care provided by ANH that accounts for its success. Information from the case [under "Marketing at Abbott Northwestern Hospital" section] and from case **Exhibit 7** can be used to support this claim. From case **Exhibit 7** we know that the percentage of people who perceived that ANH provided the best medical care for serious heart problems rose from 13.7% in 1984 to 26.1% in 1985, the year in which ANH was the site of the first artificial heart implant in a woman.

Advertising Budget: In analyzing the advertising budget proposal for 1986 (case **Exhibit 9**). two things stand out:

1. The substantial increase in the total budget from $716,600 (1985) to $1.25 million—a 75% hike.

2. The shift in the media emphasis.

With respect to the first point, Medformation's expenses show an 84% increase between 1985 and 1986. To support this rise in expenses, one has to decide which programs should receive most of the additional advertising, and the optimum number of ads to be placed in a given month. **Exhibit TN-10**, which presents the ad effectiveness as a function of ad frequency, indicates a dramatic decline in calls/ad as the number of ads per month increases.

Marketing Performance Assessment

An important objective of the case relates to the concept of assessing marketing peformance. One way of thinking about this subject is in terms of efficiency and effectiveness (thanks to Professor Tom Bonoma's work on this topic). Another approach, which is an extension of the earlier approach, is to think about assessing marketing performance in terms of four dimensions—which I call the 4 E's of marketing performance assessment:

1) Efficiency	"Doing things right" (e.g., using measures such as market share, calls/ad, bed occupancy rate).
2) Effectiveness	"Doing the right things" (consistent with the firm's goals, culture, and strategy).
3) Ethics	"Doing the RIGHT thing" (consistent with ethical principles).
4) Externalities	Unusual environmental factors, changes in law, luck, etc.

In assessing marketing performance, people often tend to think primarily of efficiency and almost take for granted the issues of effectiveness, ethics, and externalities. The case allows for very clear distinctions between these issues. **Exhibit TN-11** illustrates the kinds of points that come out in this analysis. In terms of efficiency (students would probably not use that word), one usually gets things like profits, market share, bed occupancy rate, calls per ad, and so on.

In terms of effectiveness, students typically refer to the goals of ANH (for example, being a regional center of quality health care) and ask whether ANH is doing the "right thing" to achieve its goals. Some students will also debate whether ANH's goals are appropriate and clear.

The kinds of ethical issues that come out are discussed in detail under "Ethical Dilemmas." Finally, under externalities, students voice luck and the fact that the first ever heart implant in a woman was performed at ANH as important factors.

Students should understand that all four of these dimensions should be examined carefully when assessing marketing.

Ethical Dilemmas

The case raises several potential ethical dilemmas faced by providers and payers of health care. One such issue is whether hospitals should advertise at all. Some students argue that health care is a fundamental right of individuals and consequently is not a product/service (like computers/airlines) to be marketed. They argue that marketing merely increases the cost of the service to the patient, and insist that trying to influence consumer choice is not only inappropriate but also unethical. Some other students argue that health care advertising is acceptable so long as it (1) provides accurate information that may otherwise be unavailable to consumers, and (2) does not attempt to persuade consumers to choose one particular hospital (or physician) over another. A third group of students argue that advertising of health care is not only appropriate but should be encouraged, since consumers can use the ads to become aware of and evaluate various hospitals and programs. These students argue that advertising is a good signal of the quality of care. Finally, some students propose that while advertising may be useful, the money could be better utilized for more research and for purchasing medical equipment so as to improve the quality of care. They assert that quality will win out and that those hospitals which spend money on equipment and research will gain market share in the long run.

Another ethical dilemma concerns the physician's role in hospital selection. In those situations in which the physician is the key decision maker, some students question whether he or she can really be objective in deciding on the hospital. This is not easy, they argue, because physicians are usually "active" in only a very small number of hospitals, and will obviously tend to direct the patient to their "favorite" hospital (one where the physician is well treated), not necessarily the best or most appropriate hospital.

The government's new DRG method of payment is another area for discussion. Some students argue that by requiring that payment to the hospital be based on diagnosis rather than the length of stay and collective expenses, the government is encouraging a lowering in the average quality of health care. International students can contribute greatly to this discussion by comparing this situation with what they observe in their countries.

Some of the specific actions and ideas of ANH also raise interesting ethical questions. For example, the following statement, taken from the case [section under "Project Management"], usually invokes very strong reactions: "We could have coffee and donuts provided to ambulance drivers and paramedics. This might provide them an incentive to bring patients to the ANH emergency room." The fundamental question here is whether there should be incentives for those who influence the hospital choice, since such incentives could result in the patient's not receiving the most appropriate and timely medical care. Some students vehemently point out that this idea is extremely unethical and inappropriate for a hospital. Other students argue that ambulance drivers are not so stupid as to risk taking a seriously ill patient on a longer route "just for coffee and donuts." In executive programs, some participants have gone so far as to suggest that ANH should not only provide these snacks, but should also hold a big dinner once a year for the ambulance drivers and paramedics.

Many students assert that the Medformation ads downplaying the link between Medformation and ANH is another action that borders on the unethical. They believe that downplaying this link is deceptive.

Teaching the Case

This case can be taught in a variety of ways, depending on the instructor's preference, style, and teaching objectives. We will assume that the teaching objectives are as indicated [under "Use"] at beginning of this teaching note.

A good way to start the discussion is to probe students on the nature of ANH's business. This discussion would lead to a quick but important analysis of the health care industry. Students should examine the role and strategies of the industry's various constituents as well as the extreme competitiveness of the Twin Cities marketplace.

The discussion could then focus on how health care is bought. The customer analysis discussion can be a very rich and powerful one. The instructor should encourage customer segmentation (see **Exhibit TN-3**) and target market specification. This is also a good place for discussions on the importance of and difficulty associated with evaluating quality in a service such as health care, the price sensitivity of consumers, and the separation of consumption and payment both in amount and time.

Discussion of the role of Medformation and whether the program works is a rich analytical area. Students, especially in MBA classes, do a sound job of this. The instructor should try to ensure that students develop a model of linking ads → calls → hospital use → contribution, and of evaluating the contribution per person contacting an ANH physician (see **Exhibit TN-7**).

If students focus only on the advertising aspects of marketing at ANH, the instructor should guide them to a discussion of the nonadvertising aspects of marketing directed at both end consumers and physicians.

The fact that ANH is a not-for-profit organization is most appropriately discussed after the economic implications of Medformation and WomenCare have been analyzed. This discussion should address whether it is appropriate for ANH to evaluate Medformation in terms of contribution or whether it makes more sense to use some noneconomic measures, such as the number of people who have a physician with whom they are satisfied, the health condition of Medformation users a year later as compared to a control group, and so on.

The ethical issues associated with the aggressive use of marketing programs in the health care industry must be discussed in some depth. Usually, students become very emotional and excited in this part of the discussion. The following questions (which can be varied) may be useful for facilitating the discussion:

- Should hospitals be advertising, or should they instead be spending that money on equipment and/or research?
- What impact does the government's DRG pricing have on the quality of health care?

- Is it fair to consumers that ANH recommends only ANH physicians, since the ads intentionally downplay any link between Medformation and a particular hospital?

- How would you respond to an ER product manager's proposal to provide coffee and donuts to ambulance drivers and paramedics? Is it ethical to do that?

The final part of the discussion can focus on what is really involved in assessing marketing performance. The instructor can use board space very effectively by organizing these points (as they come out during the class discussion) on the two side boards or on one large board.

At a more strategic level, the discussion benefits from doing the quantitative analysis and evaluation of ANH's marketing programs early in the class, as students tend to resist this kind of analysis once the broader issues of objectives, ethics, and so on have been raised. The instructor should try to hold off the ethical discussion until later. This needs to be done in a very tactful manner, without suggesting that the ethical issues are in any way less important than other issues. Otherwise, students may sense that the instructor wants to focus only on the nonethical issues and consequently may refrain from addressing these very important issues of ethics.

A list of suggested teaching questions is provided in **Exhibit TN-12**, and a suggestion for a board plan is presented in **Exhibit TN-13**.

Exhibit TN-1 Evolution of the Health Care Industry

	1965	1985
Structure	Decentralized: multitude of individual operators	Centralized organizations, e.g., HMOs and Supermeds
Size Market Size	\$41.9 billion	\$425.0 billion
% of GNP	5.9%	10.7%
Payees		
Patient Direct Payment	51.6%	28.4%
Third Party	48.4%	71.6%
Consumers	Depended on physicians for hospital selection	Play important role in hospital selection; ready to seek alternatives, e.g., HMOs
Government		
Involvement	Low (22.0% of PHC)[a]	High (39.7% of PHC)
Actions	Institutes programs (Medicare & Medicaid) to provide medical assistance	Introduces controls to reduce rapid expense growth
Payment	Fee-for-service	Diagnosis based (DRGs)
Physicians	Limited; shortage of specialists; 7,000 graduating/year	Surplus; no dearth of specialists; 15,000 graduating/year
Decision Making Unit	Doctor - most important Patient - minor role	Depends on condition of health
Marketing Programs		
Target Market	Physicians	Consumers
Communications Strategy	Push	Pull
Pricing	Relatively unimportant	Increasingly important
Advertising	Nonexistent	Rapidly increasing

[a]PHC = Personal Health Care

Exhibit TN-2 Financing of Personal Health Care

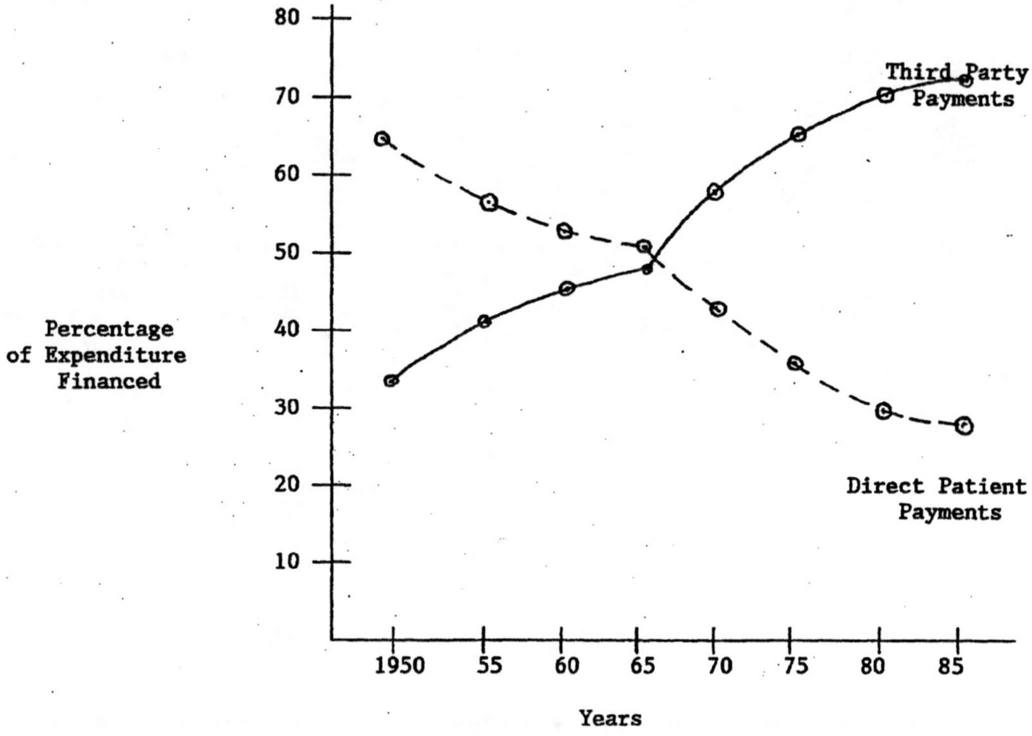

Exhibit TN-3 End Consumers

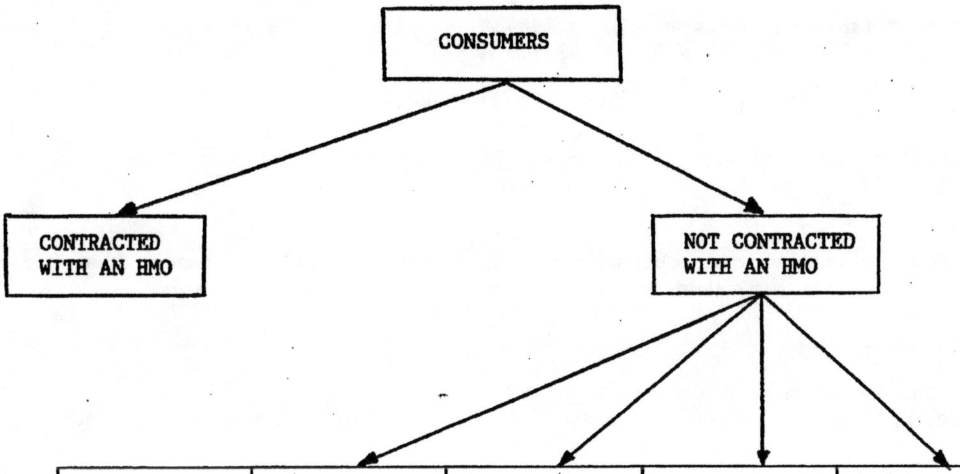

	PREVENTION	EMERGENCY	MINOR ILLNESS	ACUTE CARE
HAS PHYSICIAN	CONSUMER DECIDES	CONS/PHY/AMB DRIVER DECIDES	CONS/PHY DECIDES	PHYSICIAN DECIDES
HAS NO PHYSICIAN	CONSUMER DECIDES	CONS/PHY/AMB DRIVER DECIDES	SEARCH	SEARCH

Exhibit TN-4 Contribution from an Active ANH Physician

Number of inpatient days at ANH in 1984
= 705 x 0.712 x 365 = 183,215 days[a]

Average length of stay during 1984 = 6.28 days[b]

Hence, number of patients at ANH = $\frac{183,215}{6.28}$ = 29,174

The 400 active physicians brought in 85% of these patients. Hence, the average number of patients brought in by an active ANH physician
= $\frac{29,174 \times 0.85}{400}$ = 62

Contribution from each inpatient = $700.
Hence, contribution from an average active physician = 62 x $700 = <u>$43,400</u>

[a]From case <u>Exhibit 4.</u>

[b]From case Table A. It is assumed that the average length of stay at ANH was the same as for other hospitals in the Twin Cities.

Exhibit TN-5 Role of Medformation

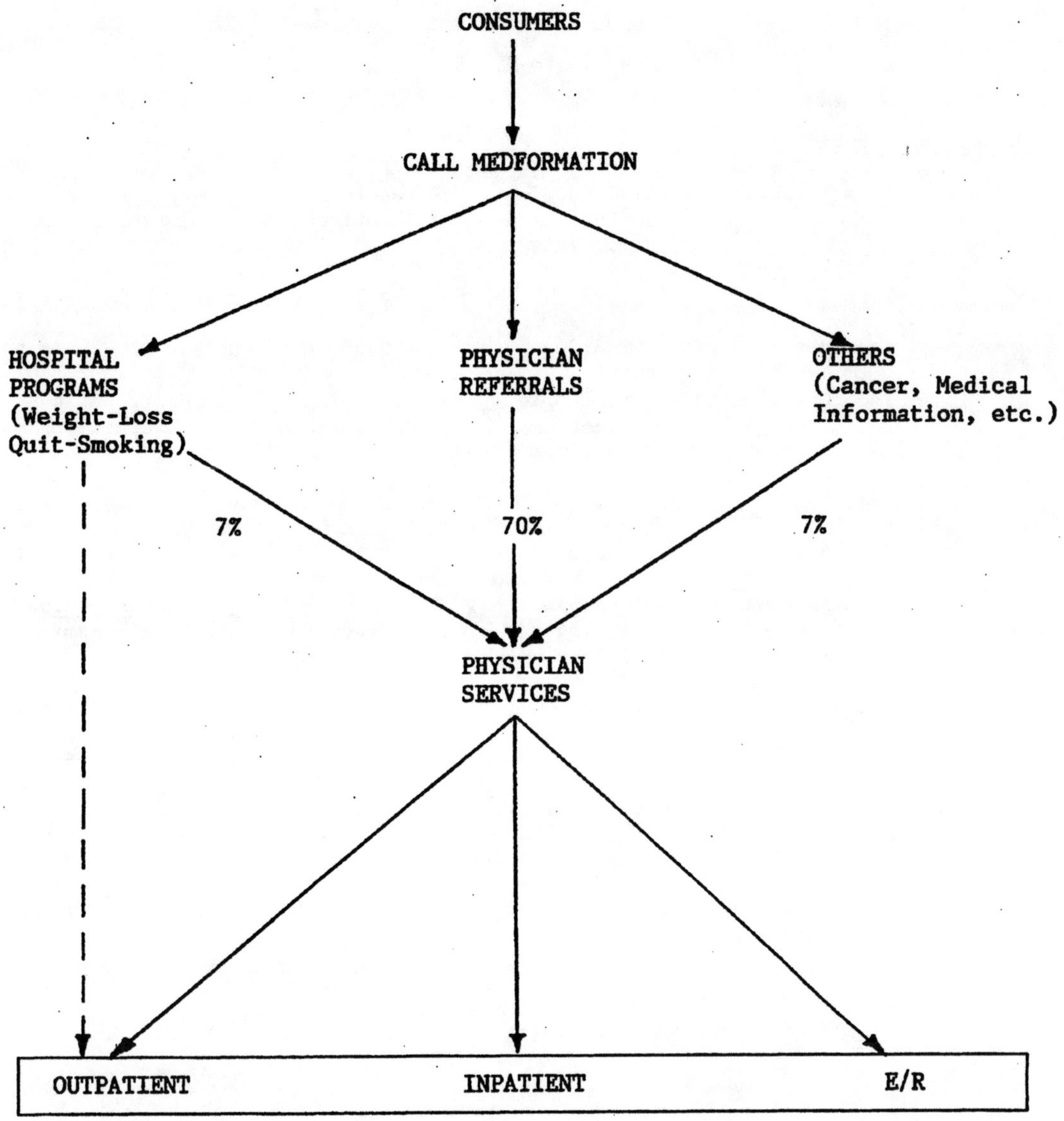

Exhibit TN-6 Contribution from Physician Referral System

Number of People Contacting Physician = Number of Calls x % Contacting Physicians

= 2,338 x 0.70

= 1,637

Gross Contributions

1. From Inpatients = # of People Contacting Physicians x % Returning As Inpatients x Contribution/Inpatient

Year 1 =	1,637	x	0.10	x	$700	=	$114,590
Year 2 =	1,637	x	0.05	x	$700	=	$57,295

2. From Outpatients = # of People Contacting Physicians x % Returning As Outpatients x Contribution/Outpatient

Year 1 =	1,637	x	0.10	x	85	=	$13,915
Year 2 =	1,637	x	0.10	x	85	=	$13,915

3. From Emergency Room = # of People Contacting Physicians x % Returning to Emergency Room x Contribution/E/R Admit

Year 1 =	1,637	x	0.05	x	40	=	$3,274
Year 2 =	1,637	x	0.05	x	40	=	$3,274

Total Contribution in Year 1: $131,779

Total Contribution in Year 2: $ 74,484

Assuming a discount rate of 10%, the net present value of the total contributions in Years 1 and 2 is: $\$131,779 + \frac{\$74,484}{1.1} = \$199,492$

Cost of 52 Ads $\left(\frac{52}{205} \times \$294,000\right) = \$74,576$

Net Contribution from Physician Referral System = $124,916 ($199,492 - $74,576).

Exhibit TN-7 Evaluation of Expected Contribution per Person Contacting an ANH Physician

	Number Returning to ANH	Contribution Per Person Treated	Contribution Per Person Contacting Physician	NPV[a] Contri-bution
Year 1				
Inpatient	0.10	$700.00	$70.00	
Outpatient	0.10	$85.00	$8.50	
Emergency Room	0.05	$40.00	$2.00	
	0.25		$80.50	$80.50
Year 2				
Inpatient	0.05	$700.00	$35.00	
Outpatient	0.10	$85.00	$8.50	
Emergency Room	0.05	$40.00	$2.00	
	0.20		$45.50	$41.36
Total Contribution/Person contacting an ANH physician:				$121.86

Hence, expected contribution/call to Physician Referral = $121.86 x 0.7 = $85.30

Break-even number of calls in Physician Referral System = $\frac{\$74,576}{\$85.30}$ = 874

[a]NPV = net present value based on a discount rate of 10%.

Exhibit TN-8 Break-Even for Weight-Loss (W-L) and Quit-Smoking (Q-S) Programs

1.	Contribution from each person attending program:	$90.00
2.	Of people attending program, number who will contact an ANH physician (70% x 10%):	7%
3.	Contribution/person contacting an ANH physician:	$121.86
4.	Total expected contribution/person attending program:	= $90 + (.07 x 121.86) = $90 + 8.53 = $98.53
5.	Contribution/caller to these programs:	$98.53 x .6 = $59.11
6.	Number of people who called for these programs:	(693 + 655) = 1348
7.	Number of people who attended (60% of callers):	809
8.	Total contribution from these programs:	809 x $98.53 = $79,711
9.	Cost of ads for the programs: $\left(\frac{37}{205} \times \$294{,}000\right)$	$53,063
10.	Net contribution from the W-L and Q-S programs:	$26,648
11.	Break-even number of people needed to attend program: (53,058/98.53)	539
		=40.0% of those who call (539/1348)

Exhibit TN-9 Break-even Analysis of Medformation

	Weight Loss	Quit Smoking	Phys. Ref.	Cancer	Med. Inf.	Others	Total
Number of Ads	15	22	52	16	15	85	205
Number of Calls	693	655	2,338	2,974	2,830	19,177	28,667
Calls/Ad	46.2	29.8	45.0	185.9	188.7	225.6	139.8
Cost/Call	31.0	48.2	31.9	7.7	7.6	6.4	10.3
% Attending Program	60%	60%	--	--	--	--	
% of Callers who Contact ANH Physician	4.2%	4.2%	70%	7%	7%	7%	
Contribution/Person From Program	$90	$90	--	--	--	--	
Contribution/Person Contacting Physician	$121.86	$121.86	$121.86	$121.86	$121.86	$121.86	$121.86
Number of Attendees	416	393	--	--	--	--	675
Number Contacting Physician	29	28	1,637	208	198	1,342	3,432
Contrib./Program	$37,440	$35,370	--	--	--	--	$72,810
Contrib. Through Hospital Use	$3,534	$3,412	$199,485	$25,347	$24,128	$163,536	$419,442
Gross Contribution	$40,974	$38,782	$199,485	$25,347	$24,128	$163,536	$492,252
Cost of Ads (@ $1434.15 ea)	21,512	31,551	74,576	22,946	21,512	121,903	294,000
Net Contribution	19,462	7,231	124,909	2,401	2,616	41,633	198,252
Contribution/Caller	$59.12	$59.12	$85.30	$8.53	$8.53	$8.53	
Break-even Number of Calls	364	533	874	2690	2521	14,291	21,273

Exhibit TN-10 Ad Effectiveness as a Function of Ad Frequency

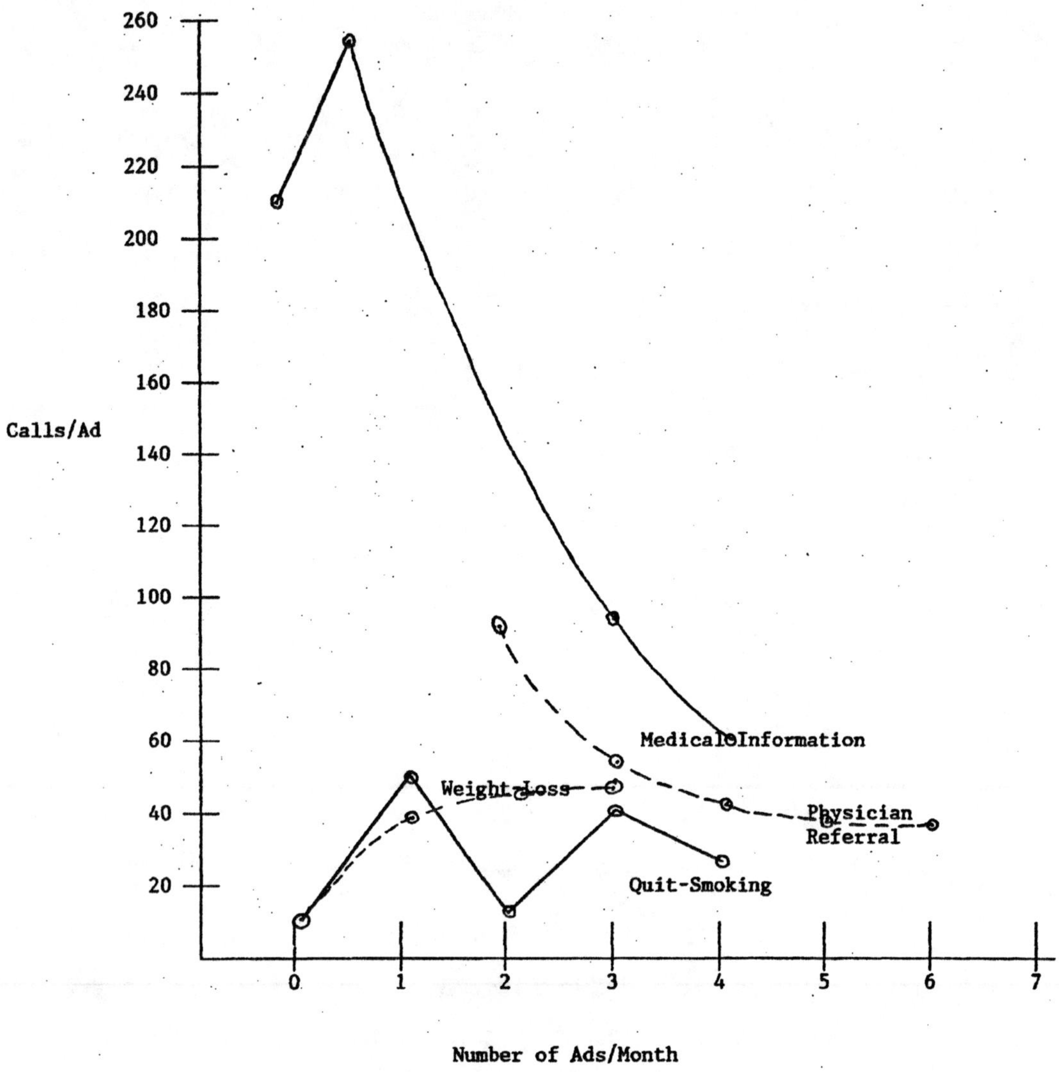

Exhibit TN-11 Assessing Marketing Performance

EFFICIENCY

"DOING THINGS RIGHT"

- Awareness
- Number of Calls
- Calls/Ad
- Contribution/Call
- Number of Participants in Programs
- Contribution per Program
- Contribution per Person Contacting Physician
- Total Net Contribution
- Market Share
- Bed Occupancy Rate
- Revenue $/Advertising $
- Profits

EXTERNALITIES

"UNEXPECTED FACTORS"

- First Artificial Heart Implant in a Woman
- Luck

EFFECTIVENESS

"DOING THE RIGHT THINGS"
(from a mission viewpoint)

- What are ANH's goals?
- Is ANH doing what is most appropriate to achieve these goals?
- Should ANH be concentrating its marketing efforts on consumers or physicians?
- Is this the best way for ANH to spend dollars? Should it instead improve its equipment and facilities?

ETHICS

"DOING THE RIGHT THINGS"
(from an ethical viewpoint)

- Is it appropriate for ANH to market itself, its products and services? If yes, for what ends?
- Is the Medformation advertising deceptive? Manipulative?
- Would you approve the request to provide coffee and donuts to ambulance drivers and paramedics to gain market share?

Exhibit TN-12 Teaching Questions

1. Should Hillestad get the money? Prove it!
2. What's ANH's business, and what does it sell? How are ANH's goals different from those of a for-profit hospital?
3. What drives the health care business, and what are the roles of its various constituents? How has the industry changed between 1965 and 1985?
4. How is health care bought? What is the trade-off between price and quality?
5. What is the role of Medformation? Does Medformation work? Is it effective? Is it efficient?
6. What is the role of WomenCare and does it work?
7. How should money be allocated? Is too much being spent on Medformation?
8. How should we measure marketing performance?

Exhibit TN-13 Board Plan

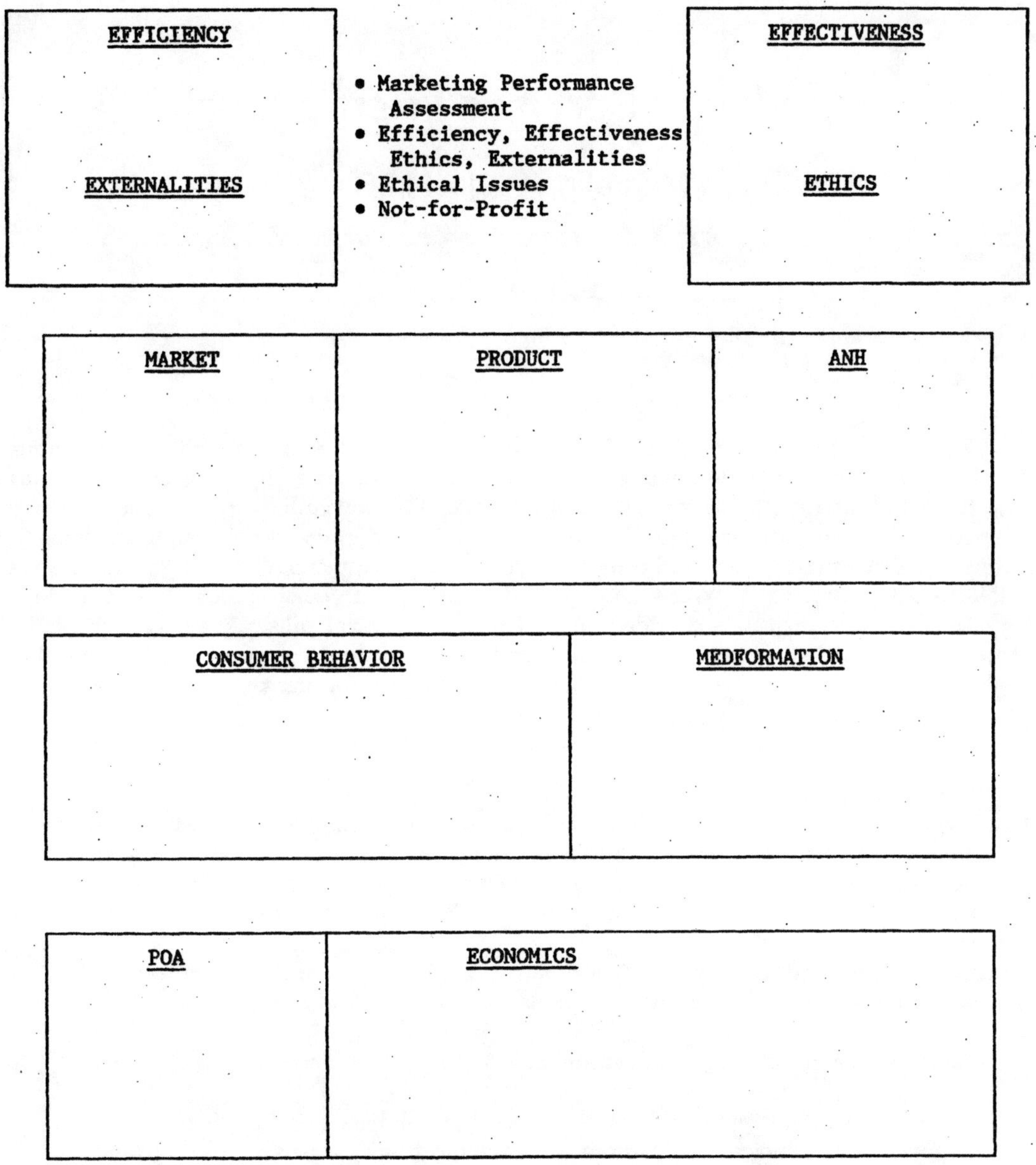

Population Services International

The Social Marketing Project in Bangladesh

Teaching Note

Synopsis

Population Services International (PSI) was a not-for-profit agency founded to disseminate family planning information and to market birth control products, primarily in developing countries seeking to curb rampant population growth. In 1976, PSI concluded an agreement with the government of Bangladesh to conduct the Social Marketing Program—a campaign using modern marketing techniques to sell subsidized contraceptives through commercial outlets. Seven years later, three PSI managers met at PSI's Washington, D.C. headquarters to discuss their 1984-86 marketing strategy for two products: Raja condoms and Maya birth control pills. They were particularly concerned that the marketing approach that had proven extremely successful for Raja was yielding poor sales results for Maya. PSI managers needed to devise a plan for improving Maya sales.

Use

This case focuses on the marketing mix, with particular emphasis on distribution channels and communications. Unlike most marketing cases, however, it raises important management issues concerning not-for-profit marketing and social marketing in a developing country. The case is best used in the communications module of a general marketing or consumer behavior course, as a contrast case to conventional marketing situations. Because of the underlying conceptual issues concerning mass-media advertising, word-of-mouth communication, and opinion leadership, it can also be used as a summary case for communications policy.

Major teaching objectives of the case are to:

1. sharpen students' understanding of consumer behavior and how it relates to a marketer's choice of mass communication versus word-of-mouth communication;

This teaching note was prepared by Assistant Professor V. Kasturi Rangan as an aid to instructors in the classroom use of the case "Population Services International," HBS No. 586-013.

2. force students to come up with criteria for measuring performance, especially when standard measures such as profits, sales, and market share appear too limited in scope;

3. expose students to the notion of social marketing—the society as a whole is expected to benefit from the program, but the marketing organization itself may or may not make a profit, and individual consumers may or may not perceive the benefits.

Analysis

Three major topics generally come up for discussion in class: the marketing plan for Maya; the nature and purpose of social marketing; and the objectives and goals of the members of the Project Council. Analysis outlines for each of the topics follow.

I. Marketing Plan for Maya

Devising a marketing plan for Maya is the heart of the case, and the first point to establish is that Maya has severe problems. It is quite clear from the case that Raja, on the other hand, has been a success.

Maya's Problems

Case **Exhibit 1** shows declining sales for Maya. Between 1978 and 1980, sales appeared to grow rapidly, from 481,000 cycles to 1,098,000 cycles, but since then sales have dropped steeply to 622,000 cycles by 1983. Case **Exhibit 8** tells the same story in Couple Years Protection (CYP) units. These data have been projected graphically in **Exhibit TN-1**; it is clear that Maya's market share is dropping while the primary market is growing.

Raja condoms, on the other hand, are doing very well. Case **Exhibit 1**, case **Exhibit 8**, and other data show that

- Raja sales have grown steadily from 9.7 million pieces in 1978 to 50.4 million pieces in 1983.

- Raja has enjoyed tremendous market share growth from 17.32% in 1978 to 59.29% in 1983. (Market share is obtained by dividing Raja CYPs by Condom CYPs—see case **Exhibit 8**.)

	Raja CYP	Market CYP	Raja Share
1978	97	560	17.32%
1979	173	330	52.41
1980	227	640	35.47
1981	316	590	53.46
1982	358	680	52.46
1983	504	850	59.29

Exhibit TN-2 provides graphs of sales and market share figures. The sales trend graph shows that the Raja and industry lines are nearly parallel after 1981, indicating that market growth came almost entirely from Raja.

The question arises: What should PSI and Bill Schellstede (country manager) do about Maya? Three options emerge from pages 11, 12, and 13 of the case:

1) keep Maya, improve retailer margins, and provide heavy communications support;

2) keep Maya, but go to market through the rural medical practitioners; or,

3) drop Maya and introduce a new product with a fresh positioning and communication strategy.

Option 1 is essentially a repetition of the Raja success formula. PSI has used intensive advertising and distribution for marketing Raja and this option suggests an extension of the same strategy for Maya. Option 2 is a radical departure from PSI's current strategy and would refocus its efforts from advertising to word-of-mouth communication. The option 1 versus option 2 debate is the central tension in the case. Option 3 is not controversial, but very difficult to address without some careful analysis of the consumers and their buying behavior. These issues are addressed under four topics, outlines for which are provided below.

These are only suggestions; student and instructor interest may generate a somewhat different outline. Regardless of the conclusions that the class may reach, it is absolutely critical for the class to analyze the suggested topic areas in order to design an action plan for improving Maya sales.

1. Market Analysis

There is no clear need or motivation for the Bangladesh people to practice family planning. The major reasons for this are:

- 85% of the population is Muslim and Islam teaches that family planning is against the will of God (page 4 of case);

- Customs and culture motivate families to have several sons and at least as many sons as daughters (page 5 of case); and

- People are generally ignorant of birth control practices (page 5 of case).

The Bangladesh government, however, wishes to curb its population's growth because the high growth rate has produced a low per-capita income (case, page 3). Twenty million couples in the fertile age group (case, page 5) were the primary target of the government's family-planning efforts. Using the aggregate market data given on page 9 of the case, and the Couple Years Protection (CYP) conversion factors given in Footnote 4 at the bottom of page 11, the effectiveness of different contraceptive methods are calculated as follows:

- *Condoms* → 85.00 million pieces divided by the CYP conversion factor of 100 = 850,000 CYPs

- *Pills* → 7.8 million cycles divided by the CYP conversion factor of 13 = 600,000 CYPs

- *IUDs* → 75,000 multiplied by the CYP conversion factor of 2.5 = 187,500 CYPs

- *Sterilization* → 300,000 multiplied by the CYP conversion factor of 7.75 = 2,325,000 CYPs.

All methods together provide a total of 3.96 million CYPs. Of the 20 million couples, slightly under 4 million couples practice family planning; thus, 80% of the target population is unprotected, highlighting the importance of the government's objective. **Exhibit TN-3** gives market share figures by product category and also by aggregate CYP numbers. From **Exhibits TN-1, TN-2, and TN-3**, the following conclusions emerge:

1. Maya's market share is dropping.

2. Private pharmaceutical firms with higher-priced products (page 12 of case), have a higher market share for contraceptive pills.

3. Raja's market share is increasing.

4. Even though Tahiti brand condoms are given away free by the government (page 8 of case), the nominally priced Raja, which consumers must purchase (albeit at a nominal price), has a commanding market share.

2. Distribution Channels

The country's retail network consists of 30,000 pharmacies, 40,000 general stores, and 30,000 pan stores. Retailers are supplied through a system of wholesalers and stockists (who buy bulk from wholesalers and sell in smaller lots to retailers). The bigger pharmacies and general stores are predominantly located in urban areas; smaller pharmacies and general stores, and most of the pan stores, are located in rural areas.

Pan stores stay open late at night and are places for men to gather and gossip. These late hours and the predominantly male patronage make pan stores ill-suited for the female shopper. PSI is very strong in this channel—an important reason for Raja's success. An interesting question is whether Maya should be sold through this male-patronized outlet; the answer is not obvious, however, because the case also tells us (first Ciszewski quote, case page 11) that women in Bangladesh do little of the shopping.

Exhibits TN-4 and **TN-5** show the profit percentages and return on investment for Raja and Maya. The profit margins and ROI look very attractive to the trade. The numbers, however, are deceptive; Raja and Maya account for only a small portion of a retailer's total sales volume. Case **Exhibit 3** gives the Social Marketing Program's (SMP) 1983 revenues as $423,000; assuming an average 40% mark-up in the channel, retail sales revenues are about $590,000. Hence, average annual sales for each of the 80,000 outlets is roughly $7.00; and with a retail margin of 20%, the average net income per store is about $1.50. Compared to the average per-capita income of $120, this does not seem to be a great financial incentive.

3. Communication Channels

There are the usual sources of mass communication in Bangladesh, and several unique sources of personal communication. Mass-communication media include radio, television, cinemas, newspapers, and billboards. Personal-communication sources include 5,000 Western-trained professional doctors, 100,000 rural medical practitioners (RMPs), 20,000 spiritual healers, and 25,000 field workers. The following observations influence the perceived effectiveness of these communication channels.

1. Women are more susceptible to personal influence than men (first Ciszewski quote, case, page 11).

2. Mass communication is effective in urban areas (case **Exhibit 9**).

3. Personal communication is effective in rural areas (case **Exhibit 9**).

4. Men seem more concerned with the economic benefits of family planning, whereas women seem more concerned with the social and health benefits (case **Exhibit 5**).

5. Maya is well-known and almost a generic name for pills (sales supervisor report, page 12).

Of the four personal communication sources, the 25,000 field workers are effective, but they concentrate on the clinical methods of family planning. The 20,000 spiritual doctors are so unscientific (and dangerous) that PSI cannot seriously consider using them. This basically leaves PSI with the 5,000 professional doctors and the 100,000 RMPs. The question of whether to include one or both groups in Maya's communication plan will provoke an interesting discussion in class—especially with respect to the RMPs, who are usually described as quacks. Students often express the following assumptions about these two groups:

Professional Doctors:

- They are well-trained, educated in English, and urbane (page 7 of case).
- They are probably biased in favor of English-sounding brands of medicines (page 12 of case).
- They are out of touch with the SMP sales force because, unlike the private competition, SMP does not call on them.
- They write prescriptions, but drugs can be bought at pharmacies without prescriptions (page 6 of case).

Rural Medical Practitioners:

- They lack formal training, but they maintain a semblance of professionalism by pursuing their professional careers and staying in touch with trained doctors (page 7 of case).
- They perform the role of friend, philosopher, and guide to their patients (page 13 of case).
- They are probably biased in favor of Bengali-sounding brand names.
- They also dispense medicines and hence, function as retailers (page 7 of case).
- They don't seem to like Maya (pages 12 and 13).
- They are ignored by the SMP sales force.

4. Reasons for Raja's Success and Maya's Failure

From an analysis of the market as well as distribution and communication channels several reasons for Raja's success emerge.

1. Appropriate selection of the brand name—Raja (page 8 of case).

2. Heavy advertising expenditure—$400,000 (page 11 of case).

3. Intensive distribution—80,000 out of 100,000 outlets carry Raja (pages 6 and 10 of case).

4. Pan stores ideally suited for distributing the product.

5. Attractive packaging—colorful, in three formats (page 9 of case)

6. Attractive retail margins (page 10 of case).

7. Heavy media allocation for point-of-purchase (case **Exhibit** 7).

Points 1 and 2 suggest that Raja was a pull brand; points 6 and 7 suggest that Raja was a push brand; and points 3, 4, and 5 can be interpreted either way. Raja's market success can be used to stimulate class debate, as many students will want to identify Raja's key success factors and duplicate them for Maya. At this stage, a comparison of Raja and Maya is inevitable. Not only are the products different, they need quite different marketing strategies. Raja is an over-the-counter consumer product with no known side effects; it is widely available and is usually purchased by men. Raja's successful marketing strategy positions it as a mass communication-intensive product. On the other hand, consumers believe Maya is a powerful drug. Many side effects (real and imaginary) have been attributed to Maya. And although men buy Maya, women apparently seek professional advice before using the product. In short, Maya is a personal communications-intensive product.

Some students will argue that Raja and Maya are complementary products, and that Raja's success is the real cause of Maya's failure. This argument would make sense if the market had been saturated, but as the *Market Analysis* section of this teaching note indicated (only 3.96 of the 20 million couples practice family planning), there is a tremendous untapped market.

Several possible reasons for Maya's failure emerge. But, interestingly enough, the discussion of pros and cons under each are fairly balanced. It is for the students to identify key reasons for Maya's failure and demonstrate how their action plan supports their analysis.

Student discussions tend to generate a lot of support for

- RMPs (versus professional doctors).

- Distribution-intensive strategy (versus communication-intensive strategy).

- Bengali name (versus English name).

- Pharmacies (versus pan stores).

Analysis of Maya's Failure

Cons	Pros
Brand Name	
- Does not have Raja-like mass appeal.	- Widely recognized. Is often mistaken for the generic pill.
- Pills with foreign names have good sales.	- A meaningful Bengali name will be widely understood.
- Professional doctors associate Bengali name with poor effectiveness.	
Distribution Channels	
- Pan stores are male-dominated channels.	- Currently has intensive distribution. Is widely available.
Communications	
- Current strategy excludes RMPs who appear very influential in the decision-making process.	- Direct communication to customers helps maintain accuracy and control of information being conveyed.
- Approaching RMPs may increase program cost.	- Mass media approach will reach the maximum number of people at minimum cost.
Price	
- Current price too low. Higher priced private brands do better.	- Priced on par with daily consumables, thus within easy reach of the masses.
- Current price too low, might be conveying poor quality.	

Student discussions tend to generate a lot of support for

- RMP (versus professional doctors),
- Distribution intensive strategy (versus communication- intensive strategy),
- Bengali name (versus English name),
- Pharmacies (versus pan stores).

But, as the analysis outlined under Market, Distribution Channels, Communication Channels, and Raja versus Maya indicates, the arguments are far more balanced than what the class may perceive. Instructors should make sure that under each analysis area, several counterarguments emerge before they move on to the next discussion area. This is absolutely crucial in order to ensure a balance among the three choices indicated on page 4 of this teaching note.

II. What is Social Marketing?

Social marketers do not have ready-made markets with consumers who express an immediate need for the product. Society's leaders believe the product is needed, but all individuals do not always share this belief. This subtle, but important, distinction is a good starting point for the discussion. Instructors can probe for parallels with other communication campaigns—those against cigarette smoking, drunken driving, etc. It is also important to note that in the PSI case, the marketing message is aimed at consumers who are, by and large, illiterate.

The entire discussion from the earlier analysis on the market and the consumer presents powerful evidence for this section. For instance, the Bangladesh government gives away its condoms free, yet Raja has the dominant share! The interesting question is, why? Is it because Raja is supported by marketing, unlike Tahiti? Some students will point out that PSI's marketing efforts are not costless to the consumer. Raja and Maya have to be purchased for a sum of money, while government-distributed contraceptives are free. The question of which method provides a greater benefit to society leads to an exciting discussion in class. Supporters of either approach should be pressed to provide quantitative support for their arguments. An illustrative benefit-to-cost calculation is shown in **Exhibit TN-6**. The numbers indicate that the social marketing project delivers enormous benefits for the society. The assumptions underlying this calculation may be debated. Under a different set of assumptions, costs may in fact exceed benefits. Nevertheless, it is useful in class to quickly get through the mechanics of the numbers, but focus on the assumptions underlying the calculations. That's where the core of the social marketing debate rests. While students are generally well-prepared with qualitative arguments concerning social costs and benefits, very few attempt to quantify them. The lack of numbers does not take away the excitement of the debate.

PSI's pricing policy (page 10 of the case) raises another interesting aspect of social marketing. The product is priced far below cost, but it is not free; thus, consumer motivation and consumer value are major issues—especially in the case of Maya, a powerful drug with major side effects. PSI's pricing is not based on cost nor value, but on parity with the price of a cup of coffee or tea!

Finally, of course, the motivations and objectives of PSI managers Harvey, Ciszewski, and Schellstede, are important for discussion. It is clear from SMP's balance sheet (case **Exhibit 3**) that there is little financial incentive for these managers. What drives them? Are they marketers or social workers, and what is the difference?

III. Objectives of the Project Council

It is not readily apparent that, despite Maya's market failure and the need to devise a new plan for it, the Project Council (the equivalent of a board of directors) is really concerned about Maya's part in the Social Marketing Program. This apparent indifference makes it useful to examine the membership of the Project Council. The four key groups are:

1. PSI, based in Washington, D.C.

2. SMP, the local organization that implements strategy. Its marketing and sales organization appears to be professional and well-managed.

3. The Bangladesh government, a key player not only because of its influence on policy, but also because it supplies competing products to the market.

4. USAID, the primary provider of funds for both project implementation (to SMP) and project supervision (to PSI). USAID also funds a part of the government's family planning efforts.

An interesting tension in the case revolves around the different objectives of each of these constituents.

PSI and SMP, for instance, are presumably eager to improve Maya sales and market share. The Bangladesh government, on the other hand, may be totally uninterested in PSI's market share—its sole concern being that family planning products reach as many people as possible. USAID's chief concern is the delivery of products in the most cost-effective manner. If Raja proves more cost-effective than Maya, then USAID will terminate the Maya program. (The Bangladesh people, of course, would be solely interested in how all this benefits them in the short run and long run.) **Exhibit TN-7** provides illustrative cost calculations. Such calculations are rarely surfaced by students in class. Nevertheless, it is extremely useful to take some time to discuss the goals and objectives of the several key players and attempt to develop quantitative measures for these goals.

Teaching The Case

There are two clear-cut starting options. One is to stay with the conventional marketing issues in the case and begin the discussion with a request for a marketing plan for Maya. The other option is to start with the idea of social marketing and discuss how it differs from conventional marketing. The first option creates a focused, decision-oriented discussion, which will then expand to include the social marketing issues. If the instructor begins with a discussion of social marketing, the initial discussion tends to be broad and philosophical, and becomes more focused and decision-oriented as the class proceeds. Both approaches have worked well for instructors; regardless of the approach, however, the three broad topics cited earlier—a marketing plan for Maya, the nature of social marketing, and the objectives of the Project Council—should be covered.

If these topics are discussed in the above sequence, a disciplined and coherent class discussion usually ensues. A more informal approach will produce a less-focused discussion, but it will also provide more spontaneity and excitement. In either situation, because of the unusual nature of the subject matter, instructors should provide summaries at the end of class. Some suggestions appear at the end of this note.

In terms of time management, the first topic (a marketing plan for Maya) requires between 50 and 60 minutes; the other two topics each need 10 to 15 minutes.

Questions for Discussion

The following list of questions often stimulate student analysis and discussion.

1. *What is your plan for improving Maya sales?*

This question will elicit as many answers as there are students. Categorizing the various recommendations under one of three options listed in the case (pages 11 and 12) will enable instructors to establish contrasts which facilitate analysis of Maya's markets, consumers, and distribution channels. With each option, several follow-up questions can help draw out student discussion.

Option One: Keep Maya, improve retailer margins, and provide significant communications support.

- How should the product be distributed? Prices and margins?
- What should the marketing message say? Why?
- Who is the consumer? How will they buy the product?
- Is Maya a communications-intensive product?

Option Two: Keep Maya, but go to market through rural medical practitioners.

- Are rural medical practitioners a help or a hindrance?
- Raja ignored RMPs successfully, why not Maya?
- How is Maya different from Raja?

Option Three: Drop Maya and introduce a new product with a fresh positioning and communication strategy.

- What should be the name for the new product? Bengali or English?
- Who are the target consumers? Urban women or rural women?
- Who will buy the product? Male or female?
- What will influence their purchase decision?

2. *What is social marketing? How is it different from conventional marketing?*

3. *Are the consumers in Bangladesh being taken for a ride by PSI?*

4. *How do you measure the effectiveness of a social program?*

5. *How will you sell your marketing plan to the Project Council?*

6. *What are the implications of this plan? How much will it cost?*

7. *Which members of the council will like your plan? Who will oppose it, and why?*

Other Teaching Observations

1. A list of possible discussion/preparation questions appears in **Exhibit TN-8**.

2. A suggested board plan is provided in **Exhibit TN-9**.

3. There is a 30-minute video in four parts that introduces Bangladesh and describes the case problem and the Social Marketing Project. Starting off the class with the first part of this video (six minutes) brings a seriousness to the class discussion by emphasizing the gravity of the population crisis in Bangladesh.

   The second part (four minutes) of the video has family-planning commercials (with English commentary). This portion of the tape, though instructive, is not essential, and may be used at the instructor's discretion. The third and fourth parts of the videotape have about four minutes of "what happened" and about 15 minutes of excerpts from motivational films on family planning (with English commentary). These two parts do not directly contribute to the teaching objectives and should only be screened after class, if at all.

4. Because of the nature of the product, women students become deeply involved in the discussions. Instructors should also anticipate student interest in the ethical considerations of the case; for example:

   - the morality of birth control;
   - the morality of marketing powerful drugs in Third World countries.

Some instructors use a good portion of the class (20 to 30 minutes) discussing these ethical and moral issues. Despite their obvious interest for students, it is usually better to avoid them—the case is rich in other areas which merit serious discussion. Also, morality is contextual: If the people of

Bangladesh have collectively decided (through their government) that family planning is good for them, there is no reason to impose one's own personal standards on this decision.

Concluding Comments

Some instructors prefer to tell their classes what finally happened in the case. Others avoid it for fear of suggesting that there is only one right answer. A brief note on the final marketing decision appears at the end of this section, but this is one case in which instructors may want to make important points that go beyond the mere facts of the case. A summary woven around some of the following themes has been well-received by past students.

1. *Consumers*: The existence of widely different perceptions of, and attitudes to, products and services (which we take for granted in Western society) offers an important lesson—especially for students interested in international marketing. We often assume we have expert knowledge when it comes to consumer behavior; serious misinterpretation, however, can follow this assumption. For example, few people realize that, in a poor country, economic and cultural factors usually encourage large rather than small families.

2. *Social Marketing*: The whole notion of social marketing—promoting a product or an idea that apparently lacks consumer demand—is an interesting one. The question of whether such activities are ethical or not is complicated but well worth consideration.

3. *Not-For-Profit Marketing*: The goals of not-for-profit marketing and the measures for evaluating them are complex; and they are further complicated by different priorities among individual constitutents. A few comments on this interesting issue, combined with comparisons to for-profit marketing situations, often helps students.

What Happened

Because of brand awareness, PSI decided to keep Maya and promote it in rural areas. The distribution channels were not changed, but the RMPs became a key part of the communications effort. SMP sales supervisors organized conferences to educate the RMPs and win their cooperation in recommending and selling Maya. One such conference is shown in the Part 3 of the videotape. However, a second pill, with an English name, Ovacon, was introduced for the urban customer. Ovacon was less powerful than Maya and was promoted through the professional doctors. A typical sales call is shown in Part 3 of the videotape. With these changes, PSI achieved tremendous success and improved its market share for birth control pills to about 20% by 1985.

Exhibit TN-1 Population Services International

Sales: Total Market and Maya

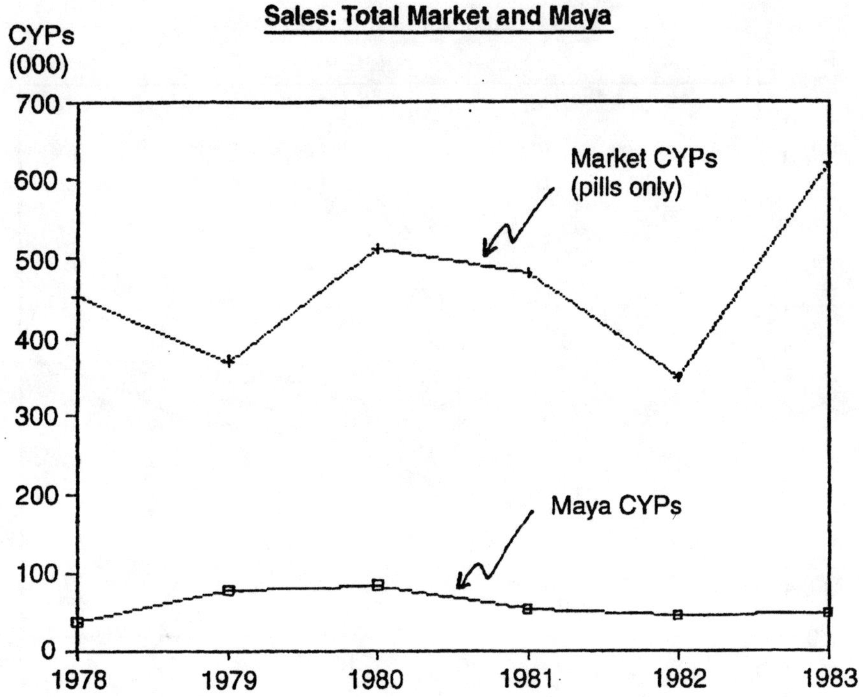

CVPs: Maya Market Share

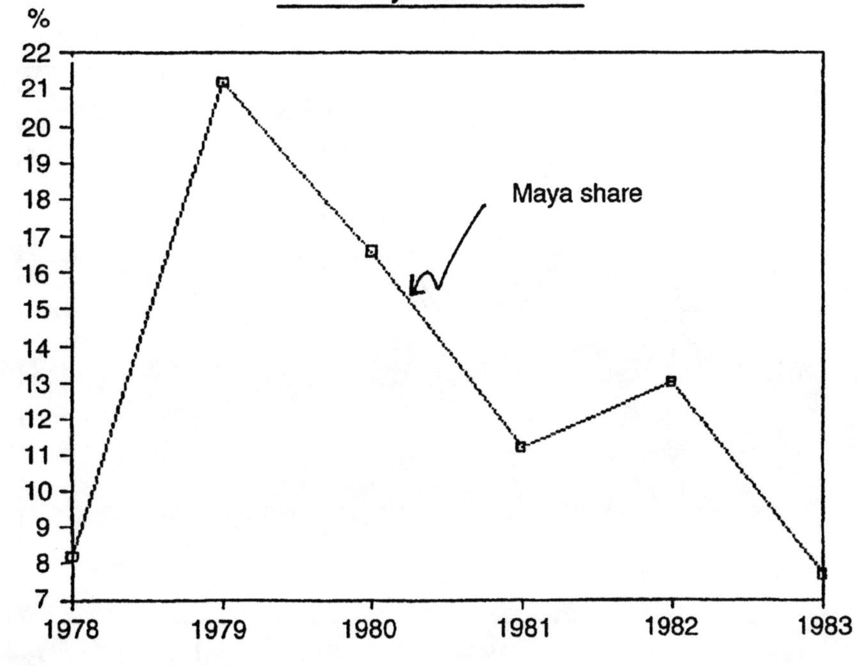

Source: Case Exhibit 8

Exhibit TN-2 Population Services International

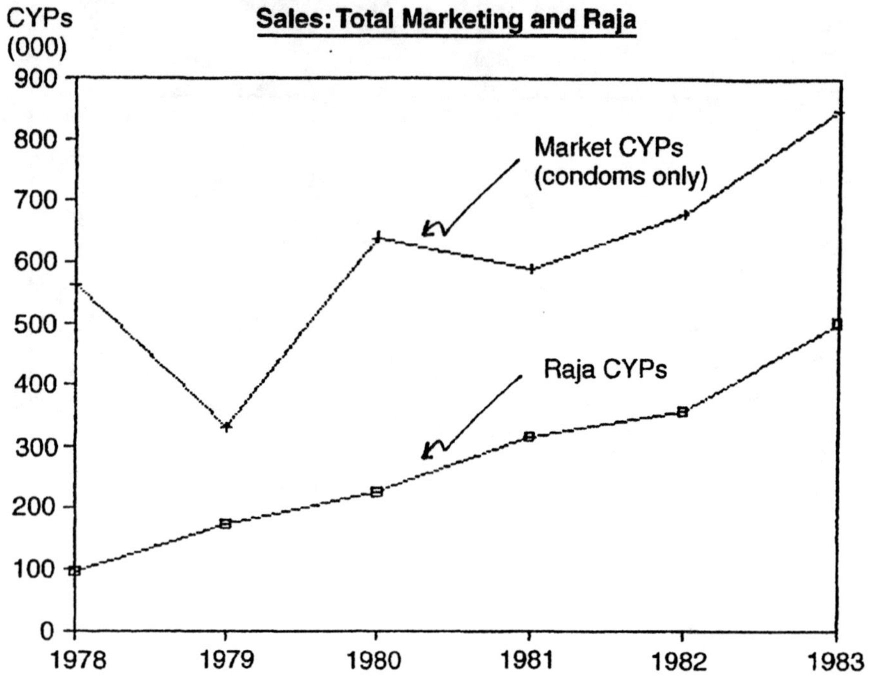

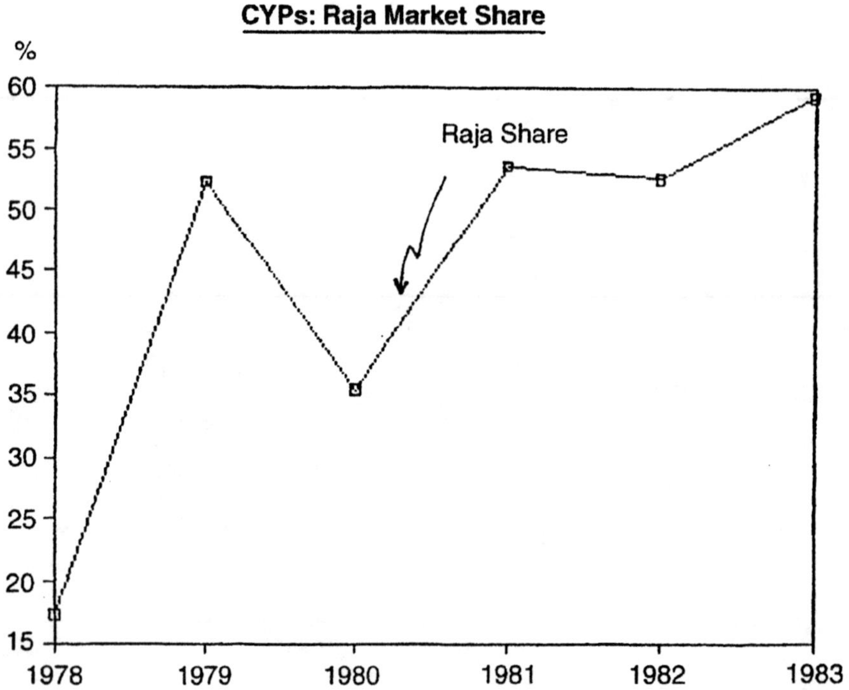

Source: Case Exhibit 8

Exhibit TN-3 Population Services International

Family Planning Products and Services: 1983 Market

Product/Service	Units Sold/Provided (1,000s)	% of Total Product Sales	Price	CYPs Provided (000)	Percentage of Total
1. Condoms					
Raja	50,000	59%	Nominal	500	13.0
Tahiti[a]	25,000	29	Free	250	6.0
Sultan	5,000	6	N/A	50	1.0
Durex	3,000	4	N/A	30	1.0
Others	2,000	2	N/A	20	1.0
	85,000	100%		850	22.0%
2. Pills					
Government	3,000	38	Free	230	6.0
Ovastat	2,000	26	High	154	4.0
Lyndiol, etc.	2,000	26	High	154	4.0
Maya	600	8	Nominal	46	1.0
Others	200	3	N/A	15	.5
	7,800	100%		600	15.0%
3. IUD[b]	75	—	—	188	5.0%
4. Sterilizations[b]	300	—	—	2,325	58.0%
Total	—	—	—	3,963	

[a]Government brand.

[b]Sterilizations and IUDs were provided by the government.

Note: PSI Share of Market: Raja 13% + Maya 1% = 14%.
Govt. Share of Market: Tahiti 6% + Pill 6% + IUD 5% + Sterilization 58% = 75%.

Source: Case, pages 9 and 11, and footnote 4.

Exhibit TN-4 Population Services International

Distribution Channels: Margins for Raja

	Cost ($)	Margin ($)	Selling Price ($)	Margin ($)
Channel:				
Wholesaler	0.29[a]	0.02	0.31	6.5
Stockist	0.31	0.02	0.33	6.1
Retailer	0.33	0.07	0.40[b]	17.5

[a]SMP selling price.

[b]Price to consumer.

Raja: Return on Investment

	Margin (%)	X	Average Inventory Turns	=	ROI%
Channel:					
Wholesaler	6.5	X	11	=	71%
Stockist	6.1	X	11	=	67
Retailer	17.5	X	7	=	122

Source: Page 10 of case.

Exhibit TN-5 Population Services International

Distribution Channels: Margins for Maya

	Cost ($)	Margin ($)	Selling Price ($)	Margin (%)
Channel:				
Wholesaler	0.45[a]	0.04	0.49	8.2
Stockist	0.49	0.04	0.53	7.5
Retailer	0.53	0.17	0.70[b]	24.3

[a]SMP selling price.
[b]Price to consumer.

Maya: Return on Investment

	Margin	X	Average Inventory Turns	=	ROI%
Channel:					
Wholesaler	8.2	X	5.5	=	45
Stockist	7.5	X	5.5	=	41
Retailer	24.3	X	3.5	=	85

Source: Page 10 of case.

Exhibit TN-6 Population Services International

CYP Benefits Achieved with SMP

	CYPs[a] Raja	+ Maya	Total SMP CYPs	Births Averted[b]
1978	97,000	37,000	134,000	33,500
1979	173,000	78,500	251,500	62,750
1980	227,000	84,500	311,500	77,750
1981	316,000	54,000	370,000	92,500
1982	358,000	45,500	403,400	100,850
1983	504,000	47,800	551,800	137,950
			Total	505,300

[a]From case, **Exhibit 8.**

[b]From case, page 13, footnote 6. Births averted = 0.25 x CYP.

Cost-Benefit Calculation for 1983:

1983 GNP = 100 million people x $120 per capital income[a].

= $12,000 million

[a]From case, page 3, last paragraph.

In 1983, if not for SMP, there would have been 137,950 more people born in Bangladesh (see table at top of page).

The benefits delivered by SMP equals:

$$\frac{\text{1983 GNP}}{\text{1983 population}} - \frac{\text{1983 GNP}}{\text{1983 population without SMP}} \times \text{Total Population}$$

or:

$$\frac{\$12{,}000}{100} - \frac{\$12{,}000}{100.138} \times 100 = \text{16.54 million in one year.}$$

What is the Benefit-to-Cost ratio? (Using costs from next **Exhibit TN-G** under SMP: operating costs):

$$\frac{\text{Savings}}{\text{Costs}} \quad \frac{\$16.53}{0.92} = \underline{18}$$

Exhibit TN-7 Population Services International

Birth Control Program Costs: Government and SMP, in 1983

Government sterilization:

Cost: $15[a]

CYPs provided: 7.75 CYP[b]

Cost per CYP: $\frac{\$15.00}{7.75} = \$1.93$

[a]From case, page 8, lines 2-3.
[b]From case, page 11, footnote 4.

SMP:

Cost: $5.143 million[a]

CYPs provided: 504,000 + 47,800 = 551,800[b]

Cost per CYP: $\frac{\$5.143}{.55} = \$9.35$

[a]Case, Exhibit 3.
[b]Case, Exhibit 8.

But, $5,143 million is not the true cost to the Bangladesh government. Only the operating costs are relevant, thus:

SMP: operating costs:

Operating expenses	:	$1,343,000[a]
Sales revenues	:	- 423,556[a]
Operating costs	:	$ 919,444
Cost per CYP	:	$\frac{\$.92 \text{ million}}{.55 \text{ million}^{b}} = \$1.67$ CYP

[a]Case, Exhibit 3
[b]Case, Exhibit 8

So, SMP is 15% more cost effective: (1.93 - 1.67)/ 1.67 = 15%.

Since the true costs of the SMP are $9.35/CYP (see above), if USAID's only objective is population control in Bangladesh, it should set up sterilization clinics, which cost only $1.93/CYP.

Exhibit TN-8 Population Services International

Possible Discussion or Preparation Questions for Population Services International

1. What is your plan for improving Maya sales?

2. What is social marketing. How is it different from conventional marketing?

3. Why does Raja work so well?

4. Explain the competitive environment in Bangledesh. Is it true we are competing with the government, which is *giving away* its goods?

5. Explain the consumption system, including buying behavior, the distribution channels, the medical community.

6. Prove your plan is an effective one. What does it cost, and what does it return?

7. How will you sell your marketing plan to the Project Council?

Exhibit TN-9 Population Services International

Board Plan for Population Services

Raja Success Factors

What is Social Marketing

Front

Action Plan for Maya

Middle

Analysis

Consumers **Channels** **Communications**

Rear

Roles and Objectives of Members of Project Council

The Dana-Farber Cancer Institute: Development Strategy

Teaching Note

Synopsis

The case describes in fair detail the funding strategies and tactics of Dana-Farber, a premier cancer research and care institution in Boston. Dana Farber runs at a deficit of about $35 million to $40 million (about 25% of its operating budget) every year, which is funded by the development office's wide-ranging fundraising efforts. The case concludes with three vignettes, each concerning a potential gift of about $1 million which is accompanied by a unique complication, making it difficult to decide whether to accept or not accept the money.

Assignment Questions

1. Which of the three fundraising opportunities described on pages 14 and 15 of the case should Dana-Farber accept? Why?
    - The $1 million from the major food company.
    - The $350K/year for three years from the up-and-coming Asian car manufacturer.
    - The $1 million from the major medical products company.
2. Would you alter the portfolio of fundraising programs utilized at Dana-Farber? How does each contribute to the mission and strategy of the institution?
3. What are the one or two major challenges facing Susan Paresky as the Chief Development Officer of this highly successful institution? How should she address them?
4. How does your development effort compare or differ from Dana-Farber? Why? Are there any lessons for your organization?

This note was prepared by Professor V. Kasturi Rangan for the sole purpose of aiding classroom instructors in the use of The Dana-Farber Cancer Institute: Development Strategy, HBS No. 599-104. It provides analysis and questions that are intended to present alternative approaches to deepening students' comprehension of business issues and energizing classroom discussion.

The $1 Million Gift from the Food Company

Against:

1. The money is tainted, because the food company is owned by a tobacco company. But cigarettes cause cancer and Dana-Farber is attempting to cure cancer: completely inconsistent with the mission.
2. Potential PR damage such an association could cause, especially after the recent overdose incident.
3. Will affect the morale of employees, especially researchers.
4. Could deteriorate the brand image and the Jimmy Fund name.

For:

1. All money is tainted. What about an investment bank with tobacco stocks? How about alcohol? Where will this stop? The check comes from the food company anyway.
2. Instead of being skeptical, let's take the money and put it to good use—at least that way we can make the tobacco company pay indirectly.
3. Take the money and use it as an opportunity to constructively educate the tobacco company. The partnership will provide the opportunity. If you turn it away, you will have no way of educating the enemy.

The $350K/Year for 3 Years Cause Marketing Gift from the Up-and-coming Asian Car Manufacturer.

For:

1. The money is clean; as long as we accept cause marketing as a legitimate way to raise money, nothing is wrong with this.
2. Gives Dana Farber an opportunity to reach new donors (Asian consumers and also Asian manufacturers).
3. The donor is willing to be an exclusive supporter of Dana-Farber.

Against:

1. Will the arrangement with a small car manufacturer preclude a bigger potential with a larger company like GM or Ford?
2. Is it the right partnership? Dana-Farber is classy, but the Asian car manufacturer is only up-and-coming. We do not know its image or the type of automobiles it intends to bring to the market.
3. Using Dana-Farber's name for commercial activity is dangerous.

4. Is Dana-Farber getting the right value for its partnership? Many students will suggest that the car company has more to gain from the association than Dana-Farber.

The $1 Million Gift from the Medical Device Company

For:

1. There is a mission match. Both are in the business of fighting diseases like cancer.

2. $500K is unrestricted and the other $500K is only restricted as far as type of research is concerned. But the outcome of the research is unequivocally Dana-Farber's intellectual property. The company is even willing to hire and place the researcher.

3. This is the way to attract committed money (smart money) to address core mission issues.

Against:

1. Stretches research priorities and leads to mission drift. Perhaps could lead to a drain on key resources (e.g., scientists).

2. What seems like an innocuous arrangement might have contractual implications. Will this company use Dana-Farber's name and endorsement (e.g., American Medical Association and Sunbeam)?

3. This is nothing but for-profit commercialism in disguise.

All in all, the argument stacks up as follows:

Food Company	Car Company	Device Company
Poor fit with morals and values	In-between	Good fit
Unrestricted money	Unrestricted	Restricted money
High risk	Low risk	Low risk
High reward	Low reward	Low reward

Interestingly, what comes out of the discussion is that in each of these cases, what looks like a tactical development office decision is actually a fairly deep strategic decision. It involves serious assessment of mission and values and perhaps calls for the Board to provide guidelines. It also involves understanding research priorities of a research-driven institution. When taught in a non-profit program, this insight is critical. Most of the time, the fundraising or development arm is seen as a tactical organization when, in fact, it has to have a place in the strategy formulation table (even if not a voice). In fact, some will argue that the external voice and wisdom brought in by the donor market could and should actually influence strategy.

What is the Dana-Farber Brand?

In response to that question, students will often identify it as integrity, classy, sophisticated, children, cancer, emotional, etc. When the issue is pressed, it will emerge that the Jimmy Fund brand is associated with kids' cancer and cure, and the Dana-Farber brand with sophisticated, research-oriented, etc. At that stage, one can get into a fairly interesting discussion of the Jimmy Fund. Dana-Farber raises a considerable amount of money and it is used in an unrestricted way, but the public's perception is that it is for children's cancer. Should Dana-Farber reposition the brand? Now that Jimmy has returned, does a new "James" brand make sense, or alternatively, the same Jimmy Fund name could be repositioned as now being in the service of pediatric and adult cancers. After all, it can be argued that discovery and basic research benefits all types of cancer and there may not be a need to fine-tune and reposition. Also, the Jimmy Fund does other things than just raise money. It builds community commitment and it brings emotive, mass appeal to an important problem. It promotes awareness, and a lot of this public image it creates may, in fact, make it easy for the Dana-Farber brand to raise money from donors, individuals, corporations, and foundations.

Jimmy Fund	Dana-Farber
Mass appeal	Narrow
Emotional	Upscale
Children	All cancer
Cancer treatment	Research

It becomes interesting to observe that the Jimmy Fund is promoted through community events and is quite costly, whereas the Dana-Farber effort, because of its focus and scale, is more cost effective. When asked the question, "should we just focus on Dana-Farber and shut down Jimmy Fund because it is less effective?" students overwhelmingly responded against the recommendation because of the value of the Jimmy Fund.

The two different revenue streams could lead to an interesting, "Who is the customer?" discussion:

	Jimmy Fund	Development Fund
Customer:	Individuals, "the little people's charity"	Wealthy individuals, corporations, foundations
Amount given	General single dollar, or small amounts (except PanMass)	Large gifts in the $000s
Involvement	More doing (walking, cycling, buying tokens)	Writing checks, serving on the board, charity events
Number of people involved	Large numbers of small donors	Smaller number of large donors
"Purchase decision"	Impulse for cause marketing, events, theater, slightly longer for commitments such as PanMass, Walk, etc.	Longer term: couple of years for major gifts, annual fund donations may be part of giving strategy.
Pitch	Children's cancer	Cancer in general—the Institute
Reach	Broad	Narrow, focused
Organizational requirements	Organization of lots of people, volunteers, etc.	Professional fundraisers

There is a tension between these two types of customers and their events. For the most part, however, the tension is only one way. The public doesn't see/hear about the upscale donors—they are part of the "Dana-Farber," not the Jimmy Fund. The more upscale, exclusive donors (and the Board) may not want to be associated with too commercial, overblown efforts believing that it erodes the reputation of the DFCI. To deal with this tension, the Institute appears to be trying to affiliate the mass market Jimmy Fund fundraising with Boston institutions such as the Marathon, the Boston Red Sox, etc. Such affiliations may make the mass market pleas more palatable to the upscale donor and in effect enhance the image of the worthiness of the venture.

One could argue that the programs under the Jimmy Fund umbrella represent an interesting evolution:

Older programs: golf, theater-can collection, special events. These are the traditional Jimmy Fund programs—broad-reach events where contributors give a few dollars for a good cause and get an ice cream or some other feel-good experience. They are excellent at raising awareness of the Jimmy Fund—although less so of the DFCI. There is also a question about the efficiency of these programs that require the organization of many, many volunteers for somewhat modest returns.

New programs such as the PanMass Challenge and the Jimmy Fund Walk. These seem to be moving to more "upscale" customers. These people are either raising or personally donating a more significant amount of money. Moreover, the events are being made more selective by their design: financial commitments, "high-quality walkers," etc. One could argue that these people make more of a personal commitment to the cause and will therefore stay with it for a longer period of time. Additionally, as these people age, presumably they form the basis for the next generation of wealthy givers. However, the introduction of "exclusivity" seems to pull the Jimmy Fund away from its historical position.

As discussed on numerous occasions and raised in the case itself, there is the question of the positioning of the Jimmy Fund. The fund has huge name recognition, although it is likely that there is also a belief that the funds raised by the Jimmy Fund go almost exclusively to children's cancer research and care. That is not the case. The question is whether this is a problem, given:

- Financially, the Jimmy Fund contributed half of the fundraising.

- The Jimmy Fund is insulated from Dana-Farber. When scandal shook, the Institute of Development Fund had to stop fundraising; the Jimmy Fund kept on going. Arguably for many people, the Jimmy Fund is separate from Dana-Farber.

- There have been huge strides in children's cancer cures and care. Some of the most pressing needs are in adult cancer—but generally people are less willing to give for adults than for sick children. Of 1.3 million cancer cases every year, only 8,000 are children's cases (case exhibit). Moreover, 80% of children's cancers are curable.

- The question is whether it is acceptable for this to continue. While the DFCI believes the above to be the case, they do not have hard evidence to back this up. Moreover, while they use both the Jimmy Fund and the DFCI on Annual Fund campaign (**Exhibit 5**), the pull is obviously toward the sick child when funds raised do not necessarily flow in that direction.

If it is a problem, what can you do without jeopardizing half of your fundraising efforts?

- Create another fund. "Finding" Jimmy creates an opportunity—perhaps Jimmy, Jr. and Jimmy, Sr.

- Leave it as is, but only use Jimmy Fund money for children's causes.

- Equally co-brand collateral pieces so that over time, people begin to see both sick children and adults associated with the Jimmy Fund. The theater clip would not just be focused on children, but also adults (mothers, fathers) with cancer.

Cause Marketing—Selling Out or Efficient Fundraising?

The DFCI has been very successful in using cause marketing as a fundraising vehicle, but the case notes several important points:

- Avoidance of conflict of interest—impact on the brand, when is a situation a conflict and when is it not?

- Not-for-profit organizations may need another skill set—one that can "sell" to corporations and create programs in concert with marketing departments, etc.

- Not-for-profits will also need to assess the value of their brand/contribution to the cause marketing effort.

- Contact at the highest levels of the organization—the CEO can make it happen.

- Divergent opinions among the Board of Directors.

- Increase in awareness of the charitable cause.

- Challenges in funds raised into areas with the greatest need. Stop & Shop–$1 million unrestricted use and thereafter money goes to the Pediatric Brain Tumor Clinic; Dunkin Donuts ultimately aligning with Rising Stars program after wanting to build the Munchkin Manor.

- Financial strength of the potential partner.

Students should discuss each of the opportunities raised in the case and then develop a working list of criteria/considerations for any cause marketing effort. The examples in the exhibit are rich in their variety and potential impact for the organization. They should be brought up for a focused class discussion.

Overall Situation Assessment on the Development Needs at Dana-Farber

Dana Farber:

Plethora of riches

- Brand name recognition.
- Board of Directors that represents the leaders of Boston.
- Lots of established programs.

But,

- Unlimited needs.
- Must raise funds consistent with their mission—research hospital devoted to curing cancer. The question to ask, "Is what we're doing related to cancer research?"
- Development resources are finite and the development office needs to focus its efforts.

Where is the Institute Financially?

Financials are difficult to interpret due, in part, to the changes related to the DF/PCC affiliation and the restructuring of care—inpatient in other facilities, outpatient at DFF. But there are some notable points:

- Looking at the deficient before investment returns, the deficit increased 2.6 times. Why?
  - Patient services revenues increased 25%, but direct patient expenses increased 31%.
  - Indirect expenses increased 20%—unfortunately, we don't know what's in that bucket—overhead costs or unallocated costs related to research.
  - Research revenues were somewhat flat.

This raises the question about how much of the deficit was related to patient care, outside the scope of the DF mission, and how much as related to research.

- While one would like to see the institute profitable on an operating basis, they do earn substantial returns on investment (again, we do need to better understand what is behind this figure—an endowment, returns on bequests, etc.).

Fundraising at the DFCI

Tables B and C outline the sources of funds from the Institute's two major fundraising arms at the DFCI. About 56% comes in from the Development Fund and 44% from the Jimmy Fund (though one could argue that it is really closer to 50%/50%, as the 44% of the annual fund's contribution is raised under the Jimmy Fund banner. Looking at the organization chart, there are five directors on the development side and five directors on the Jimmy Fund side.

In the Board of Directors' discussions, it is clear that the tone for the Institute is fundraising with good taste. Given the nature of the hospital and the position of the directors, they only want to be affiliated with the "best" sort of programs.

The Board of Directors is very important in the fundraising process—somehow involved in 50% of money raised. Reasons: introductions to other wealthy prospects, cause marketing introductions, stewardship on committees, etc. However, they also donate a lot of money. Example: in the last capital campaign, board members contributed about one-third of all funds received and probably impacted many large donors.

Teaching the Case

The case has been taught in a nonprofit program with great success. The questions and sequence outlined in this note, by and large, address this constituency. The material, however, is quite robust for use in a marketing class as well. Under those circumstances, instructors are advised to modify questions #3 and #4 offered in this teaching note. Questions such as the following would be more appropriate:

3. What does the Dana-Farber brand name stand for? How about the Jimmy Fund? How do consumers react to these brands?

4. How would you assess Dana-Farber's marketing approach to its funding community? What are its strengths and weaknesses?

Also, it would be helpful to explore the cause marketing relationship and the broader question it raises in regard to the $350K gift from the Asian car manufacturer.

Regardless of which purpose the case is being used for, starting with the three fundraising situations brings enormous energy to the class. Likewise, closing the last 15 minutes of the class with the question of "What should Susan Paresky do?" brings to closure the various issues that would have been raised.

There is a video with a couple of the Dana-Farber public service announcements and the trailer from the movie reel available for screening before class.

Bayer AG (B)

On November 2, 1994, Bayer AG purchased Sterling Winthrop's North American OTC business from SmithKline Beecham for $1 billion. Included were 140 stockkeeping units, of which 35 were Bayer aspirin items, with combined annual revenues of around $300 million. Two manufacturing plants (in Pennsylvania and Mississippi), three distribution centers, a leased research and development facility, Sterling's Manhattan headquarters and 800 employees came with the acquisition. The purchase also included the Phillips Milk of Magnesia business in Mexico and access to new analgesic and gel coating technologies. SmithKline retained the rights to two Sterling brands, Panadol and Gaviscon, throughout North America and in Puerto Rico.

The acquisition combined the eighth and ninth largest OTC businesses in the U.S. to form the fifth largest, with annual sales of $600 million. The acquisition made Bayer's OTC business the fifth largest in the world and second only to SmithKline Beecham in Europe. The reunited Bayer aspirin brand became the second best-selling OTC brand in the world (after Tylenol), the fifth best-selling brand in the U.S. (after Tylenol, Advil, Vicks and Alka-Seltzer) and the top-selling brand in Europe.

Gary Balkema, formerly with American Cyanamid's Lederle Consumer Health division, joined Bayer as president of Bayer's new U.S. Consumer Care Division. The U.S. organization reported administratively to Helge H. Wehmeier, president of Bayer Corporation, and functionally to Werner Spinner, head of Bayer's worldwide Consumer Care business unit, and represented 35% of the business unit's worldwide sales. Spinner and Balkema resolved to move quickly to realize the hard dollar cost savings and upside potential from the acquisition. For example, Miles' six distribution centers and Sterling's three were consolidated into only four sites by early 1995. A new headquarters for Bayer's U.S. OTC business was built at a cost of $28 million in Morris Township, New Jersey. Interviews of Miles and Sterling sales and marketing executives took place in November and December 1994; the first national sales meeting of the integrated sales force took place on January 20, 1995. From then on, trade customers could place a single order and receive a single invoice for shipments of all former Sterling and Miles products.

The acquisition paved the way for the renaming of the company from Miles Inc. to Bayer Corporation. The name Bayer Corporation and the Bayer cross would henceforth appear on the packages and labels as the manufacturer of all Bayer products sold in the U.S. including all the former Miles and Sterling brands. The Elkhart, Indiana plant continued in production and the main road through it was renamed Miles Avenue.

On January 30, the president of Bayer Corporation, Helge H. Wehmeier, mailed 300,000 letters from Pittsburgh announcing the name change from Miles Inc. to Bayer Corporation; an attention-getting hologram device on each letter emphasized the point (**Exhibit 1**). Around 75,000 brochures were also distributed.

Robin Root prepared this case under the supervision of Professor John Quelch as the basis for class discussion rather than to illustrate either effective or ineffective handling of an administrative situation.

Given the history of name changes from Rhinechem to Bayer USA to Miles to Bayer Corporation, a name change task force of Miles and Bayer communication specialists determined that a corporate advertising campaign was necessary. Launched in March 1995 with the tag line, "We cure more headaches than you think," the campaign focused on creating awareness of the name change among employees, customers, suppliers and the financial community. Ten geographical markets were specifically targeted. A $15 million communications budget was established at Bayer Corporation headquarters in Pittsburgh to cover the first year costs of this campaign.[1] The individual U.S. business units would be expected to share a similar expense in the following two years. **Exhibit 2** shows the first-year budget breakdown and **Exhibit** 3 depicts a sample advertisement from the *Wall Street Journal*. The Bayer cross appeared prominently in all print ads and at the end of television advertisements. Once Bayer had educated customers about the diversity of the company's business lines, the plan was to attach the values of expertise plus responsibility to the Bayer name in the U.S., as had been done previously in Germany and in many other countries.

The official date for the name change was set for April 3, 1995. This allowed several months for existing product inventories to be sold through the trade channels and be replaced with new inventories carrying the Bayer name and cross on their packages and labels. It also allowed Bayer to fly in the chairman from Germany to meet the American press in New York and explain the significance of and rationale behind the acquisition. Joining him were Helge H. Wehmeier, president of what soon was to be Bayer Corporation, and Werner Spinner, head of Bayer's worldwide consumer care business. The conference took place on January 12, 1995, and was attended by more than 100 journalists.

Early in the morning of April 3, gift packs were placed on the desks of all 22,000 Bayer Corporation employees in North America. Each gift comprised a cooler made from Bayer plastics and filled with items such as a Bayer baseball cap, a clock resembling a compact disc (for which Bayer made the material) and imprinted with a Bayer logo, a hologram refrigerator magnet that switched from a Miles logo to a Bayer logo, a commemorative issue of the company newsletter Update, and samples of Bayer OTC products, including the new Bayer Aspirin. The samples were packed in a box imprinted with the message, "Welcome to your first day at Bayer," on top of which was a greeting card from the CEO.

The Bayer aspirin product line was reconfigured. The Bayer Select line extensions were deleted. The new product line included:

- Genuine Bayer Aspirin (caffeine-free and sodium-free)
- Extra-Strength Bayer Plus (500 mg)
- Extra Strength Bayer PM (the first aspirin product combined with a sleeping aid)
- Aspirin Regimen (81 mg tablets and caplets coated to prevent stomach irritation)
- Bayer Children's Aspirin (81 mg chewable tablets in orange and cherry flavors)

Print advertisements for the new product line in 1995 (see **Exhibit 4**) emphasized "The Power of Bayer" to challenge the consumer perception that Bayer was not especially effective. Subsequent television advertisements (see **Exhibit 5**) compared Genuine Bayer Aspirin to the other major analgesic brands, stressed that Bayer could reduce the risk of a second heart attack by up to 50% and, following nine months of market research, settled on the slogan "Powerful pain relief and so much more."

During the year following the restaging of the Bayer product line, advertising expenditures reached $40 million for the product line, double those in the prior year. Special emphasis was placed on Genuine Bayer Aspirin which, in a variety of dosage forms and pack sizes, soon commanded once again 60% of brand sales. By the end of 1996, Bayer brand sales were running 17% higher than at the time of the Sterling acquisition; analgesic category sales rose by only 2% during the same period.

---

[1] Bayer AG's worldwide corporate advertising budget, excluding the U.S., was around $7 million in 1995.

Exhibit 1 Letter from CEO of Bayer Corporation

January 23, 1995

Helge H. Wehmeier
President and
Chief Executive Officer

Mr. Sample A. Sample
123 Main Street
Anytown, PA 12345

Dear Mr. Sample,

An exciting change is about to take place in the chemical industry. Starting in April, Miles Inc. will operate under the new name that you see above—the name of our parent company, Bayer.

Although you are aware of Bayer's contributions to the chemical field, most Americans associate the Bayer name primarily with aspirin. With our new name, they will learn that Bayer is one of the largest pharmaceutical, chemical, and imaging technology companies in the world, with an established track record of innovations in fields as diverse as organic chemicals, rubber, and fibers.

The Miles name is well respected but has been used principally in the United States and Canada. As the nation's thirty-third largest exporter, Miles has had to work within the limitations of its regional name while being an integral member of the worldwide Bayer group of companies. Taking on the Bayer name will make that relationship clear.

With the Bayer name, we will be uniting our identity with that of 150,000 Bayer employees in 150 countries. This will allow us to operate more effectively in today's competitive global business environment and better serve our worldwide customers, drawing on our extensive resources from around the world. More specifically, this change will enable us to more efficiently provide you, our valued partners in business, with our world-class quality products and technical service.

As you can tell, we are excited about our new name and look forward to working with you—as Bayer. On behalf of all of our employees, I wish you a happy and successful 1995.

Sincerely,

Miles Inc.
One Mellon Center
500 Grant Street
Pittsburgh, PA 15219-2507
Phone: 412 394-5551

Printed on Recycled Paper

HOLOGRAM LETTER

This letter from CEO Helge Wehmeier launched the direct mail campaign by announcing the Bayer name change to customers and business/opinion leaders. It featured a holographic logo that changed from "Miles" to "Bayer." Adaptations of the letter addressed the specific interests of each business group.

Exhibit 2 Bayer Corporate Communications Budget in the U.S.: 1995

Hologram Letter	$278,000	
Name Change Brochure	156,000	
Premiums for Employees	1,800,000	
Public Relations	775,000	
Advertising	6,760,000	
National newspapers		210,000
Local newspapers		715,000
Cable television		150,000
National television		874,000
Spot television		1,060,000
National Magazines		1,960,000
Trade publications		1,521,000
Spot radio		270,000
Total Budget	9,769,000	

Exhibit 3 April 3, 1995 Name Change Advertisement

Exhibit 4 Bayer Print Ad: 1995

Exhibit 5 Bayer Aspirin Storyboard: 1996

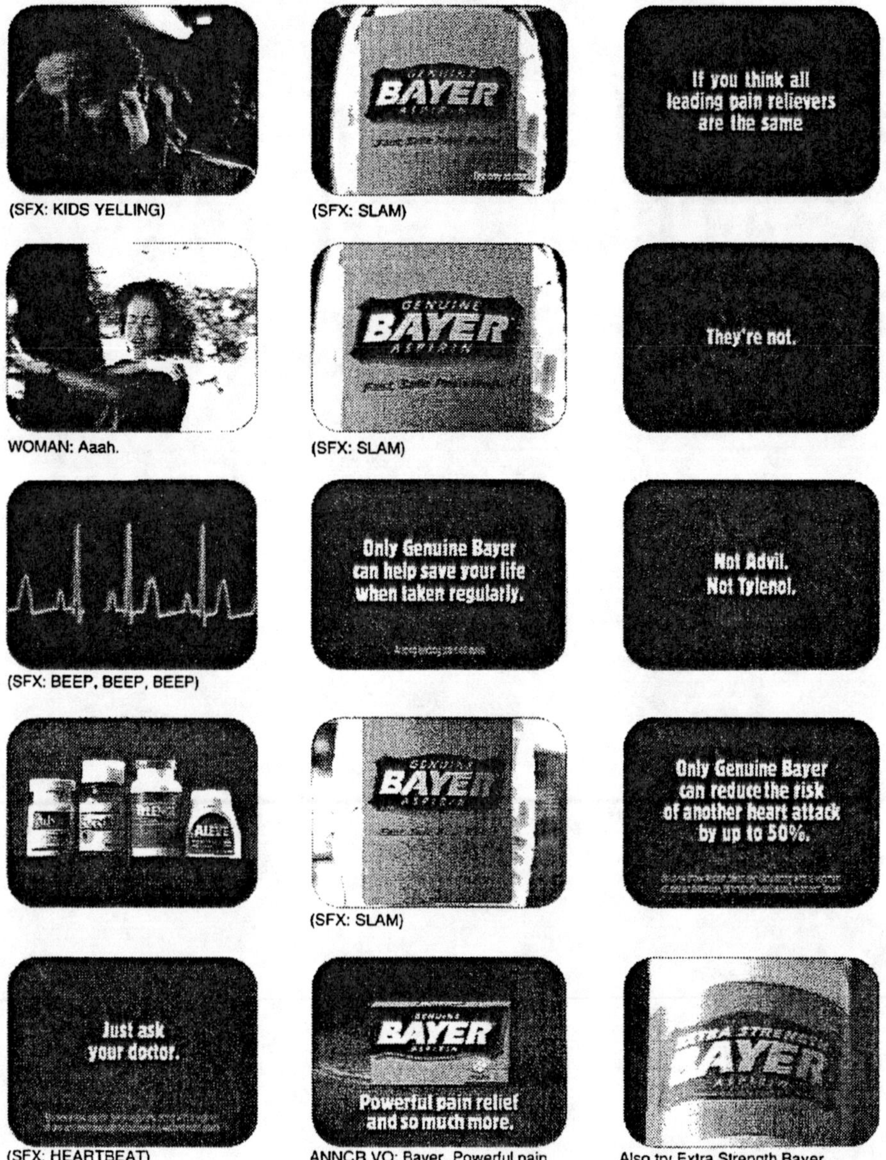

(SFX: KIDS YELLING)
(SFX: SLAM)
WOMAN: Aaah.
(SFX: SLAM)
(SFX: BEEP, BEEP, BEEP)
(SFX: SLAM)
(SFX: HEARTBEAT)
ANNCR VO: Bayer. Powerful pain relief and so much more.
Also try Extra Strength Bayer. Nothing's stronger for everyday pain.

Bayer AG (A) and (B)

Teaching Note

Synopsis

In September 1994, Bayer's top managers are meeting at world headquarters in Germany to consider paying $1 billion to SmithKline Beecham to recover rights to the Bayer name and Bayer cross trademark in North America. These rights had been confiscated by the United States government after World War I. The appropriate amount to pay to recover them depends in part on whether the Bayer aspirin brand in the United States can be revitalized and rendered more profitable.

Objectives

1. Assess the value of the rights to a brand name and trademark.

2. Highlight the benefits of owning a brand name on a global basis.

3. Explore whether or not an undermarketed brand can be revitalized.

Teaching Suggestions

The instructor can begin the class by asking the simple question, "Why is Bayer doing this?" In addition to ending years of legal maneuvers, embarrassments and frustrations, recovery of the Bayer brand name in North America is entirely consistent with the corporate strategy. Bayer wants to strengthen its position in the fast-growing over-the-counter (OTC) pharmaceuticals market. Building the OTC business in the huge North American market is essential to this effort and requires Bayer develop a stronger presence in the large analgesics category. It is worthwhile asking whether any students believe Bayer is wrong to pursue the acquisition of Sterling's North American OTC business. Some will argue that the acquisition is based on emotion rather than sound reasoning and that the price tag is too high. There may be other acquisition opportunities available to bring the Miles OTC business in North America up to critical mass. Most students, however, believe the acquisition is a good idea – in which case the instructor can ask "Why then is SmithKline selling?"

The next area for discussion is the acquisition price. Based on recent poor earnings, some students will argue that $1 billion is too much to pay, especially in comparison to the price earnings

This note was prepared by Professor John A. Quelch for the sole purpose of aiding classroom instructors in the use of Bayer AG (A) and (B), HBS Nos. 598-031 and 598-032 respectively. It provides analysis and questions that are intended to present alternative approaches to deepening students' comprehension of business issues and energizing classroom discussion .

multiples reported in **Exhibit 7**. Others argue that Bayer is lucky to be paying only $1 billion, given that SmithKline must know how desperate they are to recover the North American rights to the brand name. With guidance from the instructor, students should see that a brand's value is in the eye of the beholder and that the value of the property will differ according to who owns it.

This leads naturally to a discussion of the upside value of Bayer aspirin becoming a global brand if the North American rights are re-acquired. Of course, corporate pride will be enhanced if the flagship brand is owned on a global basis. But will the end consumer get anything out of it? Perhaps the North American consumer will benefit from improved marketing efforts and new product ideas transferred into the United States from the rest of the world.

At this point in the discussion, it is time to focus on whether Bayer aspirin's image and marketing in North America can be revitalized. The valuation of the brand rights depends, in part, on the assumptions that are made regarding possible increases in sales and profits. Most students agree that the brand has been mismanaged. The question is whether it has been mismanaged for so long that the brand equity has eroded irreparably. In the final analysis, however, Bayer does not have a choice; its corporate name and the brand name are one and the same, so it must do all it can to rejuvenate the latter to enhance the image of all its businesses operating in North America.

Exhibits TN A-E can be presented at the end of class by instructors wishing to use the case as a vehicle to discuss (a) the meaning of brands, (b) indicators of a brand's value, (c) how to calculate the value of a brand acquisition, and (d) characteristics of global brands. On this last point, it is useful to ask students whether Bayer meets the criteria in **Exhibit TN-E**. Perhaps the Bayer name is stretched thin across too diverse a portfolio of business lines and therefore lacks sufficient focus to ever be as strong as the brand names listed in **Exhibit TN-D**.

Assignment Questions

1. Why is Bayer headquarters interested in buying Sterling's North American OTC business from SmithKline Beecham? Why is SmithKline Beecham selling?

2. What are the likely reactions of the other stakeholders to the prospective acquisition?

3. Is $1 billion too much to pay?

4. Why are Bayer aspirin sales weak in North America? Can the Bayer aspirin brand be revitalized?

Analysis

1. Why is Bayer headquarters interested in buying Sterling's North American OTC business from SmithKline Beecham? Why is SmithKline Beecham selling?

The reasons for Bayer's interest are as follows:

- Corporate pride. For eighty years, Bayer has been trying to reclaim rights to the Bayer brand and Bayer cross trademarks in North America, which had been confiscated as part of war reparations after World War I. One quarter of Bayer's total sales are generated in North America, yet the company's executives cannot carry business cards with the Bayer name.

- Global branding. In 1993, Bayer was a huge $27 billion company, yet did not have control of its corporate name on a worldwide basis. As a result, Bayer was unable to conduct a global corporate identity program or a global communications program for Bayer aspirin. In addition, the global image of Bayer was being adversely affected by poor marketing of its flagship brand in the most important geographical market.

- Critical mass. By combining its existing consumer Healthcare Products business in North America (with 1995 estimated sales of $320mm) with the Sterling North American OTC business (with 1995 estimated sales of $295mm), Bayer would own the fifth largest OTC business in North America. A strong North American presence is deemed essential to a successful global OTC strategy and a strong presence in analgesics (22% of North American OTC sales) is deemed essential to success in the North American OTC market. Among other benefits, the combined organization with its extra trade clout would be a more attractive joint venture partner to distribute the OTC drugs of other non-American companies.

- Cost savings. Integration of the two businesses would increase negotiating clout with the trade; permit manufacturing, warehousing and distribution cost savings; and allow for reductions in administrative overhead and selling expenses.

- Current weakness. The Sterling OTC business has been undermarketed and poorly managed by Eastman Kodak. Sterling's U.S. OTC sales for the twelve months ending June 1994 were 15% lower than in the prior year. U.S. operating income fell 50% to $15 million in the same period, 29% below the industry average.

- Risk of non-ownership. The new owner, SmithKline Beecham, might consciously or unconsciously do a worse job than Sterling in managing the Bayer aspirin brand in North America, further weakening the worldwide image of the Bayer name.

It is worth asking students why SmithKline Beecham, having just paid $3 billion for the worldwide Sterling OTC business, is willing to sell the North American business for $1 billion just a few days later. Possible explanations include:

- SmithKline Beecham had just missed out on the acquisition of American Cyanamid and overpaid for the Sterling business as a result of not having conducted the same level of due diligence as Bayer.

- The $3 billion price stretched SmithKline Beecham's finances, so it was sensible to unload promptly a piece of the acquired business.

- The non-North American parts of the Sterling OTC business generated high margins and complemented SmithKline's product portfolio better than the North American business.

- The principal brand asset of Sterling in North America was Bayer aspirin, a mature brand which SmithKline Beecham would be unable to leverage outside of North America.

- Bayer was a willing buyer ready to pay a handsome premium for what looked to be a dying business.

- Sterling OTC's North American management had hoped to be acquired by Bayer and were disappointed to find themselves owned by SmithKline Beecham.

- Even if Bayer bought the North American Sterling OTC business back from SmithKline Beecham, SmithKline would remain the leading company in worldwide OTC sales.

2. What are the likely reactions of the other stakeholders to the prospective acquisition?

The two principal stakeholders are the North American Miles and Sterling OTC businesses that will be integrated into a single operation:

Miles OTC Business

Pros:

- The combined OTC business will probably have more clout with the trade and be more cost-efficient. The trade will welcome dealing with one rather than two organizations.
- The combined organization's critical mass of sales will be enhanced in specific categories such as gastrointestinal products (where Miles Alka Seltzer will be sold alongside Philips Milk of Magnesia).
- Exports of the former Miles products should increase if their packaging will be able to carry the Bayer name.
- Because of the recent failure of Bayer Select, Miles sales and marketing personnel may find it easier to retain their jobs in the new organization.

Cons:

- The need to sustain the Miles name will diminish, once complete rights to the Bayer name are recovered. Research data indicate that the Miles name is less well-known and less powerful than the Bayer name.
- It is unlikely that the corporate headquarters of the combined business will remain in Indiana. Many employees' jobs will be at risk.

Sterling (North America)

Pros:

- Integration with the Miles OTC business of roughly equivalent sales volume would result in a large enough company to be viable in the long run and, therefore, to warrant investment by its German parent.
- Bayer can be expected to invest in revitalizing its flagship Bayer brand in the U.S. Any corporate communications campaign for Bayer in the U.S. (using the tag line "we cure more than just headaches") would reinforce brand awareness for Bayer aspirin, and vice versa.
- Bayer is likely to be more committed to the business than SmithKline would have been.

- The medical profession will give more support to prescribing Sterling's products once they are under the umbrella of a larger research-based health company such as Bayer.

Cons:

- Product managers on other Sterling OTC brands not under the Bayer aspirin umbrella may worry about inadequate marketing support.
- Employees in functions such as sales which will inevitably to integrated may fear loss of their jobs.

The pros and cons for both organizations become evident quickly because a speedy integration is likely to be needed following the acquisition. The reasons for this are:

- Prevent Bayer aspirin's market share eroding further.
- Take advantage of the potential cost savings of integration as soon as possible. There is an opportunity cost to delay.
- Prevent competitors exploiting the uncertainty associated with delay with the trade, resulting in a further erosion of Sterling OTC shelf space.

As for the rest of Bayer's operations in North America led by Bayer's corporate executives in Pittsburgh, the acquisition would be welcomed. They would no longer be restricted from using the Bayer name on business cards, packaging and in corporate communications. This would follow the frustration of several name changes over the years, including a brief period when Bayer USA was the permitted name until Eastman Kodak challenged Bayer for using the name in non-industrial marketing contexts.

3. Is $1 billion too much to pay?

In 1970, Bayer re-secured rights to its name and trademarks everywhere in the world outside North America for $2.8 million. In 1986, Bayer acquired for $25 million rights to use the brand name in the U.S. on industrial products that had no relation to pharmaceutical or consumer health products. The $1 billion price tag looks steep compared to these earlier transactions.

The OTC acquisition transactions reported in **Exhibit 7** show sales multiples between 1.5 and 3.9 and earnings multiples between 18 and 25.5. Sales and profit figures for Sterling's North American OTC business during the twelve months ending June 1994 are $250 and $15 million respectively. On this basis, a $1 billion acquisition price implies sales and earnings multiples of 4 and 66. We are told that the 1994 sales and profit figures are 15% and 50% lower than in the prior year; on that basis, the sales and earnings multiples would have been 3.4 and 33.

Bayer corporate planners had been analyzing the Sterling OTC business for many years. Taking into account annual operating synergies growing from $25 to $44 million between 1995 and 1997, they projected operating income from the integrated business of $75 million in 1995 (on $615 million sales), rising to $182 million (on $835 million sales) in 1999. Assuming an average annual income over the period of $120 million discounted at 10% and assuming half of this income would be derived from the Sterling OTC business yields an earnings multiple of 16.

Another valuation approach combines the $44 million in annual operating synergies with the pretax equivalent of the $15 million in annual income from the Sterling OTC business (assuming a tax rate of 33%, this would be $22 million). The combined $66 million is equivalent to $44 million after tax, implying a purchase price of $440 million if we apply a 10% cost of capital, or $315 million if the restructuring costs and new corporate headquarters are taken into account. Using this approach, the Sterling OTC business in North America would have to improve its performance to generate more like $45 million in annual income ($68 million pretax) to justify the $1 billion price.

Exhibit TN-C summarizes the qualitative factors that can result in a brand's value to an acquirer being greater than the value to the existing brand owner. In addition to the factors mentioned, product and process innovations will be shared more easily between Bayer operations in Germany and North America. The combined North American OTC business will be large enough to pursue new product initiatives that may be adopted by Bayer OTC subsidiaries around the world.

Although not stated in the case, it is important to know that Bayer corporate headquarters in fact contributed $250 million towards the $1 billion acquisition cost. Bayer's North American organization had to borrow the remainder. The $1 billion was charged to all Bayer subsidiaries operating in North America (at levels proportionate to sales), not just to the Consumer Care business, on the grounds that all units derived value from being able to go to market with the Bayer name.

4. Why are Bayer aspirin sales weak in North America? Can the Bayer aspirin brand be revitalized?

Bayer aspirin suffers from the following weaknesses in North America:

- The image of aspirin is old-fashioned compared to newer analgesics in the acetaminophen and ibuprofen subcategories (see **Exhibit 5**). The brand has been undermarketed, perhaps harvested, by Sterling, partly as a result of Sterling's OTC business lacking critical mass and partly because Sterling has been something of a stepchild in the Eastman Kodak organization.

- Bayer's face-off competitive brands in the aspirin category (such as Bufferin and Excedrin) are also undersupported in marketing terms so that the aspirin subcategory is losing share within the analgesics market.

- Generic aspirin is increasing its share of aspirin sales and reducing the prices and margins that can be extracted by aspirin brands.

- The Bayer name does not have as high unaided awareness as Tylenol despite having been on the market longer.

- Aspirin is perceived by many consumers as providing less powerful and long-lasting pain relief than Tylenol and Advil. Tylenol in particular has done a good job of staking out the extra-strength position in the market. Bayer is therefore used less often than these other two brands for almost all indications (see **Table 1**).

- Aspirin has an all-purpose image in an OTC analgesic market that has become increasingly segmented.

On the other hand, Bayer sales outside North America totaled $355 million in 1993. In Germany, a youth-oriented advertising campaign (see **Exhibit 2**) rejuvenated the brand and resulted in an increase in market share from 17% to 31%. These facts suggest that the brand can be revitalized in North America.

Sterling management attempted such a revitalization by developing and launching the Bayer Select series of line extensions. However, the very term Select connotes a niche positioning and these line extensions received too high a share of the brand budget at the expense of the mainstream items in the line. In addition, several of the Select line extensions were non-aspirin based; marketing non-aspirin based products under the Bayer name caused consumer and trade confusion. In addition, the line extensions were seen as specialty supplements rather than mainstream products and, therefore, only the smaller pack sizes sold as expected. Poor retail sell-through left the trade with excess inventories and caused a 32% drop in factory sales in the first half of 1994 versus 1993. Sales of other Sterling products also suffered.

A plan to revitalize Bayer aspirin might include the following elements:

- Cancel the Bayer Select line and, through buybacks and promotions, flush excess inventories out of the trade channels as quickly as possible.

- Focus again on the flagship brand, Bayer Genuine Aspirin, which was undersupported during the launch of the Select line. The emphasis on "genuine" is necessary to counter lower-priced generics.

- Develop a primary advertising campaign that affirms Bayer aspirin as a source of powerful pain relief for frequent usage indications like headaches and arthritis. Bayer might focus on coated caplets as the product delivery form that can prevent stomach irritation since this potential problem with aspirin is often exploited by competitive analgesics.

- Develop a secondary campaign that focuses on the extra benefit of heart attack prevention. This benefit distinguishes aspirin from other analgesics and permits a unique pain relief plus prevention positioning that should appeal to aging baby boomers. Focusing on heart attack prevention as the primary positioning is unlikely to drive sufficient volume, partly because consumers find it hard to maintain a daily aspirin regimen for preventive purposes.

Postscript

The (B) case, typically distributed as a takeaway at the end of class, reports that Bayer did indeed pay SmithKline Beecham $1 billion to recover the North American brand rights. A corporate communications campaign was initiated, a new OTC headquarters established in New Jersey, and additional marketing dollars invested to revitalize the Bayer aspirin brand in North America. By August 1997, Bayer aspirin's dollar market share in the analgesics category had risen to 5.7% from 4.2% just before the acquisition. Share was gained from non-aspirin analgesics as well as rival aspirin products. Annual sales in 1997 were, however, still only 96% of the level achieved in 1988. The question remains as to whether Bayer aspirin has simply recovered its "natural" market share or can grow share further.

Exhibit TN-A

What Is A Brand?

- "The Capitalized Value of The Trust Between The Company And The Consumer"
  - (James Burke, ex-CEO of Johnson & Johnson)
- "A Tax"
  - (David Nichol, ex-CEO of Loblaw's)
- A Brand's Value Is Reflected In:
  - Attitudinal vs. behavioral loyalty
  - Customer efforts to obtain the brand
  - Dead net price premium
  - Relative market share
  - Stretchability (within/beyond core business)

Exhibit TN-B

Brand Value Drivers

- NPV of DCF of Current Business
- Discount Rate Depends On Uncertainty of Assumptions:
  - Market growth
  - Competititve actions
  - Capacity availability
  - Technology change
  - Regulations

Exhibit TN-C

Potential Value of Brand, If Acquired

- "Value, Like Beauty, Is In The Eye of The Beholder"
- Current Brand Value (to Current Owner)
  - \+ Synergies with Existing Operations (Hard $ Savings)
  - \+ Higher Sales, Gross Margins
  - \+ More Efficient Asset Utilization
  - \+ Brand Name Extensions to New Products, Channels, Geographies
  - \+ Preemption of Competition
  - \+ Reinforcement of Value of Existing Business
  - \+ Psychic Value (employee motivation, retention)
- Equals Potential Brand Value

Exhibit TN-D

Top Ten Global Brands

1. McDonald's
2. Coca-Cola
3. Disney
4. Kodak
5. Sony
6. Gillette
7. Mercedes-Benz
8. Levi's
9. Microsoft
10. Marlboro

Source: Interbrand 1996

Exhibit TN-E

Common Features of Global Brands

- Strength In Home Market
- Geographical Sales Balance
- Consistent Positioning
- Address Similar Consumers Needs Worldwide
- Consumers Value Country of Origin
- Product Category Focus
- Corporate Name

Warner-Lambert Ireland: Niconil

Teaching Note

Synopsis

The marketing director for Warner-Lambert Ireland (WL) is considering the introductory marketing program for Niconil, a transdermal skin patch designed to enable consumers to quit smoking. Niconil is to be launched early in 1990 as an ethical pharmaceutical product available only on prescription. Communications, product, and pricing decisions remain to be made.

Objectives

- Introduce the concepts of the hierarchy-of-effects, decision-making unit and decision-making process, and push versus pull communications.
- Illustrate the challenges and opportunities in developing a communications strategy for a new ethical pharmaceutical product that cannot be advertised directly to end consumers.
- Highlight the six key elements of marketing communications programs (motives-markets-messages-media-money-measurement).
- Demonstrate the importance of integrating communications policy decisions with other elements of the marketing mix and with the overall marketing strategy for a new product.

Teaching the Case

The case discussion can usefully begin with an in-depth exploration of the target consumer and the decision-making process. Instructors can ask students to profile the ideal Niconil user and then to detail the process by which the consumer moves through the hierarchy-of-effects, aided by the general practitioner and the pharmacist.

This note was prepared by Professor John A. Quelch for the sole purpose of aiding classroom instructors in the use of "Warner-Lambert Ireland: Niconil," HBS case no. 593-008. It provides analysis and questions that are intended to present alternative approaches to deepening students' comprehension of business issues and energizing classroom discussion.

This analysis sets up a subsequent discussion of the communications approaches that WL can use for a product like Niconil which, although available only on prescription, can be readily understood by the end consumer. A combination of pre-launch, launch, and post-launch communications have to be targeted at all members of the decision-making unit—the doctor, the pharmacist, the end consumer and, possibly, friends and relatives as well. Allelements of the communications mix (motives, markets, messages, media, money, and measurement) can be considered during this part of the discussion.

The case raises other issues associated with the Niconil launch regarding product policy (package count size and role of support system), pricing policy, and demand forecasting. First mover advantages, competitive preemption, and the role of communications in building barriers to entry can also be discussed. While it is important for the Niconil communications program to build primary demand for the patch and the brand, there are risks of stockouts and unsuccessful triers spreading negative word-of-mouth if demand is excessive. In this vein, instructors can emphasize to students that communications policy must be integrated into WL's overall marketing strategy for Niconil and must be internally consistent with other elements of the marketing mix.

Time permitting, instructors can ask how the Niconil communications mix would be different if it was marketed as an over-the-counter product rather than as an ethical pharmaceutical product. Clearly, the focus would shift from push to pull marketing.

Assignment Questions

1. How important is Niconil to WL and Elan?
2. Who is the target market for Niconil? What will be the demand for the product?
3. What communication policies should WL use to manage the decision-making processes of doctors, consumers, and pharmacists?
4. When should Niconil be launched? Are there prime-mover advantages? How can Niconil best establish itself against future competition?
5. How should Niconil be packaged and priced?
6. What is the role of the support program? How should it be packaged, priced, and distributed?

Analysis

1. *How important is Niconil to WL and Elan?*

As an easily understandable product with broad appeal, Niconil could raise the public visibility of both WL and Elan. WL is only the sixth largest pharmaceutical company in Ireland with 3% share of a highly fragmented market (£4 million sales out of £155 million). As the first launch of a nicotine patch anywhere in the world, Niconil promises to be celebrated as an Irish business success story.

Niconil is a significant new product in WL's portfolio and could prove an important source of exports to WL subsidiaries in Europe (73% of WL Ireland's current revenues are derived from intracompany exports). The success of Niconil in Ireland will influence Dixon's career, the reputation of the Irish subsidiary within WL, and the level of backing the nicotine patch is likely to receive from other WL subsidiaries.

Elan's worldwide reputation and visibility and its ability to sign up pharmaceutical companies in other countries as licensees for its patch will also depend on Niconil's success in Ireland. A successful launch could further strengthen collaborative ties between Elan and WL.

2. *Who is the target market for Niconil? What will be the demand for the product?*

The launch of Niconil, as a new smoking cessation option, will doubtless increase the number of people trying to quit over what it would have been otherwise. The case suggests that, in demographic terms, the target market from Niconil should include middle-aged, better educated, upper income consumers, especially women (who are more health-conscious, vulnerable to smoking during pregnancy and visit doctors more often). In addition, the best consumer prospects for Niconil are people who:

- Say they want to quit to protect their health and/or raise their self-esteem.
- Acknowledge that quitting will not be easy.
- Have tried before to quit (perhaps using Nicorette, Nicobrevin, or Accudrop) but have failed.
- Have a nonsmoking spouse or friend who dislikes secondary smoke but will provide support and encouragement during the quitting process.
- Have children for whom they do not wish to set a bad example.
- Have just recovered from a heart attack or other serious medical problem related to smoking.
- Are not subject to Niconil side effects.

Three environmental trends are persuading more and more smokers to try to quit:

- Increased information on the connection between smoking and health problems.
- Increased government taxes on tobacco products.
- Increased pressure against smoking in the workplace as a "dirty habit," especially among professionals.

At the same time, as smokers quit, those that continue constitute an increasingly hard core (with the exception of young people who are subject to peer pressure and display a bullet-proof "it can't happen to me" attitude).

The case suggests two methods for forecasting Irish demand for the Niconil patch. The relevant calculations, presented in **Exhibit TN-1**, produce quite different estimates. Obviously, demand will depend upon the price, availability, and communications campaign effectiveness. The fact that Niconil will only be available by prescription and on a nonreimbursable basis will probably result in lower sales and a slower ramp-up than if the product was available over-the-counter. Long-term, however, demand is likely to be steadier, less faddish, and less volatile.

Underforecasting demand will result in supply stockouts. Consumers unable to fill their prescriptions might then lose interest or be unable to complete the program successfully. However, since production capacity in Ireland will also be used to supply the patch to other European countries, it is unlikely to prove a constraint.

3. ***What communication policies should WL use to manage the decision making processes of doctors, consumers, and pharmacists?***

The consumer's purchase process for Niconil as a prescription product can be summarized as follows:

a. Awareness of Niconil
b. Visit to doctor
c. Obtain prescription
d. Visit pharmacy
e. Use product
f. Revisit doctor/pharmacy
g. Complete Niconil program

Some consumers may achieve awareness, knowledge, interest, and preference for Niconil before visiting their doctors. They may move through the hierarchy of effects as a result of (a) stories about Niconil in the media and interviews with WL and Elan executives that occur as a result of WL's public relations efforts, (b) the Niconil logo on "no smoking" posters in pharmacies and Niconil sponsorship of smoking cessation hospital outreach programs, and (c) word-of-mouth communications from friends, family, and Niconil users. Other consumers may become aware of Niconil and gather some knowledge from the public media, and then seek further information from their doctors during regular office visits or at specially made appointments. A third group of consumers may be unaware of Niconil until their doctors raise the possibility of using the product during office visits scheduled for other purposes.

WL plans to use several communications approaches to inform and persuade 2,000 Irish general practitioners to consider prescribing Niconil. Given the side effects associated with Nicorette, many doctors will welcome Niconil as a possible solution to the common problem of smoking. General practitioner support will depend, in part, on:

- The approval of cardiovascular surgeons and other experts on heart and lung disease who, in addition to prescribing Niconil for their own patients, may also be opinion leaders for general practitioners.

- The number of general practitioners who do not smoke (90%), who have quit smoking or tried to quit, and who discuss smoking habits with their patients (63%).

The communications program includes prelaunch, launch, and postlaunch activities as follows:

Prelaunch →	Launch →	Postlaunch
Press release	Symposium	Sales drive
Medical opinion leaders dinner	Health organization endorsements (none)	Advertising

Direct Mail

Responses to the direct mail effort will identify those doctors most likely to be interested in prescribing Niconil and on whom the subsequent sales drive can focus. The launch symposium will generate positive publicity not only for Niconil but also for WL and Elan. During the subsequent sales drive, doctors' questions about Niconil will be answered one-on-one by WL salespeople.

If 16 sales reps make 6.5 calls per day, they should be able to see all 1,600 high-priority general practitioners over 16 business days. On an ongoing basis, 4 reps making 6.5 calls per day could detail Niconil to the 1,600 doctors 4 times per year. WL decided to present Niconil last rather than first in the sales call because the expected interest in the patch would thereby lengthen the call without reducing the time afforded presentations of other WL products.

Advertising in medical journals and in medical reference books on pages adjacent to prescribing information for smoking cessation products will be pulsed to coincide with key "commitment to change" times such as New Year's. The text presents four copy approaches for Niconil advertising. Students typically make the following comments about the Niconil message strategy:

- Few doctors need to be reminded of the dangers of smoking and why patients should stop.
- The emphasis should be on support, not fear ("all they need to succeed" versus "dying for a smoke").
- The emphasis should be on why and how the Niconil method will work where others may have failed.

Other communications approaches mentioned by students include the following:

- Training seminars for doctors on the results of clinical trials, on how to select appropriate prospects for Niconil and on how to explain product usage to patients.
- Samples of the patch and the support program for doctors to use as props for these explanations (doctors will not give out sample patches since use of a single patch will not be enough to have any effect).
- Posters in doctors' offices with the easily recognizable Niconil logo can serve as a reminder.

Once a prescription is written by a doctor, it must be redeemed at one of 1,132 Irish pharmacies and the product must be paid for. WL will wish to educate pharmacists about Niconil so that they can answer consumer questions at the time of purchase. Niconil "quit smoking" posters in pharmacies and, possibly, Niconil support programs sold separately on display racks could reinforce brand awareness and confidence at this point.

Once the prescription is filled, success depends on consumer compliance. Consumers must be educated about the risks of misuse such as wearing two patches at once or wearing a patch while smoking. The following factors determine compliance:

- The support program and a toll-free support hotline.

- Follow-up visits to the doctor (at £15 per visit and 74% of the Irish population has to pay).

- Encouragement of friends.

- Level of willpower.

- Incidence of side-effects (insomnia, skin irritation).

- Perceived status associated with wearing the patch.

4. *When should Niconil be launched? Are there prime mover advantages? How can Niconil best establish itself against future competition?*

WL has scheduled the launch of Niconil for January 1990. Most students will identify the New Year, Lent, and the annual budget day when the government announces tax changes (e.g., on cigarettes) as the three periods when smokers interested in quitting are most likely to try and, therefore, when the media are most likely to carry public relations stories about smoking cessation products. Problems associated with skin irritation from the patch and suntanning argue against a summer launch, though some users may welcome the opportunity to display the patch publicly as a status symbol. Some students argue that WL could try to orchestrate a public service anti-smoking advertising campaign to coincide with the Niconil launch, or time the launch accordingly.

As the first patch brand to market in Ireland, Niconil could charge an initial price premium to the most interested and, therefore, the most likely to be successful group of potential quitters. These individuals could then further fuel Niconil sales through positive word-of-mouth. Although the ethical status of the product prevents the use of pull advertising, WL does sell some over-the-counter products and therefore should be able to apply some creative consumer marketing skills to building brand recognition for Niconil ahead of competition.

Being first to market has the following benefits:

- Quitters most likely to succeed adopt the product first. If they fail, they are unlikely to try a second nicotine patch brand.

- If market demand rises and falls quickly, nicotine patch launches by latecomers are less likely than Niconil to be profitable.

- Brand recognition can be developed such that doctors prescribe Niconil by name rather than a generic nicotine patch.

- If Niconil has a good in-stock position at pharmacies, communications efforts by follower brands are likely to boost primary demand for the patch and, specifically, for the product already in distribution, especially when doctors do write generic prescriptions for the nicotine patch. Pharmacists may not see a need to stock multiple nicotine patch brands and a Niconil volume rebate directed at pharmacies could also help maintain share in the face of competition.

5. *How should Niconil be packaged and priced?*

Each Niconil patch contained 30mg of nicotine, equivalent to that in 20 cigarettes. The single dosage level did not take account of patients who smoked fewer cigarettes per day, smoked "Lite" cigarettes, had largely quit and therefore did not need as big a dose, or who could experience side effects from a 30 mg dose. A lower (say 15 mg) dosage patch could have been included in the product line but might have complicated the communications task.

Niconil could be packaged in counts of 7 (one week), 14, 21 or 28. The issues are as follows:

- A higher count size will result in a price that may be prohibitively expensive, especially to lower income Irish consumers living from one paycheck to the next who are used to buying cigarettes by the pack rather than the carton.

- A higher count size (and price) will attract a smaller number of highly committed consumers and hence result in a higher success rate. On the other hand, a lower count size permits more flexible prescribing, will attract more triers and encourage them to check in with their doctors to renew their prescriptions and discuss any side effects as they proceed with the treatment.

- A higher count size (e.g., 28) requires that only a single sale be made and takes consumers out of the market (though this benefit will only apply when Niconil faces head-to-head competition).

- A higher count size is favored by WL subsidiaries in continental Europe which will be securing their patches from the Irish plant. To achieve production efficiencies, WL's International Division would probably prefer the Irish plant to make a standard pack size for Ireland and Europe.

WL executives are considering the two pricing structures summarized in **Exhibit TN-2**. The pricing decision depends in part on whether target consumers are more likely to focus on the price per patch, the price per package or the price of the entire treatment program. It also depends on what consumers will compare the price to. Some consumers may use the cost of two weeks supply of cigarettes as a basis for comparison (£2.25 x 14 = £31.50). Others may compare Niconil prices to those for Nicorette (£14 for a 14 day supply of the 4 mg dose), even if it has not worked for them. A third group might estimate all the money they could save in the future on cigarettes if they quit and, as a result, be willing to pay a premium price for Niconil, especially if they were convinced it would work for them. Some students argue that the lower price option is more socially responsible, others that the higher price signals quality and potency.

The implications of the two pricing options for Niconil gross margins, coverage of fixed costs and breakeven volumes are explored in **Exhibit TN-3**. Under the proposed price of £33 which yields £4 per unit gross margin, the existing production capacity of 24,000 units per year would produce only £96,000 gross margin, well short of the £200,000 launch year marketing budget. Adding the £1.2 million machine is essential and the financial impact on WL's Irish subsidiary is softened by the opportunity to export production beyond the needs of the Irish market to other WL European subsidiaries for a £2 per unit margin contribution.

6. *What is the role of the support program? How should it be packaged, priced, and distributed?*

The support program comprises an audiotape, explanatory booklet, personal contract and diary. The objectives are:

- To provide psychological reinforcement to the quitter, supplementing the physiological impact of the patch. The support program helps consumers learn the behavior of not smoking and resist the temptation to have a smoke at a customary time of day or when one is offered.

- To convince the medical establishment and the consumer that WL is providing a comprehensive, "system" solution to the problem of quitting smoking and not promising a "quick fix."

- To set a standard in the marketplace that future competitors would have to follow.

The support program could not be packaged with the Niconil patch without the Irish National Drug Board approving the entire system. Since this might have delayed the approval process, WL decided to distribute the support program separately. Research also indicated that the support program could command a mean unit price of £8.50 which would give WL a £5 unit margin (£8.50 less £3.50 variable costs per unit).

The support program could be (a) given to Niconil patch purchasers by pharmacists, (b) given by doctors to patients at the time they received Niconil prescriptions, (c) given to potential quitters to interest them in trying Niconil, and/or (d) sold separately by pharmacies. Some of the issues raised by students in discussing these options include the following:

- Pharmacies are better equipped to handle inventories of the support program than doctors.

- Doctors are more likely than pharmacists to listen to the support program audiotape in advance of distribution.

- Doctors would be less likely than pharmacies to give duplicate support programs on the issuance of second and third prescriptions.

- Doctors might wish to give the support program directly to their patients to emphasize its importance and to reinforce the importance of counseling to success. Such communications are less likely to happen in pharmacies.

- Separate sale of the support program could advertise the Niconil patch but would detract from the system image and possibly result in it being used with other smoking cessation products such as Nicorette.

Postscript

Warner-Lambert launched Niconil as a prescription product in Ireland in May 1990, the first launch of the patch in the world. Niconil was sold at retail for £33 in 14 count packs. In the first nine months, 13,000 units were sold. Breakeven was achieved by the end of the first year. The communications budget for the first year broke down as follows:

Training, manuals, brochures	45%
Support programs (distributed through doctors)	45%
Doctor meetings	7%
Sample patches for doctors	3%

Patch sales in 1992 in Ireland were 60% higher than in 1991. By year end 1992, Niconil held 57% of the Irish market for smoking cessation products. Nicorette held 31%, having received a sales boost from the launch of the patch. Nicobrevin, an over-the-counter product, held 10%. Ciba-Geigy, the world market share leader, was about to enter the Irish market with Nicotinell.

The marketing of Nicotinell, already sold in France, Germany, and Italy, would differ from Niconil in several ways. First, no support program was sold with the Nicotinell patch. Second, it was sold in three package counts (7, 14, and 28) and in two different dosage levels (30 mg. and 15 mg.) that permitted a patient to be weaned gradually from his/her nicotine dependency.

In the United States, the patch was marketed aggressively through pull advertising. The Elan patch was licensed to Lederle Labs which marketed it under the Prostep brand name. Demand in the United States grew dramatically in 1991 but tapered off by the second quarter of 1992 as a result of (a) press stories—boosted by the tobacco lobby—about smokers wearing the patch suffering cardiac arrest, and (b) unrealistic expectations and poor compliance among consumers purchasing the product. Brand market shares at the end of March 1993 were:

Nicoderm (Marion Merrell Dow)	42%
Habitrol (Ciba-Geigy)	35%
Nicotrol (Warner Lambert)	12%
Prostep (Lederle)	11%

Exhibit TN-1 Niconil Demand Forecasts

Method 1:

	30% of 2.5 million Irish adults smoke	750,000
x	10% try to quit each year	75,000
x	10% buy a smoking cessation product	7,500
x	50% who might purchase Niconil in Year 1	3,750 unit sales
	plus 60% buy a second pack:	2,230
	20% of these buy a third pack	446
	Total Year 1 (1990) Sales	6,426 units
	Rising to total Year 5 (1994) sales, assuming 90% of committed quitters buy Niconil:	11,567 units

Method 2:

	30% of 2.5 million Irish adults smoke	750,000
x	17% say they will go to doctor and pay for patch	127,500
	33% likely actual purchasers	42,500
	plus 60% buy a second pack:	25,500
	20% of these buy a third pack	5,100
	Total Year 1 (1990) Sales	73,100 units

Exhibit TN-2 Two Alternative Price Structures for Niconil

	Proposed	Premium
Price to consumer	£33.00	£61.00
Retail dispensing fee	1.00	1.00
Retail price	32.00	60.00
Tax (25%)	8.00	15.00
Retail markup (50%)	8.00	15.00
Manufacturer price	16.00	30.00
Variable cost	12.00	12.00
Manufacturer gross margin	4.00	18.00

Conclusions: The premium price delivers 4.5x gross margin per unit.

The premium price requires only 22% of the units sold under the proposed price to deliver the same profit contribution.

Exhibit TN-3 Niconil Gross Margin, Fixed Cost, and Break-even Analyses

Gross Margin Scenarios (Year 1):

Unit Sales / Unit Margin	6,426	73,100
£4	£25,704	£292,400
£18	£115,668	£1,315,800

Additional Gross Margin Potential:

Example: Assume 6,426 unit sales in Year 1 at £4 margin = £25,704

In Year 1, 10% variable cost savings in last three months of year results in additional gross margin of £1.20 x 1,606 = £1,927

Also, assume all extra capacity (14,000 units per month x 3 months less 1,606 units) is sold to European subsidiaries at £2 margin per unit = £80,788

Total margin = £108,419

Fixed Costs

	Year 1	Ongoing
Marketing	£200,000	£138,000[a]
Machine	90,000[b]	360,000
Total	290,000	498,000

[a]Assumes 50% of Year 1 advertising, promotion, and public relations costs and 100% of market research, sales force allocation and product management allocation costs.
[b]Cost for last three months of 1990 based on five-year, straight-line depreciation of £1.2 million machine plus 10% interest.

Break-even Unit Volumes (14-count packages)

Fixed Costs / Unit Margin	Year 1	Ongoing
£4	72,500	124,500
£18	16,111	27,666

Note: Because 60% of triers will buy a second pack of Niconil and 20% of these will buy a third pack, the above numbers can be divided by 1.72 to give the required number of patients. The resulting numbers can be divided by 2,000 or 1,600 to give the required number of patients per doctor.

5-703-047
REV: JULY 22, 2003

TEACHING NOTE

Life, Death and Property Rights: The Pharmaceutical Industry Faces AIDS in Africa

Life, Death and Property Rights is a case that is simultaneously about many things. It is, first of all, an account of the horrific AIDS crisis that descended upon Africa in the late 1990s. The case exposes students to the magnitude of the crisis and the human toll it continues to impose. It also, though, exposes them to the business crisis that AIDS has created, particularly for the global pharmaceutical firms that have been caught in the middle of the turmoil. Increasingly, activist groups have targeted these firms, demanding that they either donate their drugs to AIDS victims in Africa or eliminate the patents that still undergird the production of most AIDS-fighting treatment. Because the AIDS crisis is both so severe and so well known, no pharmaceutical firm can afford to ignore the activists completely. At the same time, however, full compliance with the activists' demands would be extraordinarily costly. For if the firms agree to compromise on either prices or patents, they risk undermining the very system that has allowed them both to profit and to discover lifesaving drugs. In exploring this tension, the case thus exposes students to the broader issues that surround intellectual property and the challenges that firms face as they attempt to sell intellectually-based goods across the global economy.

Case Overview and Structure

The case begins by laying out the scope of the AIDS crisis in Africa: the numbers affected, the high price of drugs, and the lack of attractive solutions. It makes clear that the tragedy is both a social calamity and a business problem, since the world's major pharmaceutical firms are being pressed from all sides to respond, somehow, to the crisis.

The case then provides a brief historical survey, describing the emergence of AIDS in the early 1980s and the response it engendered in the United States. It details the initial unwillingness of the U.S. government to deal with the disease and the growth of a powerful activist community. Although the disease proved stubbornly resistant to either treatment or cure, U.S. scientists slowly developed a menu of drugs that together offered some measure of hope to AIDS victims. By the late 1990s, the most comprehensive of these drugs, known as HAART therapy, were able to prolong both the health

---

This note was prepared by Professor Debora Spar for the sole purpose of aiding classroom instructors in the use of "Life, Death and Property Rights: The Pharmaceutical Industry Faces AIDS in Africa," HBS No. 702-049. It provides analysis and questions that are intended to present alternative approaches to deepening students' comprehension of business issues and energizing classroom discussion. HBS cases are developed solely as the basis for class discussion. Cases are not intended to serve as endorsements, sources of primary data, or illustrations of effective or ineffective management.

of AIDS patients and the quality of their lives. HAART was extremely expensive, though, with an annual per patient cost of approximately $10,000 to $15,000.

Meanwhile, just as the AIDS epidemic was coming under control in the United States and other developing nations, the disease was running rampant elsewhere in the world. In the 1990s, rates of infection began to soar in Africa, Asia and Latin America, with Africa particularly hard-hit. 3.4 million new victims were infected by HIV in 2001 alone, raising the continent's total number of victims to 25.3 million. Thirty percent of adults were HIV-positive in several African states, and population rates in 2002 were actually starting to decline.

Once this crisis has been laid out, the case takes a critical detour, reviewing the history of intellectual property rights (IPR) in western markets and the particular role they have played in the pharmaceutical industry. It describes the arguments in favor of IPR (protection of valuable property; motivation to research and discovery; encouragement, according to the U.S. Constitution, for "the progress of science and the useful arts") and the views of opponents, including Thomas Jefferson, who famously reasoned that "inventions cannot be a subject of property." Initially, as the case shows, pharmaceutical firms saw no need for intellectual property, since the "drugs" they sold were dubious elixirs mixed from commonplace materials. But as the drug discovery process became increasingly scientific, pharmaceutical firms relied more and more heavily on the patents that protected their creation. Particularly in the United States, patents were restrictive, prices were high, and drug companies reaped substantial profits throughout the later decades of the twentieth century. They also presided over major scientific advances, including treatments for typhus, yellow fever, infections, and so forth.

The next section of the case describes the global fight over intellectual property rights, exploring how U.S. firms have led the charge for global application of U.S.-style IPR, and why other states have fought instead for weaker property rights regimes. The case reviews how intellectual property rights were eventually embedded in the GATT regime under the auspices of TRIPS (for trade related intellectual property rights) and how opponents from the developing world continued to debate the merits of the TRIPS accord. The case then returns to Africa, examining how the deadly spread of HIV/AIDS led in the late 1990s to a wave of activism targeted directly at western pharmaceutical firms. The case lays out the arguments from all sides, including the activists' complaints, the pharmaceuticals' response, and the view from countries (Brazil, Thailand) that have walked an alternative policy path.

Life, Death and Property Rights ends with the pharmaceutical firms. It describes the pressures they face from the expanding AIDS crisis, the options available to them, and the problems that each of these options presents.

Teaching Assignment

Read: *Life, Death and Property Rights: The Pharmaceutical Industry Faces AIDS in Africa (2-702-049)*

Study Questions

1. How should the pharmaceutical companies respond to the plague of AIDS in Africa?
2. What strategy should they follow to protect their intellectual property rights?

3. How far should they be willing to go? What are the costs and benefits?

Teaching Plan and Objectives

In many ways, *Life, Death and Property Rights* is a very difficult case to teach. Clearly, students have to see and describe the magnitude of the problem: 24.4 million dead from the disease; 40 million living with it; 25.3 million in Africa alone (pp. 1, 4). At the same time, though, instructors have to be careful not to get too bogged down in the tragedy at hand. It is hard, understandably, to turn to other issues once one has "40 million victims" written on the board. But it is also essential, because the power of the case comes from understanding the sources and possible solutions to the crisis, in addition to the crisis itself.

With this objective in mind, I suggest a teaching plan that divides simply and explicitly into three pastures. One explores the scope of the problem; one looks at causes; one at possible solutions.

Throughout, and particularly in the last pasture, it is critical to push students to consider the role that intellectual property has traditionally played in drug discovery and the extent to which the AIDS crisis has forced a re-examination of this key relationship. Intellectually, this tension—between access to drugs and incentives for drug discovery—sits at the heart of the case.

I. Introduction (5 minutes)

Because of the complexity inherent in this case, as well as the difficulty of dealing with so much tragedy in class, I like to start the discussion slowly, pushing students to think about the many facets of the AIDS problem and dealing directly—and upfront—with the disease's human toll. I thus introduce the case simply by drawing comparisons with whatever case has preceded it in the course. I remind students that whatever we studied the day before pales as a problem when compared with AIDS.

The case we have before us today, I remind them, is extraordinarily complex. It doesn't look like a business problem in many respects, but it is. It doesn't look like it has the power to shatter one of the fundamental institutions of modern commerce—intellectual property rights—but it does. In most business cases, it's relatively clear what the protagonists need to do: they need to respond to competitors, perhaps, or find some way to lower costs, or bring a new technology to market. In this case, however, it's not at all clear how business people—or indeed any people—should respond to the crisis of AIDS in Africa. In fact, we don't even know just what this crisis is, and who is supposed to respond to it.

II. Defining the Problem (20 minutes)

Against this backdrop, I tell students that I want to start by asking a very simple question that is actually very difficult to answer.

Q: What is this case about?

Almost immediately this question catches them off-guard. It also makes them think about the case at the broadest level and tends to encourage wide student participation.

I will take nearly any response here, since my goal is expose both the sheer magnitude of the crisis and the extent to which it crosses social, commercial, scientific, and political boundaries. Students should quickly see, for instance, that AIDS is on the one hand a purely medical crisis: it involves a newly-discovered virus for which there is no cure. It has killed millions of people already, with millions more nearly certain to die. AIDS, therefore, is a medical scourge on parallel with the plagues of the Middle Ages.

By the same token, however, this case is not just about a disease, or even a medical tragedy. It is also about the social and economic structures that, to some extent at least, have impeded treatment. The case is about the lack of affordable or accessible drugs in Africa and elsewhere. It is about public policies that have done little to stop the spread of disease or eliminate the suffering of its victims. It is about the lack of health care in Africa, and the lack of funds to support such care.

Finally, and critically, the case is also about intellectual property rights—about a system that has worked superbly well in the western world to motivate and reward the discovery of drugs; but a system that is now under massive attack in Africa and elsewhere. The fight about AIDS in Africa is largely a fight over property rights; about whether the pharmaceutical companies can and should alter a system that has generated both profits and drugs for over a century.

I let the discussion go on just long enough to cover these main points. I simply record students' responses on the right side board and then proceed to the second and closely-linked question.

RSB
Disease
Death
Lack of drugs
Lack of health care
Public policy
Intellectual property
Pharmaceutical industry
Activism

Q: What is the central problem of the case?

Here, my objective is to push students harder on the topics they've just raised, prodding them to understand the full magnitude of the AIDS problem and the deep-seated issues that defy easy resolution. Once again, the discussion should cover various aspects of the problem, without any need to choose among them.

Obviously, part of the problem is purely medical. People are dying from AIDS in staggering numbers, particularly in the developing world. Instructors will not want to dwell on these numbers for too long, but the numbers should be mentioned and written on the board. 95% of new AIDS infections are in the developing world. There are 4.7 million infected people in South Africa alone. In some countries (Zimbabwe, Botswana) roughly one-third of the adult population is HIV-positive. As a result, life expectancy is actually falling across parts of sub-Saharan Africa. The number of orphans is expected to skyrocket. Given the nature of the disease's transmission, entire families have been stricken, with disastrous implications for the existing social structure. As productive workers die, they impose dramatic costs on both their employers and on society at large. Companies that produce in southern Africa now need to train 2 or 3 people for every position, knowing that 1 or 2 of them are likely to die. Companies that sell into these markets are watching 30% of their customers literally disappear. Thus a medical problem (disease) rapidly translates into both a social nightmare and a commercial disaster.

As mentioned briefly above, though, the disease itself is only part of the problem. Part also comes from the inability of Africa to deal with the unfolding crisis. As students will recall from the text, AIDS in the western world has been more or less brought under control: the disease still kills, but its spread can be contained by education and behavioral changes, and its effects forestalled through the use of powerful treatments such as HAART. In Africa, by contrast, education has been slow in some countries and ineffective in others. Because the countries and their people are poor, expensive therapies like HAART are essentially out of reach. Students should recall the price comparison listed on page 1 of the text: treatments that cost roughly $10,000 to $15,000 per person per year are simply unaffordable in countries where per capita incomes range only from $450 to $8,900. And thus the lack of both money and effective public health policies exacerbates the spread and toll of AIDS. If victims can't afford treatment; if they don't understand how the disease is spread and have no access to drugs, then they are likely to spread the disease even further.

The final piece of this complicated puzzle is pharmaceutical firms and their property rights. Arguably, drugs and those that produce them are the solution to AIDS, not the problem. Drugs are what have the potential to cure AIDS—or at least to help its victims lead longer and healthier lives. But the problem, as described above, is that nearly all AIDS drugs are far too expensive for African victims to afford. Drugs, therefore, and access to them, are perceived as part of the problem, rather than the solution. From the perspective of many Africans, as well as the activists that support them, the problem of AIDS in Africa is a problem of unaffordable and inaccessible drugs. Because pharmaceutical companies insist on high prices and on the maintenance of patent rights over the drugs they discover, there is simply no market for low-priced generic AIDS drugs. And without these drugs, AIDS patients have no hope of treatment.

Once these three aspects of the problem have been raised and explored, students will probably start to argue with one another, insisting that the problem isn't really medical, for example, or that African governments, and not US drug companies, should be seen as having exacerbated the crisis. I try to constrain the arguments until all the major points have been made, and then I openly encourage them, letting the discussion flow naturally to the next pasture.

B-1: The Problem

People Dying:

95% of new infections in developing world
1/3 adults HIV-positive in some countries
4.7 million infected in SA alone
Totals (in Africa) expected to hit 7.5 million by 2010
Totals (in Africa) expected to hit 7.5 million by 2010

Life expectancy ↓
Orphans ↑

No Way to Afford Health Care:

Drug prices ($10,000 - $15,000/year) far above average incomes ($450 - $8,900/year)
Govt. budgets can't afford
Generics unavailable
Need cheaper drugs ←→ drugs expensive; protected by intellectual property rights

Patients can't pay; governments won't pay → pharma being pressured to pay

Intellectual property under attack

III. Assessing Causality (25 minutes)

In this pasture, I want students to think carefully about who or what is to blame for the AIDS crisis. There is no single correct answer, obviously, but students should quickly see how all of the causes interact and how even those who bear little blame in an objective sense may still labor under the weight of public scrutiny. They will also veer pretty naturally into a discussion of intellectual property rights, examining how this system works and what costs it may (or may not) impose.

I start with a provocative question that follows naturally from the preceding discussion.

Q: Who is to blame for the crisis of AIDS in Africa?

If the preceding discussion highlighted all of the key points here, then this debate will emerge naturally—and almost certainly contentiously. I tend to use a very light hand in managing the class, and just push students to defend their arguments. I play devil's advocate (or let others assume the role) for every "perpetrator" mentioned. The dialogue is intense, but fairly straightforward.

For example:

Can we really blame the victims here? Well, to some extent, yes. Given the sexual nature of HIV transmission, victims that understand that transmission may consciously choose to infect others (or at least, not to prevent infecting others). If people with AIDS refuse to take preventive measures (such as using condoms or refraining from multiple partners) then one can accuse them of helping to spread the deadly virus. Likewise, if people who suspect they have HIV refuse to be tested for it, then they, too, might be held complicit.

By the same token, students should quickly note that victims may not be fully responsible for their own behavior. Many of them, after all, are purely passive—infants infected at birth, for example, wives infected by their husbands, those infected by tainted blood. Many others have not been made aware of the HIV transmission mechanism or have no access to testing facilities. (NOTE: Given the sexual nature of HIV transmission, there may be an underlying uneasiness in the class. Students may giggle, or get nervous addressing some aspects of the issue. I try simply to ignore this uneasiness and deal with the subject as analytically as possible).

Examining the role of the victims leads swiftly to the role of their governments. *Aren't governments responsible for changing or addressing improper behavior? And haven't they just dropped the ball here?* Governments, after all, are the one who should be establishing clinics and urging their citizens to be tested. Governments are the ones to run educational campaigns and provide access to drugs. Insofar as HIV/AIDS is a public health disaster, then surely public policies must bear some large portion of the blame.

The problem with this line of argument, though, is that most African governments simply do not have the resources to respond. As the case points out (text, p. 5) doctors are scarce across the continent and most countries are struggling already under massive fiscal burdens. They cannot afford to build clinics, buy drugs, or build the infrastructure that the widescale distribution of these drugs would demand. Clearly, one can fault the African governments for not doing more, but it is hard to push the full weight of blame upon them.

Which leads to the third potential "perpetrator" of the crisis, the one that receives the bulk of attention both in the case and in general public discourse.

Why should anyone even think of blaming the pharmaceutical industry? Aren't they the ones saving lives? In fact, aren't they the only ones who offer any prospect of hope to those suffering from AIDS? This is the standard refrain from the pharmaceutical industry and its supporters, and it needs to be fully elaborated and explored in the course of this pasture.

The basic argument runs as follows: Pharmaceutical companies are in the business of providing products that make people healthier. They spend vast amounts of money (between $500 and $800 million, according to the text, p. 7) developing drugs and never know which of their various compounds or procedures will ultimately result in a successful treatment. They also have to undergo years of rigorous trials before receiving approval for any drug and they make no money on the drug during the testing period. Patents, which are embedded in the U.S. Constitution, are the devices which allow the pharmaceutical companies to stay in business and save lives. Without patents, pharmaceutical firms would have no way of recouping the funds they spend during drug discovery and testing. Without patents, therefore, firms would have no incentive to develop new drugs and everyone in society would be worse off. Evidence for this point comes from **Exhibits 7a and 7b**, which show that the countries with the tightest patent protection also generate the vast bulk of new drug development.

The counter-argument is equally passionate. Patents, opponents argue, are merely state-created monopolies. They give extensive protection (7 years in the United States) to firms which then reap tremendous windfalls from them. The key bit of evidence here is **Exhibit 6** (a very popular chart among AIDS activists), which shows the drug industry consistently earning profits well above the *Fortune 500* average. (A useful and predictable bit of drama can occur by showing Exhibit 6 to a supporter of the pharmaceutical industry. The instructor can ask him or her to explain why the industry consistently outperforms its peers.) Students arguing against the industry should also cite consumer advocates (on p. 7) who claim that R & D costs in the industry are only, on average, between $57 and $71 million.

A related and critical debate concerns the role of generics, copycat drugs produced once a product's patent has expired. As **Exhibit 8** demonstrates, generic drugs are much less expensive than their patented counterparts. Opponents of the pharmaceutical industry therefore argue that if the firms were to allow for greater generic production, prices for AIDS drugs would plummet. By avoiding generic production, therefore, the pharmaceutical firms are essentially denying Africans access to life-saving treatment. Evidence for this possibility comes from Brazil (pp. 10–11), which used a strategy of generic production to vastly reduce to prices for, and access to, HIV/AIDS treatment. Once this possibility is voiced, instructors may wish to turn again to students who expressed the standard pro-patent position, confronting them with the extreme version of the argument in favor of generic production:

Q: So, by preventing competition in your market, you're apparently letting millions of people die. You're okay with that?

They will chafe, understandably, at this question and will generally respond by defending patents and protection as the necessary components of innovation. Supporters of the generic solution will then counter by asking how much protection is enough, or even by arguing that a fair amount of drug discovery comes from university or government-sponsored labs, where the motivation of patents is less direct. Debate will flow pretty quickly from here, and instructors may wish simply to let the students argue among themselves.

At some point in the discussion, though, two important points need to be raised: first, that generic drug producers are not by nature any less profit-oriented than the major pharmaceutical firms;[1] and second, that patents are not really the key problem in Africa, since most of the major firms have not patented their most expensive products there. This last point is picked up in greater detail in the subsequent (B) case.

Typically, this part of the case discussion simply runs on its own. Students are quick to take sides on the issue of patents and to argue with their peers. I try only to moderate the discussion and keep tempers under control, pushing students to argue analytically rather than emotionally. Most critically, I try to keep them focused on the underlying tension that drives this case: if patents are the key to innovation, then what will happen to drug discovery—and particularly the discovery of drugs that address the so-called diseases of poverty—if pharmaceuticals are forced to abandon, or even limit, their patents?

---

[1] At HBS, *Life, Death and Property Rights* is taught in the second year elective course, *Managing International Trade and Investment*. It follows a related case on generic drug production in India, which allows students to compare the strategies of these two very different kinds of pharmaceutical firms. See Yasheng Huang and Harold F. Hogan, Jr., *India's Intellectual Property Rights Regime and the Pharmaceutical Industry*, HBS Case No. 702-039 (Boston: Harvard Business School Publishing, 2002).

LSB
Blame:
The victims?
Their families?
Their governments?
WHO?
Pfizer?

Once all sides of this argument have been laid out, I turn the discussion away from the topic of patents and towards the strategic implications of the argument itself. Pointing to whichever students have been the largest critics of the pharmaceutical firms (or referring to groups such as Doctors without Borders, cited repeatedly in the text), I will reiterate that part of the blame for the problem of AIDS in Africa—indeed, much of the blame—appears to rest with Western pharmaceutical firms. I then ask two related questions:

Q: Is this a valid argument?

Q: If not, then why is it receiving so much attention?

The objectives here are straightforward. Students need to understand that, even if the argument against the pharmaceutical firms is not entirely persuasive, it is compelling enough to stick, and to cause massive outrage against the firms. Once the comparison has been drawn between poor, dying Africans and wealthy Western companies, the companies will be forced to respond. Almost certainly, African governments are more directly responsible for the crisis that now befalls their people. Almost certainly, there are institutions (the Red Cross, the World Health Organization, the United Nations) that are better suited for dealing with a medical crisis of this magnitude. But the pharmaceutical companies are rich; they are well-known; and they control the drugs that have the potential to save lives. Like it or not, they will be forced to respond to the crisis of AIDS in Africa.

IV. Crafting the Solution (25 minutes)

Once this realization has been voiced, the final pasture follows easily. We now know that the pharmaceutical companies have to do something. The question is what.

To prompt a wide-ranging debate, I begin here by asking students to conceive their solutions from a particular vantage point. For example:

Q: Imagine you work for Doctors without Borders. What solutions might you propose?

Q: What about if you worked for the South African Ministry of Health? For a Brazilian pharmaceutical firm? For the World Health Organization? For Pfizer?

Obviously, the point here is to prod students to see 1) how closely the proposed solutions will correspond with the proponent's own interest; and 2) how nearly all solutions will demand major concessions from the pharmaceutical firms. I record the proposals on B-2, where their range essentially speaks for itself:

B-2: Solutions

	Solutions?	
Doctors w/o Borders	**SA Ministry**	**Pfizer**
Get drugs for free NGO provision Eliminate patents	Get drugs for free NGO provision	Distribution Education Innovation...
WHO	**Brazilian firm**	
Reduced drug prices Centralized access	Generics Shorter patent lives	

Once this board is complete, I turn to two related follow-up questions.

Q: Is there a compromise?

Q: Is it feasible for firms like Pfizer?

The answers here are straightforward. Compromise will be extremely hard, since the solutions proposed by many of the most vocal groups involve dramatic measures: deeply reduced drug prices and sharply reduced, or even eliminated, patents. Firms like Pfizer will have to find some way to meet these demands without destroying their fundamental way of doing business.

V. Conclusions (5 minutes)

How instructors choose to conclude this case will depend heavily on whether or not they choose to teach the follow-up case, *Phase Two: The Pharmaceutical Industry Responds to AIDS* (703-005) as well. If the (B) case will follow, then conclusions here should probably be brief, simply highlighting the central issues and tensions of this case and setting the stage for what is to come.

I typically use something along the following lines:

5-703-046
REV: JULY 22, 2003

TEACHING NOTE

Phase Two: The Pharmaceutical Industry Responds to AIDS

Phase Two: The Pharmaceutical Industry Responds to AIDS was written as a follow-up case to *Life, Death and Property Rights: The Pharmaceutical Industry Faces AIDS in Africa.* Although it is possible to teach Phase Two without the previous case, most instructors will want to teach the two together, either in a single class or over two consecutive sessions. *Phase Two* was created to describe how the pharmaceutical industry responded to the AIDS crisis outlined in the *Life and Death* case and to provide an account of key events in this area between 2000 and 2002.

Case Structure and Overview

In structure, this case is much simpler than its predecessor. It does not introduce any new theoretical material and essentially is just an account of the industry's response. Whereas the previous case explores the AIDS crisis from a number of perspectives, *Phase Two* concentrates almost exclusively on the commercial side.

Teaching Assignment

Read: *Phase Two: The Pharmaceutical Industry Responds to AIDS (703-005)*

Study Questions

1. Have the pharmaceutical firms responded well to the AIDS crisis in Africa? Have they gone far enough in addressing the problem? Or too far?

2. As AIDS spreads across the developing world, how should pharmaceutical companies structure their relations with affected populations? With governments? With NGOs?

This note was prepared by Professor Debora Spar for the sole purpose of aiding classroom instructors in the use of "Phase Two: The Pharmaceutical Industry Responds to AIDS," HBS No. 703-005. It provides analysis and questions that are intended to present alternative approaches to deepening students' comprehension of business issues and energizing classroom discussion. HBS cases are developed solely as the basis for class discussion. Cases are not intended to serve as endorsements, sources of primary data, or illustrations of effective or ineffective management.

3. What public role, if any, should companies like Merck and Pfizer play in debates over the pricing and availability of AIDS drugs?

Teaching Plan and Objectives

Presuming that instructors have already taught the first case of this series, they can simply introduce the case as part of an ongoing analysis. I am typically extremely brief in my opening remarks, saying only that, "We pick up now where we just left off. This case describes the period from 1999 to 2002 and explores how the pharmaceutical industry responded to the expanding AIDS crisis." I then divide the class time into four pastures, exploring what the companies have done; what they still may have to do; what their response suggests about corporate strategy in a complex and high profile arena such as life-saving medicine; and finally, what the story of AIDS suggests about the evolution of intellectual property rights in the global economy. In this respect, the final pasture of the (B) case completes the analysis launched in the first pasture of the (A) case.

I. Response (20 minutes)

I begin with a basic cold call:

Q: What did the pharmaceutical industry do to respond to the crisis of AIDS in Africa?

The question basically asks for a recitation of case facts, but I think it's important here to get these facts in the classroom and on the board. With this objective in mind, instructors may wish to call on a strong student, so that the class can move quickly to the subsequent analysis. They can also ask this student, once the facts have been established, to summarize what the industry did. Essentially, as one executive states in the case, the industry "took the price away" (text, p. 3). They cut drug prices to a fraction of their retail price in exchange for getting governments and international organizations to adhere to the existing system of intellectual property rights.

RSB

Accelerating Access—negotiated substantially reduced (10% US) to governments

Money for treatment and education

Assistance to orphans (Abbott)

Diflucan for free (Pfizer)

Lower prices for drugs (AZT, nevirapine)

→ "Took the price away"

This deal raises the obvious question:

Q: How significant are these concessions?

Students can debate this at some length. On the one hand, purely in terms of price, the concessions are huge. Drugs that cost $10, 000 to $15,000 per person per year in the United States are now being offered for roughly $1,000 to $1,500 per person per year in Africa. This is a major change of heart for the industry, which has traditionally abided by a global pricing policy. Moreover, as the case describes, all of the major firms announce significant charitable programs during this time, indicating a newfound sense of responsibility towards Africa's AIDS victims.

On the other hand, however, students can easily argue that these concessions are little more than public relations, since they still do not address the underlying problems of AIDS. Even at $1,000 a year, for example, AIDS drugs are still unaffordable for the vast majority of Africans. Lowering the price has no effect on Africa's shaky system of drug distribution and insisting that governments play a role in the distribution system keeps other possible distributors (most notably NGOs) out of the process. Most critically, the pharmaceutical firms have made no concessions in the area that has attracted the loudest criticism. Rather than loosening property rights or reducing patent duration, they are actually demanding stringent patent enforcement as a condition of their deal.

To heighten debate and underscore the role of NGOs, instructors may wish to refer to the opening quote from Samantha Bolton of Doctors without Borders. When someone is commending the pharmaceutical firms' actions, simply ask:

Q: If you've done so much, then why does Samantha Bolton still want to whip you?

This question serves two important functions. First, it helps to emphasize that corporate concessions have still not come anywhere close to what AIDS activists are demanding. The key here is property rights and the firms have offered no change in policy along those lines. Second, it sparks discussion of the NGOs' role. **What are their objectives with regard to the AIDS epidemic? Why are they "whipping" the pharmaceutical firms and not the African governments? And to whom are they accountable?**

There are no right answers to any of these questions. Students should see, however, that NGOs are both powerful and mysterious players in the international economy. They have the skills and credibility to shape public opinion, especially in the face of a grave and tangible crisis such as AIDS. But they are not themselves accountable to any rigorous standard; nor are their own motives and tactics necessarily beyond reproach. This realization leads naturally to the next pasture.

Further Concessions (20 minutes)

Q: What could you do to make Samantha happy?

The central objective of this pasture is to explore all options available to the pharmaceutical industry. Students should analyze not only what the industry can do to "keep Samantha happy," of course, but also the implications of any strategic change.

Roughly speaking, there are four groups of options. The pharmaceutical industry could reduce prices even farther; they could remove patents on AIDS drugs in Africa; they could develop drug delivery and treatment systems; or they could do nothing. Each of these options imposes significant costs and raises serious questions of feasibility.

Reducing prices is in many ways the most straightforward of the options. As the case describes, the pharmaceutical firms have already made massive concessions in this direction. If they can sell AIDS drugs for $1,000 why not for $100? Or $1? Indeed, as students should be encouraged to point out, the marginal cost for producing most drugs is very small. Once firms have recouped their R&D costs in the developed world, there is no financial reason why they can't sell drugs very cheaply in developing markets.

There are, however, considerable strategic reasons that mitigate against such a policy. First, by lowering drug prices dramatically in any single market (or group of markets) the drug firms risk the establishment of a very dangerous precedent. If they lower prices in one place, why not elsewhere? If they differentiate between rich countries and poor ones, then why not between rich patients and poor ones? Moreover, the entire pricing policy of the industry is based on the notion that drug prices have to be high in order for firms to recoup the exceedingly high costs of discovery. Once this notion is called into question, the firms could face price pressure on all their drugs. Likewise, in a world of fluid boundaries, cheap drugs from one market might easily flood into more expensive territories, pushing prices downward again. Finally—and most subtly—even if firms gave their AIDS drugs away; even if they made Samantha wildly happy on that score; it's not clear that they would actually make serious headway against the AIDS epidemic. If people don't have access to the drugs or knowledge of their use, then even free drugs may be of limited value. (This distinction raises an interesting sidebar discussion: are the firms trying to keep Samantha happy or help AIDS victims? These two objectives may not always be the same).

Another option is to **focus on the weakness of Africa's drug delivery system.** Theoretically, the pharmaceutical firms could address the problems alluded to above. They could help distribute the drugs they produce; establish clinics and testing facilities; and train the medical personnel that full-fledged treatment programs will demand. Once again, though, a host of problems arises. Should pharmaceutical firms really be in the business of medical delivery? Do they have the skills to engage in such a program? And are they being fair to their shareholders if they diversify in such a massive and unprofitable direction? Is it even appropriate for private firms from one country to assume a quasi-governmental role in another?

If they stay closer to the core competence, meanwhile, and focus on **property rights**, the pharmaceutical firms are treading on their own most sacred territory. As the discussion in *Life, Death and Property Rights* will have made clear, patents sit at the core of the pharmaceutical industry. They are what have allowed the industry to prosper and to reap significant profits. If the industry compromises with these drugs, in these countries, they risk a ripple effect across their entire industry. It is exceedingly hard to imagine the industry conceding on this front.

In addition, there are two elements of the patent debate that deserve mention. First is the role of generic producers, such as India's Cipla. One could argue that it is these firms which would truly benefit from any reduction in patent production, since shorter patent lives would give them a longer period in which to sell their own products. Yet because generic producers are still profit-minded firms, there is no guarantee that even lower priced generic drugs would be either affordable or accessible to Africa's millions of poor patients. A second and related aspect is evident from **Exhibit 1.** Here we see that patents in Africa are largely irrelevant. Because the markets are so small, most pharmaceutical companies have not even bothered to seek patent protection for their antiretroviral drugs. In other words, there is nothing stopping any generic producer from selling even the most cutting-edge AIDS drug in most African markets. There is no patent protection in most of the continent (South Africa being a notable exception) and thus little reason to suspect that simply getting rid of patents would solve the AIDS problem.

Which brings us to the fourth group of options. If there is nothing that the drug companies can do to make Samantha happy—perhaps even nothing they can do to make serious headway against AIDS—then perhaps they shouldn't do anything. Perhaps they are better simply riding out the storm, sticking to their own business and waiting for the outrage against them to subside.

This is an attractive option in many ways, but almost certainly both unfeasible and unpalatable. The pharmaceutical companies are being ambushed by the activists; their reputations are staggering; and morale is more difficult to maintain. They cannot ignore either the AIDS crisis or the public relations nightmare it has become. Even if none of their options are particularly attractive, they need to find some way to respond.

LSB: Options

Do nothing

Reduce price

Remove patents

Manage drug delivery and treatment system

(Walk through implementation and feasibility of each)

Strategies of Response (20 minutes)

At this point in the discussion, it is useful to drop below the industry level and look at the actions of specific firms. Instructors can structure this in several possible ways, either asking students to suggest which of the firms did the best job of managing the AIDS issue, or posing questions about specific firms.

One interesting avenue is to compare Merck and Pfizer. Pfizer, as the case mentions, has long been the political leader among the major drug companies. It was Pfizer, for example, who championed intellectual property for decades and succeeded in getting intellectual property embedded into the operating rules of the World Trade Organization.[1] In the AIDS debate, by contrast, Pfizer has taken a backseat role, even dropping out of the Accelerating Access program as Merck took the leadership position.

Instructors can therefore ask whether this reticence makes sense.

Q: Do you as a manager want to lead the industry's response to AIDS? Is there any first mover advantage here? Why or why not?

Once again, there are no right answers but many avenues of discussion. Students should see that the responding to activism is a deeply strategic choice. Firms can decide to be first movers in this area, grabbing the spotlight that will almost certainly appear if they make serious concessions before

[1] For more on Pfizer's role in establishing the global roles of intellectual property, see Lynn Paine, *Pfizer: Global Protection of Intellectual Property Rights,* HBS Case No. 392-073 (Boston: Harvard Business School Publishing, 1992).

their rivals. Or they can decide to let their rivals move first, conceding as part of a broader, perhaps industry-wide trend. Or they can flat-out refuse to concede, ignoring the activists and their demands.[2]

During this pasture, I am generally happy to let students air their voice, intervening only to push them to complete and elaborate their thoughts. Students should see that nearly all possible strategies for the pharmaceutical firms involve heavy costs with no clear benefits. If a firm such as Merck moves first, establishing itself as the lead firm in responding to AIDS, it sets itself up for further criticism. Anything that the company fails to do will leave it vulnerable to attack—and the invidious nature of the disease means, nearly by definition, that no single firm can do all that much to affect or stem it. By contrast, however, a firm that stands by the sidelines risks receiving the full brunt of the activists' wrath. If one believes that the activists are powerful; and if one thinks that sooner or later the pharmaceutical companies are going to have to respond more forcefully to the crisis of AIDS in Africa, then there may be no advantage in waiting. Any response, though, will be both financially expensive and of uncertain long-term value.

Q: How much of their shareholders' money should the pharmaceutical firms spend trying to combat a problem that, arguably, they haven't caused?

Q: How can we calculate – or even conceive – the full costs of either fighting this disease or letting it continue to spread?

These are extremely tough questions and they need to be posed, even if not answered. I generally leave them as unanswered, simply reminding the students of both their importance and their difficulty.

Intellectual Property Rights (10 minutes)

In this final pasture, I try to tie together a powerful thread that runs through both the (A) and (B) cases. Because the topic has already been raised, presumably, in other discussion segments, this pasture need not be long. It is useful, though, to end the class with a consideration of property rights, since this is both the strongest intellectual issue to run through the cases and the most generalizable.

After summing up the previous pasture, I thus generally turn to a student who has been advocating for the strongest kind of response from the pharmaceutical industry. I ask simply:

Q: Should the industry reverse its stand on IPR, or at least alter it? and

Q: What would the implications be?

The point here is straightforward but critical. Essentially, the industry can not reverse its stand on IPR. It has fought too hard and too long for the perpetuation of intellectual property rights and it's just not clear how the industry could afford its massive R & D programs without the security of

[2] For a case that describes one firm's decision to be a first mover in this realm, see Forest Reinhardt and Emily Richman, *Global Climate Change and BP Amoco*, HBS Case No. 700-106 (Boston: Harvard Business School Publishing, 2000). For a more theoretical examination of the strategic choices around response, see Debora L. Spar and Lane T. La Mure, "The Power of Activism: Assessing the Impact of NGOs on Global Business." *California Management Review* 45, no. 3 (Spring 2003).

patents. Students can advocate shorter patents periods, perhaps, or differential patents (depending on country circumstances) but it's pretty tough to argue that the industry could survive a complete loss of IPR protection.

Moreover, as the direction of the second question makes clear, a change in this industry would have reverberations across many of the world's leading commercial sectors. Movies, software, semiconductors, biotechnology—all rely heavily on patents to motivate invention and protect rents. If the pharmaceutical industry, which has long championed global IPR, were to change course, it would put heavy pressure on these other industries as well.

A more likely scenario, therefore, is quiet movement toward a regime of differential enforcement. Indeed, as **Exhibit 1** suggests, this regime is already largely in place: pharmaceutical firms do not seek patents on many drugs in many parts of the world. Essentially, these drugs are "off patent" from the start. And they still are not produced, because the costs are too high and the market too small. Against this backdrop, the drug companies may well be able to address the problem of AIDS without destroying the global system of IPR. They can stick by their traditional support for intellectual property rights while emphasizing that most of these rights simply aren't relevant in the African context. More importantly, they can make major concessions on the price side (as they are doing by the end of this case), assuring that AIDS drugs really are accessible and affordable in Africa.

Conclusions (10 minutes)

Closing comments follow directly from the final pasture.

The most important point here is also the most obvious: the are no simple answers to the tragedy that is AIDS in Africa. The problem is enormous, the human toll tragic, and the solution far beyond the bounds of normal commercial, medical, or political action. Any real solution will take work and concessions from all sides, and will take years, possibly decades, to have real effect.

I do, however, raise several other, more specific points, most of which will have emerged from the preceding discussion.

First, I stress that intellectual property rights should not (and probably will not) be sacrificed in pursuit of a cure for AIDS. Indeed, although the system of IPR undoubtedly has flaws; although it is more relevant for the developed world than the developing, the system itself has worked—both in the pharmaceutical industry and elsewhere. Can the system be tinkered with? Yes. Can could patents be changed or shortened in developing countries? Probably. Should the world find some other way of motivating research on "poor" diseases such as malaria and tuberculosis? Almost certainly. But none of these arguments demands the elimination of patents.

By the same token, however, the visible tragedy of AIDS and the attack it has provoked upon the pharmaceutical industry show little signs of diminishing. The industry is going to have to respond to AIDS in Africa and it will be forced to make major, expensive concessions. Are these concessions "fair"? It doesn't matter. The tragedy is real and there's no one else to attack. (For example: Thabo Mbeki probably deserves a significant measure of blame for refusing to acknowledge the nature of HIV/AIDS and severely underfunding treatment programs. But Doctors without Borders is not about to attack Mbeki.)

Against this backdrop, the best strategy for the pharmaceutical industry is probably to move fast and to move big. They have already lost a great deal of public goodwill as a result of AIDS in Africa and they need to address the problem, as seriously and significantly as they can, before the political environment shifts even more dramatically against them.

To be sure, the pharmaceutical firms do not (and almost certainly should not) need to act alone. They need to work with and gain the support of well-meaning governments in Africa. They need to establish connections to local communities and to the public health personnel who will be critical in combating AIDS on the ground. They need to make links with international organizations such as the World Health Organization and with the more respected, less combative, activist groups.

None of this will be easy for the pharmaceutical firms. They are big, and profitable and not used to being attacked on so many fronts. But AIDS in Africa is not a peripheral problem for them or a fleeting trend. It is a medical disaster so big and so terrible that it has the potential to force major changes in how drugs are discovered, marketed and owned. The pharmaceutical industry can not afford to rest on its laurels in this case or simply to do business along accustomed channels. The rules of the game have changed for these firms, and the industry must change along with them.

Ciba-Geigy Pharmaceuticals: Pharma International

Teaching Note

Synopsis

The management committee of Pharma International (PHI) has to decide whether to approve the launch of an antimalarial drug in Nigeria and how this should be implemented. The case is rich in situation assessment as it raises and interrelates commercial, ethical, and policy considerations against a backdrop of criticism of pharmaceutical companies' marketing practices in the Third World.

Objectives

1. To examine pharmaceutical marketing practices in the Third World, and particularly the ethical issues that can arise (including product safety, honesty and accuracy in marketing communications, responsibilities in product testing, and exporting nonapproved products).

2. To alert students to the ethical dimensions of marketing decision making, specifically within an international Third World context.

3. To show ethical considerations as an integral part of marketing decision making, alongside commercial and policy considerations.

4. To show how situation assessment (including stakeholder analysis) helps marketing decision making, specifically in new product development.

5. To consider the limits of corporate social responsibility, how much is "socially responsible" and how that level might be determined.

Professor John A. Quelch prepared this teaching note as an aid to instructors in the classroom use of the case "Ciba-Geigy Pharmaceuticals: Pharma International," No. 589-108.

Teaching Suggestions

The pharmaceutical marketing note can be discussed prior to and separately from the case. This discussion should be restricted to 30 minutes to allow for adequate coverage of the case (40 minutes) and a concluding wrap-up (10 minutes). The focus of the initial discussion should be on improving marketing practice. It may be useful to draw some conclusions before turning to the Ciba-Geigy case. However, the note contains powerful material likely to produce heated discussion, which may make closure difficult at this stage. In any event, the bridge to the Ciba-Geigy case is that the note provides the backdrop to the Fevex decision, which PHI would presumably wish to make without incurring the sort of problems described in the note. With this observation made, a student may then be asked to "open" the case decision: Should PHI approve the development and launch of Fevex? If so, how should this be implemented?

A thorough situation assessment will provide the facts necessary for Ciba-Geigy to make the "right" decision which would be ethically and commercially sound and hence seek to avoid the problems identified in the pharmaceutical marketing practices note. Unlike many of the situations described in the note, the case does not deal with misconduct. It presents a typical product development decision for a pharmaceutical company operating in the Third World which, nonetheless, requires careful and explicit consideration of the firm's responsibilities. It can be useful to conceive of ethical issues in business at different levels: the society, industry, and the individual. Many of the ethical issues in this case are at the societal level.

The discussion should address the following questions. Given time, some attention might be given to the Servipharm initiative (as indicated below). This can, however, be ignored. The concluding wrap-up can provide the sequel to the case (see Postscript) and conclusions reached on responsible marketing practice, by pharmaceutical companies and others, in Third World countries.

There is a separate teaching note for "Note on Pharmaceutical Marketing Practices in the Third World" (No. 589-039), which can be used with this case. This teaching note includes a section covering the integration of the case and the note.

Questions

1. What is the function of the PHI management committee? What decision(s) must it make regarding Fevex?

2. What key factors emerge from an assessment of Ciba-Geigy's situation in Nigeria?

3. What criticisms might be made of the Fevex proposal by concerned consumer and health organizations?

4. Should the PHI management committee approve the development and launch of Fevex?

5. What suggestions for implementation would you make?

6. How might our analysis have differed if the product had been aspirin, a soft drink or a ball-point pen?

7. Why did Ciba-Geigy set up Servipharm? What should it do with Servipharm now?

8. What general conclusions may be drawn about marketing in Third World countries?

Analysis

1. What is the function of the PHI management committee? What decision(s) must it make regarding Fevex?

It is important to secure an early understanding of the role of the PHI management committee and the decision(s) to be made; as important as an appreciation of what it does *not* do. The management committee is not responsible for determining that the drug meets clinical and technical criteria; that is the role of the PEA, a committee of detached scientists who must approve the drug in the form proposed. (It may be noted that having a separate committee solely responsible for product efficacy is a useful control mechanism.) Furthermore, the management committee does not have to provide a detailed marketing plan for Fevex. At this stage, it merely provides approval and may make some recommendations. When the product development process is more advanced, Pharma Nigeria will be able to include Fevex within its yearly plan, submitted to Switzerland for approval. The management committee would then have the opportunity to comment on the details of the proposed implementation.

While the PEA assesses the drug's technical performance, the management committee still has a "duty of care" responsibility. (Explicit recognition of the committee's "duty of care" responsibility is another important control mechanism.) So, for example, it must judge whether the product would work and be safe in the Nigerian marketplace. Reference to the Nestle infant formula case may be useful here.[1] A product may be safe according to laboratory tests and in the country of origin, but not when used in very different circumstances in a Third World country. The management committee's decision must incorporate commercial, policy, and ethical criteria.

2. What key factors emerge from an assessment of Ciba-Geigy's situation in Nigeria?

Environmental analysis is an important part of situation assessment. This case is rich in data on broader environmental factors which will influence the Fevex decision, such as the economic and political climate in Nigeria. To be effective, the situation assessment should be focused, with a clear purpose and structure. In this case, the situation assessment should be focused on factors bearing on the Fevex decision and may be examined at three levels: global, Nigeria, and the Nigerian antimalarial market. At the global level are factors determining Ciba-Geigy Pharmaceuticals' overall policy and strategy which may be critical for such a genuinely transnational corporation. In practice many of these factors are "givens" unlikely to be explicitly considered by the management committee in making the Fevex decision, but contributory nonetheless. See **Exhibit TN-1** for an outline of the situation analysis.

Also important within the situation assessment is stakeholder analysis. The stakeholder concept suggests that stockholders are by no means the only corporate constituents who have a vested interest in the conduct and performance of a given firm. Stakeholder groups consist of people who are affected by corporate policies and practices and who see themselves as having a stake in the business.

---

[1]"Nestle and the Infant Food Controversy (A)," revised edition, University of Western Ontario case No. 9-81-A005.

PHI stakeholders include:

• Consumers	- urban Nigerians	- rich
		- poor
	- rural Nigerians	
	- visitors to Nigeria	
• Customers	- physicians	
	- health centers/clinics	
	- hospitals	
	- distributors	- pharmacies
		- patent medicine stores, etc.
• Employees	- Basel	- Pharma Main board
	- Nigeria	- PHI
		- SNNC
		- Pharma
• Stockholders	- Giba-Geigy	
	- SNCC	
• Consumer/health organizations		
• Suppliers		
• Community	- Nigerian	
	- global	
• Nigerian government		

Each stakeholder group is likely to have a different agenda and expectations. While compromise will be anticipated, PHI will have to reconcile the interests of these groups as best it can according to some set of priorities (evident below).

3. What criticisms might be made of the Fevex proposal by concerned consumer and health organizations?

Consumer and health organizations would be concerned about product safety, product proliferation and wasted resources, and aggressive marketing.

Chloroquine is well-established as an antimalarial; the PEA will confirm that the Fevex formulation is technically sound. It has been linked to retinopathy when extensively used (and Ciba-Geigy's SMON experiences heighten the sensitivity to this side effect), and there is evidence of chloroquine-resistant strains of malaria. However, its inclusion on the WHO essential drugs list, support for Third World chloroquine manufacture from UNIDO, and its use in the Nigerian federal government's program, make it more legitimate and a lower risk than alternatives such as sulfadoxine/pyrimethamine. Chloroquine resistance is not a major problem in Nigeria. Limits on continuous use would be required.

More significant product safety concerns arise from two less direct sources. Most important is the prospect of unintended consumption, particularly by children, as Fevex no longer has the safeguard of the extremely bitter taste found in traditional formulations. Against this risk, there are the benefits of the more pleasant taste reducing the likelihood of postponement of treatment (or the use of suspect alternatives) and improved compliance, without which chloroquine's efficacy is reduced in subsequent attacks and chloroquine resistance develops. In the West, chloroquine is only available as a prescription product and even in its traditional forms must have childproof packaging in West Germany.

The second concern is the OTC supply. This product requires accurate self-diagnosis and administration. There is a narrow margin of safety between therapeutic and toxic doses, requiring caution. However, most antimalarials are available OTC in Nigeria, as are many other drugs, providing treatment that for some regions would otherwise be nonexistent.

There are already 50 antimalarial brands available in Nigeria—is another one required? This criticism rests on whether Fevex is seen as a "me-too" (discussed below) and, more broadly, whether Ciba-Geigy shouldn't be addressing more serious problems than making chloroquine pleasant to taste, a criticism of Ciba-Geigy's responsibilities and priorities in serving the Third World (also discussed below).

Criticisms of aggressive marketing partly reflect similar concerns about wasted resources. Is the money on promotion well spent? Could it be better used on R&D? There is also the possibility of marketing communications misleading consumers and health care workers, particularly in countries with lower levels of literacy and education. What claims will be made for Fevex? It is no more effective than other chloroquine products (assuming consistent quality), and free medication is available for many Nigerians.

It should be noted that despite the ideology of marketing, the interests of consumers and producers do not always coincide. However, Mark Pastin has referred to the "moral superiority of the uninvolved" in criticism of public interest group challenges to corporate practices.

4. Should the PHI management committee approve the development and launch of Fevex?

On the basis of the above analysis, the arguments for and against Fevex, incorporating commercial, policy, and ethical criteria are:

For	Against
• Malaria morbidity (at least 1.4m cases) + mortality ("leading cause of death")	• Consumer/health organization criticism—targets currently sought, Ciba-Geigy a good target (Entero-Vioform and SMON)
• OTC (and associated marketing) solution to absence/decline of health care (40-50% untreated)	
• Product superiority: - pleasant to take - no postponement - improved compliance (and improved efficacy of subsequent treatments, less chloroquine resistance) - capsules highly regarded	• Product safety concerns: - chloroquine by prescription and childproof packaging in West - no bitter taste safeguard - unintended consumption, especially by children - OTC requires self-diagnosis and administration - narrow margin of safety between therapeutic and toxic dose - locally manufactured - counterfeiting
• Choroquines's safety/legitimacy - well-established (50 years) - new side effects/contraindications unlikely - "endorsement" of WHO, UN, Nigerian govt. - familiar to Nigerians	

For	Against
• Pharma Nigeria strategy - increase OTC presence (Pharma goal globally), especially in Nigerian pharm. market (70% OTC) - OTC market growth prospects - antimalarial 4th largest segment of OTC market (N10m; Pharma sales only N6m) - local production of strategic importance	• Product proliferation (50 brands) means resources wasted which could have been used elsewhere
	• Aggressive marketing - wasted resources - misleading?
• Utilization of capsule-filling capacity (60%, from 20%)	• Fevex is "me-too" - what social benefit? (Fevex no more effective than generic chloroquine) - "low tech—counter to Ciba-Geigy policy (R&D emphasis, see mission)
• PHI need to support local innovation (proposal (originated from Pharma Nigeria)	• Current competition and likely competitive reaction
• Export potential	• Capsulated chloroquine easy to copy
	• Limited OTC experience and resources (distribution, brand franchise, etc.)
	• Costs and delay of clinical trails
	• Nigerian economy - economic prospects poor - decline in pharmaceutical market - vulnerability of distribution system
	• Growing resistance to chloroquine - limits long-term prospects in Nigeria - reduces export potential
	• Nigerian production and quality perceptions also reduce export potential
	• Conflict with Servipharm (Serviquin)

Assuming continued PHI support for the development of Pharma Nigeria, an assessment of the pros and cons would likely favor approval. Fevex treats a killing/disabling disease; will reach many people through OTC supply; is a superior product in its capsule formulation, yet safely based on chloroquine; fits Pharma Nigeria's strategy and the Pharma global goal of increasing OTC presence; and, although no bottom-line figures are provided (and were not calculated by the company), can be assumed to be potentially profitable, especially given plant utilization improvements.

Many of the arguments against approval are not unique to Fevex and would be faced regardless of the product proposal. They are part and parcel of doing business in Nigeria as in many other countries: counterfeiting, testing new products, the economic situation, quality perceptions, limited OTC experience and, to a large extent, consumer/health organization criticisms. Given Pharma's commitment to OTC supply (and belief in its safety and appropriateness), the product safety and aggressive marketing concerns can be largely met by careful implementation; PHI should make recommendations accordingly (see below). So, the most convincing argument against Fevex is that it is a "me-too," an argument which in itself has ethical and policy considerations as well as the normal commercial issues.

A radical critique might well reject Fevex—and not simply (with the benefit of hindsight) because of the Nigerian political and economic situation. Consider: How does Fevex add value? This question needs to be considered not only from the narrow marketing, company-specific perspective, but also from the broader societal (macromarketing) perspective. From the company perspective, Fevex may only provide short-term success because its added value over competitive offerings is likely to be temporary. Fevex is not a "me-too" from a consumer rather than a more technical standpoint; it has genuine differentiation. However, its product superiority may soon be eroded as competitors copy the idea of capsulated chloroquine or, alternatively, seeing the appeal of Fevex (assuming Pharma Nigeria is correct about consumer resistance to chloroquine's bitter taste), improve "tasteless" formulations or retarget syrup formulations to include adults as well as children. PHI estimated a 1-2 year lead over the competition, during which time Pharma Nigeria had to become well established in a new market, if the "key player" objective is to be realized.

Company policy (see mission statement, resistance to Servipharm, etc.) favors new products based on R&D. Fevex is more in keeping with the minor product improvements of an earlier phase of pharmaceutical R&D, counter to the current trend of innovative R&D. Perhaps this trend is less appropriate in developing markets. However, more important is the recognition that increased OTC presence will come largely through this sort of initiative. Ciba-Geigy Pharmaceuticals will have to face up to the conflict between the R&D policy and the OTC goal.

From a societal perspective, what does Fevex add to improve human welfare? It is no more effective than existing treatments. Heavy expenditures on advertising, etc., particularly given Pharma Nigeria's low profile in the OTC market, may make Fevex the leading brand, but does this equate to added social benefit? These are particularly serious concerns in health care and an environment of scarce resources. Society's goal of reducing the incidence and effects of malaria may be better met in other ways. What effort is Ciba-Geigy making to develop antimalarial vaccines or, as a chemical company, safe pesticides which would control the anopheles mosquito? Simpler measures, such as reducing pools of dirty water (where mosquitos breed in urban areas), might better meet society's goal than yet another brand of chloroquine.

A reply to these charges demands an appreciation of the social benefits which marketing activities can bring and a faith in capitalism, together with acknowledgement of its inefficiencies. Fevex may be no more together with acknowledgement of its inefficiencies. Fevex may be no more *effective* than other chloroquine brands, yet it may be more *successful* in dealing with malaria because the customer orientation which marketing brings takes account of a human factor, the aversion to chloroquine's bitter taste. Moreover, Fevex marketing may help by increasing consumer understanding of the need and means to treat malarial symptoms and, through OTC supply, reach those who would otherwise go untreated.

Capitalism entails undesirable inefficiencies, inequities and externalities. Yet, it is arguably the best political-economic system so far devised. Under such a system, can private enterprise (Ciba-Geigy) be expected to deal with broader environmental factors contributing to disease (pools of dirty water with malaria, nutritional deficiencies more generally)? Private enterprise requires the right incentives to serve social good, including (as in the case of antimalarial pesticides or vaccines) governmental direction. Whose role is it to identify the social good and the means for realizing it? Marketing's externalities (too much advertising, misleading or harmful advertising/sales tactics) may be a cost which society has to bear in return for the benefits of the competitive market system. Yet it may still be argued that Ciba-Geigy could do more (see below).

These concerns may not be well articulated by students, but may emerge more in the form of nagging doubts they can't quite pin down. Provocative questioning may help in this process (e.g., what would be in society's best interests?).

5. What suggestions for implementation would you make?

As the analysis indicates, product safety concerns and the prospect of targeting by consumer/health organizations require the careful implementation of the Fevex proposal. PHI recommendations would include:

- On packaging: childproof packaging (though not used by competitors); clear instructions, written and graphic, on product use; cautions against continued use; including "keep out of reach of children" on labels.
- On marketing communications: caution in claims, incentives for sales force, etc. (This recommendation would have the broader impact of reinforcing any earlier PHI efforts to curb marketing excesses overseas.)

Market research would be required as standard procedure. As well as contributing to marketing mix refinement (e.g., form of message in advertising), it should also measure and confirm consumer aversion to chloroquine bitterness. Does Fevex warrant broad market entry with "no bitterness" as a positioning statement, or is there a clearly defined market segment which should be targeted (e.g., upscale, urban Nigerians and visitors)? PHI should also ask Pharma Nigeria whether the Nigerian government program will impact Fevex sales and why competitors haven't produced capsulated chloroquine.

6. How might our analysis have differed if the product had been aspirin, a soft drink, or a ball-point pen?

Is health care unique, even sacrosanct, requiring different standards of marketing? Arguably, it is not unique, though many in the industry would argue otherwise, and this does not provide support for the use of questionable marketing practices found elsewhere. The Fevex proposal could be usefully compared with the marketing in Nigeria by a transnational organization of aspirin (an OTC product of greater familiarity and lower toxicity), a soft drink (nonhealth product), and a ball-point pen (nonhealth product, not consumed). OTC marketing of any drug ostensibly unsuitable for nonprescription status might also be discussed. Discussion should highlight the requirement for *appropriate* safeguards to ensure product safety, balanced against benefits of the product. For example, nonprescription status increases risks of misuse but provides greater convenience and, in some cases, drugs that would otherwise not be available.

7. What general conclusions may be drawn about marketing in Third World countries?

The central criticism of pharmaceutical marketing in the Third World is that standards are lower than in the developed world. Easily viewed as "unacceptable," is this not difficult to remedy and sometimes inevitable? While the management sloppiness evident in the Bhopal tragedy is avoidable, the cultural, economic and other environmental differences between Third World and developed country operations makes uniformly high standards difficult to achieve. How, for example, can Pharma Nigeria ensure the availability of drugs when dependent upon a decentralized and unsophisticated distribution system in a country that lacks the health care infrastructure of the West? There will always be variables which the firm cannot control yet affect performance, constraints which the firm must attempt to predict and work within as best it can.

The general point that international marketing employs basic marketing principles which apply to Third World countries. These principles must, however, be applied so as to account for cultural and other differences in international markets. Conventional marketing concerns (e.g., marketing mix differences) as well as ethical concerns may be addressed from this position, though it might be argued that the Third World also has "special case" status, demanding a more philanthropic approach (see case **Exhibit 1**, Ciba-Geigy Policy for Third World Countries). In any event, as Ciba-Geigy seems to have recognized, public opinion in the West will not tolerate poor or abusive practices in Third World countries.

8. Why did Ciba-Geigy set up Servipharm? What should it do with Servipharm now?

There may be some speculation as to the reasons for the Servipharm initiative. The case states that Servipharm's purpose was to provide quality drugs, economically priced and with service support, to institutional markets in the Third World, reaching beyond the economic elite of developing countries. Yet, the operation seems hampered by internal resistance to generics, heavy overheads, and the desire to fill surplus capacity (which might conflict with a market orientation). In any event, Servipharm's sales are so small relative to the aspiration of serving 80% of the world's population that one might well question commitment to the venture, if not its rationale. At 7% of PHI sales, Servipharm realized $14 million sales in 1982, only 1-1/2 times the sales of Pharma Nigeria. Allowing for lower prices, this is small beer, and much less than should be achievable with Ciba-Geigy's backing. This initiative must achieve better sales if critics are not to charge that it serves a less laudable purpose—as a public relations exercise gaining Milton Silverman's support, while utilizing surplus capacity and learning about generics production and marketing.

9. Is Ciba-Geigy Pharmaceuticals doing enough in the Third World?

Students can be expected to express their opinions about the limits of corporate social responsibility and personal values are critical here. However, a measure of rigor may usefully be introduced by reference to the four positions delineating the limits of corporate social responsibility. This continuum could be drawn on the board and students asked to vote on where Ciba is now (as represented in the case), and where it should (and could) be. A difference would probably emerge (though evidence in the case is limited), with more students urging greater social responsibility. The implications of this verdict should be explored.

Interestingly, the argument for "doing more" may well be utilitarian. Business often defends its practices on utilitarian grounds, yet, ironically, in this instance, existing practice does not provide "the greatest good for the greatest number." With 80% of the world's population, the Third World does not receive the "best medicine" (e.g., R&D efforts on tropical diseases; $31.5 million, less than 1% of a total expenditure of $10 billion) because it cannot pay.

Should pharmaceutical companies merely act to serve their own interests, prospering parasitically on health care? Or do they have a far broader responsibility such that their purpose is not selling drugs, but contributing to the full in society's endeavor to provide health for all?

Postscript

The PHI management committee approved the development and launch of the new antimalarial in Nigeria at the August 1983 meeting. PEA committee approval was also forthcoming, subject to required clinical tests which the drug passed. However, the management committee was concerned about the possible misuse of the OTC product and recommended childproof packaging. This was not used by competitors and increased the cost of goods by 5%. A special blister pack was developed which would be opaque, so the capsules could not be seen, and with a thicker backing sheet which would make them more difficult to extract. The outer box, containing the blister pack, was printed in black, yellow, and green. Yellow was closely associated with malaria (because of the symptom of yellow urine), and so the yellow capsules in the pack were shown in yellow on the box. Full instructions (with side effects and contraindications) were provided in the leaflet insert, but also repeated in pictorial form on the box. Green was used to caution against exceeding the recommended dose and to advise storage out of reach of children. A mosquito was also shown on the box. The management committee did not make recommendations on the level or form of promotion of the product.

While Pharma Nigeria went ahead with market research and other development activities, however, the political and economic situation deteriorated rapidly. A coup reestablished military rule in December 1983, which still continues. Falling oil prices produced a severe slump in the economy, which led to a debt crisis and foreign exchange pressures. Economic mismanagement aggravated the situation and, by 1988, the economy was still suffering from high inflation and foreign exchange restrictions. Pharma Nigeria's antimalarial received a further setback when the Fevex name was found to be protected. Launched amid extensive publicity as Capquin (capsulated chloroquine) in June 1988, however, it met with immediate success. Priced at N3 to match the competition, one million tablets were sold in four months, well in excess of expectations—and supply. Foreign exchange restrictions entailed an out-of-stock situation from October 1988 to February 1989. They also resulted in a sixfold increase in the cost of goods, which left little profit margin.

Exhibit TN-1 Situation Analysis for Pharma Nigeria

Situation Factor	Nigerian Economy	Antimalarial Market
ECONOMIC	• High inflation • Overvalued currency • Low per-capita income	
POLITICAL	• Political instability • Elections in process	• Government program on malaria
LEGAL	• Pharma Nigeria 60% locally owned	• Chloroquine sold OTC
SOCIAL	• Large, growing population • 80% rural	
TECHNOLOGICAL		• Chloroquine linked to retinopathy (but on WHO list of essential drugs)
CONSUMER	• Health care declining • Capsules preferred	• Malaria = "a leading cause of death"—afflicts 1.4 million, kills 100,000 • 40%-50% go untreated • Chloroquine tastes very bitter
COMPETITION	• OTC only form of health care in some areas	• Largely OTC
COMPANY	• Pharma Nigeria managers are locals • Just entered self-medication market • Underutilized capacity	• Fevex proposal originated locally

5-303-066
NOVEMBER 5, 2002

TEACHING NOTE

Genzyme's Gaucher Initiative: Global Risk and Responsibility

Part I: Case Background and Assignment Information

Case Overview

Against the background of Genzyme's birth and development as a biotech company, this case describes the evolution of the company's global strategy and structure. In particular, it describes management's decision to provide a cure for Gaucher's disease to all sufferers worldwide, regardless of their economic situation. The case then focuses on the tension between this humanitarian commitment and Genzyme's commercial need to build a viable global business with this extraordinarily expensive therapy for a rare disease. The trigger issue that drives the discussion is a decision that must be made in Egypt where Genzyme's Gaucher Initiative has been providing free treatment to patients for several years, but its sales and marketing organization believes there is an opportunity to convert this market to buy on a normal commercial basis.

The case begins with a description of the company's start-up, and particularly the role of Henri Termeer as CEO in shaping the strategy, organization, and cultural values. Termeer brings structure and focus to the young company, in particular making a big bet—against the recommendations of his scientific advisory council and other senior management—to back an unproven therapy for a rare medical condition called Gaucher's disease. The case traces the development of this therapy, along with the difficulties of commercializing a product with an expected worldwide patient population of only 3,000 or 4,000 people. The very expensive R&D and manufacturing operations, conducted under the government's "orphan disease" category, finally results in a therapy that can cost between $100,000 and $300,000 a year to provide. The company's strategies in dealing with political pressures, regulatory hurdles, marketing access, etc. are also described.

The next section of the case describes the opening of overseas markets where Genzyme develops a unique entry strategy based on identifying a limited number of patients and a handful of physicians, then building connections among them. This community is then used as an advocacy group to help bring about the legislative change necessary to obtain reimbursement country by country.

This note was prepared by Professor Christopher A. Bartlett for the sole purpose of aiding classroom instructors in the use of Genzyme's Gaucher Initiative: Global Risk and Responsibility, HBS No. 303-048. It provides analysis and questions that are intended to present alternative approaches to deepening students' comprehension of business issues and energizing classroom discussion. HBS cases are developed solely as the basis for class discussion. Cases are not intended to serve as endorsements, sources of primary data, or illustrations of effective or ineffective management.

Underlying all of this development is a strong cultural value, built in from the earliest days, that focuses on a strong and often emotional commitment to the patient. This translates into a policy of "universal provision" that Termeer articulates frequently and passionately within the organization. Even before the product first comes to market in the United States, Genzyme sets up an assistance program to ensure that the therapy will be provided to anyone who is uninsured or otherwise unable to gain access to the product. As the company internationalizes, this universal provision philosophy is expanded abroad through the Gaucher Initiative, a partnership between Genzyme and the non-profit organization Project HOPE.

Focusing on the creation and expansion of the Gaucher Initiative, the case then describes the role of Tomye Tierney, the pioneering marketer who had opened many of Genzyme's overseas markets and then is brought back to the U.S. to head up the Gaucher Initiative. Tierney's entrepreneurial zeal is then applied to this commitment to humanitarian objectives, a mission that is not always well understood or appreciated by the sales and marketing parts of the organization.

While Tierney initially keeps the Gaucher Initiative out of markets where the sales team is focusing its energy, eventually the intersection of humanitarian care and commercial objectives has to occur. The trigger issue focuses on this intersection, which presents itself in Egypt. After several years of free provision through the Gaucher Initiative, Egypt becomes one of the program's most successful and high-profile locations. However, the sales organization believes that the country's health care system is sufficiently well developed to begin supporting reimbursement for this therapy directly. It is proposing to Tierney that the free provision program back off in Egypt so that the sales organization can develop this market for normal commercial sales. The case concludes with Tierney having to decide how she will handle the issue.

Teaching Purpose

This case can be taught in a variety of courses from marketing and strategy to international business and corporate responsibility/management ethics. Depending on the course, different combinations of the following teaching objectives (and others) might be emphasized:

- To raise the issue of the corporation's responsibility in society—especially the role of the multinational operating outside of the regulation and control of any single government.
- To explore the tension created between a company's humanitarian commitments and the commercial interests that fund them (and the underlying tension between responsibility to communities, shareholders, employees, customers, etc.).
- To explore the role of corporate purpose as it relates to the development of strategy, organization, and culture within a company.
- To illustrate the internationalization process, and particularly to explore new market entry strategies in developed and developing countries.

Assignment Information

The following questions can be assigned with the case:

1. How was Genzyme able to emerge from its marginal position in the high-risk biotech business to become a strong global player in that industry? What are its core competencies? Its core vulnerabilities?

2. What do you think of Henri Termeer's "universal provision" and "universal pricing" policies? Are they socially responsible? Commercially viable? Competitively sustainable?

3. How can the company reconcile the tension created between the Gaucher Initiative's humanitarian commitments and Genzyme's commercial imperatives?

4. Specifically, what should Tomye Tierney do about the situation in Egypt? How should she respond to Genzyme's Middle East sales organization? To Project Hope representatives? To Egyptian government officials? To her bosses, Sandy Smith and Henry Termeer?

Possible assigned reading:

Christopher A. Bartlett and Sumantra Ghoshal, "Changing the Role of Top Management: Beyond Strategy to Purpose," *Harvard Business Review*, Vol. 73, No. 3, May-June 1995, pp. 132-142.

Related materials:

Genzyme's Gaucher Initiative videotaped interview with Henri Termeer and Tomye Tierney, HBS No. 303-804.

Part II: Teaching Plan and Analysis

I introduce this case by describing how the late 1970s and early 1980s were a boom time for the creation of biotech companies in the U.S. Several have survived, but most have not. Many failed, many others were acquired (many by the big pharmaceutical companies), and a handful survived as freestanding independent companies. One of those is Genzyme. Yet, back in the early 1980s, Genzyme was a struggling little company that was supplying reagents to large research labs and dreaming of the possibility of bootstrapping itself into the biotech field. Let's first understand how this unpromising startup emerged into one of the industry's success stories. This leads to the opening question:

1. **In 1983, Henry Termeer gave up his senior position in a major healthcare company to join a privately held company selling diagnostic reagents from its small walk-up office in Boston's Chinatown. How do you evaluate his first year or so on the job?**

   - ***How did he add value to Genzyme?***
   - ***How effectively did he take charge?***

The opening question—and the follow-ups—are designed to open the case with an evaluation of Genzyme's emerging strategy and Termeer's early leadership in developing the strategic, organizational, and cultural base on which the company would grow. As students reiterate these core steps from Termeer's early history, the instructor can push beyond the reiteration of case facts to probe for inside an analysis of what Termeer was doing and why he was doing it. Among the key issues that the class should recognize are the following:

- Termeer's first priority was to have management articulate a set of strategic principles. By pushing students to analyze these strategic principles, the class should understand how

Termeer was trying to recognize the risk inherent in his industry, yet minimize it to match it to the company's limited resources. For example, the company committed to build a diversified portfolio of products that acknowledged the likelihood of product failure in this risky business, but also focused that portfolio on niches where they were unlikely to face a high competitive risk; and while the strategy was to integrate across the whole value chain in order to maximize Genzyme's ability to capture value, it also minimized the risk by funding the investments through internally generated funds or non equity instruments rather than overextending itself. Both these principles were designed to meet a third overarching goal, which was to maintain Genzyme's independence—a priority that demanded prudence in this high-risk business. (During this time period, many biotech firms found that their ambitions outran their ability to fund them, and were force to sell themselves to large pharmaceutical companies.)

- Within the diversified portfolio of products being developed, Termeer made a major bet on Cerezyme that ran against conventional wisdom and internal advice. It was a bold decision, especially for a company with such a conservative strategic philosophy, and the instructor might push students to justify Termeer's bet on therapy for Gaucher disease without the benefit of hindsight. It is interesting to have them articulate his apparent motivation. It seems that this was not just a strategic bet, but also an important articulation of the cultural value of putting patient needs first that would become so critical to the organization. Through this decision, Termeer demonstrated a commitment to meeting patients' needs that would trump both scientific rationale and financial analysis.

- At a more operational level, he also implemented control and brought a more professional management to the day-to-day activities (e.g. selling Genzyme Gene, the race horse). This was a vital first move, if the organization was to have the discipline to implement the ambitious strategic agenda he shaped for Genzyme.

A board plan for this first area of discussion is illustrated in **Exhibit TN1**.

2. **How effective a business model has Termeer and his management team created to bring Ceredase/Cerezyme to market?**

In this second discussion pasture, the students should develop a clear understanding of how this small, resource-constrained company could bring such a high cost therapy to market. This is even more surprising when they are targeting such a tiny patient population—not only in the United States, but worldwide. Students should see that the strategy they develop is quite contrary to the typical pharmaceutical company's approach of detailing physicians and visiting purchasing agents in large hospitals and health maintenance organizations. Instead, they adopt a grassroots, bottom-up, patient-oriented approach that is often highly personal and individually tailored. The kind of follow-up questions that can generate discussion might be as follows:

- ***How different is their approach from the traditional pharmaceutical companies' strategy of detailing physician and selling to hospital purchasing agents?***

- ***What do you think of their approach to enter new markets?***

- ***For example, how would you evaluate Tomye Tierney's approach to entering Korea?***

It is important to capture the business model clearly, since it is critical to the understanding of how Genzyme has succeeded. I prefer to block out the relationships and processes graphically as students describe them, building a model similar to the one illustrated on **Exhibit TN-2**. The key points illustrated are as follows:

- In the grassroots approach, the salesforce (or in the case of a new market entry, market pioneer) identifies a physician-patient relationship on which they can build. As other Gaucher sufferers are located, they are linked into a patient group and put in touch with one or two physicians familiar with the disease. Genzyme's sales organization then works to develop the critical mass necessary to mobilize this under-diagnosed and powerless group of sufferers by providing education and supporting their activities. Furthermore, by linking more of them to one or two physicians, they develop the expertise of these health care providers and make them opinion leaders on Gaucher Disease within their profession.

- Mobilizing the patient group and the physician group, the sales organization can then put pressure on insurance companies to have the treatment reimbursed. The addition of specialized "caseworkers" to support these activities again gives power to the patients in their battle to obtain treatment, and reassurance to the doctors that their work will be paid for.

- In overseas markets, Genzyme's market pioneers arrange for the drug to be imported and prescribed on an exception basis at first, using investigational new drug (IND) or "named patient" status to temporarily bypass formal regulatory and reimbursement procedures. The patient groups and physicians are then mobilized to lobby legislative bodies and regulatory agencies. With this support and pressure, legislation and regulations are eventually changed to recognize the disease and to authorize reimbursement for the therapy through the Ministry of Health.

In analyzing this market entry strategy and recognizing its power and creativity, some will inevitably express a level of discomfort about the pressure being put on health care systems to provide expensive care for a rare disease when more basic needs are not being met (e.g. the situation in Czechoslovakia described on p. 11 of the case). Others will defend the right of any individual to fight for treatment of their curable disease, and will argue that Genzyme cannot be the arbiter of which patients deserve its support. Governments must decide, and if they choose not to pay, the company's free product policy and universal provision will kick in. This debate leads into the next question.

3. **As the company is developing this business model, and even before it has marketing approval, Termeer articulates his "universal provision" philosophy. What is the rationale of such a major commitment for a company just finding its feet?**

This third discussion pasture opens up a full exploration of the humanitarian commitment that the company has made. It is important that students examine what that commitment is and discuss what the company's motivation is in making it. While most will take the commitment at face value, there will likely be some who will ascribe other motivations—a public relations exercise, to deflect government attention on the therapy's high cost, etc. The believers and the skeptics will often engage each other in vigorous debate, and after allowing this exchange about what the commitment is and what motivation lies behind it, I then ask:

- ***How effective is the universal provision in its application?***

- ***Was Amaru Ascarza treated appropriately?***

These followup questions focus on the implementation of Genzyme's universal provision philosophy and particularly on the case of the Peruvian boy whose plight is described in Exhibit 7 of the case. By moving from the abstract general philosophy to the specific case, debate will become greatly sharpened. While some will argue that Amaru and his family accepted treatment on the condition that they cooperate with the company to return to Peru, others will see this as nothing more than a cynical ploy to use the family to open a new market. Genzyme's sympathizers will point to the company's commitment "to take it as our responsibility to see they are treated," as Termeer pledges (case p. 6), while its critics may wonder just how far their responsibility extends.

The instructor might probe both sides of the argument asking the supporters if such a guarantee is not a huge commercial risk, since governments will quickly recognize they can sidestep this responsibility and rely on the company's willingness to pay. To the skeptics, the instructor might ask what alternative approach they would recommend to Genzyme. For example, should they continue to treat Amaru in Boston? Should they treat anyone who presents themselves at the company's offices for as long as they need treatment? What are the implications of this policy—for the company, the patient, and their home country?

Video Part 1: After some discussion, it can be helpful to pause to play part 1 of the video (approx. 5 minutes) which shows Henri Termeer and Tomye Tierney discussing the company's growth and philosophy. Termeer describes the company's commitment to the patients and emphasizes that they will never be used as hostages or bargaining chips in negotiations with governments. On the other hand, he insists that it is legitimate for the company to ask others take responsibility for the provision of health where they can, and to ask for patients' support in helping to make that transition. Tierney then describes the Gaucher Initiative as a part of the universal provision program and the challenges integrating it into Genzyme's commercial activities. The video provides a good transition to the next question:

4. Is the Gaucher Initiative part of the humanitarian commitment or part of the business model?

This question is usually foreshadowed by comments made in both previous areas of discussion, and the question simply allows students to bring those issues together for debate. Both sides of the argument can be made quite strongly, since the Gaucher Initiative clearly organizes patient groups and physician opinion leaders to give visibility and voice to sufferers from this rare disease. In that regard, it is creating the same kind of pressure in an environment for the treatment of the disease. But on the other hand, Gaucher Initiative has clearly been isolated from Genzyme's mainstream commercial activity by setting it up as a separately managed partnership with Project HOPE. The company's commitment to universal provision is backed by its universal pricing policy that there are only two prices for Genzyme—the normal price and free—and the delivery mechanisms for product at each of those prices is quite distinct.

The students will usually come to recognize that the Gaucher Initiative is not only an embodiment of the company's humanitarian commitment, but also part of its business model. Genzyme's explicit commitment is to treat all patients regardless of their economic situation—*but also* a strong, explicit belief that once a viable long-term support can be found (through private insurance or public health care), the company should hand off that responsibility. Such a conclusion allows the instructor to follow up with:

- ***Is this a problem? Should the two activities be totally disconnected—quarantined from one another?***
- ***Why is there tension between these two objectives? Can they manage the tension?***

These questions lead to a discussion about the legitimacy of having the Gaucher Initiative acting in a humanitarian role but also intersecting with Genzyme's business model. Some will see this as perfectly legitimate, arguing that if the two activities are totally segregated, the Gaucher Initiative will gradually erode the commercial viability of the company. In doing so it will undermine Genzyme's ability to support the overall humanitarian program.

At some stage in the discussion, the instructor may want to ask students how many patients Genzyme can afford to support with free therapy for life. This requires them to calculate the cost of this initiative (approximately $50,000 per patient per year according to the calculation on **Exhibit TN3**—the annotated version of case Exhibits 9 and 3). In a company whose profits swing from $70 million in the black in 1999 to $60 million in the red in 2000, what level of humanitarian commitment is sensible—or feasible?

Those who are concerned about the intersection of the humanitarian and commercial activities often try to formulate some criteria to define a "bright line" that divides the two. Typically, they discover that this is a difficult thing to do on a permanent basis. Most will eventually concede that the dividing line between providing free product and expecting to sell the therapy has to be constantly reviewed and negotiated—and this is what Genzyme is struggling with at the decision point that begins and ends the case.

This leads to a discussion of how the company should manage the situation in Egypt. The instructor might introduce the issue by suggesting that the salesforce is increasingly likely to focus on the most affluent of the developing markets as potential opportunities for growth. Having expanded through most of the developed countries and reaching saturation point in that expansion activity (see Exhibit 9), countries like Egypt are now prime sales targets.

5. How should Tomye Tierney deal with the issue facing her in Egypt?

To help focus the action question on both the strategic decision and the organizational one, I like to depict on a blackboard (or show as an overhead transparency) the graphic in **Exhibit TN-4** which represents the relationships that Tierney has with the various constituencies whose interests she must reconcile. In any plan of action, she has to manage up, down, out, and across to align the interests of these various constituencies as the company attempts to make the transition from provider of free therapy to a more commercial arrangement. Typically, I will ask two or three students to articulate a specific plan of action as Tierney.

- ***To whom do you talk first? What do you tell them?***
- ***At what point would you call on Henri Termeer for intervention?***
- ***As Henri Termeer, would you get involved in this negotiation?***

Video: From the various proposals, the class usually converges on some plan of action that defines how the transition might be negotiated. At this point, the second part of the video can be shown describing how the organization resolved the issue and providing some update on how activities subsequently developed.

Following a brief discussion of the video, the instructor might then conclude with a summary that picks up the key issues of the discussion, tying them to one's particular teaching objective.

Conclusion

Because of the way I use this case, my conclusion tends to focus on the following points:

- The importance of building a company's social commitments on a strong foundation of economic viability: in this case, highlighted in the need to recognize—and manage—the intersection between the company's business model and its humanitarian model.

- At a more macro level, the power of a deeply embedded corporate purpose to engage people to commit to a cause—not just work for a company.
- And at a societal level, the obligation of multinational companies to think beyond the common view of overseas operations as simply incremental marketplaces, sources of low-cost labor, or locations to play off against one another in some elaborate tax minimization or investment subsidy game. In today's world of anti-globalization sentiments mounting against MNCs they must recognize that they are not just economic entities, they are also powerful engines of social change—and with that power comes a responsibility.

Exhibit TN1 Board Plan for Question 1

Set Strategic Principles

- Diversified portfolio
- Niche markets
- Remain independent
  - Whole value chain
  - Conservative financing

Risk-minimizing philosophy

Strategic Choice

- Bet on Gaucher therapy

Embeds

Cultural Values

- Commitment to patient
  - Ceredase bet
  - "Universal Provision"

Org. Development

- Recruits and acquires expertise
  - Furbish, Salesforce
  - IG technology
- Recruits for values
  - "Practical dreamers"

Operational Efficiency

- Systems, controls
- Management discipline
- Professionalism

Exhibit TN2 Board Plan for Question 2

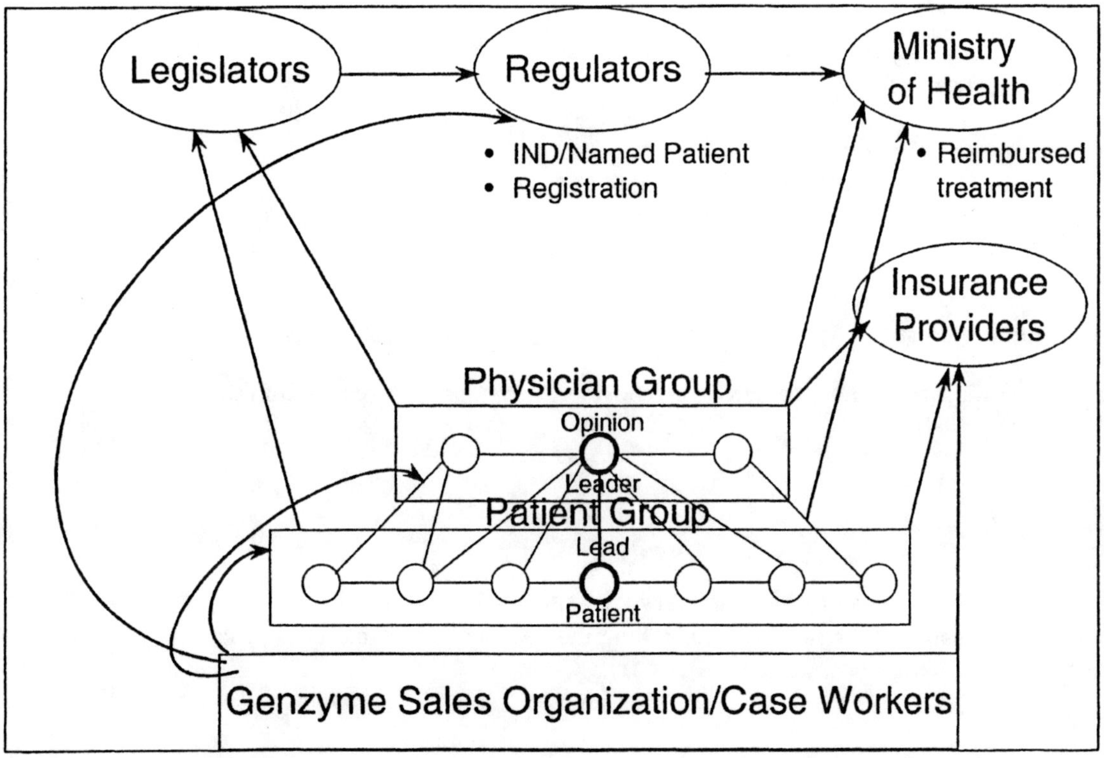

ıibit TN3 Case Exhibit 9

ıibit 9 Ceredase and Cerezyme revenues and patient growth, 1991-2001

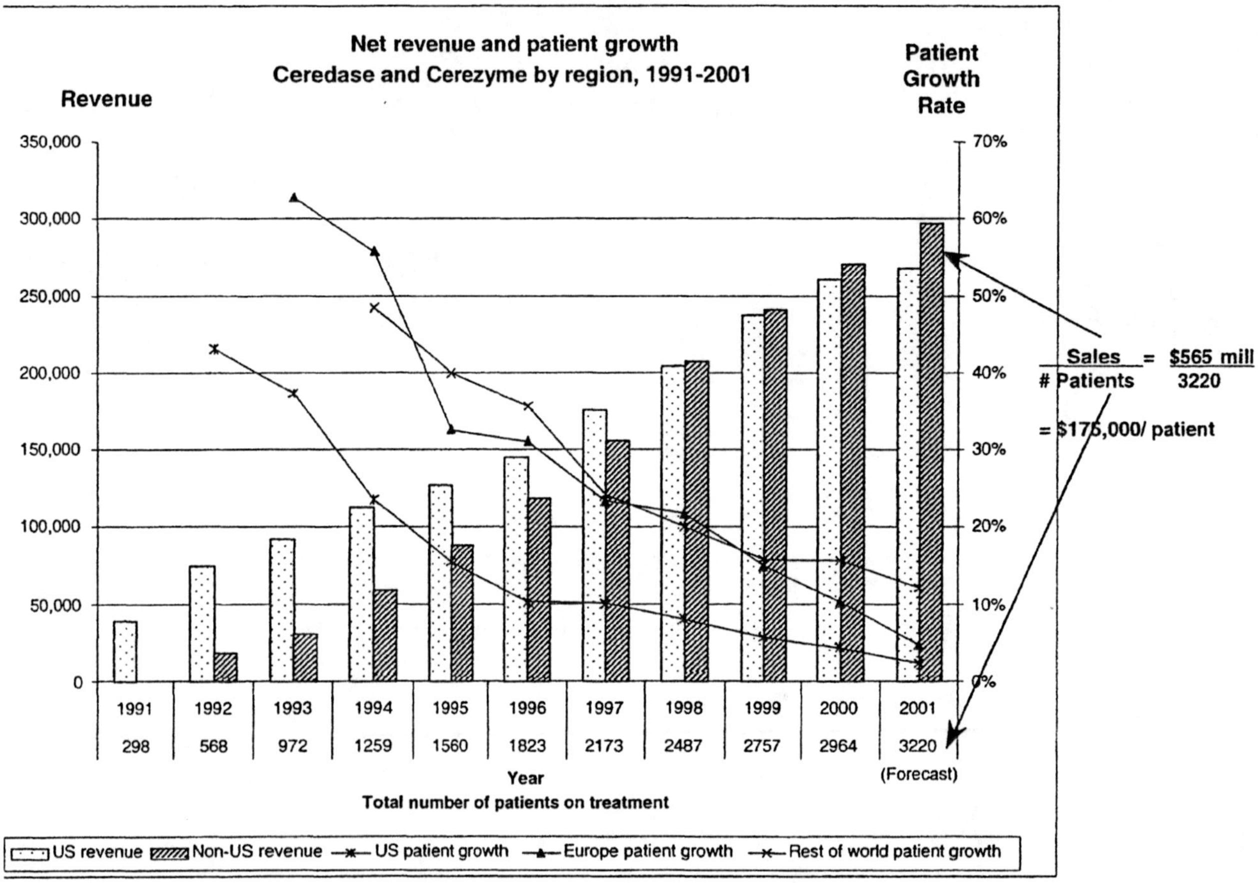

ımate of Gaucher Initiative cost:

patients (case p. 10) x $175,000 revenue/patient (from above) x 28.5% Cost of Products Sold (from ?)* = approx. $7 million in 2001.

)0 Ceredase/Cerezyme represents $530 million of total $812 million in product sales, of two-thirds he total. Given this dominance of the sales volume, taking the company average cost of product l percentage seems reasonable.

Clearly, the problem of AIDS in Africa is immense. It is a terrifying problem that demands a massive solution – but there is none in sight.

Almost certainly, the pharmaceutical firms are not to blame for the crisis. They didn't "cause" the spread of AIDS, nor can they be held accountable for the inability of most African governments to address the pressing medical demands of their citizens. However, because their drugs hold the only real hope for AIDS sufferers, and because the firms are both wealthy and widely perceived as wealthy, they have borne and will continue to bear the brunt of public criticism. The pharmaceutical firms will have to respond – quickly and decisively – to the AIDS crisis. We'll examine this response and see how effective it's been when we turn to our (B) case.

If instructors will be using *Life, Death and Property Rights* as a stand-alone case, however, they will probably want to conclude more fully, saying something about how the pharmaceutical industry has indeed responded to the AIDS crisis and what implications this response is likely to have. For information about this response, instructors will probably wish to read either the case itself or the accompanying teaching note.

Essentially, though, the industry made a major turn-around in 2000, when five leading firms offered the World Health Organization a fairly remarkable deal: they would sell AIDS drugs in Africa at a sharply reduced price as long as the WHO agreed to help maintain property rights and distribute the drugs. It was a basic trade-off, compromising on price in exchange for the perpetuation of property rights. (This may well have been a compromise suggested by students during the final pasture of class).

But this compromise was not sufficient. The price of AIDS drugs remained too high for nearly all consumers in Africa (roughly $1,000 to $1,500 per patient per year) and few governments were willing to engage pharmaceutical firms on their offer. Matters reached a head when Cipla, an Indian firm producing generic AIDS drugs, announced bargain basement prices for its own non-patented drugs: only $350 per patient per year. This prompted the major firms to slash their own prices as well, and to agree to let NGOs, in addition to states, distribute their products.

As of 2002, therefore, the pharmaceutical firms had made major price concessions in order to stave off further attacks on the patent system. They were basically willing to distribute drugs below their generic price—and to donate millions of dollars in charitable aid—in order to maintain U.S.-style protection for intellectual property rights. This is almost certainly a wise concession. For in the long run, it is hard to imagine how the western pharmaceutical firms could maintain their underlying business model without the security of patents. But it is still not clear whether their bargain will hold. As the AIDS epidemic sweeps across Africa and elsewhere (predictions for infection rates in China, India and Russia are equally grim) the pharmaceutical firms will be pushed to offer more and more drugs, at lower and lower prices. These reduced prices will engender resentment in the developed markets (why should poor patients in America pay more than rich patients in Africa?) and facilitate a potentially vast gray market for drugs. Concessions for AIDS drugs, moreover, are likely to ignite similar concessions for equally deadly diseases, including malaria and tuberculosis. Will the global system of intellectual property rights be able to withstand this assault? It's not clear. But if the AIDS epidemic manages to shake this system even a little bit, the implications—not only in the pharmaceutical industry, but wherever intellectual property rights hold—will be profound.

Exhibit TN5 Board Setup/Overhead for Question 5

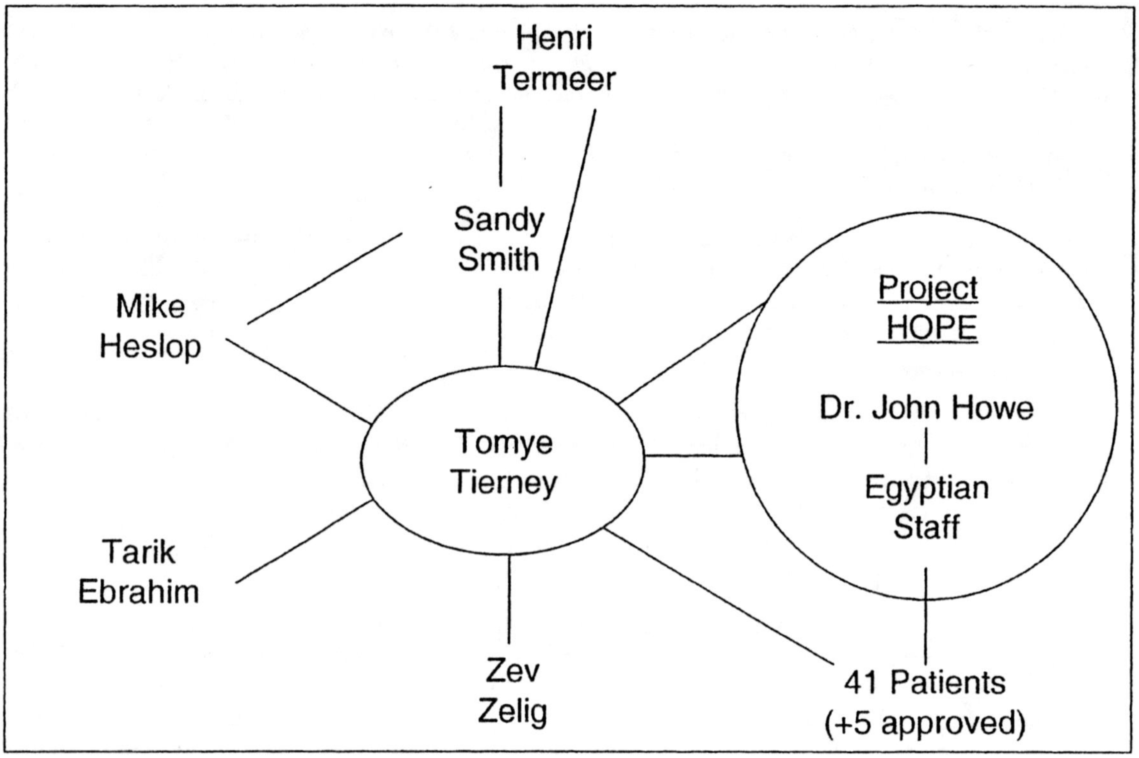

Exhibit TN4 Case Exhibit 2 *Ceredase/Cerezyme sales $530 million (65% total)*

Year ending December 31	2000	1999	1998	1997	1996	1991	1986	1981[a]
Revenues:								
Product sales =	$811,897	$683,482	$613,685	$529,927	$424,483	$72,019	$9,770	$2,167
Service sales	84,482	79,448	74,791	67,158	68,950	21,503	-	-
Revenue from R&D contracts	6,941	9,358	20,859	11,756	25,321	28,394	2,366	-
TOTAL REVENUES 28.5% sales	**$903,320**	**$772,288**	**$709,335**	**$608,841**	**$518,754**	**$121,916**	**$12,136**	**$2,167**
Costs and Expenses:								
Cost of products sold = 28.5% sales	$232,383	$182,337	$211,076	$206,028	$155,930	$33,164	$5,421	$936
Cost of services sold	50,177	49,444	48,586	47,289	54,082	14,169	-	-
Selling, admin & general	264,551	242,797	215,203	200,476	162,264	39,118	5,084	838
Research & development	169,478	150,516	119,005	89,558	80,849	27,232	2,285	57
Purchase of in-process R&D	200,191	5,436	-	7,000	130,639	-	-	-
Charge for impaired asset	4,321	-	-	-	-	-	-	-
Amortization of intangibles	22,974	24,674	24,334	17,245	8,849	-	-	-
TOTAL EXPENSES	**$944,075**	**$655,204**	**$618,204**	**$567,596**	**$592,613**	**$113,683**	**$12,790**	**$1,831**
Income (loss) before unusual items	**($40,755)**	**$117,084**	**$91,131**	**$41,245**	**($73,859)**	**$8,233**	**($654)**	**$336**
Investment income	$45,593	$36,158	$25,055	$11,409	$15,341	$12,371	$889	-
Interest expense	(15,710)	(21,771)	(22,593)	(12,667)	(6,990)	(2,088)	(194)	(92)
Equity in net loss of unconsolidated affiliates	(44,965)	(42,696)	(29,006)	(12,258)	(5,373)	-	-	-
Affiliate sale of stock	22,689	6,683	2,369	-	1,013	-	-	-
Sale of equity securities	15,873	(3,749)	(6)	-	1,711	-	-	-
Minority Interest	4,625	3,674	4,285	-	-	-	-	-
Sale of product line	-	8,018	31,202	-	-	-	-	-
Sale of GENE_TRAK	-	-	-	-	-	4,065	-	-
Credit from operating loss carry-fwd	-	-	-	-	-	8,387	-	-
Other revenue (expense)	5,188	14,527	-	(2,000)	(1,465)	2,726	-	-
Income (loss) before income taxes	**($7,462)**	**$117,928**	**$102,437**	**$25,729**	**($69,622)**	**$33,694**	**$41**	**$244**
Provision for income taxes	(55,478)	(46,947)	(39,870)	(12,100)	(3,195)	(12,848)	0	(165)
NET INCOME (LOSS)	**($62,940)**	**$70,981**	**$62,567**	**$13,629**	**($72,817)**	**$20,846**	**$41**	**$79**

Source: Adapted by casewriters from Genzyme Corporation Annual Reports.

[a]Note: 1981 results cover the period from company inception on June 8, 1981. (Source: 1986 IPO Prospectus.)

Note that "lumpy" R&D due to buy-back of limited research partnerships (case p. 4) and expensing of acquired companies' R&D premium. This led to losses in 1996 and 2000.